LARCENY
GAMES

LARCENY GAMES

SPORTS GAMBLING, GAME FIXING AND THE FBI

BY BRIAN TUOHY

ISBN: 978-1-936239-77-1

10 9 8 7 6 5 4 3 2

FERAL HOUSE
1240 W SIMS WAY
SUITE 124
PORT TOWNSEND WA 98368
WWW.FERALHOUSE.COM

DESIGNED BY GREGORY FLORES

CONTENTS

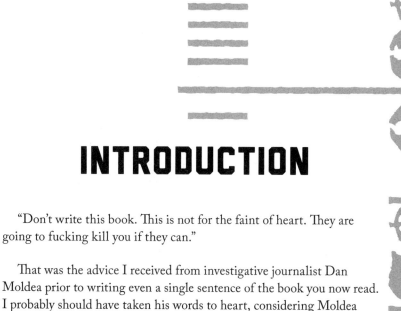

INTRODUCTION

"Don't write this book. This is not for the faint of heart. They are going to fucking kill you if they can."

That was the advice I received from investigative journalist Dan Moldea prior to writing even a single sentence of the book you now read. I probably should have taken his words to heart, considering Moldea knows of what he speaks. In 1989, his book *Interference: How Organized Crime Influences Professional Football* was published, perhaps the only book to investigate game fixing/point shaving in the National Football League (or in any of the professional sports leagues, for that matter). The book, Moldea claimed, destroyed his career. "Sometimes I wish they would've killed me," he lamented. "I really do because it just stopped me. I had a fucking great career going and it just stopped me."

Why? Because the NFL is a $10 billion-a-year business with several prominent government and corporate ties (CBS, NBC/GE, Disney/ESPN, and FOX, to name but a few) which does not like when people write or broadcast negative things about it. The late, great broadcaster Howard Cosell expressed fear of the NFL's power over the media back in 1985, writing, "The NFL, you see, monitors and collects just about everything that is written about it in newspapers and magazines and said about it on radio and television. Apparently, [Joe] Browne [the NFL's director of information] and his troops go so far as to tape my twice-daily radio reports, which I find a particularly frightening aspect of the NFL's never-ending quest to dominate the media. Like the CIA and the FBI, the NFL has its own enemies list—and I got the distinct impression that I was at the top of it."[1]

In the case of *Interference*, the NFL was not caught unaware that Moldea's book was forthcoming, and the league gave him the same treatment it had with Cosell. "These guys [NFL security] were out there following me," he said. "They would have a tape of every show, they would transcribe every show. I mean it was unbelievable what they did. The effort they put into dealing with me...." To top it off, veteran NFL beat writer Gerald Eskenazi was assigned by the *New York Times* to review Moldea's book. In his critique of *Interference*, Eskenazi accused Moldea of, among other things, "sloppy journalism." Moldea responded by pointing out the factual errors in Eskenazi's review, demanding a retraction, and then suing for libel when the *New York Times* refused to budge. Initially, Moldea won his case, but it soon turned into a lengthy court battle, falling an appeals ruling shy of the Supreme Court. Though publicly supported by the president of the National Book Critic Circle, the *Columbia Journalism Review*, and the *Wall Street Journal*, Moldea lost.

"I sued the *New York Times* for libel in a case that lasted longer than World War II," he recounted. "I wanted to fight the NFL, and I ended up fighting the *New York Times*. It was bullshit. It took the heart of my career right out of me. I was fighting the bullshit the *New York Times* pulled on me and the NFL was behind it all the way....The *New York Times* critic had lied about me. I sent a letter to the editor which they refused to publish, and then they claimed that I was the one restricting free speech. When do I get my free speech here? The guy wrote lies about me and I'm not allowed to respond to it?"

It is quite possible that the same thing will happen to me with the publication of this book. And I'm foolish enough to take it one step further by not just investigating game fixing and point shaving in the NFL, but in the National Basketball Association (NBA), Major League Baseball (MLB), soccer, tennis, and boxing as well. Moldea even asked me, "Are you independently wealthy? Because they can sue you. They can make your life completely crazy. That, to me, is fearsome."

The problem at the heart of this is the fact that I shouldn't have needed to write this book. All of the information presented here should have already been part of many sports fans' knowledge base…if the sports media was actually doing its job. This book should not have my name on the cover; it should have been written by Bob Costas or Dan Patrick or Jim Rome or any one of a number of prominent sports media pundits. But it wasn't. It's not backed by the likes of ESPN, NBC Sports or *Sports Illustrated*. In fact, I doubt any of those outlets will even recognize this book or the facts upon which it is based. If they do, it will only be to marginalize or mock this work as that of mere "conspiracy theory" because what is alleged in these pages threatens not just the status quo, but more importantly the billions of dollars earned every year in the world of professional sports.

This tome also threatens the livelihood of organized crime in the United States. Although sports gambling is seen as a victimless crime, in truth 99 percent of all sports gambling in the U.S. is done illegally with the vast majority of those untold billions of dollars funneled directly to the mob. It is their top moneymaker, followed closely by the loan-sharking activities which often accompany gamblers who cannot pay off their bookies in time. When games are fixed today—and believe me, games are being fixed today—the money wagered on these rigged contests is being trafficked through these mob-backed bookmakers, whether they are located on offshore websites or in the backroom of some local pub.

Much of what follows is taken directly from Federal Bureau of Investigation (FBI) case files. These investigative files were obtained through multiple Freedom of Information Act requests, a resource which the NFL, NBA and MLB do not possess for interested parties. The FBI held over four hundred files directly related to sports bribery which is the legal term for game fixing and/or point shaving. These covered everything from horse racing to boxing to college athletic events to the NFL, NBA and MLB (with a notable exception of the National Hockey League). The files are quoted directly. However, though some of these investigations date back 50 years or more, there is still vital information which has been redacted by law. (By the way, the government no longer blacks out what they don't want you to read. Instead a white box omits the tantalizing information.) This is indicated within these pages thusly: [redacted]. Sometimes it is just a name. Other times several sentences or entire pages were blocked. Because of this, a few files were rendered incomprehensible and were not included. However, most investigations relating to professional sports are discussed here. Sometimes the names of those involved remain unknown, yet in many instances a little research and the connecting of a few dots led to the revelation of the suspected guilty parties. For fans knowledgeable of the history of their favorite sports, some of these names will surprise you.

Remember, too, when reading the tales of these investigations, that this is only the information of which the FBI was aware. It doesn't mean these were the only players, coaches or referees suspected by those in the know to have fixed games or shaved points. Like many criminal acts, much goes unreported and uninvestigated for a variety of reasons. This is merely a starting point. How much deeper the rabbit hole goes remains to be known. I just hope that by the time I reach the bottom, I don't need the name of a good lawyer. Or it won't be the NFL or NBA I'll have to worry about. It'll be my wife.

THE SAGA OF
TIM DONAGHY

The story of 13-year veteran NBA referee Tim Donaghy is the most recent, and next to the 1919 Black Sox, perhaps the most discussed case of game fixing in professional sports. The problem is—and most people have this completely wrong—Donaghy was neither arrested for nor sent to prison because he fixed games. The two crimes he pleaded guilty to were conspiring to engage in wire fraud and transmitting betting information across state lines, not game fixing. There were a few reasons why. One, the FBI did not attempt to prove Donaghy fixed a single game. Two, for their own financial reasons the NBA had no desire to see Donaghy convicted for fixing a game. And three, Donaghy wasn't about to admit to a crime neither of those two entities were accusing him of committing.

The Donaghy case destroys several myths that surround sports gambling and the likelihood of game fixing. These include: games cannot be fixed today; athletes, coaches and referees are paid too much to even consider fixing a game; the FBI is watching for anyone attempting such a crime; the leagues and their security divisions, with their background checks, official reviews, etc., would know before anyone if such a plot were attempted; the sports gambling community would tip off a league if suspicious betting was occurring; and lastly, anyone attempting to fix a game would make it so obvious that everyone would know. These are merely comforting thoughts. The truth is there may have been a bigger cover-up surrounding the Donaghy case from the NBA and the gambling community than with the criminals who were arrested for their participation in this plot.

Tim Donaghy's problem was he was a compulsive gambler. He bet on everything: golf, football, casino table games and more. It wasn't long before he broke the ultimate taboo as an NBA referee and gambled on basketball. As he told me, "It was just something I did because I needed the action. I was betting on something every night." Donaghy started betting on NBA games, including games he was officiating, late in the 2003–04 season. This trend continued as he then bet on 30 to 40 of his own games in each of the following seasons: 2004–05, 2005–06, and 2006–07. Pete Ruggieri, who booked the bets Donaghy made through his friend Jack Concannon, said Donaghy only had success in wagering on basketball when the bets were on games in which he officiated.

In betting lines for NBA games, a point spread movement of one-and-a-half points is considered significant. A two-point move is rare, and anything above and beyond that would be suspect unless an injury or other influential factor became known. This is due to the fact that NBA betting lines are quickly determined and bet into, as during the season, games are played nearly every night. According to author Sean Patrick Griffin's research, the games in which Donaghy officiated between 2003 and 2006 had a line movement of one-and-a-half points or more 18 percent of the time.[1] This did not go unnoticed.

Early in the 2006–07 NBA season, Donaghy went 10–0 betting on games in which he officiated. But he abandoned gambling with Concannon and Ruggieri as he felt he wasn't making enough from these repeated victories.[2] Instead, Donaghy decided to bet with an old acquaintance, James "BaBa" Battista. At this time, Battista was one of the most influential sports gamblers/"movers" in the world. Once Donaghy was betting with Battista, the percentage of games in which Donaghy officiated and the line moved one-and-a-half points or more doubled to 36 percent. Even more telling, the percentage of Donaghy games between December and April 2006–07 that had a similar one-and-a-half-point or greater swing was 43 percent.[3]

Battista nicknamed Donaghy "Elvis" because "I knew he was going to do whatever it took to win. Elvis could set the tempo of a game, and affect the outcome of the game. To me, Timmy was 'Elvis' a.k.a. 'The King' because I had been winning so much on his games."[4] Battista explained to author Griffin, "Once I knew what side Elvis liked, I'd get to work. I'd bet, like, a hundred and twenty thousand in Europe, then maybe thirty to fifty thousand at a few outs in Asia, all of it before people were gonna start betting in the U.S. The hope was that I could get some money accumulated over there without affecting the offshore and U.S. markets. I had the most sophisticated computer setup moving these games, and I was trying to filter the game through Europe, Taiwan, Vegas, and the rest of the U.S. I would use money from the sharp guys to bet around fifty thousand dollars and invest it betting on the games the wrong way. I was just sabotaging the market. So, if I wanted to take seven on a game and the game was four-and-a-half and five, I'd lay the four-and-a-half and five. The followers would lay the five-and-a-half and six, and force the bookmakers to go to seven. Now, it was sitting around seven, and I'd be taking back the seven. I'd be sending people offshore, 'Go get me half a million plus seven.' Bookmakers were in a frenzy because the lines were moving so much, and they were getting opened up to being middled. The lines would move from three, to four, to five, to six, to seven. They were fucked. If I laid four and four-and-a-half and the game went to seven and I take seven, and the game lands on five or six, the bookmakers were getting destroyed. I had people in England betting for me, people in Taiwan, and the money would filter back into the United States. No one had any idea where the action was coming from."[5]

That wasn't completely true. The lines were moving at a ridiculous clip. Some gambling insiders knew something was amiss. Battista even stated, "That's why bookmakers knew something was going on. These were the most respected bookmakers in the world. They didn't cheat on the numbers, and they were very good at what they did. The lines were moving so much, and it wasn't like there were injuries or anything else that could account for the big line moves. People couldn't do anything about what I was doing, and the best they could do was take the next number. Sometimes you'd see a line go from two or two-and-a-half all the way up to eight, and that started happening a lot."[6]

While this was going on, Donaghy's picks—at least the ones made in the games he worked—were winning time and again. It's nearly impossible for a professional gambler to win over 60 percent of his bets, yet Battista claimed he posted a record of 37–10 (79 percent) on games in which Donaghy officiated. In doing so, he also claimed to have bet $1–$2 million on each of these games in 2006–07, compared to just $10,000–$20,000 on a normal NBA game.[7] This accounting seems a bit off, however. Donaghy stated to me, "I was told by the FBI that he [Battista] was betting $75,000–$100,000 a game," while Donaghy was only getting $2,000–$5,000 per game for his "picks." If Battista and Donaghy were hitting at nearly 80 percent, even just during those prime months in 2006–07 they worked together, Battista should've won $16 million or more. Yet by his own admission, Battista was in the hole by the time he went into rehab for a drug addiction in 2007 (which ended his work with Donaghy) and still owed money to various cohorts as of 2011. Of course, maybe not all of the $1–$2 million he wagered was his own, as Battista moved money for some of the world's biggest sports gamblers.

This should make one wonder exactly who else knew what Donaghy and BaBa were up to. "No one can know just how widespread the knowledge of [Battista's] stone-cold NBA locks was, but there is little dispute among the world's big-time betting community that by early 2007, word within that crowd was that Tim Donaghy was fixing games and only a fool would have ignored Battista's ridiculously obvious wagering success."[8] When Battista entered rehab, the scheme continued. Battista told author Griffin, "There was a group of guys who I had been using in Asia.

There were still getting the bets and were moving lines on [Donaghy] games and crushing over there, and bookmakers were getting pissed. By then, everybody was jumping on Donaghy's games….Talk on the street was nuts, and everybody in the gambling industry knew what was going on. I found out from Tommy [Martino, who was arrested with Donaghy and Battista] one day when I called him from rehab that Pete was shutting everything down because he said the games were moving too many points, and we were attracting too much attention."[9]

If this was such common knowledge, where was the NBA? Where was its security division? Where was the warning to the league from the gambling community whom the NBA claimed to have worked so closely with? There appeared to be only one lone voice of dissent in all of this, a call that went unheeded. It came from Kenny White who at the time was CEO and head oddsmaker for Las Vegas Sports Consultants, the world's largest oddsmaking company. "[White] researched betting trends involving Tim Donaghy and submitted a report to the NBA in the fall of 2007. Of this situation, White told the *Las Vegas Review-Journal*, 'They never called back to discuss it or anything.'"[10]

Despite all of this behind-the-scenes knowledge, the FBI stumbled across Donaghy and Battista purely by accident. A wiretapped conversation from an unrelated organized crime case mentioned the control of an NBA referee. Donaghy was eventually tipped off about the investigation and turned himself in, confessing. This was an intelligent decision as cooperating with the FBI allowed Donaghy to control the message. His story was to be followed while Battista's side went unheard. Donaghy put forth the tale that he was able to pick winners based on his inside information of the NBA and how his fellow referees normally called games. This proved somewhat inaccurate, but the FBI followed along.

Donaghy wasn't about to admit he fixed games. There was no reason to. The FBI did consider pursuing this angle, but in order to take that aspect of the case to court they would have had to be able to prove it. There was little evidence. The FBI watched 14 of Donaghy's 2006–07 games and found nothing of note. They cannot be blamed for this. As Griffin wrote, "…even those who believe Donaghy influenced outcomes do not think he made 'wrong' calls to affect games. Rather, they contend Donaghy consistently made calls for violations which are commonly not enforced. These calls would not be considered 'incorrect' during reviews by various parties, and wouldn't necessarily stick out because Donaghy had a reputation for being a referee who called a lot of fouls. Simply stated, Donaghy could have easily called a game 'tight' against a team he bet against, and 'loose' against a team on which he had wagered. None of this would have raised eyebrows, since there was no reason to question his integrity at the time. I have interviewed several basketball experts and pro gamblers who each believe Tim Donaghy influenced game outcomes, and yet these parties almost universally agree that viewing game tapes is a fruitless pursuit because there is so much subjectivity involved."[11] The government's ultimate conclusion was summed up in a letter of recommendation written on Donaghy's behalf for his sentencing which stated, "There is no evidence that Donaghy ever intentionally made a particular ruling during a game in order to increase the likelihood that his gambling pick would be correct. He has acknowledged, however, that he compromised his objectivity as a referee because of his financial interest in the outcome of NBA games, and that this personal interest might have subconsciously affected his on-court performance."

The FBI interviewed experts in the sports betting world about Donaghy and his games, but never examined the unusual line movements associated with them. No one in the gambling community revealed anything of note to the FBI in these regards, either. Yet gambling expert, author, and former radio show host Larry Grossman revealed to me that many in fact did know the facts the FBI sought: "For the population of basketball bettors who are sophisticated and monitor every call and every everything, it was obvious that [Donaghy] was making certain calls in certain games that were favorable to certain sides."

The man simply known as Vegas Runner took this idea one step further. As someone who once worked side by side with Battista and today operates as a professional sports gambler and writer in Las Vegas, Vegas Runner revealed to me the key ingredient as to why this slipped through the cracks. It was a problem of an improperly preconceived mindset. "You know why [no one recognized the fix]? Because it was professional sports. These guys were under the misconception that you can't fix a professional sporting event because of the fact that these guys make too much money. A line moving didn't wake anybody up in the NBA. They were thinking, 'Okay, it's the wiseguys. They're on a hot run, it'll cool off.' But at the end of the day, these books out here seeing a line move in the NBA, seeing money coming in on the NBA, it didn't even register that these games could be fixed because it was pro. But I could promise you, if it was college, they would've been all over it. If it was UW-Green Bay versus Cleveland State and all of a sudden the line moved three or four points, and this happened five, six times in a row? And it went 5–1 or 6–0? Rest assured they'd be all over it. But if it was an NFL game, a Major League Baseball game, an NBA game, they just don't think it's touchable. They'd say to you, 'What are you going to do, approach Michael Jordan to fix a game? Pay Kobe Bryant to fix a game? How much can you possibly pay them?' They're under that thinking, that these guys are unapproachable." Even after the Donaghy scandal, these notions remain prevalent which is all the more frightening.

Once the FBI was involved in the case, the question again could be raised: where was the NBA? The FBI met with NBA commissioner David Stern and other league officials on June 15, 2007, but the story didn't break in the media until July 20. What was the NBA doing during that missing month? Circling their wagons. First, the NBA sealed a new television rights deal with ESPN/ABC and TNT on June 27. Then Donaghy resigned—he was never fired—on July 9. (In fact, had the FBI not become involved in this case, Donaghy could very well be an NBA official today.) Finally, Commissioner Stern held his press conference, stating at one point, "I can't believe it's happening to us." Yet as Jack McCallum of *Sports Illustrated* wrote in 2007, "No league can know everything about the private lives of its employees, but one league source says, 'When I heard that a referee was in trouble with gambling, I knew right away it was Donaghy.'"[12] Why would this be? Because the NBA *had* previously investigated Donaghy for his gambling habits, way back in 2005. At that time, the league only looked into his casino gambling (which was still a violation of the collective bargaining agreement between the league and its officials' union), failing to examine whether Donaghy's rampant gambling had spread elsewhere.

The NBA had absolutely nothing to gain by having the feds convict Donaghy of fixing games. Such a result would wreck the league's integrity, not preserve it. The arrest was bad, and Donaghy's damning accusations against the league were easily written off by a compliant media as mere "conspiracy theory" (despite his passing a polygraph test), but his contribution in fixing a game had greater ramifications. "[Battista] thus did not envision the NBA's 'investigation' getting any closer to the truth, since Battista could only imagine what implications there would be for the league if it concluded (let alone announced) that one or more referees were either active in, or privy to and/or profited from, the influencing of games by one or more referees. 'You're talking players' contracts and clauses being affected, teams not making the playoffs and losing revenues, fans pissed at the league for not preventing a rigged product from being put out there. How could you even start to calculate the losses to all sorts of people who could sue? In my eyes, there was no fucking way the NBA was ever going to document Elvis or anybody else fixing games.'"[13]

Battista was correct. The NBA's internal investigation, which was actually labeled a "compliance review," was led by Lawrence B. Pedowitz, a former chief of the Criminal Division in the United States Attorney's Office for the Southern District of New York. The ultimate determination was that Donaghy acted alone and did not fix any games (though this investigation examined only 17 games Donaghy officiated and did not speak to anyone within the gambling community). It is interesting to note, however, that Pedowitz discovered that 52 of the NBA's roster of 57 officials had broken their collective bargaining agreement with the league and had engaged in some form of gambling. This information was offered up by the offending officials even though they were neither the true focus of the investigation nor under oath. That being the case, with Donaghy already in federal custody and their jobs on the line, did those officials reveal the entire truth of their gambling habits? During his polygraph examination, Donaghy answered as "true" that officials often bet on which player would commit the first foul in a game. That didn't make it into what's now known as the Pedowitz Report. So what else is missing? To make matters worse, instead of firing those 52 officials as Stern could have, he announced that league rules would be rewritten to allow NBA officials more leeway to legally gamble. And the NBA was worried about its integrity because of Donaghy....

But the NBA wasn't out of the woods just yet. In June 2008, Donaghy's defense attorney John Lauro met with retired FBI agent Phil Scala who worked the Donaghy case until he was forced into mandatory retirement midway through the proceedings. "Scala told [Lauro] that the investigation yielded at least five to six other individuals of interest—including NBA referees—who could have been further investigated but that time, scarcity of resources, and statute issues had precluded it."[14] Donaghy would go on to write in his book, "To this day, I don't fully know why the individuals Scala felt were worth of investigating escaped further scrutiny. Maybe the U.S. Attorney's Office felt that my conviction sent an appropriate message, or that while more investigation might uncover wrongdoing, they would not be prosecutable offenses. Maybe the fact that my story had broken removed the element of surprise that could have aided an extended probe....Maybe political strings were being pulled to make sure I was cemented in the public's mind as the 'lone assassin.'"[15]

The notion of other referees fixing games is not beyond the realm of imagination. Battista told Griffin, "Do I think stuff like this, involving corrupt officials, is going on in other leagues? Absolutely. Do I have direct evidence of other officials? No, but the money involved is too big to ignore. You have to consider the financial situation for these officials. Yeah, they're making good money, but not when you compare it to the players they are working with. Look, the officials in pro sports are traveling all the time, too, and it's a fucking grind. They're making pennies compared to the athletes, and people get jealous, not to mention how much scrutiny they're under and how much shit they have to take from players, coaches, and fans. You're gonna get a certain percentage of officials who say, 'Fuck these ungrateful people,' and do what they think they have to do. So, you can see how they would rationalize selling information and betting on games. Also, don't forget how much some people like to gamble—once somebody owes a bookmaker some cash, who knows what they'd do to pay off their debt?"[16]

SO YOU WANT TO BE A PROFESSIONAL SPORTS GAMBLER

Archeological evidence shows that organized sport dates back to the rise of civilization. Not so coincidentally, there is similar evidence indicating that since the advent of sport, people have been wagering on the outcomes of those events. Gambling, it seems, is natural. It's who we are as humans. Artifacts relating to the dawn of the Olympics in ancient Greece have shown that the Greeks bet on athletics with great zeal. Should we be surprised then that there is also evidence from this period of athletes being bribed to under-perform, to fix the outcome in favor of those offering a cash reward? "The first recorded incident of actual cheating occurred in 388 B.C. when the boxer Eupolus of Thessaly bribed three opponents to take a dive. Olympic corruption peaked under Roman influence; in A.D. 67, the Emperor Nero bribed the judges to include poetry reading as an event. They also declared him the chariot champion, overlooking that he fell out and never finished the race."[1] Sport may have never been the pure ideal in which we all want to believe. For in the 2,000 years since these incidents, little has changed.

Today, sports gambling exists as a profession. Few have the fortitude, time, instinct and bankroll to make a living at it, but those that do—known as "sharps"—are indeed circulating amongst us "squares" in the general gambling public. It seems like such an easy living, that more sports fans would have the knowledge capable of gambling successfully on the games they love so much. Looking at it objectively, it's just the matter of picking the right side of a 50-50 proposition. Patriots or Jets? Cubs or Cardinals? Lakers or Celtics? Ali or Frazier? Heads or tails? That's it. That's as complex as it really gets. You form an opinion on a contest, back it with a monetary wager, and wait to see if it's correct. Yesterday doesn't matter as past performance isn't an indicator of future success, and tomorrow never comes. It's all about right now, this game, this outcome, and whether you'll stuff your pockets with the spoils of victory or only your hands as you sulk home a loser.

As sports gambling evolved in America since the late 1800s, complicating factors have arisen to foul up the simplicity inherent in what is still a 50-50 chance. In order to gamble, one has to have someone else with which to bet. Not everyone is willing to gamble on every event. And occasionally the two people wanting to gamble both prefer the same side because each party "knows" who is going to win. This created an opportunity for risky entrepreneurs, leading to the development of bookmakers (a.k.a. bookies) and odds. Bookmakers—those who took or "booked" bets—filled the void created by timid gamblers. They were the ones with whom anyone could bet no matter which side they preferred. The odds bookmakers created became their weapon, allowing these wagers to occur only if bettors were willing to sacrifice monetary return for opportunity. But the odds are a trick. They are an illusion, an assumption created on the gamblers' perception of a future event. While the odds may indicate that Team A should beat Team B nine out of ten times, what if this one game about to be played is that mythical tenth game? This is what sports gamblers must battle against—their own ideas.

A modern sports gambler need only pick the right side of that 50-50 proposition 52.38 percent of the time to break even. Anything above that is profit. "I can promise you that the best on the planet, the guys that are the sharpest in the world," professional sports gambler Vegas Runner revealed, "they're lucky to hit 57 percent, 58 percent [of their bets] in the course of a year. Most pros aim for 55 percent. If you could hit 55 percent, you could make a living. A damn good living. Anything above that is a bonus." If someone can win 58 percent of his bets, why couldn't he hit on 60 percent or more? Some claim to have such a talent. What would this higher percentage potentially earn for a gambler? As professional gambler Steve Fezzik wrote, "Do you know what a bettor could make hitting at 60 percent? Let's assume you start with $1,000 you were planning to buy a couch with. Instead, you decide to take a pot shot with it. You choose to play only one game a day, and wager what would normally be an insane 10 percent of your bankroll each play, laying -110. A little over five years later you wind up with a 1,200–800 record (60 percent). Guess how much money your $1,000 will grow to? $10,000? $50,000? Nope. $550 billion. Yes, that's BILLION. It sounds ridiculous, but believe me, the math completely supports it. So the next time a guy tells you he is a 60 percent handicapper, you might want to confirm whether he is a multimillionaire. If he isn't, it is likely he either: 1) cannot hit 60 percent or 2) is one horrific money manager."[2]

A LINE DRAWN IN THE SAND

Originally, sporting wagers were made with odds, much like horse racing is bet today. If you placed a $20 wager on a team that was listed as 5-1 (or 5 to 1) and they won, you'd get back $100 (five times the $20 bet). This was all well and good, but sometimes the odds weren't enough. For one, certain contests did not lend themselves to the creation of odds which would attract wagers. Sometimes the event in question was seen as being so one-sided bookies didn't want to offer odds. Plus bookies didn't like trying to make a living off of their clients' losses. It made them appear lecherous, as if they enjoyed watching their clients lose. Bookmakers saw themselves as offering a service. They were in effect a betting exchange, a go-between that took in and distributed money amongst gamblers who didn't know how to connect with other like-minded individuals. As any good capitalist would, the bookies didn't think this service should be offered for free. Over time, the bookies began to charge a "vigorish" or "vig" (or "juice") on every wager made. At first, bettors would have to put down $6 to win $5 (with the bookie keeping the rest). Today, the standard is wagering $11 to win $10. This gives the "house" a 4.54 percent advantage which creates the situation forcing a gambler to win more than 52.38 percent of his bets to be profitable.

By charging this vig, the bookie remains neutral. What he wants more than anything is a situation in which 50 percent of the money is bet on one team and 50 percent is bet on their opponent. When the game ends and the winners are paid with the losers' money, the bookie would be guaranteed a five percent profit from the vig. That can make for a fine living. But that's in a perfect world. Rarely does a game create an exact 50-50 split on wagers. A bookmaker—be it the Caesars Palace sports book or Bernie the bookie down the block—can deal with a game where wagering becomes slightly one-sided. But the last thing they want to see is wagers on the game come in at a differential of 70-30 or worse. When that occurs, and it occurs more often than you think, the bookmaker has a clear rooting interest and can lose big with the wrong result.

Baseball is still bet upon based on odds. This is often called the "money line" or sometimes the "dime line." The money line represents a conversion from a team's theoretical chance of winning into odds against a dollar. A team that is given a 60 percent chance of winning would be favored at -150 (or -$1.50, meaning for every $1.50 bet, the winner gets only $1 in return). A team priced at -200 is believed to have a 66.7 percent chance of winning. Typically, the odds set on a baseball game list a team as -110 if the game is considered an even match. If a gambler wagers $11, he would win $10, which maintains the bookies' usual vig. But these odds can change, depending on which team is favored (in baseball this is often based on the starting pitchers). A favored team may be listed at -120, while the underdog is +110. This would mean it would take a $12 bet to get back $10 on the favorite, but a $10 bet on the underdog would earn $11. Usually, the difference between the favorite and the underdog won't vary by more than ten cents (hence the term "dime line"), but it can and often does happen. This can create a 20-cent or more differential, with the favorite -140 and the underdog +120. Professionals will often avoid betting under such circumstances, but recreational gamblers don't. And bookies make their profits when underdogs win which usually occurs about 45 percent of the time.

As can be seen, the odds alone can sway a smart gambler away from placing a bet. Even if a game appears to be a "sure thing," are you really willing to risk $150 or $200 to only win $100 when you should normally be risking only $110 to win the same amount? This is the baseball bettor's dilemma. Fortunately for those wanting to gamble on basketball and football, the odds and the sometimes exorbitant amount needed to lay down on a bet are no longer the norm (though you can still bet on the money line if you like). No, those days have vanished thanks to the creation of the point spread, a.k.a. the line.

To those unfamiliar with the point spread, here is a quick tutorial. Say the Detroit Lions are playing the Seattle Seahawks, and the Lions have a 10–1 record on the year while the Seahawks are an anemic 3–8. Instead of offering potentially lopsided odds on this game as was once the case, the bookmaker now offers a number; in this example, nine points. As the favored team, the Lions are listed as minus nine points (-9) or said to be giving nine points to the Seahawks. That simply means that the Lions would have to win by ten points or more for a gambler to win his wager. The reverse option is also available. Bets on the Seahawks getting nine points (+9) mean if the Seahawks lose by less than nine points or win the game outright, the gambler wins. If the game ended with the Lions winning by exactly nine points, it's considered a "push" and all money is returned. All bets, whether for the Lions or the Seahawks in this scenario, would pay off at $11 to $10, guaranteeing the bookie his vig.

The point spread came into existence in the late 1930s as a new way to bet college basketball. Though the name of the person who originally devised it has been lost to history, it's believed that Chicago bookmaker Charles McNeil first offered it as a betting option. Originally, the point spread was known as the split line. Using the previous example between the Lions and Seahawks, the split line would have been set at 10/8. To bet the Lions, gamblers would need the team to win by ten points or more. For the Seahawks, they would have had to lose by eight points or less. This was a subtle, yet significant difference. Why? Because with the split line, had the game ended with the Lions winning by exactly nine, it was not a push. No money was returned; the bookmaker won all bets. As the bookies' acuity increased, more games ended in the middle of the split line's numbers causing bettors to shy away, especially in football where teams often won by three, seven or ten points. The loss of business forced the bookmakers' hands, leading to the refinements of the modern point spread system.

THE LINE'S ORIGINS

The line set on a game has to originate from somewhere. It's not released by the leagues with the announcement of the day's officials. For quite some time, point spreads were disseminated throughout the nation having originated mainly from a single source. This was the "Outlaw" line, named as such due to the illegal nature of sports gambling.

Beginning after World War II, Leo Hirschfield set what was known as the Minneapolis Line. Based in Minnesota because of its central location which assured fast mail times and a solid long-distance phone infrastructure, Hirschfield sent his numbers to thousands of illegal bookies spread across the nation. Besides setting the line, Hirschfield's company published the *Green Sheet* which was a tout sheet offering insights and recommendations on upcoming games. In other words, he set the line for the bookies then published a newsletter giving bettors ideas on how to beat it, profiting from both ends. Though those that used his services were breaking the law, Hirschfield's business was 100 percent legitimate.

During the 1950s–'60s, the Outlaw line came under control of the mafia based in New York City. Soon it was transferred to the Chicago mob where it was overseen by a sports gambling genius, Frank "Lefty" Rosenthal. Robert DeNiro's character Sam "Ace" Rothstein in the Martin Scorsese film *Casino* was based on Rosenthal. Lefty was no angel. He was in deep with the mob and fixed games—the known fixes included college football and basketball. But his influence helped legitimize sports gambling when he arrived in Las Vegas in the 1970s.

Prior to then, the sports gambling scene in Las Vegas began in the 1940s when mobster Mickey Cohen brought in the horse racing wire. Come the 1960s, casinos did not possess sports books. Instead, independent race and sports books dotted Las Vegas, most of which were named after famous horse racing tracks. Harry Gordon opened perhaps the most influential one in the 1960s on the spot where the Paris hotel/casino stands today—the Churchill Downs Race & Sports book. One of Gordon's first decisions was to hire Bob Martin to create his sports betting lines. "Bob Martin was an absolute genius at making numbers (point spread, money line and odds) to book with. Nobody ever completely knew what he did or how he came up with his numbers, numbers he booked to, numbers that could get two-way action (bettors wager on both teams). Bob said, 'when it fits like a glove, you know it's the right number.' Bob Martin was king of odds makers. He was the judge of the sports betting world. His word could settle disputes anywhere in the country. Just ask Bob, and whatever Bob Martin says goes. No one has ever filled that universal position since."[3] Like Hirschfield and Lefty before him, Martin's line tended to be *the* line everywhere.

The 1960s also saw two major changes take place within the sports gambling world. On the plus side was the creation of the "totals" wager, today often referred to as the "under/over line." A bet on the totals is a bet on whether the amount of points scored by both teams in a game—be it baseball, football or basketball—is either more or less than the number the bookmaker lists. "Bill Dark was the creator of the totals. Bill was the first to ever book totals. His original total was a Dodgers game with Sandy Koufax pitching. Bill made the total something like three. As a bookmaker, Bill could drive his players crazy. He was known to take the phone off the hook when he had the money on a game the way he wanted it."[4] But the major negative came in 1960 when the federal government gave sports gamblers a one-two punch in the form of the "Kennedy Law." Passed as an initiative against organized crime, it made it illegal to place a bet from one state to another. It also imposed a ten percent "excise tax" on all wagers. As the icing on the cake, all bookmakers—whether legal or illegal—were forced to purchase a $50 yearly stamp/license from the government in order to book a bet. Needless to say, these actions initially curtailed the action of sports gamblers everywhere. While some bookies came out of the woodwork to follow the letter of the law, many dove further into the shadows.

Scott Schettler, the former head of the Stardust Race and Sports book, worked in Las Vegas during this innovative era. In his book *We Were Wiseguys and Didn't Know It* he explained how the bookies got around the government's demands. "At that time, there was a 10 percent federal tax on race and sports bets, which neither players nor bookies could overcome. The sports books operated on maybe 3 percent. You can't win 3 percent and pay 10 percent of the gross to the feds. Likewise, the sharpest player on the planet couldn't survive paying a 10 percent tax, penalty, extortion, or whatever you call it. You couldn't book or bet in a compliant, legit book. So the books figured out a way to get out of the 10 percent federal tax long before I hit town. For the bettors who were known and trusted, we would write an 'R' on the bottom of their ticket. The 'R,' just in case anybody would question, stood for 'tax refund,' but it had a different meaning for us. All Las Vegas books had their own system but essentially served the same end. If a bettor was an 'R' customer (known and trusted), we would write his ticket for 10 percent value, i.e., a $100 bet was written for $10 but with an 'R' on the bottom. This way when we checked out, graded the ticket, and he cashed it, it was worth the full $100 wager. To the bean counters, it was worth $10. When the 'R' customer cashed it, the cashier would see the 'R' and knew it was really a $100 wager….It had to be done to stay open."[5]

Luckily the sports gambling community had someone with clout on their side. Nevada senator Howard Cannon pushed legislation through Congress in 1974 cutting the ten percent tax on sports wagers down to just two percent. Nine years later, it would drop to its current 0.25 percent. Cannon's legislation breathed new life into sports gambling in

Las Vegas, and in August 1975, the Union Plaza opened the first sports book within a hotel/casino. Linesmaker Bobby Martin was brought in to run the operation as his line continued to be the trusted number. But Lefty Rosenthal did the Union Plaza not one, but one hundred better. He opened a massive 9,000 square-foot race and sports book at the Stardust hotel/casino with room for six hundred gamblers. Lefty's pride and joy catered more to horse players than sports bettors (times have clearly changed), but both were blown away by the size and scope of the operation. "[Lefty] built a mammoth race and sports book with ceilings three stories high. The race and sports boards were a couple stories high themselves, reaching almost to the ceiling. They were big enough to require catwalks and ladders behind them, so odds and results could be put in by hand, much like the Fenway Park or Wrigley Field scoreboards. He installed a state-of-the-art satellite TV system with a monster theater screen and a complement of smaller screens to bring in games and races other books didn't even acknowledge as existing. He had a maintenance crew assigned exclusively to take care of the satellite system and TVs."[6] The Stardust book also became the first to pay off winning tickets 24 hours a day.

At first, the Stardust relied upon Bob Martin's numbers to create their odds. But in 1983 Schettler took over, and instead of taking one man's opinion for the line on a game, he relied upon himself and a cast of four characters: Jerry the Hat, Michael "Roxy" Roxborough, Bobby "the Owl" Beghtel, and Kenny White. With their expertise, the group would "just hash [the line] out off the top of our heads." But very soon their line, their odds were relied upon and quoted throughout the nation. "A lot of the other places were timid, but we weren't," Schettler recounted. "It was our line. We crunched the numbers ourself, put up a virgin line, and opened up every morning like a bank at eight o'clock. And there would be a mob of people. Money from all over the country, through their beards in Las Vegas, would bet that line." During its heyday in the mid-to-late 1980s, sharp bettors would participate in a lottery just for the privilege to line up to have a crack at the Stardust's opening numbers. "They [the serious players] were looking for weak spots in our line, of course. If they found a weak spot—so what?—they still had to win the game. If they won the game—so what?—they'd be back in the morning for new openers. Look at it like this: We were all passing the same $20 bill back and forth. Only we held it for 20 days, and the players held it for ten."[7]

As the atmosphere of Las Vegas changed with the influx of corporate money in the 1990s, so too did the sports books. Schettler left the Stardust in 1991, seeing the writing on the wall. "Las Vegas nowadays," he said, "they don't take that much money on bets. They're corporate-owned. In my day, individuals owned the books and they were all gamblers. You could just take whatever you wanted. But nowadays it's corporate-run and the guys wear suits and ties and shake their heads up and down, yes and no. They don't take much money and they're scared to death to lose. It's a little different atmosphere now. If you tried to come out now and bet a few hundred thousand on a game, automatically you alert somebody. [In fact, every sports book wager over $10,000 in Las Vegas requires the bettor to show his identity and give a Social Security number.] Back in my day, it was just a routine thing. Guys would bet that much every day. We had guys that would bet a hundred thousand a day. It just kind of blended in."

Just how corporate-controlled are the Las Vegas sports books? Cantor Gaming, which according to one published report in 2011 took 40 percent of all sports bets in Las Vegas, runs the books at the Tropicana, the Hard Rock, the Cosmopolitan, and at its flagship location, the M Resort. The M has become the place to wager for sharp bettors. And while most Vegas sports books don't have predetermined limits, only the M boasts it will book any size bet on any game. (The Philly Godfather laughed at the M's boast, telling me, "No chance. They would be broke in a week." Many other professional sports gamblers echoed this sentiment.) Cantor has been looking to become *the* name in Las Vegas sports gambling and to expand its operations. Its sights have been recently set on commandeering the Bally's group of nine Vegas sports books, including the Rio and Caesars Palace. The other major player is MGM, whose sports betting halls include itself and eight others like the Mirage and Treasure Island. Betting in any one of these connected sports books is like betting in them all, as each ring of books possesses the same odds and lines. The only difference is if you want to pretend you're placing your bet in New York, Paris, or ancient Egypt.

THE NATURE OF THE BEAST

There are three very important facts to remember about the line. First and foremost is that the point spread does not necessarily signify which team bookmakers believe will win a game. It is not based solely on two teams' strengths and weaknesses; it is based largely on the public's perception of those factors. In other words, if the Lions are favored by nine points over the Seahawks with an under/over line set at 45, it's not because the bookmakers think Detroit will beat Seattle 27–18. No, the line is set at those specific numbers because this is what bookmakers believe the public will think the final score may be. As former sports book director at Caesars Palace, Vincent Magliulo wrote, "The purpose of the betting line is to balance the action. It is not a prediction of an event's outcome. Wagering is an opinion of bettors that is backed up with monetary gain in mind. As a bookmaker, the goal is to attract equal amounts of money on each side, not necessarily to split the opinions equally."[8]

A member of Schettler's crew and the onetime president of the oddsmaking service Las Vegas Sports Consultants, Roxy Roxborough expanded on this idea. He wrote, "The line, or odds, is the key to running a successful sportsbook….Linemaking involves handicapping the bettors who create the bulk of the action. Suppose the Giants are a two-point favorite over the Saints and there are 101 bettors interested in the game. One hundred of those like the Giants at -2 for $55 to win $50. The last bettor likes the Saints at +2 for $5,500 to win $5,000. The line certainly didn't split the opinions of the 101 bettors. However, it did split the money, which is the most any oddsmaker or bookmaker can ask."[9]

Another key fact to know about the line is that it is not universal nor stagnant. It moves. Often. It is adjusted, pushed, pulled, and outright manipulated. Of moving the line, Magliulo wrote, "In bookmaking, as in all casino games, there is a need to limit liability. This is where line movement comes into play. It is rare that the opening line or price will attract equal amounts of money on both (or all) sides."[10] While injuries, weather conditions, or other unforeseen incidents may cause a line to move, more often than not money is the deciding factor. If the Lions at -9 created a situation where a majority of the money being wagered is on the Lions, the books will move the line to perhaps -9.5 or -10 in an attempt to entice bettors to take the other side, trying to balance the action.

Those sharp players, the kind that used to stand in line for the opening numbers at the Stardust? They serve a valuable purpose for the books. In a sense, their bets are votes on the validity of the line. "Before the offshore markets opened up where you could get down so much action with the click of a mouse," Vegas Runner explained, "we [the sharp bettors] were more or less an asset to the bookmakers because by letting one of us bet into them, they knew how to adjust their lines. It'd also stop other wiseguys and professionals who were going to piggyback that play from getting that same number [because the line would have already moved]. You have to remember that professional bettors don't look at these as teams; we strictly look at numbers. It's all about getting down at the right number. [In football] if the point spread is -2.5, I like Team A. But if the point spread moves to -3.5, Team B is more attractive, knowing that 3 is one of those numbers that a [football] game ends on 11 to 16 percent of the time. So I want to be on the right side of that 3. Recreational gamblers don't get it. They bet teams, not numbers. If they're going to bet the New England Patriots at -7, when they call their bookmaker and get -8.5, they're still going to bet it. But a professional bettor knows how important every half-point is, and there's no way he's going to lay 8.5 at that point."

In the days when news of line movements traveled much more slowly, betting coups could easily occur. Underground bookies reliant upon the Outlaw line to set their numbers wouldn't always know if it was truly accurate for each game. Not recognizing a good number from a bad one could cost a bookie dearly. Lacking today's widely available sports information, those early bookies weren't informed of every team and every game. Sharp bettors who did their homework were quick to take advantage of this ignorance.

Bookies had their advantages as well. Even in the days when the crew at the Stardust was setting the line for America, most gamblers wouldn't realize that the number they were betting on Sunday just before kickoff was completely different from the one released six days earlier. With value packed into every half-point, not knowing the line had bounced around prior to placing a wager equated to a cardinal sin (unless, of course, it ended on the number you wanted). Another trick available to bookies was to shade lines. For example, a New York bookmaker may add an extra point or two to the Jets-Broncos line, making the Jets a -9 favorite rather than the -7 it was listed at everywhere else. How could he get away with this? A wise bookie would know most of his customers were "homers" and would bet on the local team no matter the spread—and most didn't know the spread until they asked their bookie. It was easy pickings. Even so, a wise gambler with the proper connections and knowledge could exploit this variance in the line as well.

The casino sports books weren't immune to this either. As Schettler wrote, "Say we [at the Stardust] open UCLA at -4 over USC. UCLA gets bet up to 5.5 or 6 [by the first bettors of the day]. The other sports books hang up our 6 or maybe 5.5. They're assuming we took all the risk and they're safe with a 6 or 5.5. At the end of the day, they would only get one-way action, all +6, +5.5, +5, and 4.5. We had UCLA money on the way up to -5.5 and -6 and USC money coming back the other way at +6, +5.5, +5. We had two-way action; the books that hung our numbers at their zenith would have one-sided business. We usually needed a side of course, big or small, *but* we also had two-way action."[11]

"There are so few real bookmakers anymore," lamented Vegas Runner. "Most of today's guys are bookkeepers, not bookmakers. There are a select few that know they are strong when they put out a number. Now, even the biggest ones here on the Strip—the MGMs, the Caesars—they're looking at line screen. And if they see a sharp book like Pinnacle or the Greek or CRIS Sports offshore move their line, they're not going to have an opinion on their own. They're going to move it, too. We call this 'moving it on air.' No real bookmaker would do this. You'd have to bet into them for the line to budge."

Because the line may change due to the amount of money bet on a particular side, this opens the line up to manipulation. When I asked Schettler if people attempted to manipulate the lines, he was quick to respond, "Of course! Absolutely! That was a daily battle. That was when we did it all by hand. We didn't rely on computers. When the computers came in, we just ignored them. We still went by our instincts. The line? The line was definitely manipulated. You could swing the line, you know? That was not a problem."

For the guys with the clout to move a line—and not just anyone can—there is a strategy behind manipulating it. If the Lions sat at -9, but the sharp player wanted the Seahawks *if* they were at +10, a few well-placed bets on the Lions could get the books to start moving the line toward that magic number. Some players mimic or "piggyback" on sharp players' bets. When this occurred and even more money came in on the Lions, the line would be forced to move to   -10 or maybe even -10.5. At that point, the sharp bettor who put this scheme into motion would come in and bet heavier on the Seahawks than he had on the Lions and get the number—maybe even a better number—that he originally wanted. The first money bet was willingly sacrificed for a wiser, more calculated wager that hopefully results in greater rewards.

Betting syndicates, like the type James "BaBa" Battista ran when working with Tim Donaghy, have the power and cash to bend point spreads to their whim. There are only a handful out there, most of which have nicknames like the Scholar Group, the Kosher Kids, the Asian, or Tiger. But the king of the hill was once known as the Computer Group. Now it's better known simply by the name of its leader, Billy Walters. "Billy's smart. Probably the smartest gambler there is," Schettler claimed. "He's the best right now. He can influence the line just by looking at a game." Manipulating the line was part of Walters' m.o. "He would use us," Schettler explained. "They would come in the morning and bet with us at the Stardust on the games they wanted to lose. So say USC is playing UCLA and they wanted UCLA, well, they would come in and bet on USC. We would change the line, and the whole country would wait for us before they put up their line, even the illegals around the country. Well, Billy and his crew had successfully altered the line,

an army of informants to give him the lines at all the different sports books now could log on to a website and see every number on a single screen. So, too, could the sports books. They could see what their competition were doing, when the lines moved, and to what number. Now when a big, number-altering bet is placed, it is instantly known the world over. To utilize runners today, a syndicate must coordinate their bets like a precision air strike and hit books all over the world with the right number at the same time before they witness the line movements.

And the entire world is certainly in play for sports gamblers. Enterprising folks have opened up online sports books in several Caribbean countries where sports gambling is legal, creating new outlets for desirous bettors. Many European and Asian countries have legal sports wagering as well. All of these can be utilized by gamblers with the proper connections. Shockingly, these foreign outlets can be used to manipulate the lines in the United States. "Most people in the U.S. don't even have a passport," Vegas Runner explained. "They don't realize how big the world is. There's so much going on in the Asian market, the European market, before we even wake up. And a lot of the guys that get the most respect are the ones that can manipulate the market the most. They set a lot of the games up by simply sprinkling some money early in Asia or Europe on one side so the line moves, and it keeps moving, and the other followers that aren't in the know think it's a sharp play and they start piggybacking it and eventually the line goes up, up, up, and come later through the U.S. market, they bet the side they really like in the first place. So now instead of getting the Browns at +6, you get them at +8." This isn't too far removed from the manipulations seen within the world's financial markets. In fact, to listen to some sports gamblers talk, you would think they are discussing stocks, not football games. The teams are companies; the lines are their prices; and the bets are investments. It is day trading with the results seen on ESPN and in *Sports Illustrated*, not CNBC or the *Wall Street Journal*.

There is a major drawback to all of this offshore gambling—getting one's money out of a foreign country. Many a gambler has been burned by less-than-reputable offshore books which either take their sweet time in paying off or simply don't pay at all (What are you going to do? Fly

too often, he becomes a sharp himself and his action may be limited. There's also the issue of wagering a large amount on a side on which the book is already heavy. This is getting to be a bigger problem in the age of corporate-controlled books because they are always looking to limit liability. But perhaps the biggest problem of all is that large bets tend to move lines. With so many books now interconnected, one big bet can shift the point spread at eight or more books. This is why gamblers need multiple outs.

The more places a gambler can bet, the more he can get down on a game. And when a bettor sees an edge that needs to be taken advantage of, there can never be too many places where he can bet. In the pre-computer age of sports wagering, the line moved slowly after a number-changing bet. Gamblers could send their runners literally running to the next book down the Strip to get a bet down on a good number before it moved, or else they could hit the phones and bet, bet, bet with every illegal bookie available until the line changed. It was a race, but a fair one.

When the Internet was introduced, all this changed. "Don Bessette came up with the first public Internet line service. [Jimmy] Sirody would call the Stardust line changes in to him, and Bessette would update the computer manually for his original thirty-five customers. Bessette would later sell to Al Corbo, and then it became known as Don Best....that's how they started, across the Strip from the Stardust, in a small upstairs room."[13] The Don Best subscription service is still going strong today and is run by Kenny White, formerly of Schettler's linemaking crew at the Stardust.

Don Best gave its clients up-to-the-second line changes at all the major sports books. Well, most of the time. The man known as the Philly Godfather admitted in a podcast interview with Vegas Runner posted on Pregame.com that sometimes Don Best would hold up sending out the line changes to their customers until certain bets of their own were made. Legal? That's a bit of a gray area (for the record, Philly Godfather is no longer affiliated with Don Best). But the Don Best service curtailed the need for runners. Gamblers like Lem Banker who once relied upon

nia—feeding me lines. They wanted to follow my games. So they'd give me the lines and they'd all be different. But I could never do it again." Billy Walters uses runners as well, though technically his associates skirt the law by being considered "investors," putting up their own money for a share of the profits. Even so, one of his runners was charged in 2011 with stealing nearly $500,000 from Walters' gambling enterprise known as ACME Group Trading. The arrest brought further scrutiny to Walters' group's activities.

While Las Vegas sports book operators may not openly admit it, they know who the runners are. They even "comp" them. Why? "Because they become an asset," claimed the aptly named Vegas Runner. "When I was running on the Strip, I never hid the fact. They knew who I was." The reason the job exists is because big-time bettors cannot be everywhere at once. What these gamblers and syndicates need are "outs" or places to bet. Because the sharp players are considered as such due to a reputation of being consistent winners, they are often limited in the amount of money they can put down on a game within a particular book. A sharp may want to bet $100,000 on a certain game, but the book may limit him to only ten percent of that. Why? Simply because they are "sharp." And in certain cases—especially when a book is heavy on the side the sharp wants to play—the book is outright afraid of losing. This is where the runner comes in handy. The known sharp may only be able to get $10,000 out of his desired $100,000 down, but the runner can appear as a separate, independent bettor while actually increasing the sharp's bet without the book's knowledge.

Of course in this day and age, this isn't as easy as it sounds. For one, a book—be it legal or illegal—is going to look suspiciously at a newbie walking in wanting to wager thousands of dollars on a game. ID will be required, and questions will be asked. Gambling writer Michael Konik chronicled his adventures as a working runner in the book *The Smart Money*. Konik wrote that in initially placing money on account with the sports book, he had to create a plausible backstory for himself, otherwise his wagers may have been denied. If trust is built between the gamblers and the book, bigger bets are often allowed; however, another problem crops up in actually getting the money down on a bet. If the runner wins

and then they'd just go to all different places around the country and bet the other side. It was pretty neat."

Schettler seemed impressed with Walters, partly because he respected the bookmakers. "Billy and his crew also put out false games because they knew people followed them. They didn't want to put all the book-makers out of business, so they'd put out false games, false moves, and all the dumbbells, no matter what those guys bet, they would just blindly bet [what Walters did]. It was really funny. You'd listen to these bettors: 'Billy Walters has USC.' 'No, he's got UCLA!' They don't know who the hell he's got. It was just a riot." At the Stardust, Schettler even welcomed Walters and his crew because they were useful. "[Walters] supposedly won like $25 million in one year. So I said, 'I don't care what they win. They could win $25 million, and I hope they do because if I do my job correctly, and balance my books, I'm going to make $500,000 in juice."

There is just one small problem with these betting syndicates. They're illegal. The syndicate in and of itself isn't illegal, but they often employ "runners." Runners are lackeys who place bets on the syndicates' behalf. This is called "messenger betting," and aspects of it, such as being paid to place bets for others, are against Nevada state law. This activity also raises questions under federal law. The IRS has always had interest in the activity because of the potential lack of reported, taxable winnings. The agency renewed its efforts in examining messenger betting in 2011, getting the attention of the major Vegas bookmakers. At that time, IRS Special Agent in Charge Paul Camacho was quoted in the *Las Vegas Review-Journal* as saying, "Many out-of-state operations use runners to lay off bets in Vegas. A word of caution to those acting as runners for bookies: You are obligated to inform the casino who you are conducting the transaction on behalf of. Withholding information will cause a false Currency Transaction Report to be filed. Willfully causing a false CTR is a felony. Federal forfeiture statutes also may apply, making the vig the worst bet in town."[12]

Using runners to place bets is not a new invention. "When I was successful years ago," legendary sports gambler Lem Banker told me, "I had runners all over the country—New York, Miami, Chicago, Califor-

down to Aruba to collect? Good luck finding the guy(s) sitting on the other end of that Internet connection). Also, the U.S. government has cracked down on this illegal (or to some, quasi-legal) form of gambling. "In 2000, Jay Cohen became the first person to be convicted of running an illegal offshore Internet sports gambling operation. Cohen, co-owner of World Sports Exchange, based in Antigua, was sentenced to twenty-one months in prison and was fined $5,000. Six years later, David Carruthers, the former chief executive of an online company called BetOnSports, and ten others were indicted on Wire Act violations. He was sentenced to thirty-three months in prison in 2010 after pleading guilty. BetOnSports, which was based in London, took in $1.25 billion in 2004. No less than 98 percent of the revenue came from bets by U.S.-based gamblers, according to court papers."[14]

In 2006, the Unlawful Internet Gambling and Enforcement Act was passed. It granted the federal government the power to go after payment processors, credit card companies, and banks which route money sent to and from gambling companies. Aimed squarely at offshore Internet casinos and poker websites, the law covers international sports books as well. There are loopholes for offshore books to skirt this law, but most are time-consuming. In this age of instant gratification, few gamblers want to sit and wait for their winnings, especially when there are other bets to be made. The federal government has already enforced this law by setting up false payment processing websites, an act that ensnared ten offshore sports books in 2011 with some involved pleading guilty. A result of this action has been to scare some offshore book operators from setting foot on U.S. soil, further complicating things for enterprising bettors.

Of course, there are alternatives to these alternatives. "Every guy that I know that is a professional bettor does 90 percent of their stuff outside of Vegas," said Vegas Runner, "and not necessarily offshore. Offshore there's really just a handful of reputable books. And most big-time bettors do not want to put their bankrolls in a foreign country in a non-interest-bearing account. A guy betting $20,000 or $50,000 a game would have to give the book $1 million upfront. To put $1 million in a non-interest-bearing account does them no good. But they do use the reputable offshore books where it's more or less a credit basis, but the rest use locals." "Locals" in Vegas Runner's parlance doesn't mean local Las Vegas books. He is referring to illegal bookies operating within the United States.

THE MOB

The last thing one must remember about the line is that sports gambling outside of Nevada (with a slight exception) is illegal. A little clarification is in order: It's perfectly legal for two people to bet on a game or for a group of people to have a Super Bowl pool as long as 100 percent of the money put in is paid out. The legal trouble arises when there's a fee associated with these wagers such as a bookie's vig. On the federal level, no law exists that outlaws individuals from betting on games. However, the Wire Act of 1961 does prohibit sports gambling operations from accepting wagers, as the law made the transfer of gambling information across state lines—which covers all forms of communication, whether written, phone or Internet—illegal. Even so, no individual bettor has ever been arrested or tried for gambling on sports (many bookmakers, however, have not been as fortunate). But on a state level, there are laws that prohibit gambling on sporting events, though few gamblers have been prosecuted. To hammer this gambling prohibition home, the 1992 Professional and Amateur Sports Protection Act (PASPA) barred states from legalizing sports gambling or creating their own, state-sponsored sports betting programs. The only exceptions were states that had previously legalized it: Nevada, Delaware, Oregon, and Montana. By law, these four states could only have forms of sports gambling that each allowed prior to the passage of PASPA. In other words, Delaware could allow betting on NFL parlay cards as it had in 1976 (which the state did re-legalize in 2009) but it could not have single-game betting or open full-service sports books as are allowed in Nevada. Currently the state of New Jersey is fighting PASPA, hoping to legalize sports gambling on all levels to coexist with the legal casino operations in Atlantic City. However, as the state's case slowly turned from one about sports gambling into an argument over state's rights and the Tenth Amendment, their prospects of winning slipped away. New Jersey was dealt a crushing loss early in 2013, but plans on appealing the ruling—all the way to the

Supreme Court if need be.

To the uninitiated, what follows is perhaps the most shocking statistic you will read in this book. In 2008, the total amount wagered in the legal Nevada sports books was $2.57 billion. When the National Gambling Impact Study Commission (NGISC) issued its final report in 1999, it estimated that anywhere from $80 to $380 billion a year was gambled illegally in the United States. In other words, possibly only one percent of all the money gambled in the United States on sporting event is done so legally.

"Despite the enormous amount wagered illegally every year, the United States has lapsed into a general approach of non-enforcement of illegal sports wagering laws, both at the state and federal level," wrote Anthony Cabot, a lawyer specializing in gambling law. "Law enforcement efforts to deal with illegal sports wagering have declined dramatically in the past twenty years. In 1960, almost 123,000 arrests were made for illegal gambling. FBI arrest statistics reveal that all gambling arrests in the United States have steadily declined since 1994 and totaled less than 10,000 in 2008. In contrast, the number of illegally wagered dollars has increased dramatically. In 1983, only $8 billion were wagered on sports in the United States compared to an estimated $380 billion in 2009.

"Many factors have contributed to this decline in arrests. First, law enforcement has reallocated its limited resources to more serious crimes. Second, federal laws and prosecutorial policies have become increasingly confusing and contradictory. Therefore, prosecutors may be less anxious to test the laws in fear of creating bad precedence. Third, the penalties assessed against those who violate betting laws are generally low, and often do not justify the time or expense of law enforcement. Fourth, improvements in technology have made it more difficult to detect and prosecute offenders. Attempting to apprehend and prosecute gambling operators in foreign countries is often a challenge. Fifth, the public does not perceive gambling as a serious crime or even a crime at all: office pools on sporting events, such as the NCAA basketball tournament and the NFL Super Bowl, flourish. Championship games are frequently marked by 'friendly' bets between governors. Finally, the media has contributed to the public perception of sports gambling as an enjoyable and legal pastime. For example, wagering on fantasy sports is widespread. Additionally, the NGISC claimed, albeit somewhat incredibly, that because point spreads are available in almost every major U.S. newspaper, many people do not know that sports wagering is illegal. The fact that newspapers post point spreads shows that the public enjoys wagering on sporting events. Because most states have laws against sports wagering, law enforcement is placed in the uncomfortable position of enforcing laws that are unpopular with the public."[15]

"You've got a tremendous demand out there, and someone's going to provide for it," said former FBI Special Agent Tom French. Who will do that? Who can handle $380 billion in bets a year? "Bookmaking is probably one of the biggest moneymakers for the mob," French continued. "It's sports betting, it's horses to a lesser extent, and numbers, too. Sports betting is huge for the mob. All five families. And right on the heels of that is loan sharking because of people who cannot pay off their bets." French should know. He worked cases for the FBI's New York bureau from 1971 until 1998, spending 15 years as a supervisor. As part of his assignment, he worked sports bribery cases as well as making sports bribery presentations to teams in all of the major leagues.

While some parents are surprised to discover their child is dealing illegal drugs, many sports gamblers may be shocked to learn that their local bookie is connected to the mob. Perhaps not directly, but the roots of organized crime's control over the illegal sports gambling market run deep. Here's how: Say you bet $50 on the Chicago Bears in their game against the Dallas Cowboys this weekend with your local bookie. No big deal, right? But the bookie is loaded with one-sided action on the Bears. So to help balance his books—because remember, he is looking to profit mainly from the vig, not losing wagers—he himself makes a bet on the Bears with another, larger bookie he knows in Dallas. The Dallas bookie was facing the same problem—too many bets on the Cowboys and nothing on the Bears. The one bookie's Bears bet helps the other balance his books, and perhaps vice versa with the Dallas bookie betting into the other with the Cowboys. This is called a layoff bet. As smaller bookies bet into larger ones, all of this layoff money is funneled through the system to bigger and bigger bookies, the biggest of which are mob-controlled. The mafia even created a nationwide system starting in the 1950s to run this layoff operation. It has never ceased to exist. So while you think your $50 is just bet with "your guy," even if he isn't directly working with organized crime, it's likely your $50 will sooner or later land in some mobster's lap.

Of course nowadays you don't need to call your local bookie. That's time-consuming, and perhaps monitored by the authorities. The best way to reach your man is through a pay-per-head site. "Ninety-nine percent of bookmakers now don't answer phones," explained Vegas Runner. "They have you go on a website, to a pay-per-head." These websites usually charge the bookmakers $10–$15 per customer/head a week to run the bookmaker's operation. Using the website's software, the bookie can assign accounts to each of his bettors and track everything through there. Players book their bets through the site and the bookie tracks each account's status without ever interacting with the bettor, except perhaps to settle up at the predetermined time or amount. Limits with local bookies are dependent on how sharp you are perceived to be and basic trust. A loaded square bettor likely can bet more through locals than through Vegas.

Who is monitoring all of this illegal, underground action? Who is looking for unusual line movements or manipulations? No one. It's the Wild West. Even within the relatively small community of serious sports gamblers, unusual activity is spotted all the time. The problem is that who is an honest, law-breaking gambler going to go to with such information? The mob? The feds? Or would it just be better to keep your head down, your mouth shut, and try to profit from this special information you suddenly possess?

THE ULTIMATE INSIDE INFORMATION

One of the earliest entries in the FBI's file on sports gambling is dated from February, 1958. It reads in part, "In general discussion as to how [redacted] was making a living since he had no particular visible means of support, [redacted] stated that 'every once in a while' a person in his position would receive information to the effect that the star basketball player in one of the major games would not be 'playing' that night. He indicated that this information would become available through gambling circles shortly before the sporting event, basketball in this instance, would begin. He further indicated that this information would affect odds on the game, particularly as in regard to the 'point spread.' When [redacted] was asked whether this information indicated that the player in question would not be 'playing,' whether that information indicating he was sick, or whether the game had been fixed, [redacted] stated 'no comment.'"

"You're as smart as your information." Words to gamble by, courtesy of the pro Lem Banker. Every gambler, no matter which game of chance he chooses to specialize in or wager upon, is seeking an edge. A little something that gives him a leg up on the house or his opponent. Blackjack players count cards. Poker stars know the percentages and read opponents' tells. Even slot machine players seek out certain machines and payouts. For the sports gambler, yes, hard work and number-crunching are part of the job. The willingness to put in a 60- to 80-hour work week examining numerous games, their associated numbers and line movements only to perhaps see value in one game out of the 14 posted in a day is a good start. But the edge the pros often seek comes in the form of inside information.

It could be as simple as the weather conditions. A change in the officiating crew. Perhaps whether or not a star athlete is going to play in the upcoming game. Is he injured and out? Or is he in the starting lineup? And if he's going to make a go of it, is he 100 percent? Seventy-five percent? Twenty-five percent? What if a player is sick, vomiting? Maybe he was out partying all night. Maybe he's a drunk, or an addict. Maybe he's having marital problems, or just broke up with his girlfriend…or boyfriend. Inside information can come in many forms, and every variable can easily affect the outcome of a game and thus the bettor's wager upon it. "The organized-crime gambling syndicate believes that inside information is necessary in order to discover what a member of a team is doing or might be doing. Aside from the rare fix, inside information is the commodity that professional gamblers will bank on. The mob wants to learn everything it can about the players' health, their marital problems, deaths in their families, drug dependencies, internal team problems, and anything else that might affect on-field performances, especially those situations that are not immediately reported in a public forum."[16]

For this inside information to be of value, it has to be relatively unknown. Lem Banker wrote, "I get inside information all the time; sometimes it's good, but most of the time the bookmakers and pricemakers know about it and the price becomes inflated. What happens is the bettor pays retail instead of wholesale. If you get original information when it's still fresh, you have a good shot at winning. Unfortunately, most people are followers and, in most cases, they will lose."[17] When I spoke with Banker, he elaborated by giving examples. "I had [inside] information, but I also had a good feel for the stuff. Matter of fact, when Willis Reed was hurt for the Knicks when they were playing the championship, I think it was against the Lakers, a guy called Joey Goldstein, he was a New York guy and knew Madison Square Garden, he was a friend of mine. We didn't know if Willis Reed was going to play. That's when the Knicks had Dave DeBusschere, Walt Frazier, Bill Bradley...and so he called me a couple of hours before the game, and he says 'Reed's going to play. He's suiting up.' So I made a big bet on it. But I had a lot of friends. Larry Merchant [sport author and commentator] called me once, as the Raiders were playing at home, playing the Jets I believe, and he called me and told me Joe Namath's not going to play. He's hurt. Stuff like that. A lot of friends going out of their way, a lot of good tips."

Can gamblers still get these insider tips today? "Not as much," Banker flatly stated. "It all comes over the computer. They have so much information." Which is true, given the saturation of ESPN, FOX Sports, Yahoo! Sports, etc. within the sports information market, it is rare for something to seemingly go unnoticed. Of course, even at a spry 80 years of age, Banker isn't as active as he once was in the gambling trade. Yet he's still savvy enough to spot when something's amiss. "But they hold back on information, too. I have this Don Best service and they flash the injuries, but somebody knows about it beforehand because all of a sudden you see the line movement five minutes before the injury [is announced]. So there's a lot of inside stuff."

To find it, a gambler has to mine everywhere for a nugget of pure information. Much like having plenty of outs for making bets, multiple sources of information are necessary to make informed wagers. The Philly Godfather used to hire "readers" to get the best inside information. "At that time readers were invaluable," he revealed. "You could literally find an article on a college team like New Mexico State that was in a local paper that mentioned the quarterback hurt his ankle at practice and his backup will be playing. No one else would know about this until game time, so you could actually wait until game day and bet the game. Now if a player on Weber State catches a cold, the whole world knows in a flash." But the need for such information has not subsided. "Inside information for us was and still is everything," he continued. "We were sure that the best handicappers in the world could make a better line than us, but if we had information the handicappers didn't then we gained a major edge." Like the Philly Godfather, Billy Walters was known to pay guys to pick up out-of-town newspapers at the airport, paying stewardesses for papers left behind on flights in order to search them for information on teams and games. Before the Donaghy scandal in the NBA, knowledge of which officiating crews were overseeing which games was dynamite. Even today, over/under lines on NBA games can immediately shift when the officials are announced each morning. Vegas Runner hasn't bet a baseball game without knowing who's behind home plate, checking how the umpire's tendencies matchup with the pitchers' tendencies on the mound.

But real inside information comes directly from insider sources. It's not going to be found amongst the general public. As strange as it may seem, the athletes themselves could be a source. "These things could be a very innocent remark," explained former NFL security chief Warren Welsh. "Some players are so clean they don't even know what they've just said in the sense that it could be used against them. I think probably from time to time there's some stuff that gets out that shouldn't." Most of the time, however, it is not an innocent remark that makes the bettor's day. It is information that is sought out, paid for, or even blackmailed out of people. And it is all of value.

Former professional sports gambler James "BaBa" Battista explained this in *Gaming the Game*: "The inside information was always the key. So, whether that meant buying someone or being someone's friend and being there for them, that was the business of getting the right information. Our information was coming from all sorts of people all around the country, whether it was about the betting lines or sharp bets in Vegas, or inside stuff about players, coaches, or refs and stuff like that.

"We really started developing a network of people giving us information, especially people who owed us money. A lot of times you'd have somebody owe money who couldn't pay off their debt in cash, so they'd offer something else instead….Sometimes, people could help us get inside information, like this guy who delivered food into Veterans Stadium. His way of paying us back was relaying back certain information from inside the stadium. Another time, we had this guy who owed us money report to us just before a Chicago Cubs baseball game at Wrigley Field. We needed to know whether the wind was blowing out or blowing in before the first pitch, and that was his only job—call us with a report about the outside flags and the wind. Shit like that was pretty common after so many people owed us money."[18]

That was just the beginning. Battista seemed to develop an army of insiders, all willing to provide him with the information needed to place winning bets more often. "'There was a college coach…who would give us what we called our 'Big East Game of the Week.' We'd give him the point spread on a game to pick once a week, and he'd tell us who he liked, taking into account the spread. He had such incredible insight on stuff we couldn't have known. That was the first time I knew inside information was being transferred between parties. You always heard stories, but I thought a lot of that was bullshit. I started realizing that there was *so much* inside information being traded. We had a bookmaker friend of ours who had a college basketball ref that bet games with him. One time, the bookmaker called and asked us if we could get three hundred thousand down for him on Georgetown plus-seven because the ref was on the take. No matter how good you are with numbers, you're not going to win more than 55 to 58 percent without inside information.

"Sportswriters—journalists—are really the key. There are so many variables into a team that guys like journalists who are around the team can help a bettor understand. It could be the mood of a team, and whether or not they are tanking the season late in the year because they're already out of the playoffs. It could also be access to a team trainer, who is giving more detailed information than the public has. The reporters look like they're gathering information for stories, but some of that stuff is being transmitted to big-time bettors. I used to deal with a guy who used to routinely get into a certain locker room all the time, and let me know what was going on with that team. He was in there on a day-to-day basis, and the information was incredible.

"A bookmaker or bettor might pay a reporter in cash for his services, but they are most commonly paid in bets or excused from prior betting losses. Battista developed relationships with reporters and with trainers, expressly to groom them as inside sources. [Battista] offers a tidy example of how these shenanigans manifest in betting circles. It involves a Philadelphia Eagles game in which star running back Brian Westbrook's injury status was not known until just before kickoff. 'He was questionable but we got a call out of the locker room before anyone else that he wasn't playing,' Battista says. 'The Eagles were favored by ten points, and the over/under was something like 52. Well, Westbrook being out of the offense was a big deal. The total moved like six points. We bet the dog and buried the under. The under hit and the dog covered.'

"The inside information didn't have to come directly to Battista or his partners for them to benefit. The Animals [Battista's group] often knew who among the world's bettors possessed such knowledge and piggybacked bets accordingly. 'We were trying to pick everyone's pocket,' Battista says. 'The Poker Players were picking 60 to 65 percent in baseball. We knew they had inside information, and these guys were con men at their best. They weren't just conning people at the poker table. Those guys had bundles in their pockets and friends everywhere. If they bet a baseball game, there was a reason why. We found out later that they also had handicappers working for them, but their success had a lot to do with the inside information they were getting....'

"'We also moved baseball games for a guy named Doc Johnson, who was The Computer's handicapper back in the 1980s. During football sea son, Doc would have his "Big Ten Game of the Year" and the line would move like six or seven points, because he had inside information. If the quarterback was out the night before a game, or if he had gotten in a fight, Doc fucking knew. Some of the things he knew were ridiculous.'"[19]

Vegas Runner worked with BaBa and his crew. "Back in the day before the Internet, I remember working in that office and we'd hear some crazy information come through," he explained. "Was it true, was it not? I had no idea. But I remember betting on teams, the same team, five or six times in a row and the call was an 'open order.' When they would yell out 'open order' that means bet as much as you can at any number because it was so rare. That means everyone get on the phone and until they take this game off the board just keep hammering it. Minus five, six, seven, eight, nine—it doesn't matter. Thirty minutes later, we'd see the game taken off the board. Now why did it [the open order] happen? I have no idea. But I know those open orders cashed in at a high clip, that much I can promise you." These "open orders" Vegas Runner described fly in the face of gambling logic. If you find a good number on a game, you bet it—bet it heavy, even—but you back off once the numbers move. That wasn't happening in these instances. It was almost as if on these rare occasions, it was a sure thing. As if the fix was in.

A fixed game—one in which it's known a player, coach, or referee is working with a gambler or mobster not to cover the spread—is perhaps the greatest form of inside information one could possess. The knowledge of what a game's outcome will be prior to it being played is akin to insider trading on Wall Street. There is little else a gambler could ask for; it's his ultimate dream.

But can it happen? Can games be fixed today? The overwhelming consensus of the leagues, their fans, and the general public would say "no." But those in the know would say otherwise. When I posed this question to former FBI Special Agent Tom French, he responded, "Personal opinion? Absolutely. In a heartbeat. In a New York minute."

"Has there been fixes?" pondered Larry Grossman, author of the sports gambling how-to book *You Can Bet On It*. "I don't know. I would say, if I had to say yes or no, I would say 'yes.' Look, how much shit goes on that nobody ever hears about? So to think that [the sports leagues] are purely without any kind of black mark is naïve. Before Donaghy was caught, was anybody talking about refs doing any kind of shenanigans? 'Oh, no, that couldn't happen.' Then all of a sudden Donaghy did it and people are saying, 'Wow. Maybe that could happen.'" Spurred on by the idea, Grossman continued, "There's a lot of different ways to do it [fix a game]. There's no question in my mind that it can be done. There's really very little question in my mind that it has been done. But look, you can't prove it. I could never tell you this game was fixed or that game was fixed, but it's hard for me to believe that there are no shenanigans going on whatsoever anywhere. That just doesn't jibe with the human condition. People just, like I say, they have larceny in their souls."

Lem Banker concurred, "Is it possible to fix games today? Yeah, sure, especially in basketball. You get a top scorer or a rebounder and because there're only five men on the floor, you'd have 20 percent of the team right there. Football's harder because a guy misses a block or something and the coach is liable to take him out. But anything's possible." Banker should know this better than anyone. He counted "Lefty" Rosenthal as one of his personal friends.

Lefty was a known fixer of games. "Rosenthal had a long list of team personnel who received money in return for supplying him with inside information. In 1960, while working for Angel-Kaplan [wire service] in Miami, Rosenthal was charged with conspiring to fix a basketball game between New York University and West Virginia University during the regional finals of the NCAA tournament in Charlotte, North Carolina. He had offered a bribe to one of the NYU players. Rosenthal pleaded *nolo contendere* and was fined $6,000.... [David] Budin [one of Rosenthal's co-conspirators] also told [North Carolina] state agents that he 'had given [the] New York District Attorney's office enough information to make a similar investigation involving football. That this would be almost as big as basketball, but that New York never did anything about this. Budin further stated that in his opinion fixes had never stopped.

That this was especially true in professional football.'

"'Rosenthal was always trying to fix something,' a former associate says. 'I'd tell him, 'Lefty, this team can't win.' And he'd say, 'Just watch.' He must have had somebody on the other side. He thinks everything is crooked. He just doesn't breathe clean air.'

"Two years later he was indicted for attempting to bribe Michael Bruce, a halfback for the University of Oregon, prior to a 1960 football game against the University of Michigan. On September 23, 1960, according to Bruce, Rosenthal and an associate offered Bruce $5,000 for his help in throwing the game—which was to be played the following day; another $5,000 for successfully soliciting the cooperation of the team's quarterback; and $100 a week for providing Rosenthal with inside information."[20] In May 1962, Rosenthal was indicted in New York as a co-conspirator related to fixing basketball games across the country between the dates of November 20, 1957 through March 17, 1961—over 72 games in total. His co-conspirator was convicted. Rosenthal was not.

Of course, Lefty was the mob's guy. Considering the mafia controlled (and continues to control) the illegal bookmaking trade in this country, it's little wonder that someone like Lefty wasn't constantly out on the prowl attempting to fix games. In fact, that may just be the case.

Michael Franzese is the son of mob hit man John "Sonny" Franzese and in the 1980s rose to the ranks of capo in the Colombo crime family. While earning $6–$8 million *a week* as a member of the family, Franzese was known to fix games, including, allegedly, New York Yankees games. Franzese was never arrested or convicted for game fixing, nor did he even seem to be investigated for the crime. But today, free from the mob as a born-again Christian, Franzese—without naming names—often talks about fixing games. As Franzese wrote in his own book *Blood Covenant*, "I never underestimate the power or ability of my former associates. We didn't control the underworld in this country since the turn of the century for nothing. In the real mob world, Tony Soprano would have been found dead in the trunk of a car soon after he spilled his guts to that cagey therapist. We can't take anything away from these men. They know their business, and they're good at what they do. No one knows that better than I do."[21]

Repeated yet unsuccessful attempts were made to interview Franzese for this book. However, author Declan Hill talked with Franzese for his book *The Fix: Soccer and Organized Crime.* At that time, Franzese told Hill, "My personal opinion as one who has been involved in organized crime and gambling is how easy it is to do....It is very easy to get a professional athlete to come 'on side.' We would spend a lot of time trying to get these guys to do this....We would deliberately target them....Heck, a lot of the time they would come to us!...Athletes like to gamble. They are confident, aggressive risk-takers. All the things that make them good athletes make them good gamblers....Once they got in trouble with us, we got them to do things for us. They would shave points, you know, maybe not try so hard. Or just share information, let us know what was going on."[22]

"People say 'you can't fix a game,'" laughed Scott Schettler. "That's nutty. Of course you can fix a game! You can get to anybody." When asked if there were times during his tenure at the Stardust that certain bets and outcomes raised suspicions, he replied, "Yeah. After the fact. We'd be overloaded on a game and we'd sit there and watch it on TV and all of a sudden you see the quarterback throw the ball right into the linebacker's hands. There are things that happen after the fact. We weren't too worried about it before the fact. Except in horse racing. With horse racing, you really had to be on your toes. But sports, there's so much money involved, if you were going to fix a game, you'd spread the money around and a fixed game just blended in with everything else. Even if they said, 'Yeah, we fixed it, you're not going to get your money back, blah, blah, blah,' at the end of the year, it wouldn't even matter. Can you understand what I'm saying? There's so much involved."

Schettler's point should not be overlooked. As the head of America's leading sports book, he never cared if a game was fixed. It wasn't even considered because at the end of the day, it didn't matter. Why? If his job was done correctly, half of the bettors lost and half won as it would have been with any game, fixed or not. The book's handle on each and every game was so huge, a little extra money sprinkled in didn't set off any alarm bells. The only people the fix mattered to were the ones attempting to control the outcome.

And this is still ongoing today.

"A lot of guys I know that move money for sharps," Vegas Runner revealed, "they say it all the time, that they've seen patterns and they'll piggyback it. Not knowing where it's coming from, not knowing who's getting down, but all of a sudden they see a small school and they find out this offshore book that they have a contact in is taking $20,000 bets on or against this team. All of a sudden, three or four straight times, that guy won. You gotta understand these guys are going to piggyback that without having to know for sure. And that goes on all the time. People don't talk about this enough.

"The sharpest guys aren't on that side of the counter [the bookmaker's side]," Vegas Runner continued. "They are on my side. We see things all the time. It's in no one's best interest to start yelling 'fire' and wanting investigations, you know what I mean? We're just the opposite. We're trying to make as much money as we can off of it…if it lasts, without caring how it happened."

A GOOD DEFENSE...

"In theory," began Larry Grossman, "the greatest arm of keeping an eye on the games is Las Vegas because they know who makes what bets and they know when something funny is going on, like when that Arizona State college team was being fixed [in 1994]. They saw a bunch of people coming in that they never saw before betting wild amounts of money no matter what number [was posted] all over town, and you know, the people that are running the sports books know each other and talk to each other and they'll say, 'Be on the lookout for this guy or that guy.' It becomes relatively obvious to the powers that be in this town. So as far as being a policeman for these leagues, Las Vegas certainly wants to see an honest game probably more than just about anybody."

In a sense, Grossman is correct. Vegas does not abide cheats, and the sharps that run the sports books should be the first line of defense in spotting a potentially fixed game. However, there's a "but." As Grossman added, "But just because the powers that be want an honest game doesn't mean that people with larceny in their souls like agents, players, friends, etc. [haven't fixed a game]. To think that there's not one person that has done anything over the last 20 years, I think, is rather naïve. I don't know an example, but if I had to make a bet and the answer was known, I would bet 'yes, it happened.' I mean, how could it not have?"

One of the defenses each league employs in watching for fixed games is to monitor the betting lines. This is especially true in the NBA and NFL. In the case of the NFL, this watchdog action dates back to the late 1940s. As former NFL and AFL owner Harry Wismer wrote, "[NFL commissioner Bert] Bell…[hired] an investigating force of former FBI men to concentrate on gamblers and report to him anything that might involve the league. Bell, unlike some baseball magnates, didn't bother to have the players trailed. Instead, he had his staff frequent the haunts of the bookies and gamblers to find out firsthand if any players, coaches, or owners were associating with them….

"Bell ran his own 'wire service,' calling all over the league each Sunday morning and checking his information. If anything were out of the ordinary, he could know immediately and be in a position to act. But no matter what safeguards Bert and the league would put up, there was and is always a way for gamblers to get information. The only way games can be kept free of outside influence is to count on the integrity of the players and officials."[1]

It's a bit disingenuous for NFL officials to be frequenting the same gambling halls it banned its players from visiting, but it served a vital purpose. How else could an institution like the NFL know what was going on within the underbelly of the sports gambling world? As the Las Vegas sports books grew in stature, the league would eventually station a security agent there to watch for unusual line movements and the "unnatural money" that pushed them. When I asked Scott Schettler about the authorities monitoring the line and its movements while he ran the Stardust sports book, he replied, "The FBI, they used to monitor the line from Las Vegas. Bob [Martin] was in contact with the FBI. Or rather,

A GOOD DEFENSE…

the FBI was in contact with him. And they'd ask him questions about the line, fluctuations, this and that." What about the leagues themselves? "Yeah. The leagues, too, but they're hypocrites." Why would Schettler call them hypocrites? Perhaps because when I asked if the NBA or NFL ever directly contacted his office—the biggest, most influential sports books in Las Vegas at the time—about their lines, he said, "No. Never."

Who did the league talk to in Las Vegas if not the sports books? Lem Banker, who at one time was perhaps the biggest sports gambler in town. "Did you ever hear of Warren Welsh, head of NFL security?" Lem asked. "He was a friend of mine, and they'd help me get tout services ["touts" are usually scam artists who inflate their winning percentages to get gullible customers to buy their picks on upcoming games]. As a matter of fact, he came over to my house and listened to some of the recordings on these tout services." As for the line, Lem recounted, "The NFL used to call me early in the morning before the first game was played and see where the late money moves were on the line. I would give them the latest line, or unnatural money, that's what they would call it. And there was money movement and rumors, but there's always rumors when big money shows up on the right side of a game."

But even the sage advice and input of Banker wasn't enough for the league. During a 1979 FBI investigation centering on two NFL referees for their alleged participation in fixing games (which is discussed later), the FBI's file revealed that a source within the league told the Bureau that the field security representatives for the NFL "are responsible for developing confidential sources who are bookmakers, and provide the field security representatives with the odds in the particular city up to the final moments prior to game time. These odds are called in by the field security representative to the NFL main office in New York and are recorded on the enclosed closing line spread sheets. [redacted] explained that a quick check of the closing line spread sheets would disclose any abnormalities in the betting practices across the U.S. which might include a large bet." To make this crystal clear, NFL security—at one time at least—associated with known bookmakers in every city in which the NFL had a franchise. Former NFL security chief Warren Welsh confirmed this, albeit with a little spin added. He told me,

"Maintaining that liaison was important. The security reps were required to have a contact with either a bookmaker per se or somebody in an intelligence unit from a police department to get the line information in their particular city. In most cases it was probably through an intelligence unit, like the Chicago PD." What should bother fans is that these bookmakers were criminals, possibly even tied to the mafia. Did the NFL turn them in to the FBI or local law enforcement? Apparently not (and the FBI seemed to have little issue with this as well). Why? Because the NFL was using the bookmakers as a guardian of the game. Were the illegal bookies being 100 percent honest 100 percent of the time with the NFL? The league could only hope so, because they had no one else to turn to for this information. It's akin to asking the fox if the hen house is safe.

Included within this FBI file were seven handwritten NFL closing line spread sheets. One problem: these sheets only listed the closing line. There were no line movements recorded of any sort. There was no way to see where the line started, how it moved, when it moved—*if* it moved—just where it finished. Granted, NFL security agents were to remain in contact with these bookmaking sources throughout the week, ostensibly to monitor line fluctuations, but listing just the closing line without any other information associated with it isn't useful. And in fact, this entire methodology may be worthless.

For starters, when visiting Las Vegas, I spoke to several sports book employees, from ticket window operators to management. If they were all speaking freely and honestly, not one person gave the idea of fixing games a second thought. The very notion was often derided and dismissed. For the select few who considered the possibility, they concurred that the last place today's fixer would be betting was in Las Vegas. And that's the key fact. Considering that perhaps only one percent of all sports wagers made in the U.S. are done so legally in Nevada, an intelligent fixer is going to hide his bets within the hundreds of billions of dollars wagered illegally every year. So when a league like the NFL states it's watching the lines in Las Vegas, it sounds great to the general public. Yet in reality, doing so is a waste of time. Yes, Las Vegas is going to pick up on line fluctuations—*because they happen all the time*—but are

A GOOD DEFENSE...

those sports books really going to sniff out the unnatural money bet on a fixed game? Quite simply, no.

Of course, detecting a fixed game by only watching line movements may be fruitless. " That's like trying to detect insider trading from watching share prices rise and fall," claimed author Declan Hill, who is one of the world's foremost experts on game fixing in soccer. "It's a good indication that there may be something wrong, but it doesn't tell you much besides that the share price went up or down. There may be some very good reasons that are totally legitimate that the odds would fluctuate on a game. And there's ways of fixing games where the odds don't move at all….if you fix it for the weaker team to lose [a game they are already expected to lose], that's not going to shift the odds. So betting odds are, I don't want to dismiss it out of hand, but what these gambling companies and betting monitoring systems are doing is basically just reading the newspaper, saying we can detect insider trading from the newspaper. My take is, no, it's *way* more complicated than that. There's also an element of hucksterism in it. I don't live and die by my bets. I don't gamble. And I know that it's not possible what they are claiming. So how can they with a straight face claim these things?"

The perfect case study to prove Hill's point is the Tim Donaghy scandal. Vegas Runner was betting on those allegedly fixed Donaghy games. He claimed that even at the time the fix was on, he had "no idea" because Battista "never told anybody." But what about the system in place to detect these line movements due to unnatural money? The system the NFL and NBA are reliant upon to stop any potential fixer in his tracks? "Any professional sports bettor, I mean a serious sports bettor, or a betting syndicate, they are going to see that something's wrong here eventually," claimed Vegas Runner. "The reason the market is efficient is because the market has the ability to correct itself. So what happened here [in the case of the Donaghy games] was it never corrected itself. These lines— we were betting the over on these totals, and the lines were moving three or four points. Eventually the market should've corrected itself, it should've balanced out, but it never did. Even a lot of sharp bettors out here in Vegas that I've spoken to since then that had no idea, that didn't have the resources to monitor it and realize that something wasn't right.

These guys went broke because they were betting against these moves. Because going in, they saw that there was value on the under, and then they saw the line moving three, four, five points and now there was even *more* value. And they were waiting for the market to correct itself while betting it, betting it, betting it, and they're still getting killed, not understanding why." In other words, there were unusual line movements caused by large wagers—the supposed tip-off—and even though professionals were losing by being on the wrong end time and again, nothing was done. Instead, Vegas Runner pointed out, "A lot of guys were piggybacking these plays. They didn't know why. They just saw a pattern. But as for the casinos here, and offshore, nobody knew for a long time."

He chuckled. "That's why I laugh when people say, 'Oh, no way. Games are never fixed.' I wouldn't go as far as being the guys that you hear in so many places that think every game is fixed. Every time they are on the bad end of a half-point loss, they assume it was fixed or that they are following some kind of script. Those guys are even crazier than the ones that don't think anything ever goes on. But there's a happy middle somewhere in there."

THE LEAGUES' PRIVATE CIA

Each professional sports league possesses its own private police force known as League Security. There is scant information regarding these entities, and each league's department seems to relish its secretive status. While it may sound like an exaggeration, these security divisions are staffed with former members of the FBI, CIA, DEA, and Secret Service as well as local law enforcement. James M. Cawley is currently the senior vice president of security for the NBA. Prior to obtaining this position, he worked security for Goldman Sachs and was once the Special Agent in Charge of the New York branch of the Secret Service. Oddly enough, the current vice president of security and facility management of Major League Baseball is Bill Bordley, who also worked for the Secret Service. Bordley spent over five years of his service time on President Bill Clinton's protection detail. As for the NFL, its current chief of security is Jeff Miller, who previously served as the commissioner of the Pennsylvania

State Police.

In late 2011, I was fortunate enough to interview former NFL security chief Warren Welsh. Though retired from the NFL since 2007, Welsh wanted to clear our talk with the head of the league's public relations department, Greg Aiello, before officially speaking with me. Aiello apparently green-lit our conversation. Welsh graduated law school in 1961 and then joined the FBI where he worked several organized crime cases. Most of these involved gambling matters, including a few run-ins with Lefty Rosenthal. "I can remember him looking at me with those steely eyes," Welsh recounted, "and telling me, 'If you get me fair and square, I'll go.'" Welsh did in fact arrest Rosenthal once, only to see him bribe guards for food and other items before getting released. This sort of behavior "was just in his blood," Welsh claimed. He left the FBI in January 1969 in order to take jobs in the private sector, including a stint working security for NBC. Then in 1980, Welsh landed the position as chief of security for the NFL, which he held until 1996. Less than two months after resigning the post, Welsh returned to the NFL as a consultant for the league's drug-testing program.

"Jack Danahy [NFL security chief from 1968 to 1980] established the security network," Welsh said, "and I came in. I told everybody, 'I'm just going to get through the first season and look and see what we've got here, and there could be changes or there won't be.' Well, as it happened, at that point these were mostly retired FBI agents and were maybe a little old. Between the first and second year, there was an almost complete turnover of these security reps."

While Welsh cleaned house, the basic formation of the security division remained intact. Besides a unit stationed at league headquarters, for each city the NFL has a franchise, two security representatives are posted, a primary and an alternate. It also placed one member in Las Vegas who was "close to the action and had contacts with the various bookmaking concerns." Their prime directive? "In very broad terms, it was the integrity of the sport," stated Welsh. "If you say, 'What does that entail?' you're looking at things and your major emphasis would be on things that could possibly—not that they are or have been—but that could possibly interfere with the integrity of the sport. And certainly coming in right at the top of that list, we always looked at gambling and drugs."

"Part of [the security representatives'] responsibility," Welsh continued, "had to do with maintaining a liaison with various law enforcement agencies in their particular area." What was meant by "liaison"? Welsh elaborated, "Some people are of the opinion that you wouldn't have this close relationship because the FBI was trying to make cases if there were violations of law, and the NFL security people wanted to keep a tab on that and would keep things to themselves. And that just wasn't the case. I would say there was a fairly free exchange of information. If there was something that was very, very, I don't know, secretive, and could not be told to another body, then people respected that. It was a relationship where sometimes they had lunch together, sometimes they probably talked over the phone, and other times they might meet at sporting events or whatever. But I would say it was a good relationship that existed between the NFL security department and the FBI or DEA, whoever the agency might be."

Besides coordinating efforts with law enforcement officials, each league's security conducts thorough background checks on its employees. In his book *Inside the Meat Grinder*, former NFL umpire Chad Brown described the process he had to endure to move up from the college ranks to become a member of a NFL officiating crew. After receiving a letter informing him he was a candidate for the NFL, Brown was interviewed, or as he wrote, "interrogated" by NFL supervisor Jack O'Cain for about two hours. Brown then had to complete both a written intelligence and a psychological examination. Having jumped through those hoops, he was then a finalist which opened him up to a background check. An NFL representative explained this process to him: "We call current employers, past employers, friends, relatives. We do a detailed financial history, interview neighbors, and do an extensive education history. We will often interview a former teacher. In your case, we've decided to interview your second-grade teacher."[2] The NFL did in fact send a private detective to interview Brown's neighbor. He discovered that only because the misdirected investigator rang Brown's doorbell by mistake. According to the NFL, it subjects all of its referees to this sort of background check every three to four years. Though unconfirmed, it's hard to imagine each league's vetting process isn't similar in scope.

Potential players, too, endure this sort of treatment from the NFL. In a March 2012 article written for 101ESPN.com, former 11-year NFL front office executive Tony Softli wrote, "At the yearly NFL Combine, once the players arrive in Indianapolis and upon checking in and receiving their hotel room, they are greeted by NFL security representatives. All 300-plus participants fill out and sign a release form for a standard background check. Like any other corporation in America, the NFL conducts this to see if there are any red flags prior to the prospects becoming professional football players. While all 32 teams spend thousands of dollars performing their own background checks, the goal is to find information on all players that the other teams may not have or receive, creating an uneven playing field. Several days prior to the draft, each team's security director makes a call to compare their findings to their own investigations. NFL security information helps in last-minute decisions on all players to clear red-flag issues or potentially take the player off the board. This process of double-checking with another source limits any major mistakes when it comes to character."[3]

Softli's conclusion is laughable, especially when on more than one occasion potential first-round NFL draft picks have admitted in interviews to using marijuana, only to see their draft status remain unaffected. If buying and using illegal drugs isn't a "red flag," then what is? Softli did admit later in this article, "Like in other professional sports or walks of life, it's not a big secret and is well documented that many NFL players have made both minor and major mistakes when in public."[4] This was putting it mildly. NFL players as well as athletes from all of the major professional sports leagues seem to be in constant trouble with the law. Every season, players are suspended by their respective leagues for drug violations, be they for performance-enhancing or recreational substances. There are arrests for DUI, assault and battery, weapons violations, spousal abuse; the list goes on and on.

I asked Welsh if NFL security would turn information of criminal acts over to the FBI or local law enforcement, or would the league handle the problem in-house? "If somebody locally, let's say the security rep in Buffalo," he responded, "if they discovered something, they would come back to the NFL [headquarters] in New York and discuss it." Notice he didn't say that NFL security would immediately go to law enforcement. The league needed to know first. Welsh continued, "But just because of it being a much larger organization, more than likely information was going to come from the local law enforcement agency prior to it coming from within NFL security." In other words, NFL security was more reactionary than proactive. "Yeah, I would say that's true particularly with the prominence of drugs." Obviously the likes of the DEA or FBI were better suited to deal with such investigations. "We weren't another law enforcement agency," Welsh added. "But there wasn't any cover-up or anything else. With the trust issue, there was certainly information that was shared with us that couldn't go anywhere because of a pending investigation that could very easily amount to somebody being put on trial and going to jail. So you had to respect that, too."

Though Welsh asserted that "there wasn't any cover-up," a few ob-servations need to be made. For starters, despite researching this subject matter for over six years, I cannot find a single instance of law enforce-ment praising a league—be it the NFL, NBA, or MLB—for its assis-tance in a criminal investigation regarding one of its players or person-nel. Perhaps these types of comments do not make news reports. Perhaps their cooperation is simply understood. Yet the leagues never appear to be the source for any deeper, penetrating law enforcement investigation of one of their own. If league security exists to protect the integrity of the game, why is this true? Why was it when Tim Donaghy was brought in by the FBI for gambling on NBA games did the league seemed shocked by the revelation? Same goes in the case of former player and then-current Phoenix Coyotes assistant coach Rick Tocchet, who was arrested for running a bookmaking ring which booked bets from NHL players. Why didn't NHL security know this before law enforcement took him into custody (and why did the NHL allow him right back into the league as head coach of the Tampa Bay Lightning)? When Chicago Bears wide receiver Sam Hurd was arrested on federal drug charges in 2011 for attempting to obtain his yearly salary's ($700,000) worth of marijuana and cocaine *a week* from an undercover agent, why did NFL security appear completely unaware of the situation? Shouldn't these security divisions be ahead of these scandals rather than behind?

This then begs the question of what really is the security division's purpose? Is it to protect the integrity of the game, or simply the *appearance* of the integrity of the game? The correct answer may be the latter. As FBI agent Tom French told me, "You're talking about a multi, multi, multimillion-dollar enterprise. Anything that even tarnishes that is something that they had to handle as fast as possible and as quietly as possible." That sounds like the definition of a cover-up. In his book *Interference*, Dan Moldea made a similar claim against the NFL's security division. He wrote that no fewer than 50 legitimate investigations of corruption within the league were either suppressed or stopped thanks to NFL security's relationship with the various law enforcement agencies. Perhaps those lunches, meetings and "liaisons" Warren Welsh discussed in relation to his security department meant a little more than would be apparent.

An example of this sort of sweetheart relationship surfaced in a scandal surrounding Joe Namath's infamous nightclub, Bachelors III. Author Mark Kriegel wrote in his biography of the legendary quarterback that Bachelors III had been investigated by the Manhattan District Attorney, the New York Police Department (NYPD), and the FBI by the spring of 1969. Jack Danahy, who was head of NFL security at the time, met with the NYPD's chief of detectives about Namath. "Danahy was informed that Namath's regulars included con men, fences, bookmakers, and of course made men—exactly the kind of guys you'd expect to find in a hot East Side joint. The cops already had an undercover working inside, and the phones were tapped. 'The police were giving me the heads-up with the agreement that I would get Joe off the license because they wanted to make a bust on the place,' says Danahy. 'They didn't want to embarrass the National Football League. It was a big favor to me.'"[5] How many more favors were done on the behalf of each league will likely never be known.

It's rather astonishing that though players have been arrested for a wide assortment of crimes and have been suspended for seemingly just as many rule violations in recent years, not once has a player been punished for gambling. How is that possible? Do players, coaches, and referees simply not gamble? Of course not. Go to any popular bar in Las Vegas and ask the bartender which celebrities he has seen come through. Inevitably, the names of prominent and active major league players will be mentioned (and those players aren't in Vegas simply for the sightseeing). However, gambling in and of itself is not banned by the major leagues. Were Welsh and his staff ever concerned with members of the NFL gambling legally? "Not really," he said. "There wasn't a prohibition, but on the other hand, if any information ever came that somebody was hanging out and losing money, those were things that were certainly looked at. But the idea of someone going to a casino? No." What about gambling on other sports? "If you take a conservative approach, and say, 'Well, the way it's written is you can't gamble on NFL games,'" Welsh related, "well, there's also a part in that policy that talks about associations. And in order for you to associate with, say, a bookmaker on college sports or baseball, then it seems to me you're getting very close to the line."

That "line" Welsh mentions is again league integrity, and perhaps nothing strikes at the heart of that more than a gambling athlete. Even if it's done "just for fun," the sight of a professional athlete betting upon a sporting event instantly raises questions in fans' minds. "If he's betting on this game, what else is he betting on?" "Is he losing?" "Is he in debt?" "Does he know something no one else does?" "Is the fix in?" Undoubtedly, this is why each and every sports league's first rule for players, coaches and referees forbids wagering upon games within one's respective sport. The punishment for breaking this rule is banishment. But do they all really abide by the prohibition? Pete Rose didn't in baseball. Art Schlichter didn't in football. Can those truly be the only two players/coaches out of the thousands that have come and gone over the years to break this taboo? No. They were simply the only two who were caught and publicly fingered as gamblers. Many more got away with it, and continue to do so today.

Gambling, however, isn't game fixing. And doing the first does not mean a player committed the latter mortal sin. However, given the nature of gambling—a "hobby" in which only the true experts routinely succeed—it is an excellent gateway to a player rigging a game. Therein lays the danger. It's exactly why league security makes player gambling one of its top priorities…sort of. When Dan Moldea interviewed Warren Welsh's predecessor Jack Danahy for *Interference*, he asked whether there had been attempts to fix NFL games while he ran the division. Danahy responded, "I'm sure there were. I think that in 90 percent of the cases, the ballplayer didn't even bother to report it. He didn't want to go through the hassle."[6] If 90 percent didn't bother to report it, how many might have gone ahead and fixed a game? Apparently NFL security didn't know, nor did they seem to want to know such an answer. As for Warren Welsh, he told me, "You have to have your eyes open as these are things that can conceivably happen. The other part of it obviously, if it's conceivable, did it ever happen? Insofar as I know in my years there was not a fix, but we were certainly ever vigilant and tried to understand if there was any switch in the line at the last minute or whatever, to look at those things."

Welsh further expanded on the notion of game fixing by saying, "There might have been some things that people loved to talk about, particularly if you had two skilled football teams and for whatever reason the quarterback has a bad day, people wonder and say, 'Ah, well, the fix was in.' But it's like separating the wheat from the chaff, I guess…. Strange things happen, and it's hard to put your finger on why. I happened to be in the FBI at the time and I went to Super Bowl III, the Jets and Baltimore, and it was, you know, one of those games. And Namath said before the game, 'We're going to win,' and I guess there are some people that felt that there was something wrong with that game."

In the end, Welsh sounded adamant that while he was in charge, NFL security left no stone unturned. "I don't think there was anything that came to our attention in the security department where we said, 'Throw away this piece of paper. This wasn't worth the ink to write it.' I think it behooves you to at least look at it and the best thing to do is to put it to bed. One way or the other." Does the NFL overprotect itself? "No," he said. "Obviously it's very big business. But the idea that they are too big to be investigated, I don't think that that's the attitude. I think once there's information that there's something wrong, that's normally all you needed to start looking at something. If there's something wrong, it's going to be looked at. I don't think there are intentional cover-ups in any of these areas."

THE FEDERAL BUREAU OF INVESTIGATION

Would a league inform its fans if a game was fixed?

The problem with any league's security department is that it is beholden to its master, the league, not to the fans. They truly want to maintain the appearance of integrity at the very least; that cannot be questioned. But though the leagues are public entities and profit from fans spread across the country, it is in each league's best interest to keep any and all signs of corruption out of the public's eye. Certainly, they possess the ability to do this. They can conduct internal investigations of players, coaches, referees, owners, and franchises, and keep all findings private. They are not obligated to make anything public. Whether a league even chooses to react to something discovered in such an investigation is entirely up to them as well. For fans, then, all they can do is trust.

At one time, the Federal Bureau of Investigation was the fans' best friend in terms of monitoring for potentially fixed games. As will be shown, this fell by the wayside over time; however, it was never the FBI's job to police the professional leagues. The Bureau was tasked with investigating federal crimes, and for quite some time fixing a game wasn't such a crime.

The FBI did not seem to take an interest in sports gambling or game fixing until 1957. One of the first pieces of information it obtained was the following: "It is further noted that U.S. Attorney George MacKinnon, St. Paul, Minnesota, advised the Bureau on October 17, 1957, of an alleged conspiracy between a former college basketball referee [redacted] of Godfrey, Illinois, and gamblers [redacted], a Minneapolis bookmaker, and [redacted] of St. Louis, Missouri. This was reportedly a conspiracy to control the 'point spread' in games refereed by [redacted] in the Missouri Valley Conference beginning in 1954. This matter was the subject of an article in the national magazine entitled 'Sports Illustrated,' March, 1957.

"U.S. Attorney MacKinnon had advised the Department of his theory in which he feels that because this gambling exists he believes the students and the public as well, who paid good money to see an honest game and who have a right to expect honest refereeing, have had a fraud perpetrated upon them. On December 26, 1957, when the Criminal Division asked us to inquire into the 1954 situation mentioned above, this matter was called to the attention of the Attorney General by memorandum dated 1/3/58." Following this was a handwritten note from FBI Director J. Edgar Hoover (signed simply "H.") which asked, "Have we any idea just what Fed. Statute might apply?"

Hoover received his answer shortly thereafter. "With regard to the Director's inquiry as to just what Federal statute might apply to the alleged gambling activities in connection with national basketball games, this is to advise that according to U.S. Attorney MacKinnon, St. Paul, Minnesota, it is the Fraud By Wire Statute, Title 18, U.S. Code, Section 1343: 'This statute provides punishment for whoever transmits wire radio or television communications in interstate commerce for the purpose of any scheme to defraud or for obtaining money by means of false and fraudulent pretenses.'"

This statute had nothing to do with sports, and the FBI didn't seem to believe in U.S. Attorney MacKinnon's theory. Instead, it decided to take a closer look at sports gambling. However, from reading the file, it appeared as though the FBI needed an education on the subject first. On February 19, 1958, the Bureau talked with an informant who gave them a basic tutorial. This began with the opening, "National sporting events apparently continue to be basis for widespread gambling operations. Information furnished by a Potential Criminal Informant [PCI] provides a revealing glimpse into current bookmaking activities based on national sports." This informant told the FBI that he had "nationwide bookie contacts enabling him to place bets as high as $15,000 on a particular basketball game." He continued, "One handicapper in Ohio is alleged to have devised his own system for mathematical computation of odds based on a home-made computing machine. This machine has been named 'Univac' after the much-publicized commercial computer." But in getting to the nitty-gritty, the informant advised, "As a result of his experiences in bookmaking, the PCI says he is of the opinion that basketball referees are generally better able to 'throw' a game the way they desire than is a coach or a player. He claims that bookmakers are prone to accept higher bets on baseball games because they believe there is little or no chance that a baseball game is 'fixed.' The PCI cites doctors, lawyers, and some wealthy businessmen as the biggest gamblers. The 'professional bettor' is described as one who has a tip which will alter the outcome of a game or who is in a position to 'fix' a game. The professional bettor bets heavily on the game through a 'beard'—an agent who protects the gambler's identity by placing bets in his own name among various bookmakers."

While the Bureau attempted to get its collective head around the subject, Congress passed the Wire Communications Act of 1961. This was just one of several anti-racketeering laws passed at the time, meant in large part to curtail the activities of organized crime. Since gambling—especially sports gambling, which is the only form of wagering specifically mentioned within the Wire Act—had been one of the mob's largest sources of income, the bill was meant to suppress illegal bookmaking operations. Subsection (a) specifically read, "Whoever being engaged in the business of betting or wagering knowingly uses a wire communication facility for the transmission in interstate or foreign commerce of bets or wagers or information assisting in the placing of bets or wagers on any sporting event or contest, or for the transmission of a wire communication which entitles the recipient to receive money or credit as a result of bets or wagers, or for information assisting in the placing of bets or wagers, shall be fined under this title or imprisoned not more than two years, or both."

The Wire Act did allow for a few exemptions. For one, the law did not make sports gambling illegal. It merely made the transmission of such information a criminal offense. Secondly, though their information could and would be used to place wagers, sports media outlets were given a free pass for reporting sporting events and outcomes. The Wire Act also allowed state-to-state bets if both states possessed legalized sports wagering.

As the Wire Act was signed into law, on June 30, 1961, New York senator Kenneth Keating introduced S. 2182, a bill to amend Title 18, U.S. Code to effectively create what became known as the Sports Bribery Act. Keating stated, "The bill would make a Federal crime any conspiracy in interstate commerce which sought to influence by bribery the outcome of any sporting event." For the FBI, the key in this proposed legislation was that "The bill also includes a prima-facie proof clause that is unique in that a showing of proof of bribery is prima-facie proof of a scheme in commerce to influence a sporting contest." The FBI recommended the bill, writing in part, "This proposed legislation would be another vehicle by which legal pressure could be placed on gamblers, racketeers and hoodlums who associate themselves with amateur and professional athletic contests." Despite this backing from the FBI and its relation to the Wire Act, Keating's bill languished.

In the meantime, the FBI ramped up its general investigation into sports gambling across the nation. It first sent directives to each Bureau field office, requesting that a preliminary survey be conducted to determine how much (if any) sports gambling was ongoing. As the field offices reported back to headquarters, the results were varied. Some saw widespread sports gambling, others reported it minimal to nonexistent. From there, again through every major field office, the FBI attempted to set up "two or more" sources/contacts/informants for future use, specifically seeking sports gambling information and potential fixes. In many cases, the Bureau had specific individuals in mind—some of whom they had worked with in the past, and many of whom were either bookmakers or otherwise involved in sports gambling. However, many of these contacts were active and meant to be kept under wraps as to not blow their cover. A few were developed under the FBI's "Top Hoodlum Program." Occasionally certain field offices were told *not* to contact certain individuals about this program, and some potential contacts were rejected due to being "too close" to professional or college sports. As the Bureau instructed its field offices, "You should insure those persons contacted clearly understand that the FBI does not intend to police any sports activity nor are we conducting any widespread investigation of college or professional sports. The purpose of these contacts is to insure that we are alerted to any possible violations within our investigative jurisdiction arising from sports activities."

In February 1962, the FBI considered creating a news article "setting forth the provisions of the new laws and how they would apply to the efforts of gamblers and others to 'fix' or predetermine the results of the events." Though Hoover approved of the plan, the Bureau was unsure as how to best disseminate this information. Ultimately it was decided that both national sports wire services—the Associated Press (AP) and United Press International (UPI)—would be provided the article so that "the sports staff of virtually every newspaper in the country will receive this item." At this same time, the FBI discovered that "only 36 of our 50 states now actually prohibit bribery in connection with sporting events and that in those states where such is not prohibited the new legislation would not apply. This, of course, will be taken into consideration in the preparation of the type of article proposed herein." The 14 states which did not have a law on the books to prevent game fixing were Alaska, Idaho, Kansas, Maine, Montana, Nevada, New Hampshire, New Mexico, North Dakota, South Carolina, Utah, Vermont and Wyoming.

A month later, on March 1, 1962, the FBI released the following to the AP and UPI: "Future bribery scandals of the type which have rocked the sports world in the past may well be the topic of investigation by the Federal Bureau of Investigation. Federal jurisdiction over such crimes is derived from the law prohibiting the interstate and foreign travel or transportation in aid of racketeering enterprises, one of several anti-crime bills enacted in 1961.

"An FBI spokesman explained that a 'fix' or attempted 'fix' of a sporting event would be a Federal violation under the following circumstances:

"(1) An individual travels in interstate or foreign commerce or uses any facility in interstate or foreign commerce with intent to unlawfully influence the outcome of a sporting event;

"(2) Such individual actually influences or attempts to influence the outcome of the event;

"(3) The method he uses (extortion or bribery) is in violation of the laws of the state in which committed.

"The FBI requests that anyone possessing information indicating a violation of the above law immediately contact the nearest FBI office, telephone number and address of which can be found on the first page of telephone directories."

While the FBI sought the public's assistance, Senator Keating continued to try to get his bill passed. "This bill would provide the authority our law enforcement agencies need to prevent gamblers from corrupting college and professional sports," Senator Keating said. "It would halt the contamination of sports by organized gambling syndicates by punishing any players or officials, as well as gamblers, who attempt to corrupt these games for personal gain. It would cover schemes to affect the point spread in a contest, as well as to throw the game entirely, and would apply to every case in which interstate facilities—such as the telephone or the mail—have been used to carry out the conspiracy." As if that weren't enough, Senator Keating implored Congress to think of the children. "We must do everything we can to keep sports clean so that the fans, and especially young people, can continue to have complete confidence in the honesty of the players and the contests. Scandals in the sporting world are big news and can have a devastating and shocking effect on the outlook of our youth to whom sports figures are heroes and idols." Senator Keating ultimately won. The Sports Bribery Act passed in 1964.

By that time, the FBI had established a nationwide network of informants to help it investigate and enforce the newly enacted law. And as a law, the Sports Bribery Act was relatively straightforward: "Whoever carries into effect, attempts to carry into effect, or conspires with any other person to carry into effect any scheme in commerce to influence, in any way, by bribery any sporting contest, with knowledge that the purpose of such scheme is to influence by bribery that contest, shall be fined under this title, or imprisoned not more than five years, or both."

One question remained. How do you prove a game was fixed? This was one riddle the FBI could not solve, as it never obtained a conviction in any investigation of a fix within the professional sports leagues. Not in Major League Baseball, not in the National Basketball Association, and not in the National Football League. Why is that? Could it be that none of those leagues ever saw one of their games fixed? Or is it more likely that proving such a case beyond a reasonable doubt is near impossible?

The problem for law enforcement generates from trying to differentiate a fixed game from a regular game. How does one do that? Can you tell a player's "bad" game from an intentionally "bad" game? Quarterbacks throw interceptions. Running backs fumble footballs. Linebackers miss tackles. Home runs are hit. Walks are issued. Ground balls bobbled. Free throws are missed. Shots are blocked. Fouls are called. All of this occurs in every game played. So what's the determining factor?

The obvious answer is evidence, yet this always appears lacking in an investigation of a fixed contest. Concrete evidence, outside of the money passed between cooperating parties, is nonexistent. Nothing is written down. What then is available with which an investigating agent could use to make a connection between the player/referee and the gambler/mobster involved? A confession would be ideal, yet how does one obtain a confession to a federal crime in which no solid evidence exists? If the FBI was on its toes and a bit lucky, it could obtain information via a wiretap, catching the two involved parties communicating with one another. Yet when information about a fixed game comes after it's been played—after the bet is made, after the line moves, after the "bad" game, after the payoffs are complete—what use would the wiretap be? Sadly, there is little else on which to base a case. Without this sort of proof, both guilty parties could be properly arrested for game fixing, instantly maintain their innocence, and be freed by the end of the day. Case closed.

Tom French, who investigated sports bribery violations as a Special Agent for the FBI, agreed with this assessment. "The only way we were ever able to prove a lot of those cases," French stated, "was having somebody crack. Break down. And/or we had a wire someplace and you picked up a few conversations. I mean, to look at a film, you could look at a film all day long and say, 'Aw, man, that guy looked lousy today,' but so what? He had a bad day. People have bad days." The cases French alluded to were mostly investigations of rigged New York-area horse races, though he did participate in the investigation of *Goodfellas* mobster Henry Hill fixing Boston College basketball games in 1978–79.

Even so, throughout the 1960s and 1970s, the FBI initiated several investigations of game fixing in professional sports. What sort of tip provided strong enough information upon which to open an official case file? "I think an assessment of the information itself," French related, "and then to see preliminarily if there was a way to corroborate this. In other words, if they get information, you look at the source first of all and you see how credible he is. Let's say a guy says, 'I was up at the race track the last four nights and I'm telling you, something's going on, etc.' Well, why? 'Because I had a horse that should win tonight and I'm telling you, this guy came out of nowhere and won, and I just know something's going on.' You look at that and go, 'Okay. I'll index it and file it and if something else comes back on that, then maybe we'll take a look at it.' But then, on the other hand, a guy says to me, 'Hey, I know a guy who taking bets from a basketball player.' How do you know that? 'Well, he bets with my friend.' Oh, he does? Who's your friend? Then you say, 'Well, maybe we got something here.' Then you'll open up a case and take a look and see what you can do, look at the investigative possibilities to corroborate this." Yet to corroborate this must be difficult. "Extremely," he stated. "Extremely hard to do. What you need to do is jam up somebody to turn him against the other people, like the NBA referee."

Yet even in the Tim Donaghy case to which French refers, though three of the conspirators were sentenced to jail, not one was convicted of fixing a game. Why? No one was charged with it, no one admitted to it, and no one within the FBI or NBA attempted to prove it. Hence, no games were fixed. Or at least that's the story.

At one point the FBI had a special file designation for sports bribery investigations. At some time in the late 1980s-early 1990s, they shut it down and rolled those investigations into other organized crime and/or gambling-related files. By then the network of informants and bookies the FBI established at the time of the passage of the Sports Bribery Act had faded away as over 20 years passed since it was first organized. Even during this heyday, the FBI had more pressing issues to contend with than whether or not last night's Celtics game was fixed. President John F. Kennedy, his brother Robert, and Dr. Martin Luther King Jr. were all assassinated. Riots were occurring in major cities across America. College-aged radicals and hippies were challenging both the police and the status quo. The Watergate break-in took place. President Nixon resigned. The Cold War was ongoing. And organized crime seemed to have its dirty paws in every scam and crime committed. Despite the Wire Act, despite the Sports Bribery Act, where did the FBI's attention need to be focused? On a fixed NFL game, or on something more urgent and of true national importance?

The FBI appeared to grow weary with its sports bribery investigations. All the money, time and effort poured into chasing mob-connected bookies and the rumors of fixed games proved fruitless. Bookies, if convicted, rarely faced stiff penalties. And with the athletes, coaches, and referees connected to potentially fixed games, the Bureau seemed somewhat content to hand off these investigations to each league's security department, even if the league's conclusions always ended with the phrase "all parties involved were absolved of any wrongdoing." By the 1980s, President Ronald Reagan shifted the FBI's focus completely, cutting back its investigations into gambling and bookmaking. This was partly due to Nevada senator Paul Laxalt, one of Reagan's closest friends. Senator Laxalt complained that Las Vegas was infested with FBI and IRS agents, even though organized crime was no longer a problem there.[7] The FBI was instead tasked with Reagan's pet project, fighting the "war on drugs."

Yet the professional sports leagues were fighting their own war on drugs at the time. In an attempt to combat it, they too enlisted both the FBI and the Drug Enforcement Agency (DEA) to assist in warning athletes and coaches about the dangers of drugs…and the gambling that

A GOOD DEFENSE…

was sometimes associated with it.

SPORTS BRIBERY PRESENTATIONS

The *Los Angeles Times* wrote on June 16, 1983, "The heavy use of cocaine among some college and professional athletes has increased the chances that players might shave points or fix games for illegal book-makers, a top federal agent said Wednesday.

"Tony Vaccarino, the FBI's national coordinator for gambling and sports bribery investigations, said the use of cocaine puts many athletes in a position where they can be compromised to fix games.

"'I think there is a strong likelihood it does exist,' Vaccarino said of the possibility of games being fixed. 'It can be easily done—especially in the over-under, where a bettor bets on the total points scored.'

"Vaccarino said the athletes who are heavy cocaine users sometimes end up becoming distributors to support their habits and are easy targets for organized crime figures to extort favors from.

"'We know many big-time athletes are involved in a very large scale using cocaine,' he said. And despite the huge salaries paid some of the top players, he added, 'The price of cocaine is very, very expensive.'

"Vaccarino, speaking at a seminar on gambling and drugs at the National Assn. of Collegiate Directors of Athletics convention, said sports betting is such a big business in this country that bookmakers will do anything they can to gain an advantage over the bettors."

Three years later, *Sports Illustrated* also explored the dangerous combination of drugs and gambling. The authors wrote, "One major, almost universal misjudgment made by pro sports executives is the assumption that the astronomical salaries paid to players are a near-perfect deterrent to any temptation to fix games. [NFL commissioner Pete] Rozelle has said, 'The only blessing about the crazy salaries players are getting these days is that they don't need the money they could get by fixing games.'

The NBA's security director, Jack Joyce, agrees: 'One of the big things in our favor today is that players' salaries are so great that the possibility of someone paying them off is greatly reduced. Of course, I'm not saying it can't happen.'

"Indeed, the way it can happen is with the addition of drugs to the sports environment. Joyce himself says, 'We've always been aware that if a fellow does get into cocaine heavy, well, he can go through $200,000 or $300,000 a year. So then the bad guy can come to him and say, 'Why are you putting up so much bread for coke? Tell you what, we'll give you all the top-quality stuff you need. All you have to do is give us two, maybe three games a year.' Peter B. Bensinger, ex-chief of the Drug Enforcement Administration and now president of a Chicago firm dealing with drug and alcohol problems in the industry, is alarmed about the same thing: 'Someone on coke is the perfect prey for the gambler. A coke habit can easily bankrupt millionaires. It costs $5,000 to $8,000 a week. Suppliers can control a man's play, get him to perform all sorts of deeds in exchange for high-quality stuff.'"[8]

Of course that never once happened.

But athletes did use drugs. My word, did they use drugs. Especially cocaine in the 1980s. Major League Baseball had the most public problem with the drug, but they weren't alone. As Kansas City Royals pitcher Vida Blue said after being busted for drugs in 1985, "The public thinks the three Kansas City players and I are the only athletes in professional sports who used drugs. Let me tell you something: if you were to make a case against everybody who uses drugs in pro sports, you might have to close down some of the teams."[9]

Author Aaron Skirboll did an incredible job chronicling the MLB's cocaine era with *The Pittsburgh Cocaine Seven: How a Ragtag Group of Fans Took the Fall for Major League Baseball.* Most of the revelations about cocaine in baseball stemmed from the case at the center of his book in which seven small-time drug dealers were convicted of supplying cocaine to several prominent 1980s-era MLB players. The list of players Skirboll cites as users included: Dave Parker (who claimed Mike Schmidt used), Rod Scurry, Dale Berra, Lee Mazzilli, Lonnie Smith (who claimed to have seen a FBI list of one hundred MLB players thought to be users), Tim Raines, Lee Lacy, John Milner, Enos Cabell, Keith Hernandez, Al Holland, Jeffrey Leonard, Dusty Baker, Pascual Perez, Gary Matthews, Dickie Noles, Joaquin Andujar, and J.R. Richard. Also on that list was Mark Liebl, who sold cocaine to the aforementioned Vida Blue and his Royals teammates Willie Wilson, Willie Aikens, and Jerry Martin, as well as to other unnamed members of the Boston Red Sox, Oakland A's, Chicago White Sox, and Minnesota Twins.

The two FBI agents at the center of this investigation were astonished by what was happening within baseball. Skirboll wrote, "Despite the fact that no players were set to be arrested in Pittsburgh, one thing became clear to the agents as their investigation unfolded: cocaine was the first thing many of these players thought about in the morning and was at the forefront of their daily activities. While [FBI agent] Ross was amazed to learn what was really going on in baseball, [FBI] Agent Craig found it unnerving. He certainly wasn't surprised that players were using drugs, but he was shocked at the scope and extent of it. A lifelong baseball fan, he says his faith in America's national pastime was severely shaken. 'I'm not sure I ever got over it—that exposure to the underbelly of professional athletes.'

"For a large number of players in the early 1980s, their passion for cocaine began to surpass their passion for the game. It was all about hooking up for the present moment or setting things up for later. As for the games, it was merely about getting by.

"'I started losing interest in things. I didn't care about the game. The majority of the time we were in a hurry to get the game over with and do it all over again,' [St. Louis Cardinals outfielder] Lonnie Smith told the *New York Times* [August 19, 1985]. He also spoke of the pregame discussions he had with his adversaries. 'We would have conversations sometimes,' he said, 'trying to find out who had connections, who could get something. It was usually during practice before a game, loosening up, running sprints, talking to guys.'"[10]

One of the FBI files Skirboll uncovered showed the true depth of cocaine in baseball at the time. The 13-page memo was sent from Pittsburgh to the Bureau Director. It read in part, "[U.S. Attorney] Johnson has maintained that this case is not an investigation of Major League Baseball. It is an investigation of several cocaine dealers who gained access to ballplayers through various introductions and advanced their drug trade through these associations. Nonetheless, baseball has been inextricably involved throughout the course of this investigation. Players have used their status to take known dealers into locker rooms of their teams. Players have introduced known dealers to their friends and teammates, and have facilitated the distribution of cocaine to other players. They have furthered a code of silence regarding other players known to have serious cocaine addiction and to assist these players in continuing to use cocaine. They have recommended known dealers for employment by their team. They have invited known dealers to travel with their team on road trips to sell cocaine in other Major League cities. They have invited known dealers to their homes and to homes of their friends for social occasions. Non-player team employees have furnished cocaine to young players. A player agent furnished cocaine to his client during World Series competition. A player allowed a known dealer to live in his residence during the off-season. Players allowed known dealers to use their hotel rooms while on road trips. Players bought cocaine from dealers while in groups and used cocaine with them. Players continued to associate with dealers even after being advised that dealers were known by the team and league security offices. During investigation, players stated they had been advised in 1981 or 1982 that two subjects in this case had been identified by League Security and players notified of same. This did not stop players or dealers from continuing their cocaine trafficking in and around stadiums. When contacted for background on one of the subjects, the commissioner's security office could not provide any information on subject or memorandum pertaining to subject. This subject shortly thereafter gained employment with a team. This employment was a result of player recommendation. It was also apparent during investigation that teams and league failed [to] take aggressive action to prevent player-dealer relationships when identity of drug-using players was apparent to many in and out of baseball. A dealer was confirmed to have used inside information gained from player to bet on games. It was also common for dealers to be heavy gamblers."[11]

Despite the prevalence of cocaine in baseball, players remained virtually punishment-free. Though 11 players were suspended by MLB Commissioner Peter Ueberroth prior to the 1986 season as a result of the revelations surrounding the Pittsburgh Drug Trial, ultimately not one missed a single game of baseball. What was worse was that, "[i]n time, Peter Ueberroth made one last-ditch effort to get something accomplished in regard to drugs. He called a meeting with Donald Fehr, during which he made a request that bowled the union boss over. As former union chief Marvin Miller later recounted to writer Allen Barra, 'When they finally got together, Ueberroth asked Fehr if the union would agree to testing, 'even if it was just for the sake of public relations.' Don told me his jaw dropped; when he told me, mine dropped.'"[12]

The NBA beat MLB to the punch, becoming the first league to institute a drug testing policy in 1984 because, if you'd believe it, basketball was even more infested with drugs than baseball. A famous 1982 *Los Angeles Times* article stated that 75 percent of NBA players were using drugs at the time. Few doubted that number; however, in the first ten years the drug-testing program was in place, only six players were caught and suspended by the NBA. Of course at this time, the league was not testing its athletes for marijuana, which was considered to be the most widely used substance.

That did not mean cocaine was not part of the NBA lifestyle. An FBI investigation from the early 1980s connected at least three members of the New York Knicks to a known cocaine dealer. These players were likely fixing games in exchange for the drug (this is discussed in full later). Another FBI file stated, "It is noted that Salt Lake City teletype dated May 1, 1983, identifies seven (7) NBA players who are or have been 'contacts' or middlemen for cocaine distribution and identifies twelve (12) distributors of cocaine to NBA ball players." This FBI source also "alleged narcotics use in the National Basketball Association in sixteen (16) different cities [the NBA had 23 franchises at the time]." By July 1985, this investigation had been ongoing for 22 months with the FBI as the lead investigative unit. On June 26 and 27, grand jury testimony was presented with 19 subjects indicted on 127 criminal counts. The FBI did not want the NBA to be aware of this (and apparently NBA Security did not know), writing, "SU agrees with FBI HQ that those players' actions as 'middle men' should be considered subjects of a conspiracy to distribute narcotics. Immunity for cooperating witnesses and/or informants as developed should be made on a case-by-case basis, and with coordination with the appropriate [U.S. Attorney's] office. SU also agrees that no contact should be made with any representative of the NBA; however, it is anticipated that NBA representatives will initiate contact with the FBI. These contacts should be handled uniformly and in such a manner to avoid deliberate or accidental 'announcement' by the NBA or players union of FBI investigations into sports bribery and narcotics." Despite this, no players were indicted or convicted in this probe.

The NFL wasn't devoid of similar issues either. "In April 1981, NFL Security announced that for nearly five months it had been investigating several members of the Denver Broncos for cocaine use. Subsequently, more serious questions arose when the Colorado Organized Crime Strike Force revealed that 'eight to ten' Broncos players had accepted the cocaine from known Denver gamblers and bookmakers. In return, according to law-enforcement authorities, the players supplied the dealers with inside information about Denver's games....Five alleged cocaine dealers, two of whom were major gambling figures in the Denver area, were arrested and convicted in connection with the case. No one from the Broncos team was charged. However, three players—linebacker [and current ESPN analyst] Tom Jackson, safety Billy Thompson, and return specialist Rick Upchurch—were reprimanded in a letter from commissioner Rozelle."[13]

A year later, *Sports Illustrated* published an article detailing the tribulations of Don Reese who had played for three different NFL teams prior to being busted for buying cocaine. In the piece, Reese explained, "What you see on the tube on Sunday afternoon is often a lie. When players are messed up, the game is messed up. The outcome of the game is dishonest when playing ability is impaired. You can forget about point spreads or anything else in that kind of atmosphere....I've seen dealers literally standing on the practice fields of the NFL, guys everybody knew. They're not there to make the game better. What they do, and what they know about the players, can't possibly be good for the game."[14]

While the NBA had perhaps 75 percent of its players on drugs in the 1980s, Steve "Mental Case" Durbano, who played in the National Hockey League from 1972 until 1979 and spent seven years in prison for attempting to import $500,000 worth of cocaine into Canada, claimed up to 25 percent of all players in the NHL used drugs. Not to be outdone, Minnesota Vikings Hall of Famer Carl Eller told the *New York Times* in June 1982 that more than 40 percent of NFL players use cocaine. It should come as no surprise then that "during the 1980s… according to law-enforcement officials, no fewer than nine NFL teams—the Cleveland Browns, Dallas Cowboys, Denver Broncos, Miami Dolphins, New England Patriots, New Orleans Saints, San Diego Chargers, San Francisco 49ers, and Washington Redskins—found themselves the targets of investigations in which players had been allegedly given drugs by gamblers who were looking for an on-field edge."[15]

Given the gravity of the situation, something needed to be done. The major leagues, along with the NCAA, came together with the FBI and DEA in 1982 to design a solution. This became the sports bribery presentation program. From the FBI's file on the subject: "During recent months, professional and college sports teams have received extensive local and national media attention revealing that certain well-known sports figures have admitted using illicit narcotics during and after scheduled season games. In addition, these reports indicate that numerous members of various teams have, in fact, been using illicit narcotics for many years during their college and professional sports careers. There is also an indication that use of illicit narcotics by athletes has become commonplace during social encounters in various parts of the country.

"Specific allegations have been acted upon by the FBI, NCAA, and professional sports conferences involved with minimal results at times. The professional sports conferences have indicated that they have established rehabilitation programs for certain players that have been heavily involved in the use of illicit narcotics.

"FBIHQ has discussed this important problem with various collegiate and professional sports officials and the general consensus is that the illicit use of narcotics by athletes in this country is considered a possible major problem with possible criminal repercussions involving athletes.

"FBIHQ has authorized the organized crime section to formulate a special task force consisting of FBI and DEA agents trained in sports matters to make a presentation to professional sports teams outlining each Agency's responsibilities in this area....This approach by the FBI, in cooperation with DEA and the professional sports conferences, is an unprecedented opportunity to utilize our criminal investigative experience in the areas of narcotics, bribery, extortion and illegal gambling activities....

"On 10/21/82, selected DEA and FBI Agents met at a conference held in the Washington, D.C., area to discuss future plans regarding the above sports presentations. Also in attendance at this conference were officials from the professional sports conferences, the NBA, NFL, and NHL. The results of this conference revealed a most cooperative attitude by all attendees with a general feeling that this FBI/DEA agent group can assist professional sports and meet our investigative responsibilities in sports bribery and narcotics matters. The attitude shown by the professional sports officials indicates that the assigned agent personnel will be receiving their full cooperation in communicating to the owners of the professional sports teams the objectives of this group, i.e. each agency's responsibility regarding illicit narcotics, illegal gambling matters and the possible exposure of the athletes to criminal types. In addition, it was established that this program would be informative for the professional teams and would furnish them the opportunity of cooperating with the government regarding any possible illegal activities in the professional sports field."

Like with drug testing, the NBA started the ball rolling by being the first league to receive these presentations beginning in late 1982. In 1983, MLB, the NHL, and the NFL all joined as well.

What did the presentations consist of? According to the FBI's file, "FBI Agents are requested to give consideration to the following points during their presentations: 1. Objective of program with emphasis placed on developing an awareness by the athletes attending regarding possible criminal problems. 2. Federal Statutes involved. 3. Criminal and civil penalties. 4. Possible loanshark activities. 5. Importance of advising appropriate law enforcement agencies regarding any extortion attempts to the players, their families or close friends. 6. Interesting case examples regarding any of the above."

A joint press release from the FBI/DEA in 1983 further explained, "The Agents will emphasize that persons engaged in organized crime, gambling and illegal narcotics transactions, for their own monetary gain, use any means at their disposal to corrupt players engaged in professional sports. The need to maintain the integrity of sports in the United States is utmost in this program approach."

Greg Stejskal was a 31-year veteran of the FBI prior to retirement. He was one of the first agents to make these presentations, beginning in 1982 at the request of University of Michigan college football coach Bo Schembechler. Over the years, he gave over one hundred presentations to various college and pro teams. "When I first started doing the sports presentations, there wasn't any training required," Stejskal recalled. "But later, all presenters were required to go through training at Quantico. Then we had periodic conferences with representatives from the pros and NCAA present."

Stejskal explained what he focused on when making these presentations to teams, outside of the necessity of relating the dangers of drugs and gambling. "I would emphasize avoiding being in the wrong place at the wrong time, the double standard with media. For example, if you're an athlete and do something wrong, it's going to get media attention even if it's relatively minor. I also talked about performance-enhancing drugs. The message was similar for both pros and college, but the emphasis might be different depending on the audience."

How did the players respond to these presentations? "Generally our reception by athletes was positive," Stejskal stated. "One way you gauge is by demeanor, another is amount of questions. One thing I required after doing it for a while was to have the coach present. If he's not, players get the message it's not important." Though Stejskal liked having the team's coach present, the FBI decided early on that "team owners and management [should be] excluded from the presentation question-and-answer period. This has been found to be an effective rapport-building technique between the players and the special agents making the presentations. Furthermore, a fluid dialogue is enhanced when players are comfortable in the belief that their questions will not be subject to interpretation by those with whom they engage in contract negotiations."

"The other thing, quite honestly, that was the biggest hindrance to management, especially in baseball, was the union," stated Tom French, who was also an 11-year veteran in making sports bribery presentations. "We couldn't even go in to do the speeches until the union gave us the okay. And it was touch and go there for a while....They [the union] were afraid that management was using us as a tool for negotiations against a lot of these guys. It was pretty contentious as I remember between the union and Major League Baseball." If players asked certain incriminating questions which management overheard during these presentations, obviously those players could be singled out for various reasons later. This is why the union was so protective and leery. Of course, the unions were the reason drug testing took so long to implement and expand in the first place.

By 1989, some of the steam the program had began to evaporate. The NFL seemed to be the first league to lose interest. "It is noted that the Raiders canceled the scheduled September 4, 1989 presentation and no new date has been set. Although the team members were attentive during the presentations, it was obvious that management of the Bears and Seahawks had other priorities. Seattle, in fact, requested at the last minute that the presentation be cut from the original 60 minutes to 30 minutes. Despite earlier confirmation, the Bears claimed to be surprised by the visit and requested that the presentation be shortened. Both organizations complained that the teams had already been exposed to drug and gambling presentations by the NFL and questioned the need for our presence. Unlike the baseball presentations when the agents are able to talk individually to the players during practice following the presentations, no such opportunity occurred with the NFL teams, with only a limited amount of time available for questions. If these programs are to be effective it is suggested that consideration be given to: 1. Coordinating with NFL Security to avoid duplication of subject matters covered; 2. Presenting subject matter at pre-season when time is not so limited due to actual game preparations; 3. Encourage NFL to schedule presentations on a day when presenters have more interaction with the players in a less formal and structured environment."

"After a while," French related, "the message would get old." He would know, having made over 150 sports bribery presentations during his tenure. "If you were a ten-year veteran, you've heard the same thing over and over for ten years. So then they tried to become a little more innovative. The security people for the leagues, they'd bring in bad guys like Michael Franzese. They brought him in one time to scare them a little. 'I'm a wiseguy and I'm your worst nightmare.' Or they'd bring in a hooker dressed like a librarian and she'd be talking about something, then they'd ask, 'Do you know who she is? She seems like a very nice lady,' and then they'd reveal it. Crazy stuff, just to shake things up."

Bringing in former mob capo Michael Franzese corresponded with the creation of a video titled "Gambling with Your Life" to use in these presentations. Produced in the mid-1990s with the cooperation of NBA Productions, "Gambling with Your Life" was narrated by Greg Gumbel and featured both Franzese, who as mentioned earlier claims to have fixed numerous sporting events, and mobster Henry Hill, who participated in the Boston College basketball point shaving scandal. Both Franzese and Hill were prisoners at the time and were given special permission to cooperate in making the video. The film crew traveled to Las Vegas to interview and film "individuals involved in the gaming industry, casinos, [and] cooperating sources" as well as others "who have been involved in gambling and/or sports bribery cases in the past."

Franzese wrote about the experience in his book *Blood Covenant*. "I was contacted by Major League Baseball and the NBA and asked to come and speak to their players and league personnel about gambling and organized crime. The leagues were becoming very proactive in attempting to educate the players about the dangers gambling and organized crime could present to their careers and to their very lives.

"Imagine, a former organized crime member actually standing in the middle of a group of professional ball players and telling them to beware of gambling, bookmakers, and men in pinstriped suits.…There is truly a dark side to an athlete's involvement with gamblers and organized crime figures, and I knew it firsthand.…Inviting me was a bold move on the part of the heads of security for both leagues and the NCAA, which also participated in the program. They were agreeing to bring a genuine, notorious mob capo into the midst of their leagues' most prized assets. It was a risk, a huge gamble with a potentially devastating downside. What if I wasn't on the level about this transformation thing from mob guy to good guy? Just let me get the ear of one athlete. Oh, what I could have done."[16]

The use of Franzese was interesting. He claims to have fixed games, yet he was never investigated, indicted or convicted for doing so. At the same time, during his heyday in the Colombo crime family, none of the leagues would admit to a fixed game. One of the two apparently isn't telling the whole truth. Would the FBI and the major leagues use a known liar to speak to players about gambling and game fixing—because Franzese continues to be hired by professional teams to speak about these subjects today—or would they use someone who knows exactly what he's talking about?

It also raises the question: why give these presentations at all? For example, if the NFL is honest in its claims that it has never had a game fixed in its history, with only two recognized attempts (the last coming in 1971), then why worry about informing its athletes of these dangers? It should be a non-issue because it never happens. Why go to all the trouble? "It's for liability," claimed French. "At the end of the day, if it happened, they could say, 'Well, we did our best.' I think that's what [the leagues] were doing. They were touching their bases. 'Hey, we have a program in place to inform these athletes on how to prevent these things and we're doing the best we can.'"

An attempt was made to acquire a copy of "Gambling with Your Life." The FBI has not, as of this writing, provided one. Yet even without seeing it (which would come in a redacted format), by reading the file about the video, apparently it discussed some hot-button issues because

A GOOD DEFENSE...

certain rules came along with using it. The FBI wrote, "The professional sports leagues consented to the distribution of the training video with assurances from FBIHQ that several restrictions would apply to its use by Agent personnel in the field. The restrictions imposed by the professional sports leagues include the following:

"1.) No portion of the training video shall be broadcast or provided to the local or national media; and

"2.) Use of the training video for purposes other than the FBI Sports Presentation Program is strictly prohibited by the participants of the video and the professional sports leagues (NBA, NFL, NHL and MLB).

"The aforementioned restrictions were derived from contractual agreements between the participants in the video and the professional sports leagues prior to production. Any deviation from these restrictions by Agent personnel could result in civil penalties."

Today, the presentation program continues, albeit in a truncated form. In 2006, oversight of the program was transferred to the Organized Crime Section of the FBI's Asian Organized Crime Unit. This development is interesting because, as detailed later, international sporting events are being fixed worldwide—mostly by gambling syndicates based in the Far East. The switch is no coincidence. The FBI took notice and reacted accordingly.

In a similar regard, MLB requested the FBI's assistance in 2006 in creating a new training video "which will address issues specific to Major League Baseball." The general outline of topics to be addressed included "I. Gambling: (A) Organized Crime (1) Inside the U.S. (2) International; (B) How does an illegal sports book work?; (C) Internet Gambling/Off Shore Sports Books; (D) How this can effect [sic] the integrity of the game; (E) Case examples of how athletics have been compromised by illegal gambling. II. Targeting of the Athlete by criminal elements: (A) International nature of the league; (B) Blackmail; (C) Fraud schemes; (D) Exposure to the criminal element through social circles; (E) Lower level crimes (examples: hotel room burglary, robbery)."

Looking back on his years in making these presentations, French observed, "You know what the funniest part of this whole thing was? And this is just my own perception on this, was they were more concerned—the management and the leagues—they were more concerned about the gambling more than they ever were about the drugs. And I used to look at it and say, 'The drugs are what compromises these guys.' And I used to have a DEA agent come in with me [the DEA was excluded from the program in 1990]. But the drugs weren't a real concern. But the gambling, they were afraid that if there was a gambling scandal in their sport, then that would really ruin them. I guess they figured that drugs come and go...I don't think they ever made the connection that if a guy is high on drugs, you could get him to do anything for you. They seemed to compartmentalize it. This is the gambling. This is the drugs. And I always said, if I was the owner of a team, I'd be more concerned about the drugs, not that I wouldn't care about the gambling, but the drugs can lead to the gambling part of it. The squeeze, you know?"

BOXING

"Boxing is the only jungle where the lions are afraid of the rats."
— Jack Newfield

"Boxing? Forget about it," said the Stardust's Scott Schettler. "You could say, 'We're going to fix this fight,' and the people would ignore it, bet their money, and go to the fight anyways. They just didn't want to believe it. You could say, 'Cassius Clay is going to knock out Sonny Liston in the fourth round' ahead of time, and people would say, 'Nah, that's not true,' and they'd still bet and go pay for a ticket."

That is the biggest problem with boxing. It is the easiest sport to fix. In an event where only two athletes face each other, a person wanting to fix a fight need only get to one fighter. The other—the certain winner—is effectively superfluous. The fixer needs only control the desired loser. A bribe, perhaps sweetened with a wager on the fighter's behalf, may be all that is necessary to get him to take a dive. Given that the history of boxing is filled with champions that struggled to reach the top, this may seem too simplistic. Too easy. Yet that same history, hidden beneath reams of stirring stories from the boxing realm, shows fixed fights have occurred even on the biggest of stages.

Face it: boxers box because of the paycheck attached to each fight. Most come from poor socioeconomic backgrounds. There haven't been many champions toting a degree from Harvard or Yale alongside their spit bucket. If a better opportunity or more money awaits a loss rather than a win, it may be too tempting to pass up no matter the fighter's commitment to his craft.

If he proves to have a greater sense of honor, then there are other, less sure ways to fix a fight. Having either a referee or the fight judges in one's back pocket may be the perfect safety net to ensure that the chosen fighter wins...even if it wasn't deserved. Any fight fan could rattle off a number of matches in which the presumed winner has victory snatched away because of the judges' decision—the most recent example coming in June 2012 in the bout between Manny Pacquiao and Timothy Bradley. Often times such controversial decisions benefit more than just the winning fighter. A wise boxing promoter can seize the sudden opportunity of an unpopular decision to create immediate interest in a rematch which will further line everyone's pockets—even the shafted loser.

JACK DEMPSEY

Jack Dempsey, the heavyweight champion nicknamed "the Manassa Mauler" by writer Damon Runyon, once rivaled Babe Ruth as America's top sports icon. Though his fame has faded since his championship heyday in the 1920s, allusions to Dempsey's greatness are peppered within modern pop culture from *The Godfather* to HBO's *Boardwalk Empire*. In 2003, *Ring* magazine named him the seventh best puncher in boxing history. He posted a record of 60 wins, 51 of which came by way of knockout, against seven losses, eight draws, and five no decisions.

He fought his first professional fight in 1914, and five incredibly busy years later, won the title of heavyweight champion of the world from Jess Willard on July 4, 1919, with a third-round knockout. Before winning the heavyweight belt, Dempsey may have thrown a fight.

Dempsey's record stood at 33–1 by the end of 1916. He was just 21. His first fight in 1917 was against Jim "the Pueblo Fireman" Flynn on February 16 in Salt Lake City. Flynn wasn't seen as much of a challenge for the up-and-coming Dempsey, but just ten seconds into the fight, "Flynn caught Dempsey with a left to the jaw that sent him to the canvas on his knees. Dempsey not only was counted out, but stayed down for another twenty seconds."[1]

This was an auspicious start to the year for Dempsey. After being knocked out by Flynn, his next three fights consisted of a draw, a loss by decision, and then another draw. He righted his ship for the next two fights with a win and a knockout of his own, but then stumbled again with a pair of draws. After that, however, he would lose only one more fight on his path to winning the heavyweight championship.

But that knockout loss to the Pueblo Fireman remained curious. It proved to be the only time in all of Dempsey's professional career in which he was knocked out. And it had happened so fast—ten seconds into the fight. With all of the hoopla that surrounded his career, most forgot it ever occurred. But then "in a column more than a decade later, Joe Williams, a widely known sportswriter for the Newspaper Enterprise Association, wrote that Dempsey had 'laid down, as the boys say,' in the fight. 'I understand he got three hundred for taking a synthetic belt on the whiskers and that he carried the money tucked away inside his trunks when he entered the ring.'"[2]

While some may see that as being a bit farfetched, given that Dempsey was 33–1 at the time and on a seeming path to greatness, another person—one more intimately associated with the fighter—seconded William's opinion. Dempsey's first wife, Maxine Cates, claimed after their divorce in 1919 that Dempsey did in fact dump the Flynn fight because he needed the money. Considering the fight came in Dempsey's youth not long after his days of Colorado saloon-fighting under the name "Kid Blackie," this may be more of a reality than rumor.

"Even Flynn seemed surprised at the knockout. 'Well, it was this way,' he explained some years after his most notable victory. 'I hit him with a one-two. But just put it down that I didn't exactly knock Dempsey out. He just forgot to duck.'"[3]

The next fixed fight Dempsey would participate in cost him the heavyweight crown. Only this wasn't because Dempsey took a dive; it came as a result of a conspiracy against him.

"In June 1928 Arnold Rothstein placed his hand upon a bible, swore to tell the truth, and proceeded to perjure himself: 'I don't bet on football or boxing.'

"He didn't lie about football. Football made him uncomfortable. Twenty-two men running around in a dozen different directions. Too many variables; too much to fix. But A.R. lied about boxing. In his crowd, boxers were *everywhere*. Everyone *followed* boxing. Everyone *bet* on boxing.

"Boxing meant big money. Not for everyone, but certainly to A.R. and his political friends, people who protected you and made things happen or not happen."[4]

Yes, it is quite possible that Arnold Rothstein, the man most known for masterminding the fixing of the 1919 World Series, rigged the first heavyweight title fight between champion Jack Dempsey and contender Gene Tunney in 1926.

"In the month leading up to the fight, Dempsey had been a prohibitive favorite at odds ranging as high as 4-1…but on the day of the fight, as thousands of New Yorkers descended on Philadelphia, a flood of money was wagered on Tunney, dropping the odds to 12-to-5 on Dempsey. Some 'betting commissioners,' as the *New York Times* referred to major bookmakers, said 'they had never seen anything like the change of heart on the part of bettors that took place today.'"[5] The likely cause of that "change of heart" stemmed not from the belief in Tunney's ability to beat

Dempsey, but because Rothstein and his right-hand man, former feath-erweight champion Abe Attell, were ringside—and Rothstein's money was on the underdog Tunney.

For his part, Dempsey was not up to the task of defending his title that night. At the weigh-in prior to the fight (which took place the night of the fight, unlike today's weigh-ins which occur the day before), Dempsey looked ill, even unsteady. Being under the weather—both figuratively from an unexplained illness and literally as the fight was held at the outdoor Sesquicentennial Stadium in a rainstorm—sapped Dempsey's strength, giving Tunney an easy ten-round victory. While Tunney claimed the title, Rothstein collected his vast winnings.

The plot behind the fix is a bit hazy. But what is known is Tunney and his manager William "Billy" Gibson obtained a "loan" for $20,000 for "training expenses" just prior to the fight from Philadelphia gang lord and sometimes fight promoter Maxie "Boo Boo" Hoff. It's proba-ble that Hoff didn't actually grant this loan; Rothstein did. Rothstein's connection to Tunney derived from Abe Attell, who had perhaps saved Tunney's life a few years earlier. In 1923, Tunney fought and lost a brutal fight against Harry "The Human Windmill" Greb during which he lost upward of a quart of blood. As circumstances would have it, Attell was at that fight, saw Tunney's post-fight condition, and being a former fighter himself, rushed to a nearby pharmacy to retrieve a coagulant to stop the bleeding. The two became friends. So close of friends that Attell was at Gibson's side prior to the Dempsey fight and in Tunney's locker room afterward. No one seemed bothered by the pair's friendliness, even though Attell was a known associate of Rothstein's and known for his role in the fixing of the World Series. That aside, the deal agreed upon between Boo Boo and Tunney's camp was that should Tunney lose to Dempsey, Tunney and Gibson simply had to pay back the $20,000. No juice, no commission. However, if Tunney won and became champ, he had to pay back the $20,000 and Boo Boo received a 20 percent stake in Tunney's future earnings, likely worth $200,000 or more at the time.

The entire episode seemed unnecessary. Tunney's take of the gate for the title fight would have easily covered his $20,000 expenses, so why bother to get the loan—especially from a mobster? On top of that, the terms offered were absurd. For Boo Boo to loan that kind of money and not expect something on the back end of the deal, no matter the results, was out of any mobster's character. Plus, for Tunney and his manager to give up 20 percent of future earnings meant they were either desperate (for which there was no evidence) or else they knew what the loan really meant—a certain victory over Dempsey—which would have been worth the Faustian deal.

So how did they pull it off without Dempsey's participation? On the day of the fight, "Dempsey arrived at the Broad Street train station in Philadelphia at 6:40 p.m. aboard a private car. Along the way, Dempsey began to feel week and queasy, and by the time he got to the Adelphia Hotel, he felt worse and vomited several times. By then…the others in his party were concerned….Dempsey chalked up his discomfort and the vomiting to something he had eaten, maybe the olive oil he took each morning before breakfast."[6] That's right. To aid in digestion, Dempsey had the habit of drinking a glass of olive oil every day.

From this sudden-onset illness, two conspiracy theories sprung up, each of which centered on the idea that Dempsey was poisoned prior to fighting Tunney. The first suggestion came from an Atlantic City police captain named Charles Mabbutt who oversaw security at Dempsey's training camp. Mabbutt theorized that Dempsey's coffee cream had been spiked. But the more likely scenario involved that ill-fated glass of olive oil. This was administered to Dempsey by bodyguard Mike Trent. Why is this more believable? Because the day after the Tunney fight, Trent was fired. No reason was ever given for his dismissal.

Given the surprising nature of Tunney's upset victory, others had suspicions about the fight as well. The most prominent was famed sportswriter Ring Lardner who had himself lost $500 betting on Dempsey. "In a letter to Scott and Zelda Fitzgerald [Fitzgerald wrote *The Great Gatsby* in which the character of Meyer Wolfsheim was based on Arnold Rothstein], close friends of Lardner and his wife, who were in Europe, Lardner wrote that the fight was a 'fake, a very well done fake.' Lardner's conclusion was based on a conversation he had after the fight with Benny

Leonard. The former lightweight champion had always been close to gamblers and told Lardner he suspected the fight had been fixed. That may explain why the Great Bennah [Leonard] had picked Dempsey to win by a knockout in a newspaper column before the fight, but then bet heavily on Tunney to win....

"Because of the risk of a libel suit, Lardner could not write that the fight was fixed, or even that he thought it was, unless he had ironclad proof. So, to get the matter off his chest, Lardner set it down in his letter to the Fitzgeralds. Apparently by saying it was a 'very well done fake,' Lardner suggested that Dempsey had made it look legitimate by going the distance, even though that meant taking a beating. Yet Lardner knew that fighters who agree to throw a fight almost always go down early in a bout and are counted out. Apparently Lardner, if he really did believe that Dempsey had taken a dive, felt that Dempsey was too proud a fighter to feign being knocked out, and thus had agreed to lose, but to last the ten rounds if he could and absorb whatever punishment Tunney might administer, which turned out to be substantial."[7]

Dempsey himself sensed something wasn't quite right about his loss to Tunney. When a rematch was scheduled between the pair in 1927, Dempsey wrote an open letter to the *Chicago Herald and Examiner* accusing Boo Boo, Gibson, and Attell (whom he called "the tool of a big New York gambling clique") of fixing the first fight on the basis of Boo Boo's "loan" to Tunney. Dempsey went a step further in the letter, claiming he was told "there's something phony about this fight [their rematch]." Tunney denied Dempsey's charges, labeling them "utter trash."[8] But there were rumors swirling about a possible fix in the Dempsey-Tunney rematch. This time, it was Tunney who was suspected of a willingness to take a dive in a *New York Journal* report which correctly detailed his connection to Rothstein and Attell. Tunney denied the accuracy of the article, and thanks to his clean-cut, learned reputation, he was given a free pass. However, when Rothstein was murdered years later, he had the name and address for Billy Gibson, Tunney's manager, in his possession.

Dempsey's letter was more right than wrong. The underworld was clamoring for a piece of the action in their rematch. Al Capone announced to reporters—with a telling wink, as if to say the fix was in—that he had bet $50,000 on Dempsey to beat Tunney. Big Al's bet was based on erroneous inside information. Capone heard that a local referee, who had a side job of running a speakeasy, was going to be named the third man in the ring with Dempsey and Tunney and that this gentleman had already made a large wager on Dempsey. The fellow did not get that call.

That didn't stop Al. Capone was willing to go a step further to ensure his bet came home. "Years later, Ed Sullivan, who covered Dempsey's camp for the New York *Daily News*, wrote that five of Capone's henchmen had turned up at Dempsey's training site and said Capone was prepared to have 'the right man' referee the fight if Dempsey's brain trust paid a fee of fifty thousand dollars….Dempsey, Flynn, and company of course turned down the proposal." But Dempsey did send a handwritten note of thanks back to Capone, and Capone in turn sent flowers to Dempsey's wife.

"Perhaps because of the swirl of rumors about a fight that had been fixed by either Capone or Rothstein and Attell, Dempsey's camp began to worry about his food. To make sure that no one would tamper with anything on Dempsey's menu, Leo Flynn brought in his wife, Katherine, to cook for the former heavyweight champion. Up until then, because of the suspect olive oil or coffee cream that Dempsey had ingested before the first Tunney fight, Jerry Luvadis was designated to sample whatever Dempsey was going to eat. That prompted W.O. McGeehan of the *New York Harold Tribune* to write, 'As long as the Greek lived, Dempsey could eat.'"[9]

The ensuing second bout between Dempsey and Tunney would go down into boxing legend as "the Long Count." Dempsey, knocking Tunney down in the seventh round, failed to go to a neutral corner as was dictated by a new boxing rule. Because of his inaction, the referee took extra time to escort Dempsey to where he needed to be prior to picking up the ten count on Tunney. Given a few extra seconds to recuperate, Tunney gathered his wits and held on to survive the round, ultimately winning the fight to retain his title. The controversy surrounding the

"Long Count" was so great it erased any memory of the possible fix in their first fight. It also caused a huge upswell in sympathy for Dempsey who retired after the fight, propelling him even further into the national consciousness. This soothed Dempsey, allowing him to forget how a conspiracy may have cost him the heavyweight championship.

PRIMO

A few short years after Dempsey walked away from boxing, Primo Carnera arrived in America from Italy with a 16–2 record. Nicknamed "The Ambling Alp," Carnera was huge even by heavyweight standards, standing 6'6" and tipping the scales at 265 pounds. The problem was that despite his hulking size, Carnera hit with the ferocity of a declawed kitten. Thus when Carnera's manager sold the fighter to mobster Owney "The Killer" Madden, the only way for Madden to earn a profit on his investment was to fix Carnera's fights—all of them. "Carnera, they realized, could only win the heavyweight title if they lined up opponents who would be rewarded financially so long as they agreed to fight not to win. Good-natured and naïve almost beyond comprehension, Carnera proved easy to mold.

"Through the connivance of the mobsters, a well-connected and dishonest manager in a former felon named Billy Duffy, along with a slew of other disreputable boxing managers of fighters willing to take dives, Carnera won his first twenty-four fights by knockouts, with most of them occurring in the first or second round."[10] These fights didn't last long because fighters willing to take dives wanted to get out of the ring as fast as possible. No need to take extra blows to the head when the end result was predetermined. The fans assumed that Carnera's power matched his size, that the knockouts were legitimate, not that the fix was in. Being so gullible, Carnera didn't even know his fights were set up, making him the perfect front.

Carnera only lost once in his first 32 American bouts—in a fight the mob thought they didn't need to fix. One opponent, Leon "Boom Boom" Chevalier, realized mid-fight that Carnera was a powder puff and decided to beat him. "Aware that such things might happen, the mobsters in control of Carnera made it a point to ensure that one of each of his opponent's cornermen was in on that particular night's charade. So when Chevalier returned to his corner between the fifth and sixth rounds, the mob's cornerman ran a sponge with either resin, red pepper, or some other visually impairing irritating substance across his eyes that served to temporarily blind him. Even while floundering around the ring and barely able to see in the sixth round, Chevalier still managed to land a number of punishing punches. But suddenly, following several light blows by Carnera, one of Chevalier's seconds, Bob Perry, threw a towel into the ring, the fistic symbol of surrender by a fighter's corner, whereupon the referee awarded the fight to Carnera on a technical knockout as the crowd—including hundreds of Carnera supporters—erupted with boos."[11]

Even with seemingly obvious fixes like these, Carnera continued to "win" and march toward a title fight while becoming a folk hero for Italian-Americans everywhere. In 1932, he won 24 of 26 fights—the two losses again coming in fights his controllers assumed were unnecessary to fix. After a streak of 15 victories, Carnera was granted his title shot against heavyweight champion Jack Sharkey in June 1933. The mob's reach extended even to Sharkey, who dropped in the sixth round on what some observers thought was a phantom uppercut thrown by Carnera. No matter, Carnera was the new heavyweight champion of the world.

The mob backed two title defenses for their fighter, and then let him box an honest match against Max Baer in 1934. Outweighed by 54 pounds, Baer still knocked down Carnera 12 times before the referee mercifully stopped the bout. Now a former champion, Carnera was abandoned by the mob who had robbed him of all his fight earnings over the years. Soldiering onward, he managed to win his next three bouts against bums before being KO'd by Joe Louis in 1935. Carnera lost three more fights, and then retired, broke, moving on to a career as a professional wrestler.

In both the cases of Dempsey and Carnera, organized crime showed what sort of influence it could have in the fight game. With Carnera, the mob effectively purchased a heavyweight champion. But this would prove to be small potatoes considering what came after World War II.

THE GRAY

1949 marked the incorporation of the International Boxing Club (IBC). It was the brainchild of Truman K. Gibson, Jr., a Chicago attorney who joined the boxing game through a relationship with the heavyweight champion Joe Louis. Funding for Gibson's venture derived from James D. Norris and his partner Arthur Wirtz. The pair owned the Chicago Stadium, Detroit's Olympia Stadium, the St. Louis Arena, and had a significant interest in New York's Madison Square Garden. The names of Norris and Wirtz may be familiar to fans of the National Hockey League (NHL). Norris' father, James E. Norris, owned the Detroit Red Wings and had both the James Norris Memorial Trophy, a yearly award for the NHL's top defenseman, and the former Norris Division named in his honor. James D. Norris and Wirtz co-owned the Chicago Blackhawks which is still owned by the Wirtz family. Both Norris Sr. and Jr. as well as Wirtz are honored as members of the Hockey Hall of Fame.

Gibson originally met Joe Louis during World War II when he assisted in setting up an exhibition tour through army bases in Europe and North Africa for the champ. Later, when the government chased Louis for back taxes, Gibson helped him create Joe Louis Enterprises, Inc. "The deal through which Norris and Wirtz purchased from Joe Louis Enterprises contracts binding the four leading contenders to the title Louis abdicated, contracts that thus gave the IBC exclusive promotional rights to the heavyweight championship.

"Once in control of the heavyweight title—won by Ezzard Charles over Jersey Joe Walcott in the IBC's inaugural presentation—the organization set out to place under contract and deliver to its fold the leading contenders in every principal division. As it succeeded, the IBC of Illinois grew into a network of tentacle entities: the IBC of New York, the IBC of Missouri, the IBC of Michigan, and various other related companies. Norris and Wirtz gained control of the Madison Square

Garden Corporation; Norris became its president, Wirtz its vice president and treasurer. Exclusive television contracts were negotiated with NBC for the weekly Friday-night fights, with CBS for the Wednesday-night fights."[12]

As the IBC's board of directors, Gibson, Norris, and Wirtz controlled the championship fights in all of the major weight classes for ten solid years. The IBC also held over one hundred fights a year in conjunction with the Wednesday and Friday night fights while running smaller clubs in both Chicago and New York City that acted as "talent feeders" for the more prominent bouts. Then, in January 1959, the IBC came to a crashing halt. The Supreme Court found the IBC to be a monopoly, in violation of the Sherman Anti-Trust Act, and conspiring to control the promotion of boxing in the United States. The downfall of the IBC would lead to the 1960 Senate Subcommittee on Antitrust and Monopoly in regards to professional boxing which sought to determine (a) organized crime's influence in the sport and (b) if there should be a national commission set up to oversee it.

What that Senate subcommittee would soon discover was that it wasn't Gibson, Norris, and Wirtz as the IBC that controlled professional boxing; it was The Gray who did.

Actually, he was known by several monikers. Uncle. Ambassador. Our Friend. The Southern Salesman. The Cousin. The Man. Mr. Gray. The Gray. But his given name was John Paul "Frankie" Carbo. He was a mafia hit man. And he ran professional boxing.

In 1958, the Chief Assistant District Attorney for New York County and head of the Rackets Bureau Alfred J. Scotti called Carbo "the most corrupt, corrosive and degrading influence in the sport of boxing."[13] In truth, that may have been the least of his sins.

Frank Marrone, a detective for the office of the New York County District Attorney, investigated Carbo for over ten years and actually put the cuffs on him in 1959. In testimony before the Senate Subcommittee in 1960, Marrone detailed Carbo's criminal history:

"Mr. Carbo's first conflict with the law came in 1915 at the age of 12. At that time he was sent to the Catholic protectory....Since that time Mr. Carbo's police record shows 17 arrests for vagrancy, suspicious character, assault, robbery, grand larceny, violation of the New York State boxing laws and five arrests for murder.

"Mr. Carbo, the first time, was charged in 1924, when he was indicted for the killing of a taxicab driver in the Bronx. He subsequently took a plea to the charge of manslaughter and was sentenced to two to four years in Sing Sing. Mr. Carbo was a fugitive in this case for four years before his apprehension.

"Carbo was also arrested for homicide September 1931 for the killing of a Philadelphia beer baron in a room in an Atlantic City hotel.

"Again in July of 1936 he was arrested in Madison Square Garden for the underworld murders of Max Hassel and Max Greenberg, henchmen of 'Waxey' Gordon.

"On Thanksgiving Day in 1939, Harry Schachter, alias Harry Greenberg, also known as 'Big Greeney,' a member of Murder, Incorporated, was assassinated outside of his home in Hollywood, California. Indicted for this murder was a notorious New York gangster, Louie 'Lucky' Buchalter, and the following: Benjamin 'Bugsy' Siegel, Emanuel 'Mendy' Weiss, Harry 'Champ' Segel, Frank Carbo.

"Al Tannenbaum, a member of Murder, Incorporated, subsequently testified in the murder trial of the above that 'Bugsy' Siegel and Frank Carbo killed 'Big Greeney.' He testified that Carbo fired five bullets into Schachter, and that 'Bugsy' Siegel drove the getaway car. This trial resulted in a hung jury, and a witness who was to testify against Carbo in the second trial fell or was pushed from a hotel window in Coney Island. [This witness] was Abe 'Kid Twist' Reles. Carbo was not retried for this homicide.

"Mr. Carbo's interest in the sport of professional boxing began in the early 1930s. For a number of years he virtually monopolized the middleweight division. Some of the middleweight champions over whom he had control or 'had a piece of' were 'Babe' Risko, Teddy Yarosz, Freddie Steele, and Solly Kreiger.

"He had made his influence felt in every division from flyweight to heavyweight. His range of influence ranged from lowly seconds to the president—or former president—of the International Boxing Club of New York. He is on speaking and friendly terms with almost everyone connected with the sport of professional boxing. He and Mr. James D. Norris have had a close personal relationship for a number of years. So close was this friendship that on the afternoon of October 1, 1959, Mr. Carbo met with Mr. Norris in Norris' automobile in Newark Airport, Newark, NJ, and there they had a conversation that lasted over three hours.

"This was just prior to the commencement of Mr. Carbo's trial in New York County for the violation of the New York State boxing laws, to which he pleaded guilty and received a two-year sentence."

Shortly after highlighting Carbo's criminal career, which left out that Carbo may have in fact been the trigger man who killed his former partner "Bugsy" Siegel, the subcommittee's counsel and staff director Paul Rand Dixon had the following exchange with Marrone:

Mr. Dixon: "Do you think present-day boxing is operated competitively at arm's length, or that it is controlled?"

Mr. Marrone: "It is well controlled."

Mr. Dixon: "What do you mean by 'controlled'? Who are the people you think who are controlling it? What is your opinion on that?"

Mr. Marrone: "I think I can briefly state for the record that Carbo's influence in boxing is unique and that he controlled a racket solely and to himself. There was no one else that was over him. He controlled a boxing racket by himself.

"The result was that there was not any prominent fighter in these United States that he didn't have control over, have a piece of, or owned outright.

"In addition to that, I would say that he had a strong influence over boxing managers, matchmakers, and promoters in every major city in the United States."

Mr. Dixon: "...This control would appear to me to serve as an excellent vehicle for betting purposes."

Mr. Marrone: "Yes, it does."

Mr. Dixon: "Certainly, if you know who is going to win, you are in an excellent position to take it out on the sucker public by putting a bet, aren't you?"

Mr. Marrone: "Just like money in the bank."

Mr. Dixon: "In other words, you are not gambling; you are betting on a certain thing, aren't you?"

Mr. Marrone: "Right."

Mr. Dixon: "Do you think this possibly has influenced some of these racketeers to move into boxing, because so much money is bet on boxing?"

Mr. Marrone: "Yes."

Mr. Dixon: "When a man is going to go down or even when a fight might end in a certain round, there is quite a point that is gambled on, is it not?"

Mr. Marrone: "Yes."

Mr. Dixon: "How long, in your opinion, has this condition been going on in boxing?"

Mr. Marrone: "Thirty years."

Mr. Dixon: "How long?"

Mr. Marrone: "Thirty years."

Mr. Dixon: "Do you think this permeates the whole game, the game where the money is?"

Mr. Marrone: "Yes, more so today because of closed television."

Mr. Dixon: "Television has influenced the game, too?"

Mr. Marrone: "Absolutely. There is more money [in television]."

As this question-and-answer session progressed, Marrone indicated that the investigation into the television end of boxing showed that it, too, was coming under organized crime's control. Of course, since Carbo was working hand in hand with Norris and the IBC to set up matches for both NBC and CBS, should this have come as a surprise? Television was a moneymaking machine, and it helped create a beneficial loophole for boxing and its promoters. Fights that weren't sanctioned in one state could be held in another with the bout televised into the area that initially said "no," making it a moot point where a fight was physically staged.

Marrone was then questioned by Peter Chumbris, another counselor for the subcommittee:

Mr. Chumbris: "…on the basis of the ten years that you have looked into this problem of boxing, would you say—have you formed any opinion as to the number of fixes that result in every week or twice a week boxing in the United States, particularly in New York where you—

Mr. Marrone: "You will have to explain what you mean by 'fix,' first—a dump?"

Mr. Chumbris: "'Fix' is where one or two or both of the contestants in a fight have agreed to lose. In other words, the fight would be fixed where one would win or one would lose, and it might be that one contestant is the one who is going to take a dive or it may be known to both."

Mr. John Bonomi (another counselor): "May I say with regard to that question, Mr. Chumbris, that there is another situation and that is where ring officials are fixed."

Mr. Chumbris: "I am glad to have that amendment and I accept it. Don't make a reckless answer. If you have not formed any opinion on that, I would rather you would tell us truthfully."

Mr. Marrone: "I would say from experience that a fixed fight, as you describe it, does not happen too frequently. Ordinarily, the fighters in the ring are not aware that the fight is fixed."

Senator Philip Hart: "Did you say 'the fighters,' plural?"

Mr. Marrone: "Yes; the fighters."

Mr. Chumbris: "Do I understand that it is infrequently?"

Mr. Marrone: "A fix as you describe it."

Mr. Chumbris: "Suppose you give us another illustration of a fix so that we will know how prevalent it is, so that the men who have control can be assured when they place $100,000 or $200,000 or $500,000 in bets will know that their bet is going to be safe?"

Mr. Marrone: "For example, if you have two fighters in a ring of almost equal ability, it should be a very close fight, and if you can influence one of the judges to see it your way, you have got the best of it going in.

"In addition to that, unbeknown to the fighter himself, most fighters are playboys, and a manager will overlook his dissipating so that his stamina will be down for the night of the fight. If he has to go the distance, he won't have the strength to go all the distance powerfully. He will probably lose by a close decision. That is another way of fixing a fight."

Mr. Chumbris: "How many instances would you say there are where the fighter was either doped or given some form of medication or something is put in his food to, let's say, affect his fighting ability?"

Mr. Marrone: "We have had a couple of them that I know of personally."

Clearly there was more than one way to fix a fight, and a man with Carbo's level of control had all of these tools and more at his disposal. The Gray's influence in the fight game was vast, really too vast to completely cover here. However, Truman Gibson Jr.'s testimony before the subcommittee should suffice in painting a more exacting picture of Carbo's reach. Gibson was asked, "During this period from 1949 to 1959 [when Gibson was a boxing promoter for IBC], have you dealt with certain managers throughout the country who are known as Carbo-controlled?"

Gibson responded, "I dealt with many managers that it was reported he was friendly with. The line between the control and friendship is very difficult, because in the very nature of this business the actions were not always on a businesslike basis or not on an open-and-above-board basis, so that it is very difficult to separate the line between the friendship and the control which calls for certain conclusions. But there were many managers that it was reported, and we dealt with them as a matter of fact, as friendly with or charged to be friendly with Carbo."

Gibson was then questioned about several boxing managers. The first was Frank "Blinky" Palermo—the "reputed numbers king of Philadelphia"—who managed lightweight champion Ike Williams, welterweight champion Johnny Saxton, and soon-to-be heavyweight champion Sonny Liston. "Blinky" was in fact Carbo's number two, his lieutenant, and would be later convicted alongside him when they attempted to gain control of welterweight champion Don Jordan. (Carbo's third was Gabriel "Gabe" Genovese who also held considerable sway in the boxing world.) But as a manager, Palermo was just the tip of a very dirty iceberg. Gibson also identified the following managers as being either "friendly with" or "controlled by" (was there really a difference?) Carbo: Herman Wallman (welterweight champion Johnny Bratton), Bernard Glickman (welterweight champion Virgil Akins), John DeJohn & Joseph Netro (welterweight champion Carmen Basilio), Willie Ketchum (featherweight champion Davey Moore), Anthony Ferrante (lightweight champion Bud Smith), Felix Bocchicchio (heavyweight champion Jersey Joe Walcott), Ernie Braca (middleweight champion Sugar Ray Robinson), Emil Shade & Angel Lopez (welterweight champion Kid Gavilan), Sammy Richman (co-manager of middleweight champion of Marcel Cerdan), Lou Viscusi (both featherweight champion Willie Pep and lightweight champion Joe Brown), "Rip" Valenti (welterweight champion Tony DeMarco), and Johnny Buckley (middleweight champion Paul Pender). Note that this list consisted just of managers of champion fighters. Gibson testified that Carbo also controlled or was "friendly with" several of the major boxing promoters around the nation, including the Miami Beach-based Chris Dundee whose brother Angelo Dundee would later train both Muhammad Ali and "Sugar" Ray Leonard.

The million-dollar question that follows from all of this is, did Carbo exercise this power to fix fights? The answer is undoubtedly yes.

In Barney Nagler's 1964 book *James Norris and the Decline of Boxing*, Nagler describes just one of the lesser-known instances of Carbo's control:

"[Welterweight champion Kid] Gavilan met [Johnny] Saxton in Philadelphia on October 20, 1954. The bout was a travesty. Neither fighter landed a vital blow. Saxton was inept, indifferent, and a failure. Gavilan was only slightly better. The fight was malodorous, but the decision was even worse. The decision went to Saxton.

"The entire country had seen the bout on television. The outcry was widespread. Dan Parker, writing in the *New York Mirror*, said: 'Jack Kearns told some friends before the fight to send in all they had on Saxton who, he said, couldn't lose. In New York many fans who tried to put money on Saxton were told that they could bet only on Gavilan. After the fight, Palermo said there would be no return match for Gavilan. And before and after it, Goombar Carbo lavishly entertained fight mobsters from all over America at a hotel suite. He had good reason to celebrate.'

"A few days after Saxton's unwarranted coronation, Carbo ran a party at the St. Moritz Hotel in New York. Gavilan was present. He walked up to Carbo and in Cuban-accented English, said, 'Mr. Blinky Palermo told me that they do whatever you want. That's what he told me. And if that's what you told him, for what they do to me I want my return match.'

"'Right,' Carbo said.

"Gavilan was never given a chance to regain the championship. There were mob obligations elsewhere."[14]

Perhaps the most famous fight Carbo fixed was the bout between "The Raging Bull" Jake LaMotta and Billy Fox in 1947. LaMotta was managed by his brother Joey, and both refused to play by Carbo's rules. The LaMotta brothers did everything on their own with success dependent on Jake's iron jaw. Yet because Carbo was so influential in boxing, no matter who LaMotta fought, no matter who he defeated, he could not secure a shot at the middleweight title. Being labeled the "uncrowned" middleweight champion did nothing for him. He desired the real thing. So, like many before him, LaMotta was forced to swallow his pride and knock on The Gray's door.

As LaMotta testified before the subcommittee: "When I signed for the Fox fight, after a couple of weeks I received an offer of $100,000 to lose to Billy Fox [who was managed by "Blinky" Palermo], which I refused [LaMotta would never divulge who offered him the $100,000. When asked if he was afraid of telling the subcommittee who was behind the bribe, LaMotta replied "I ain't afraid of none of them rats."]. I said I was only interested in the championship fight. It was said it could be arranged, a championship fight might be arranged.

"That is all I heard for about a couple of weeks, and while in training I hurt myself and I went to a doctor and the doctor examined me and took X-rays and found out I had a ruptured spleen. He said I couldn't possibly fight, but I thought I could, and I started training again, and I instructed my sparring partners to concentrate their punches on my face, which they did.

"But as the fight kept getting closer, I found out—I realized that I had no strength in my arms. So, therefore, when I was told again, if I would lose to the Fox fight, I kept stalling them off because I still felt I could win. But as the fight kept getting closer, I realized that it was going to be kind of difficult.

"But toward the end, when I realized that I couldn't possibly win, I said I would lose to Billy Fox, if I was guaranteed a championship fight."

That is exactly what transpired. Fox beat LaMotta with a fourth-round TKO. LaMotta, in a statement prior to his testimony, explained his actions (or non-actions) in that fight. "I was going to lose the fight, either by decision or knockout. I made up my mind I would never go down….I was hit many times but it did not bother me. I was not hurt….I just stood helpless and he [Fox] was pounding away and the referee stopped the fight."

Due to his poor acting skills, suspicions were immediately raised. In the ensuing investigation, LaMotta was suspended from boxing for seven months, not for fixing the fight—which he denied at the time—but for covering up his spleen injury. A year after returning to the ring, LaMotta would get his title shot against Marcel Cerdan in June 1949 and win.

Carbo was tied to the entire affair. He made a killing betting on Fox as LaMotta began as an 8-5 favorite. By fight night, the odds swung heavily the other way, making Fox a 3-1 favorite and stopping many bookies from accepting any bets on him. (Fox, by the way, was unable to testify before the subcommittee as he was confined to the Kings Park State Mental Hospital, having last held a job as a pin setter in a New York City bowling alley.) Then, in partnership with one of Cerdan's managers, Carbo set up the 1949 title fight for LaMotta. Upon winning the middleweight title, a clause in LaMotta's pre-fight contract kicked in, awarding Norris and the IBC exclusive rights to LaMotta's title defenses for the next three years. He would retain the title until squaring off with Sugar Ray Robinson on Valentine's Day in 1951 in the Norris-owned Chicago Stadium, a fight which LaMotta would coincidentally lose in similar fashion as he did to Fox—by TKO.

While Sugar Ray Robinson was a preeminent middleweight champion of that era, he somehow remained free of Carbo's control. That didn't mean he was completely clean, however. In Robinson's FBI file, a memo from July 17, 1959, stated: "[Bureau files] contain numerous references indicating that Robinson has been associated with hoodlum elements—as have substantially all top members of the boxing profession. The New York Office has reported in the past that Robinson's bar in Harlem has catered to prostitutes. Although he was suspended by the New York State Athletic Commission for 30 days in 1947 for failing to report a bribe at the time the bribe was made, and although there have been allegations regarding fixing of fights in which Robinson has been a contestant, informants have recently stated that Robinson and Floyd Patterson are the only prominent Negro fighters not controlled by the Frankie Carbo hoodlum group."

Robinson was in fact worried about Carbo's influence in boxing. He personally sent a Western Union telegram to FBI director J. Edgar Hoover on August 13, 1959. This read: "[New York] District Attorney [Frank] Hogan this week exposed new evidence of Frank Carbo Jim Norris axis involved in attempting to steal my middleweight title. I urge your bureau to investigate alarming underworld penetration into boxing on national scale as indicated by testimony linking [Carmen] Basilio and his managers to Carbo [Robinson had lost his title to Basilio in 1957, then won it back from him in 1958]. My full cooperation available to any steps you deem necessary to rid boxing of gangster influence. Am confident your investigation will. New York State Commission recognition of me as champion and reveal why other states have attempted to wrongly deprive me of my title."

Sugar Ray's plea to free boxing from the hoodlum element was a bit disingenuous. While in the Army during World War II, Robinson went AWOL and missed his ship overseas due to "amnesia" brought about by headaches. After a stay at a VA hospital, Robinson was diagnosed as in a "constitutional psychopathic state, inadequate personality, and mental deficiency, moron level (mental age 10 years, 6 months)." Perhaps those shortcomings aided him in becoming a great boxer as he posted a remarkable record of 173 wins, 19 losses, and six draws. Yet it is believed he participated in fixed fights, including one in which his mental problems worked against him. "Early in his career, in December 1942, Sugar Ray Robinson was supposed to carry Al Nettlow for the full ten rounds of a fight in Philly. But in the third round, when Nettlow hit him with a nasty right, Ray lost his temper, hit him with a left hook, and Nettlow was counted out."[15]

The FBI was well aware of the next allegation of Robinson's participation in a fixed fight. The following is taken from a December 8, 1955 letter from FBI agent William Whelan to J. Edgar Hoover:

"You will recall that Sugar Ray Robinson and Rocky Castellani fought a ten-round decision fight at the Cow Palace in San Francisco on July 22, 1955, in which the decision was awarded to Robinson. Recently, members of the Racket Squad of the San Francisco Police Department and, also, [redacted] of California Attorney General Pat Brown's office, have indicated that the outcome of this fight was probably arranged in advance. The allegation has been made that shortly before the fight there was a meeting between representatives of the two fighters and the promoter or the representative of the promoter at which the details of this arrangement were discussed.

"It was pretty much common knowledge that persons surrounding middleweight boxing champion [Bobo] Olson were hopeful that Robinson would win and many of them gave an indication that they were prone to believe that he would.

"From a boxing promotional standpoint, particularly of the people surrounding Olson, two fairly good fights might come out of this match if Robinson won. They figured that a Robinson-Olson fight would provide a good drawing card in a city like Chicago, particularly in view of the fact that Robinson had twice previously defeated Olson. Then after Olson would dispose of Robinson in such a fight, he could be matched with Castellani in his home town of Cleveland or some other large city and it would be a fairly good drawing match. It was true that Olson had beaten Castellani a little over a year ago; however, in the interim he had been floored by light heavyweight Archie Moore.

"[redacted] for the California Attorney General, is known to have stated that all of these rumors, in his view, indicate that there is some sort of collusive action going on between the IBC promoters and the managers. Robinson states that he does not think that any money passes hands, but that the payoffs are essentially made in favorable promotional arrangements. Using this one fight as an example, Robinson, Castellani, and Olson all get two fights apiece. The other payoff is probably in the realm of private bets that are laid as a result of the arrangements."

Hoover's response to Agent Whelan's claims was anti-climactic when in December 1955 he wrote: "I appreciated the detailed account you set forth in your personal letter of December 8 with reference to the Sugar Ray Robinson-Rocky Castellani fight in San Francisco last summer which, as you say, is very interesting and does raise all kinds of doubts. It does seem that these people would someday awaken to the realization that if they engage in such tactics, they are certainly following a very shortsighted view."

Neither Hoover nor anyone else within the FBI seemed to pursue Robinson for his involvement in this curious fight and subsequent arrangement even though it was semi-prophetic. Robinson's next fight was indeed against Olson and was held at the Chicago Stadium. However, Robinson didn't lose; he KO'd Olson in two rounds. Perhaps the idea of including Castellani in the scheme faded the same way his career did after losing to Robinson, as he won just five of his next ten fights before retiring. As for Sugar Ray, he fought a rematch with Olson five months later in Los Angeles in which Olson was again knocked out, this time in four rounds.

Another champion of that era, lightweight titleholder Ike Williams, also saw his career marred by fight fixing and the reach of Carbo and Palermo. Despite earning nearly a million dollars during his career, by 1960 when he testified before Congress, Williams was working a $46-a-week job. While a boxer, Williams originally attempted to be his own manager. This was a total failure. Working on his own he "could not even get a sparring partner." Why? The Managers' Guild boycotted him, deeply hampering his budding career. His savior from that blackballing was "Blinky" Palermo who agreed to "straighten things out" with the Guild in exchange for becoming Williams' manager. He could not afford to say no.

Though Palermo brought Williams the lightweight championship of the world, he also outright stole from him. Williams testified that after two separate title fights in 1948, Palermo refused to give Williams "five cents" of either $32,000 purse, despite his contract stipulating a two-thirds take from each. According to Williams, Blinky told him "times were tough" and that he had spent it. Williams, however, still paid taxes on the unreceived money.

As if that weren't bad enough, Palermo approached Williams at least three times with offers to throw a fight. Senator Estes Kefauver asked Williams about these offers, to which he replied, "Yes, Senator. I have received several bribes. All fighters receive bribes. I will say even the biggest fighters that ever lived. I will say Joe Louis and Jack Dempsey, I will say some guy, some nut, would come to them, even with Dempsey." First, Palermo told Williams of a $100,000 offer to lose to Kid Gavilan in a January 1949 bout. According to Williams, Palermo told him, "You are doing all right, you don't need the money. I wouldn't take it, if I was you." Williams listened to his manager, but still lost the fight in a split decision. Asked by the subcommittee if he was sorry he didn't take the money, Williams replied, "I am sorry I didn't take it....I lost the fight anyway, although I thought I won it. Most of the New York papers gave me the fight....but the officials, they called it against me, and that is their business, so I guess they know more about it than I do."

Less than a year later, Palermo again brought Williams an offer to tank a fight. The amount dropped to $30,000, but the notion was the same: lose to contender Freddy Dawson. Palermo again suggested Williams not take it, to "use your own judgment." Williams concurred. Ten minutes before the fight was to take place, a friend of Williams warned him that "they are going to take the fight from you." Williams quickly had the press brought into his dressing room, told the assembled members he had a story for them after the fight, then went out and won a unanimous decision against Dawson. Williams believed his pre-fight action may have prevented the judges from robbing him of the victory, but he was still brought before the Pennsylvania State Athletic Commission and fined $500 for "stirring up" trouble by questioning the honesty of the judges.

Then in 1951, while holding the lightweight championship belt, Williams learned of a $50,000 offer to lose his title to Jimmy Carter in their May 25 bout. Carter's manager was Willie Ketchum, known to be Carbo-controlled, and the fight took place in the Norris-controlled Madison Square Garden. Williams once again rejected the offer, but to no avail—he lost to Carter in a 14-round TKO. This story prompted the following exchange between Williams and counselor Bonomi:

Mr. Bonomi: "So that when you rejected the bribe offer of $50,000, you actually lost an awful lot of money anyway, didn't you?"

Mr. Williams: "I lost the greatest thing I ever had in my life when I lost the lightweight title, Mr. Bonomi."

Mr. Bonomi: "Did you feel the same way after the bout with Jimmy Carter as you felt after the Gavilan bout: that you lost the bout anyway; you should have taken the bribe?"

Mr. Williams: "No, I felt differently. I'll tell you, Mr. Bonomi, I was injured very seriously before the Carter fight, and, speaking for myself, I should have taken the money, but I didn't take it. I should have taken it, because I said—I was due to fight Art Aragon in Los Angeles 18 days after the Carter fight, and, speaking for myself, I said even if I beat Carter, I would not be able to beat Aragon in California. So I said actually I should take the money, you know. I should take it. But I didn't, and I lost the fight anyway."

Senator Kefauver: "You feel better that you didn't take it, though, don't you?"

Mr. Williams: "I do not, Senator; believe me, I don't."

Williams went on to be even more candid in his discussion with the subcommittee on the subject of fighters "carrying" an opponent:

Mr. Williams: "'Carrying a fight' means let the fellow go ten rounds or let him go 15 rounds, instead of trying to knock him out. I'll say, more or less, all fighters at one time or another during their career have carried someone….a lot of times the fellow will have trouble getting fights. Maybe he is too good for the fellow or the fellow knows he hasn't a chance of winning, so in order to fight, you carry him, you know, instead of knocking him out…."

Senator Kefauver: "You mean you make such an agreement before you start the fight?"

Mr. Williams: "It has happened."

Senator Kefauver: "Is this agreement made with the fighter or who would make the agreement? Would you make the agreement directly with the fighter or would Mr. Palermo make the agreement with the other fellow's manager?"

Mr. Williams: "Well, Mr. Palermo has never done that, to my knowledge, but it has been done with the fighters and with the managers also."

Senator Kefauver: "You have done it yourself?"

Mr. Williams: "Yes; I have carried fighters….I have carried fighters just to get the fight. I promised the manager that I would not knock him out or try to knock him out, because if I tried to knock him out, they wouldn't fight me…."

Senator Everett Dirksen: "It wasn't really a spirit of charity that made you carry a fighter, was it, if you could dispatch him in two rounds instead of going through ten rounds of punishment, you would do it? You wouldn't be impelled by charitable sentiments to let him stay on that long?"

Mr. Williams: "It wasn't always just thinking about charity or anything, but sometimes you would get a rematch to fight the fellow again or sometimes you did it because maybe you are having trouble getting fights and the fellow fights you, you know, if you'll go along with him, so you do it for your own benefit as well."

Senator Dirksen: "Wasn't it also, in part, perhaps, that money was wagered on how long a fighter would stay, how many points, so that if the betting was that he wouldn't stay eight rounds, that would mean odds one way; or if he wouldn't stay six rounds, the odds would be another way?"

Mr. Williams: "You are absolutely right. The fighter is wrong there. You know, you are not supposed to do any betting either. So the fellow who is doing the wagering, he is wrong also."

Senator Dirksen: "I haven't pressed you on the names of those who may have been carried, but when you do or it was suggested that you carry a given fighter, and you felt that you knew in what round you could dispose of him, did you bet on your own fights?"

Mr. Williams: "I have bet on myself on fights to win."

Senator Dirksen: "Substantially?"

Mr. Williams: "Yes. I have bet on myself several times and sometimes, usually, most of the time, I bet to win by a knockout…but I have bet to win and I have lost that also."

Senator Dirksen: "Is it customary for managers to bet on the fights, too?"

Mr. Williams: "Managers bet sometimes on the fights."

Senator Dirksen: "Do they bet heavily?"

Mr. Williams: "Yes; they do."

Senator Dirksen: "It is speculative, of course, as to how much money changes hands on a fight. Would you have any estimate of the amount of money that there has been wagered upon any given fight?"

Mr. Williams: "I know one manager that bet $100,000 on his fight...."

Senator Dirksen: "If it is not a clean game...and if as the fighters climb in between the ropes they don't do their best and they are free from pressure and free from bribe offers, it is something of an imposition on an American when in good faith he watches those fights, isn't it?"

Mr. Williams: "Yes; it is; yes, sir."

While light heavyweight champion Ike Williams was grilled by Congress, heavyweight champion Rocky Marciano was fawned over by the subcommittee. Considering that Marciano retired as champion with a perfect record of 49–0 (the only undefeated heavyweight champion in history), one would be hard-pressed to think he was involved in a fixed fight. But Marciano may not have been as guilt-free as he appeared, for within the Senate's questioning of Norris, one thing stood out: Marciano's manager Al Weill's close association with Frankie Carbo.

Norris testified that Weill was not just Marciano's manager, but IBC of New York's matchmaker. He was asked, "You knew of Mr. Weill as being very, very friendly with Mr. Carbo, did you not?" Norris replied, "Yes, I did." Norris was later asked, "...Carbo's influence with Weill was great, and that Weill, as the manager of Rocky Marciano, did not fight Harry Matthews until Carbo told him to?" Norris responded, "That is correct. That was my understanding how the match was made....I spoke to Weill time and time again over the period of a few months asking him to box Harry Matthews, saying it would be a good fight, it should be an easy fight, that I thought Matthews had been built up, wasn't a good fighter, and I don't know why but he didn't want to, and Weill later told me, he said, 'If I hadn't talked to certain people, I would never have taken that match for you.'" Those "certain people" happened to be just one person, Frankie Carbo. (For the record, Norris was right. Marciano knocked out Matthews in two rounds.)

Others were well aware of Carbo's connection to Weill as well. In a secretly taped conversation between IBC treasurer "Honest Bill" Daly and trainer/promoter Jack Leonard presented as evidence to the subcommittee, the two discussed the cozy relationship between Carbo and Weill. Daly told Leonard, "He's close now with the Gray. He's very close with Gray. Weill is. Very close. Inseparable, they are…Frankie don't like him as a person…but—" Leonard interrupted, "He cut up millions with him." As Daly retorted, these were simply "Business transactions, that's all."

The only person brought before the subcommittee who didn't seem to know of the connection between Weill and Carbo was Rocky Marciano:

Mr. Nicholas Kittrie (counselor): "Mr. Marciano, you were talking about the underworld trying to take over different fighters and so on. Has the underworld ever tried to cut into you?"

Mr. Marciano: "No, sir. I was just very, very lucky. I was fortunate that I came around the right time. I was blessed with stamina and I was on the scene at the right time, and I was lucky enough to have a manager who protected me from all outside influences. He was the master and I listened to my manager all the way through boxing, and I was very fortunate, I believe."

Mr. Kittrie: "Who was your manager?"

Mr. Marciano: "My manager was Al Weill…."

Mr. Kittrie: "You feel that your keeping out of the influence of the underworld was actually due, in great degree, to his protection; is that right?"

Mr. Marciano: "Yes. I believe that Al Weill was the boss as far as I was concerned, and I sort of took orders from him."

Even though Marciano never admitted knowing Carbo despite his manager's relationship with the gangster, Carbo's reach may have helped Marciano remain undefeated. In his book, *The Devil and Sonny Liston*, author Nick Tosches interviewed Truman Gibson. "Gibson told me that of perhaps a thousand fights promoted by the IBC, he knew of only three that were fixed….The biggest of them was the dive Archie Moore took in his 1955 New York title bout with Rocky Marciano. It was Marciano's last fight, and the fix ensured Marciano would retire undefeated." On the surface, this appears debatable as Moore knocked Marciano down in the second round with a quick right, only the second time in his career Marciano was dropped. Referee Harry Kessler did aid Marciano in his recovery from the knockdown, giving him a few more precious seconds than should have been allowed, but Marciano never appeared to be seriously hurt by the blow that sent him to the canvas. He would quickly turn the tables on Moore, knocking him down four times before the fight was stopped in the ninth with Marciano winning by technical knockout. Fixed or not, Marciano's take of the gate in this fight was nearly $500,000, part of which went to manager Al Weill. The question remains as to how much Weill might have passed along to Carbo.

Carbo's downfall—and by extension, the downfall of the IBC—came not long after Marciano's victory over Moore. A New York County grand jury began an inquiry into prizefight fixing after a match between welterweights Virgil "Honey Bear" Akins (who was Carbo-controlled) and Isaac Logart at Madison Square Garden on March 21, 1958. Logart was the favorite and dominated until the sixth round where he was knocked down twice, then simply quit fighting. The referee counted him out while he was standing, stopping the fight at the count of eight though only seven seconds remained in the round. Logart's corner didn't protest, and three months later, Akins won the vacated welterweight title. Meanwhile, as the grand jury's investigation deepened, James Norris quit the IBC on April 18.

How exactly did a supposedly respected businessman like Norris get tangled up with Carbo in the first place? When the IBC formed, Carbo was a known entity, but wasn't mixed up in their business. However, when the IBC attempted to hold a bout between Jake LaMotta and Rocky Graziano in 1949, Graziano suddenly developed a last-minute "illness" canceling the match while the Managers Guild staged a strike with picket lines surrounding Madison Square Garden. As Gibson testified, "we [the IBC] became concerned with all of the elements that would interfere with our keeping our contracts: the organization of managers; the fact of the Carbo friendship with managers over the years, which result in our making certain decisions of policy with respect to operating a business that grew into a very big business." Counselor Bonomi asked, "And was that policy that you finally decided on—to cooperate with these underworld elements?" To which Gibson replied, "No, not to cooperate, but to live with them….What we wanted to do was to maintain a free flow of fighters without interference, without strikes, without sudden illnesses, without sudden postponements….We had to put on fights that were interesting. We had to get ratings for our sponsors; we had to avoid any element of a fixed or corrupt fight over which we might not have knowledge, but which the sponsor or public would have immediate knowledge, if any such course of conduct as that resulted…. We wanted to have fights where the results were not predetermined on television. We wanted to get ratings for our sponsors and the fact that we persisted for nine years would seem to indicate that we satisfied the sponsors." Bonomi then asked, "In order to satisfy the sponsors and have a free flow of fighters, you decided to live with Carbo, is that right?" Gibson didn't hesitate, saying, "We decided to live with Carbo, with the Managers Guild, and with all of the elements that were facts of life that we had to contend with."

In questioning Norris, Counselor Dixon laid it out bare, stating, "We have been talking about some very important fights here, and various difficulties have been described with those fights and invariably, Mr. Carbo's name was mentioned. Many of the problems seem to disappear because Mr. Carbo, by some method, seemed to have straightened them out." Norris agreed. He may have been reluctant to deal with Carbo to make the IBC what it was, but he did so nonetheless because Carbo had the control. Power, coupled with the almighty dollar, made Norris join forces with a murderer in order to provide interesting boxing matches to the American public.

That is not to say Norris was a victim; far from it. He never cut ties with Carbo and even willfully employed Carbo's future wife, Viola Masters, as his own personal secretary. Norris did admit to Congress that he was "embarrassed" by the entire situation, and that it affected some relationships he had both in the NHL and in his other passion, horse racing. So why didn't he do more to clean up the sport and by extension his own reputation? Norris claimed that he did. He offered J. Edgar Hoover, of all people, $100,000 a year for ten years to join the IBC, saying to the newspapers of the time, "He is the only man in the world that would regain the confidence of the public, the newspapermen, and the integrity of boxing." That hiring, of course, never materialized. In fact, it backfired on Norris, who told Congress, "I was not very popular with Mr. Carbo or anybody else for quite a period of time after the newspapermen printed this story."

All that remained in boxing once Norris and the IBC were demolished was Carbo. Even though at the time of the Senate Subcommittee Carbo was serving a two-year stretch in prison, he, along with "Blinky" Palermo, continued to run much of the boxing world. So much so that he was brought in to testify before Congress. During his questioning, Carbo answered nothing, repeatedly taking the fifth by invoking the Amendment nearly 30 times. At the end of his pointless testimony, Senator Kefauver asked, "Mr. Carbo, we are about to excuse you and, before we do, do you wish to avail yourself of this last opportunity of answering some of these questions upon reconsideration, or upon consultation with your attorney, Mr. Brodsky. We will give you this opportunity of doing so. Do you wish to consult with your attorney?"

The Gray leaned over and momentarily spoke with his attorney, then addressed the Senator. "There is only one thing I want to say, Mr. Senator."

Senator Kefauver expectantly responded, "Yes?"

"I congratulate you on your reelection."

FLOATS LIKE A BUTTERFLY, STINGS LIKE A BEE

If one man ever lived up to philosopher Thomas Hobbes' famous quote, "The life of man, solitary, poor, nasty, brutish, and short," it may have been Sonny Liston. Though Liston would become heavyweight champion with a first-round knockout of Floyd Patterson in 1962, his life prior to that moment was one of struggle, violence, and prison. As a boxer, he was mob-controlled from day one, so much so that untangling which mobster owned which piece of Liston is nearly impossible (though a prominent name in that discussion is "Blinky" Palermo). He was an unpopular champion, outright hated in some circles because of this criminal past and brutish nature. But in the ring, he was an unstoppable force. He lost only one fight on his way to the heavyweight championship, that coming in a fight against Marty Marshall who broke Liston's jaw in the fourth round. Liston still went the distance, losing on a split decision.

Liston took the heavyweight crown from Floyd Patterson in what may have been a fixed fight. In March 1963, the FBI received information from a well-known manager in the fight game. This source was connected with Philadelphia mobster Angelo Bruno, whom the source admitted he once ran to when threatened by Palermo and Carbo when he refused to have one of his fighters tank a match as ordered. He told the FBI "that during the recent Patterson-Liston fight, Patterson reluctantly agreed to 'take a dive.' It was agreed by all parties concerned that the fight would go five or six rounds as closed circuit television demanded a reasonable duration or the fight would be criticized severely by the public. Patterson, avoiding any possibility of getting hurt, surprised all by going down in the first round. Patterson's reasoning was that Liston is not the hardest man to knock out [many would argue that point] and Patterson feared he may accidentally knock Liston out, thereby placing himself in a dangerous situation with those arranging the result of the fight. Patterson was of the opinion that he, Patterson, would win the return bout and a third bout would be a real moneymaker.

"At present, Liston is very reluctant to go along with [redacted] and others and have Patterson win [the second bout, fought on July 22, 1963]. Liston, for personal reasons, mainly money, wants to remain champ. To date, no specific word concerning the outcome has been let out.

"One of the main questions facing those controlling boxing at the present time is 'Will the public buy a second fight' after Patterson's dive at such an early round. Ticket sale (advance) will determine if a third fight would be profitable and the outcome of the coming (April 1963) return fight [which was postponed due to a Liston knee injury] will hinge upon the April gate. If a good gate is evident, Patterson will win and a third fight scheduled. If the public refuses to back a second fight, a third fight is unlikely and details for the second fight will be settled prior to the April fight.

"Patterson, Negro fighter, is basically a good fighter but has never fought a name fighter who was not 'set up.'" This source would later claim that "in the boxing business this is common knowledge for those close to boxing managers and fighters."

Oddly enough, in a *Sports Illustrated* article published less than two weeks after the first Patterson-Liston fight, Gilbert Rogin wrote that fans openly questioned whether the fight was fixed to set up a lucrative rematch. Rogin himself, however, dismissed the idea, choosing instead to believe the drama in the ring after Patterson's knockout when it took a few minutes for his trainers to assist the fallen champ back to his corner. In the end, the FBI's source proved more accurate. The rematch, held in the Las Vegas Convention Center after a Miami locale failed to generate ticket sales, saw Liston again knock out Patterson in one round to retain his title. There would be no third match, though Patterson would continue boxing for nearly ten more years.

Liston's next fight in his short-lived reign as champion matched him with Cassius Clay, soon to be known to the world as Muhammad Ali. When the pair squared off on February 25, 1964, the machinations behind the scenes indicated that all the characteristics that made Liston great—his power, his ferocity, his anger—were going to be his undoing. This, in turn, would launch the career of the most iconic fighter in boxing history.

The first Clay-Liston fight was held at the Convention Hall in Miami Beach. Chris Dundee, the Carbo-connected promoter who had set up other Liston bouts in the city between 1958–60, was charged with selling this fight as well. Despite having a direct connection to both Liston and to Clay, thanks to Dundee's little brother Angelo serving as Clay's trainer, there was little to hype. Liston was a prohibitive favorite, with odds on Clay being as high as 8-1. It seemed inevitable that no matter how much Clay talked about winning the fight, Liston would pound his mouth shut in the ring. As a result, only about half of the 16,000 available tickets sold for the bout.

To make matters worse, prior to this fight Liston allegedly sexually assaulted his former bodyguard "Moose" Grayson's wife, Pearl. If this had become public, Liston's popularity would have sunk even further, making him a worse ticket than he already proved to be. Foneda Cox, Liston's sparring partner, told author Nick Tosches, "[The mob] made a settlement with Moose. They paid Moose off. I don't know how much, but a lot. I think they even bought him a house. The Mafia picked up all of Sonny's tabs when Sonny got into trouble. I think maybe they got sick of it."[16]

Adding to the backroom pre-fight drama, "Long before the fight—the contract was dated October 29, 1963—Inter-Continental Promotions, of which Sonny was a partner, had contracted with the eleven-man Louisville Group [which controlled Clay] to purchase for fifty thousand dollars the rights to promote Clay's next fight after the Liston match. This was a staggering amount to pay for the future rights to a single bout by a fighter who was seen as facing almost certain defeat in his upcoming match with Liston. Jack Nilson [who was first Liston's "adviser" then took over as manager], trying to explain the suspect pre-fight contract, said that 'Clay represented a tremendous show-business property.'" Nilson later said, "We never dreamed Sonny would lose the title." The contract was just "a lucky fluke."[17]

But Liston did lose the bout—and his heavyweight title—to the underdog Clay in what turned out to be a very bizarre fight. Despite being angry at Clay for all of his pre-fight trash talk, Liston didn't come out of his corner with purpose. Later, when Clay returned to his corner in the fourth round and answered the bell for the fifth, he screamed about something being in his eyes which effectively blinded him. Though Clay held Liston at bay throughout the fifth round with a straight arm pressed against Liston's face, the champ, who had a longer reach than Clay, allowed him to linger without taking advantage of the one presented. Then, when the bell rang to start the seventh round, Liston refused to answer its call. He remained on his stool, surrendering his title to Clay because of a shoulder injury that numbed his left arm. While this may not have been faked as two different doctors, including one immediately after the fight, claimed they could detect an injury in his beleaguered arm, recall that Liston's only loss prior to this came via a broken jaw—an injury with which he fought through without a title being on the line.

The fight's unusual and anti-climactic ending, coupled with the general belief of the boxing world that Clay couldn't beat Liston, raised suspicions. Perhaps the most important one was that of the state of Florida, which investigated the result. "On March 23, State Attorney General Richard E. Gerstein of Florida announced that, after a month's investigation of the Liston-Clay fight, it had been decided that there was no evidence of foul play. However, he said, several other circumstances surrounding the fight were 'questionable'.... Gerstein also said he wondered why Liston would pay fifty thousand dollars for the right to choose Clay's next opponent and promote his next fight 'unless he or his managers knew the outcome of the fight in advance.'"[18]

But how far did the Florida State Attorney really go with the investigation? Author Tosches found three people—two of whom held close ties to Liston—who seemed to not just think but know the fight was fixed. The first was Liston's sparring partner Foneda, who told the author, "He told me, he said 'Foneda, I'm going to tell you. I've got to lose one, and when I do, I'm gonna tell you.'"[19] Foneda didn't travel with Liston to Miami for the Clay fight. Instead, he bet on Liston, later regretting the action as it felt to Foneda that the Clay fight was the one Liston "had to lose."

Lowell Powell was Liston's bodyguard on the night of the Clay fight. He had already bet on Liston to win—$3,000 to $4,000—and wanted to put down more. Powell related what Liston said after he told the champ about increasing his wager: "He said, 'Don't put any more money on me, man. Two heavyweights out there, you can't ever tell who will win.' He said, 'You've got enough money bet.' That's as far as he would go with me. So, later on, after it all happened and he lost the fight, I said, 'Sonny, why would you let me lose my last penny on a fight and you knew you were gonna lose it? You could've at least pulled my coat.' He said, 'With your big mouth, we'd both be wearing concrete suits.'"[20]

Tosches also found Patsy Anthony Lepera, a "gangster" from Reading, Pennsylvania. He told the author that his faction—including members of the Lucchese family—wanted to put $100,000 on the fight, same as the Philadelphia faction had. Lepera put $25,000 down on Clay personally. The bets were laid off through Cleveland and Vegas, and as he said, "These guys took the other mobs." While watching the fight, Lepera stated, "This guy didn't just take a dive—he did a one-and-a-half off the high board. It was so bad, I figured we blew everything. It worried me—I already spent my end. But no, everybody got paid off."[21]

Despite the questions surrounding this fight, the FBI never examined it. That did not hold true for the rematch.

By the time of their second bout, Cassius Clay was no more. He had changed his name to Muhammad X (after his friend Malcolm X), then to the more familiar Muhammad Ali due to his relationship with the Nation of Islam. The controversy surrounding both the new heavyweight champ and the bout that gave him that title caused a significant problem for fight promoters: no one would license a rematch. As a result, after 35 to 40 cities turned down the offer, the second Liston-Ali bout was fought in the unusual location of Lewiston, Maine on May 25, 1965. Well, "fought" may be too strong of a word as the bout barely lasted two minutes.

Legendary sports gambler Lem Banker was one of Liston's trusted friends. Of the fight, Banker said, "People would stop and ask Liston, 'What happened in Lewiston?' Sonny would say, 'Three things went wrong: Robert Goulet forgot the words to the National Anthem. Second thing, Jersey Joe Walcott, the referee, missed the count. And third, I forgot to get up,' trying to make a joke out of the thing."

But it was no joke. Liston, a slight 8-5 betting favorite, was dropped in the first round on a "phantom" punch thrown by Ali. Liston's reaction to the blow was suspect: he fell on his back, rolled to his stomach, attempted to get up, fell, and then finally climbed back to his feet, never in a rush. Though Liston had actually been counted out at 12, the fight was allowed to continue for a few moments before officially stopped. The fans on site erupted with boos, followed by chants of "fake" and "fix." The reaction angered Ali enough that he yelled at ringside fans, even though in a post-fight interview he claimed he didn't feel himself connect with the punch that floored Liston.

The FBI began investigating this fight immediately. "On 5/26/65, informant advised that the rumor amongst people in the fight game was that Liston 'took a dive.' Informant had no specific positive information to support this statement. Informant said that regardless of who was fronting in the handling of Liston, he is still controlled by the underworld, namely Frank 'Blinky' Palermo, who has been described by various investigating agencies, including the Kefauver Committee in 1960, as an underworld figure who had control in boxing."

Everyone had an opinion on what happened in Lewiston. The FBI's Chicago office provided the following theories:

"All sources furnished substantially the same information regarding Liston's defeat in that they agreed that the result of the light blow thrown by Clay in the first round was attributed to Liston's character. All described Liston as a 'dog' in the boxing field. This term is applied to a fighter who though he possesses the appearance of a fierce competitor lacks the necessary qualities of courage and the will to win...."

"[redacted], former manager of several Chicago boxers, who was at ringside at Lewiston, Maine, reported Liston appeared sluggish and dazed during the approximate 25 minutes in the ring prior to the actual bout. [redacted] theorized Liston may have been under the influence of a narcotic or similar substance...."

"[redacted], Chicago boxing promoter and promoter of the teleprompter version, is of the opinion that possibly the heat during the long wait in the ring prior to the fight coupled with Liston's age sapped his strength and slowed his reflexes causing his early downfall....

"[redacted], heavyweight competitor who has fought Liston, is of the opinion Liston felt loss by decision was inevitable, hence, took the easy way out. [redacted], from personal experience, states Liston is extremely difficult to hurt much less knock down, making knockout by Clay ridiculous."

Another interesting story developed from a source through the FBI in New York, who was described as a "close friend" of Liston:

"[redacted] bet $12,000 on Liston to win the first Liston-Clay title bout [information later changed the amount to $5,200]. After losing this, [redacted] asked questions and allegedly heard that Liston had taken a sizable payoff to 'take a dive.'

"According to [redacted] one or more oil men from Texas had bet a large amount on Liston to win. [redacted] believed that the person or persons holding this money approached Liston and offered him a very sizable amount of money to throw the fight. [redacted] advised PCI [Potential Criminal Informant] that it was his belief that Liston was approached directly in this regard and personally agreed to throw the fight, but stated no one would ever be able to prove it.

"At the time of the second Liston-Clay fight in Maine, [redacted] again intended to bet on Liston; however, when [redacted] reached Maine he was told by someone whom he would not identify, that he should not bet on Liston, as the fight was definitely fixed and Clay could not lose. The PCI stated he could not be sure, but to the best of his recollection, [redacted] mentioned that someone from Las Vegas had paid Liston to throw the fight. [redacted] also advised the PCI that Clay was not aware that both fights had been fixed and Clay is allegedly under the impression that he won both fights fairly."

A different FBI source claimed "there was no doubt in his mind that the second Clay-Liston fight held in Lewiston, Maine, was fixed and that Liston took a dive in this fight." This unnamed source worked with

Liston in St. Louis, Philadelphia, and Denver, and claimed to be one of Liston's "few friends." He told the FBI the first Clay-Liston fight wasn't fixed, but that Liston in fact injured his shoulder which caused him to quit. Afterward, a struggle ensued over control of Liston between Palermo and Philadelphia mob boss Angelo Bruno, which Bruno ultimately won.

This source continued: "[redacted] further explained that the hoodlum element decided to get rid of Liston inasmuch as he kept them in the spotlight and kept getting pressure on them by his numerous entanglements with police authorities. He said they considered Liston to be a very unpopular champion and since they controlled the promotion of every title fight and did not need actual control of the champion, they ordered Liston to take a dive in the second Clay-Liston fight.

"Mr. [redacted] further advised that Liston is very ruthless and enjoys a reputation of being hot-tempered, and he further advised that Liston was ordered to take a dive in the first round in the Clay fight inasmuch as the hoodlum element was well aware of his hot temper and the fact that if Clay made Liston angry enough, Liston would forget his orders and would knock out Clay."

Though the fight was in May, the FBI was still investigating the possibility of a fix into December when another angle to the story appeared in this file. "On 12/28/65, [redacted] reiterated as in past contacts, he had no doubts that the second Liston-Clay fight was fixed, as a result of outside influence brought to bear on Liston. Informant of opinion Clay totally unaware of any irregularity on the part of Liston.

"Informant [redacted] was in contact with Liston immediately after the bout. He recalled that Liston's wife [redacted] remarked to him, 'I just wouldn't allow him to keep going and maybe get hurt.' Informant was of opinion that she was aware that the outcome of the bout was inevitable, that Liston must lose, and that he was told by her to take the first opportunity to 'bow out,' rather than stay the 15-round distance and possibly incur injury. According to informant, [redacted] greatly influences Liston's actions...."

"Informant, [redacted] especially Liston, was at ring-side in Lewiston, Maine, 5/25/65. Knowing Liston's tremendous capacity for absorbing physical punishment, he termed the 'knock out' of Liston ridiculous. To illustrate Clay's punching power, he noted that recently Clay was unable to knock out aging Floyd Patterson who was light, smaller, and suffered from a severe back injury. [redacted] current heavyweight contender Ernie Terrill, recalled that immediately after the championship fight between Clay and Liston, he spoke briefly with [redacted] in a Lewiston, Maine hotel room. [redacted], who had 25% of Liston's contract and who is also a close associate of Philadelphia hoodlums Angelo Bruno and Frank Palermo, made a remark to informant in a voice of authority, 'Forget it, Terrill would not have fought Liston anyway.' According to informant, [redacted] prior to the bout, displayed absolutely no interest or anxiety in connection with the forthcoming fight, indicating to informant that [redacted] also had inside information regarding the outcome of the bout." Ali did in fact fight Ernie Terrill, but not until February 1967 when they faced off in the Houston Astrodome for the WBA World Heavyweight title, which Ali won in a unanimous decision.

One final theory was put forth by an informant. This fingered Ali's new friends, the Nation of Islam, as being behind the fix. "The only rumor that source has heard of late, which he has not been able to talk over with Liston, is the rumor which says that the NOI [Nation of Islam] may have threatened bodily harm to Liston's family if he did not take a dive in the second Liston-Clay fight. It is the source's opinion that while Clay is too young and strong for Liston, Clay does not have the power to stop Liston in one round." The FBI deemed this source as highly credible, writing "This office has no reason to doubt the reliability of [redacted] and it is pointed out that during the past six months this source has furnished reliable information to this office." Interestingly, the FBI had similar information from the get-go, writing, "On 5/25/65, [redacted] whose identity should be kept confidential, [redacted] Madison Square Garden, advised Liston could knock out Clay if everything was legitimate in the fight. [redacted] stated that he was concerned about the Black Muslims getting to Liston and having him throw the fight for fear of death. [redacted] was thoroughly questioned concerning this statement and explained that he had no specific information to substantiate this opinion, but he felt that the Black Muslims were a bad group and would go to any extreme to protect their champion."

Lem Banker confirmed this final theory as being the correct one, based on his close personal relationship with the one-time champion. According to Banker, the real reason Liston "forgot to get up" in Lewiston was, "The Black Muslims had just killed Malcolm X, and there was a threat on Geraldine—that was Liston's wife's daughter—and Sonny took a fucking dive." Liston took this threat very seriously, especially since Malcolm X was murdered by members of the Nation of Islam just three months prior to the rematch.

Liston would have been right to worry. The FBI had been examining the Nation of Islam, including their connection to Ali. One particular faction within the group that seemed worrisome was the Fruit of Islam. The FBI described them as such: "On July 10 1963, a source advised that the Fruit of Islam (FOI) is a group within the Nation of Islam (NOI) composed of male members of the NOI. The purpose of the FOI is to protect officials and property of the NOI, assure compliance of members with NOI teachings and to prepare for the 'War of Armageddon.' Members of the FOI are required to participate in military drills and are afforded the opportunity to engage in judo training. The FOI is governed by a military system wherein the members are controlled by general orders similar to those issued by regular military organizations." Just after beating Liston in the first fight, Ali had effectively become property of the Nation of Islam. Protecting him—in any way—was essentially protecting an asset. To threaten Liston's step-daughter as Banker claimed would ensure Ali's victory and keep the title belt—and any money related to it—under the Nation of Islam's control.

As for the FBI, they hesitated talking to Liston. A Chicago-area source stated Liston was "extremely depressed" after the fight (another source claimed Liston was "crying like a baby" in the locker room), but that by late December 1965 he might be ready to talk, although he warned, "Liston is extremely antagonistic toward law enforcement officials and members of the Caucasian race in general." The task then fell to the Denver Office, but it wasn't sure how to approach Liston. "It is noted that on two occasions during the past year Agents of the Denver Office have contacted Liston and on one of these occasions he appeared to be reasonably cooperative but on the other he exhibited a highly antagonistic attitude and refused to talk to Agents." There was no indication that the FBI ever did interview Liston regarding this fight.

Despite the knowledge the FBI possessed, including the correct information about the fight being fixed and why, the FBI noted, "...no Federal Grand Jury or other action is contemplated in this matter unless Congressional Committee investigation indicates such action warranted." That never came to pass.

After winning and retaining the heavyweight title in these two questionable fights with Liston, Ali's career became the stuff of legend. Epic fights with Smokin' Joe Frazier, George Foreman, and others followed over the next ten-plus years. But very late into Ali's career, the FBI had suspicions about one of his final fights.

Ali squared off against former U.S. Marine "Neon" Leon Spinks at the Hilton Hotel in Las Vegas on February 15, 1978. Though he won a gold medal in the light heavyweight division at the 1976 Olympics, Spinks had only fought 31 rounds of professional boxing prior to this fight. In a shocking split decision, Spinks pulled the WBC and WBA heavyweight titles out from under Ali's feet. Though there is a slim possibility this fight was fixed, it's more likely the rematch was the one rigged.

The second Spinks-Ali fight was scheduled to take place in the Superdome in New Orleans on September 15, 1978. Prior to that date, the FBI learned the following: "On Sept. 5, 1978, [redacted] Hilton Head Island, S.C., reported that during conversation with [redacted] made statement to the effect that he thinks Spinks may have been offered something not to win the next fight. Spinks and his associates spent several weeks at Hilton Head Island, S.C., around June 1978, during which time [redacted] became acquainted with [redacted]. [redacted] became fairly good friends with [redacted] and had occasion to socialize with him several times.

"On Sept. 5, 1978 [redacted] telephonically contacted [redacted] at St. Louis, Missouri, at which time [redacted] reiterated that Top Rank Incorporated is trying to influence Spinks to lose the upcoming heavyweight championship fight. [redacted] agreed to speak to the FBI at New Orleans where he will arrive on the evening of Sept. 5, 1978."

When this informant followed up with the FBI, the story continued: "[redacted] advised he overheard in a conversation between [redacted] Top Rank, Inc., [redacted] and [redacted] that they planned to induce Muhammad Ali to throw the 2/15/78 fight with Spinks as well as a possibility of inducing Spinks to throw a subsequent rematch with Ali. [redacted] further stated that Spinks is supposedly scheduled to throw the fight on 9/15/78. [redacted] refused to take a polygraph examination until after the fight and he observes whether or not, in his opinion, Spinks throws the fight." The informant also "claims that all of information discussed in conversation at Las Vegas has come to pass except loss of fight by Spinks on Sept. 15, 1978, at New Orleans...."

"[redacted] stated if Spinks does in fact lose fight, he is willing to confront [redacted] and Spinks and/or others concerning alleged conversation at Las Vegas. [redacted] is willing to wear a body recorder and/or transmitter during these confrontations." The FBI did not follow through on the informant's offer to wear a wire, though perhaps they should have. The 36-year-old Ali beat a listless 25-year-old Spinks in a 15-round unanimous decision to win back his WBA title (Spinks was stripped of the WBC title because he refused to fight number-one contender Ken Norton prior to the rematch with Ali).

Was the fight rigged? Bob Arum, who founded and is still CEO of Top Rank Inc. today (which the informant claimed was behind the plot), said Spinks was "drunk every night for two weeks before the fight."[22] Not exactly the way to prepare...unless you know the result ahead of time. Spinks would say after losing, "My mind wasn't on the fight."[23] It's also interesting to note a quote from Ali prior to the rematch. Ali told *New York* Magazine, "Do you know if I beat him the first time I wouldn't have got no credit for it? He only had seven fights...the kid was nothing....So I'm glad he won. It's a perfect scene. You couldn't write a better movie than this. This is it. Just what I need. Competition. Fighting odds. Can the old champ regain his title for a third time? Think of it. A third time. Do or die. And you know what makes me laugh? He's the same guy. Only difference is he got eight fights now."[24] Granted, Ali knew how to sell his own fights, but setting up the first fight with Spinks, which he lost, to make a victorious comeback in the second—which would make history as Ali became the first heavyweight to ever win the title three times—is exactly the scenario the informant gave to the FBI...before it took place. Sadly, the FBI could not get their source to follow up with them as he had promised after Spinks lost. The case was then closed.

DON KING & ABC

George Santayana once wrote, "Those who cannot remember the past are condemned to repeat it." This held very true in the history of boxing, for as soon as Frankie Carbo and the IBC faded from memory, Don King and ABC filled their vacancy, running a similar con job much to the sport's detriment.

Don King was very much like Frankie Carbo. Both were affiliated with the mafia (King was connected to John Gotti who once slapped King around), got rich off the backs of honest boxers, and were murderers. Prior to entering boxing, King was tight with the Cleveland mob, making nearly $15,000 a week as the leading numbers man there in the mid-1960s. He had shot a man dead in "self-defense" in 1954. Then in 1966, he beat Sam Garrett to death because he owed King $600 from a winning numbers bet. Though convicted of second-degree manslaughter in this case, King bribed his way through the trial, eliminating witnesses and paying others to change their stories. King even bribed the presiding judge, which spared him from a life sentence. In all, he served less than four years for Garrett's murder.

Once freed from prison, King finagled his way into the boxing game through George Foreman, getting the champion—who had just beaten Smokin' Joe Frazier in Jamaica—to agree to a bout with Ken Norton, in a deal literally consummated in a bathroom stall. King went to Jamaica seemingly as part of Frazier's crew (though he wasn't officially with Frazier), but he left on the arm of the victorious Foreman. "Time and again over the next eighteen years, King would switch loyalties, abandon a loser he had called his the day before, and insinuate himself into the life, dreams, and income of a new champion."[25] King instinctively knew how to do this. "He knew how to [talk to black fighters]. He knew how to ingratiate, con, charm, brown-nose, befriend, impress, amuse, and seduce fighters. He knew their language, their weakness, their psychology. He knew how to give them a self-image, an idea of their role in history, how much money they could make if they only had 'proper management.'"[26]

King was far from being proper management. He was a thief. In his 20+ years in boxing, he was the subject of nearly one hundred lawsuits initiated by fighters and managers who claimed King had screwed them. While King's story, like that of Carbo's, is too expansive to fully cover here, the tale of his United States Boxing Championship (USBC) run in conjunction with ABC Television should be telling enough.

The USBC was originally praised by both the *New York Times* and *Sports Illustrated* for giving a legitimate shot to a lot of hardworking but unrecognized fighters. But as Jack Newfield wrote, "Almost from Day One the tournament was a scam, a good idea corrupted in its cradle."[27]

King's plan was hatched in 1976 when he brought the co-managers of Chuck Wepner (the "real-life Rocky Balboa"), Al Braverman and Paddy Flood, to Don King Productions (DKP) as matchmakers and talent scouts for his conceptual all-American tournament of champions. King then sold this to ABC as the United States Boxing Championship. He was promised a return of $1.5 million (later raised to $2 million) in exchange for a tournament of 48 fights, creating 23 hours of boxing programming. "It was King who had persuaded Roone Arledge, the president of ABC Sports [and creator of *Monday Night Football*], to bankroll the tournament. To safeguard ABC's interests, Arledge got King to agree to two stipulations. He was to use Jim Farley, the chairman of the New York State Athletic Commission, as a consultant charged with selecting referees and judges for the matches. He was also to use *Ring* magazine as his source for fighters' records and rankings. But soon the whispers of favoritism, kickbacks, falsified records, and rigged ratings began to threaten the integrity and the success of the tournament."[28]

As the ink still dried on the contract between DKP and ABC, King began to pay off Johnny Ort of *Ring* magazine to get his fighters ranked higher than they should have been so their entry into the USBC tournament seemed justified. "Only fighters allied with Flood, Braverman, Ort, or their friends were allowed into the tournament, which meant good paydays and television exposure. Ort began to manipulate the *Ring* magazine ratings to justify the entry of some fighters, or to justify the exclusion of others [Ort even added two wins to one undeserving fighter's record while creating fictional fights for others]. Some boxers who wanted admission were told they had to kick back a portion of their purses, or they had to get rid of their present managers and turn their careers over to King."[29]

Some within the boxing world tried to warn ABC things were not right, but none would listen to reason. King drew up a contract all fighters had to sign—to which ABC's lawyers agreed to the wording—stipulating that any fighter who won the tournament would be under King's control for the next two years. In other words, King was using ABC, its money, and exposure to create a stable of fighters for himself. Meanwhile, "some of the most talented young fighters in America—all black and Latin—were being excluded from the tournament."[30] This included a young Marvin Hagler whose co-manager Goody Petronelli was told he would have to pay a kickback to Flood to get his fighter into the tournament. Petronelli wrote a letter to ABC Sports' Arledge detailing these allegations, but he never received a response. It was apparent that King wanted to hijack Hagler from his managers. Instead, when Hagler later became middleweight champion, he refused to work with King.

There were two white knights fighting against King, though they made for an unlikely pairing. One was ABC Sports' Alex Wallau who, unlike his boss Arledge, paid attention to the rumblings of discontent from the boxing universe. The other was a boxing-loving geek named Malcolm "Flash" Gordon who possessed shoeboxes full of information on every known fighter then in action. Together, they researched the fighters DKP included in the tournament and proved that their standings were inflated and that Ort was falsifying records. Four of the fighters King denied entry to included Hagler, Marvin Johnson, Matthew Franklin, and Eddie Gregory—all of whom went on to become world champions. In fact, only 25 of the 50 fighters allowed in the tournament were deemed "qualified" by Wallau and Flash. Armed with this knowledge, Wallau sent two memos in December 1976 to ABC Sports vice president of program planning Jim Spence (among others at ABC) which were so damning, they should've stopped the tournament before a single fight was staged. Spence would later claim he never had the time to read either memo in full.

Meanwhile, Flash, who had already been self-publishing a boxing newsletter with a circulation of a few thousand out of a printing press in his bathtub, began railing against the King/ABC fights. Despite this, *Sports Illustrated* ran a four-page spread written by Mark Kram on the upcoming tournament in their January 3, 1977 issue. Kram actually wrote, "There are American champions to be made—honestly. The last word is so important; the champions here cannot be made in the back room, they must be made in the ring." He was wrong in that assessment, but apparently for the "right" reasons. Kram was forced to resign from *Sports Illustrated* a few months later for accepting "gifts and gratuities" from King. *Sports Illustrated* never made a public announcement regarding the reason for his termination.

But the wheels really began to come off the United States Boxing Championship when on February 13, 1977, "The Fighting Frenchman" Scott LeDoux lost his heavyweight bout to opponent Johnny Boudreaux by a highly controversial decision.

In a stroke of genius, King staged the first two series of elimination-style bouts on the warship U.S.S. *Lexington* and at the U.S. Naval Academy in Maryland. As each location was federal property, both were outside the jurisdiction of any boxing commissioner. This granted King a great deal of authority over the bouts, including determining who the referees and judges were, and as the FBI would point out, "The United

States Naval Academy did not receive any of the funds from this fight and is only to receive reimbursement from the promoter, Don King, for actual expenses incurred in physically setting up the ringside and bleachers in the field house."

In the fight in question, Boudreaux was given the victory in an eight-round unanimous decision despite the fact that those watching thought LeDoux clearly won. ABC commentators Howard Cosell and George Foreman both "repeatedly expressed their incredulity that Boudreaux had been declared the winner" as LeDoux had scored the only knockdown in the fight, sending Boudreaux to the canvas in the third round. Immediately after Boudreaux's hand was raised by the referee, chaos erupted. Angered by the judges' decision, LeDoux attempted to kick Boudreaux, but missed, instead kicking Cosell's toupee off his head. When Cosell re-composed himself and interviewed LeDoux about the decision, he told the world on live television, "Odds are against you—that's a Braverman fighter—King's people, they own Boudreaux. They're not going to give you the decision. I said if I beat the guy bad on national television, they can't steal it from me. They did it. They stole it from me. As far as I'm concerned, it's what hurt boxing for the last ten years, decisions like this and there is nothing you can do about it. I got mad but I apologize for it. That's not the place to fight. I did my fighting in there. I should have left it there because that's where it's supposed to be."

This sent more than a few red flags aloft. The FBI immediately initiated an investigation. One of the ringside judges told the FBI, "He felt LeDoux would have won this fight, if the judgment had been based on the point system, rather than the round system." That sounded all good and well, but the person acting as the liaison between the Naval Academy and DKP told FBI another story. This unnamed individual told the FBI that he had sat ringside, near Cosell and close to Boudreaux's corner. "He recalled at the end of the fight [redacted — a judge] got up and passed him, making the comment, 'I got to get out of here because I think I made a bad decision.' **[redacted]** returned a short time later commenting to the effect, 'I made the right decision,' after the decisions of the other judge and referee were announced in the ring. **[redacted]** believed this was an unusual thing for a judge to do."

When the FBI subpoenaed Don King Productions in regards to this bout, they "have met with a decided lack of cooperation from officials at DKP." King was supposedly in Puerto Rico at the time and "not available for interview." As of April 1, 1977, "Three judges of fight interviewed and denied fight fixed." As if they were going to tell the FBI otherwise. Yet one of LeDoux's handlers told the FBI, "that after the fight was over, Boudreaux was standing dejectedly in a neutral corner. He advised that he heard one of Boudreaux's seconds say, 'Jump around, they are going to give you the fight.'"

Interestingly, Boudreaux's former manager was cut loose just prior to signing up for the tournament. This man had been with Boudreaux since the fighter was 13 years old, putting in nearly 12 years of service by the time of his dismissal. He told the FBI: "Don King and [redacted] allegedly are close friends and this is why Boudreaux got in the tournament. [redacted] stated that he has heard through the boxing circle that the entire U.S. Boxing Tournament was fixed and that Johnny Boudreaux and [redacted], who is controlled by Don King, were supposed to fight for the championship."

The FBI also learned "Boxer Johnny Boudreaux advised he paid [redacted] $3,000 for acting as his advisor. [redacted] manager of Scott LeDoux, advised $1,500 of LeDoux's purse went to [redacted]. [redacted], World Champions Magazine, advised LeDoux before fight that he could not win against Boudreaux. [redacted] advised that [redacted] had told LeDoux that he would be cheated out of decision because 'they' own 100% of Boudreaux."

Despite the serious possibility that the LeDoux-Boudreaux fight—perhaps the entire tournament—was fixed, ABC met with King several times yet decided to continue the tournament. ABC did make one decision before moving forward: they removed Wallau from all ensuing broadcasts. At about this same time, Madison Square Garden president Michael Burke sent Arledge a copy of Flash's newsletter (giving Arledge at least five separate newsletters detailing King's behind-the-scenes actions), but again, ABC did nothing.

The FBI, having learned that King and *Ring* magazine were in cahoots regarding fighters' rankings prior to the tournament, finally had their chance to interview the ringmaster himself. "King stated that allegations that he had paid off the press were completely false; however, he did consider the allegations to be flattering, because they suggest that he is a powerful enough figure to control the press....During the entire course of this interview, King insisted that the statements made in the press condemning himself, his company, and Farley, as well as Ring Magazine, were the work of other promoters and television networks who were jealous of his promotion of the U.S. Boxing Championship tournaments and the subsequent television rights he had obtained from ABC. King made direct statements to the effect that there is core racial motivation from these attacks. Both King and [redacted — his attorney] agreed, however, that it is probable that Ring Magazine had provided DKP with misranked [sic] boxers and that the rankings in the Ring Yearbook were erroneous." That was a whopping understatement. When the *1977 Ring Record Book* was released, Wallau and Flash compared it to the 1976 version and saw that at least 50 phony fights showed up in the 1977 version that were not in the 1976 copy. When this evidence was presented to the network, it finally compelled ABC to pull the plug and investigate the issue just before the heavyweight final between Larry Holmes and Stan Ward, both of whom were conveniently managed by King.

ABC's internal investigation was led by attorney Michael Armstrong. This was a whitewash revealing little more than what Wallau and Flash already had uncovered, despite being 327 pages long. It found no criminal conduct, but "a good deal of unethical behavior by individuals involved in the administration and organization of the tournament....The Armstrong Report essentially said everything went wrong, but nobody violated any laws. Once again, Don King was the unsinkable survivor."[31] Adding to that insult, "The Federal Communications Commission found that the tournament was unquestionably tainted, but investigations by the Congress, the FBI, the attorney general's office of the state of New York, and the U.S. District Court for New York State's Southern District (Manhattan) yielded not a single criminal indictment."[32]

Nonetheless, by this time King controlled heavyweight champion Larry Holmes whom, in typical fashion, he stole from his original manager. Holmes had "worked" for King before. He claimed that King ordered him to "carry" Billy Joiner in a December 1975 preliminary fight in order to fill time prior to the main event. But Holmes became angry when Joiner went after Holmes in the first two rounds, so Holmes floored him in the third. King was so mad he only paid Holmes $300 of the promised $1,000 until Holmes berated King into fulfilling his pre-fight promise.[33]

King then worked more magic. After Leon Spinks upset Muhammad Ali in early 1978, King convinced WBC president Jose Sulaiman (the two would work together several times over the years) to strip the Bob Arum-controlled Spinks of his title. This act essentially ended the successive line of heavyweight champions dating back to the late 1800s (King would capitalize on this in 1986 by getting $3 million out of HBO to "re-unify" the heavyweight championship he helped destroy). Sulaiman then named the number-one-ranked Ken Norton the interim champ and ordered him to fight the winner of the Holmes-Shavers fight. This bout was an ABC production—even after the DKP/ABC tournament had been revealed as a sham. It all worked out wonderfully for King, as he owned Norton, Holmes, and Shavers. After Holmes beat both fighters, King controlled the heavyweight title for 12 straight years until Mike Tyson lost to Buster Douglas in 1990.

Tyson wasn't originally a King-controlled fighter. Instead, he spent the early part of his career demolishing King's heavyweights (Trevor Berbick, Bonecrusher Smith, Tony Tucker, and Tony Tubbs, to name a few). But both of Tyson's co-managers died prior to him winning the heavyweight title: Cus D'Amato first in 1985 and Jim Jacobs in 1988. This left him emotionally crushed, lacking anyone in which to confide, as both had been father figures in his life. This was when King stepped in, making his move on Tyson during Jacobs' funeral—literally while Tyson was standing next to the casket. King was able to infect Tyson's mind against his trainer Kevin Rooney and new co-manager Bill Cayton. Tyson signed to fight Michael Spinks for the heavyweight title in 1988, and fired Cayton just prior to the bout. After unifying the heavyweight title by beating Michael Spinks in 91 seconds, Tyson fired Rooney, putting his career completely in King's hands.

Two years later, Tyson was signed to defend his title against a non-King opponent in Buster Douglas. Too busy living the high life, Tyson barely trained and King's people didn't try to get him to. He didn't even bother to watch film of Douglas' previous fights. So it was no surprise that by the eighth round, Tyson was behind on points. Sitting ringside, King sensed his fighter was doomed if he didn't get a knockout. Just then, Tyson dropped Douglas with a solid right uppercut. Douglas wasn't hurt and took time to catch his breath, rising at the count of nine. Seizing the opportunity, King went ape, screaming at WBC president Sulaiman that the referee should've counted out Douglas. Instead, Douglas knocked out Tyson two rounds later. King wasn't about to lose his crown jewel of the heavyweight title that easily. An hour after the bout ended, he continued to berate Sulaiman and the WBC as well as the WBA to withhold recognition of Douglas as the new champ, claiming Douglas received four extra seconds of time because the referee delayed in starting his count. Since Sulaiman was seen as King's puppet (and WBA president Gilbert Mendoza was little better), many feared King and Tyson were going to steal back Douglas' rightful title. Luckily, King's effort failed.

Like Carbo before him, King's stranglehold over boxing diminished over time. He was able to escape more than one FBI investigation, including a 23-count indictment for tax fraud and conspiracy which sent the vice president of Don King Productions (and his likely mistress), Constance Harper, to prison. This didn't mean boxing was suddenly free and clear of the corruption that has plagued it since the sport began. Many decisions, like the famed 1992 "draw" between Lennox Lewis and Evander Holyfield, remain highly controversial. Far too often boxing fans are subject to a trilogy of fights between the same two pugilists, with one fighter winning the first and the other taking the second, leaving a highly lucrative third fight to "settle the score." Fights are undoubtedly still fixed, but discovering exactly which have been is a daunting task. Few are willing to dig beyond the spectacle in search of the truth. And now with the rise of mixed martial arts and the Ultimate Fighting Championship, should it surprise anyone if this sport is corrupted in exactly the same manner as boxing, given the similarities between the two? All it takes is one fighter...

INTERNATIONAL GAME FIXING

"The fundamental problem is that anyone can fix a game now, and that *really* is the problem. It doesn't take a gang; it doesn't take organized criminals anymore. All it takes is a working Internet connection and some connections into a team or athletes, and then anyone can fix. You have the ability, once you have the connections on the team, just to place a bet around the world. You bet on a game that has high liquidity, or you bet the way the market is going anyway, or you just make a number of bets that are all under the radar screen so to speak, and away you go. So this nonsense now that we smashed a gang and blah, blah, blah, is missing the fundamental point: now anyone can fix."

So says Declan Hill, perhaps the world's foremost authority on game fixing in the world's biggest sport, soccer. Hill authored the international-al best-seller *The Fix: Soccer and Organized Crime* in which he not just proved that soccer matches are being fixed worldwide, he actually infil-trated a working group of game-fixers and witnessed them doing their dirty work. That investigation caused him to fear for his life. In fact, the first time I talked to Hill on the phone, he made me swear I wouldn't reveal his location to anyone. He related stories of how he rearranged his hotel room or blocked the door in case someone who wanted him silenced would break in to kill him, jokingly adding, "I don't know what the extra ten seconds or so would have done for me, but it helped me sleep better." Does he still worry about his safety now, some four years after his book's publication? "Much less so than I used to. Publicity's helped, but most of the guys that I identified have been arrested."

That's the key point Hill casually mentions in passing. Internation-ally—that is, outside the United States—games have been fixed and game-fixers have been arrested and sentenced to jail. Where are the ESPN or *Sports Illustrated* headlines detailing these minor triumphs of justice? Nowhere to be found. Within America, the notion that a game could be fixed appears absurd. Perhaps it is because the major sports news outlets believe that Americans aren't interested in cricket, soccer, or tennis. Maybe a game-fixer getting busted after the fact isn't deemed newsworthy. Or perhaps it has more to do with the millions of dollars invested by the likes of FOX Sports, ESPN and others into promoting, advertising, and broadcasting the international soccer and tennis matches now commonly found on U.S. television. A wee bit of censorship, or at least the omission of such stories, will keep American fans believing that the games they are being pushed to watch with a rooting interest are as clean as the NFL, NBA, etc. supposedly are.

But they're not.

Take for example the insanity surrounding the Chinese Professional Baseball League (CPBL). Formed in 1989 and based in Taiwan, the league has had nine teams, only four of which remain. The others are defunct, mostly due to game-fixing scandals. Prior to its 1997 season, the CPBL saw 18 players, a team manager, and two bookies arrested, convicted, and jailed for fixing games. Most of these players came from one team, the China Times Eagles. Their roster was so decimated that the league's other six teams had to lend them players so the team could complete the season. The Eagles didn't return in 1998. In July 2005, the catcher for the La New Bears and a coach from the Macoto Cobras were arrested for game fixing and instantly banned from the league. This was only the beginning. In total, police would arrest 15 players (from all but two teams in the CPBL) as well as gangsters and bookies in their sweep. This game-fixing group, police claimed, collected over $3 million during their run. The investigation revealed that coaches and players were often blackmailed, terrorized, and/or offered sex in exchange for throwing ball games. Favorite targets were foreign players from Panama and the Dominican Republic who were offered upward of $5,000 to fix a game. As a result, a team translator who acted as a go-between for gangsters and players was arrested as well. Three years later the dmedia T-Rex team completely disbanded due to game-fixing revelations. Then the following year, the Brother Elephants team lost the CPBL's equivalent of the World Series, immediately after which their manager along with a handful of his players (as well as players from two other teams) were arrested and convicted of fixing games. Despite the fact that attendance has drastically declined and those fans who do attend games are often heard shouting instructions to players (which are obeyed), the league persists.

Baseball's distant cousin cricket isn't free from corruption either. In February 2011, three members of the Pakistani cricket team and an agent were arrested after a sting operation conducted by the *News of the World*. However, the players of the Pakistani team weren't game fixing per se. They were bribed to spot-fix. The difference is slight but perhaps more dangerous. While game fixing often pertains to either outright losing a game or at least losing via the point spread, spot-fixing is much more subtle. Often in a spot-fix, a player (or referee) is paid to foul at a certain time. Because in the sports gambling world one can wager on nearly anything within a game, gamblers can even bet on when or if a player, for example in soccer, earns a yellow or red card in a match. A player or referee obviously has control over such a foul. Therefore, a sly gambler with an inside edge can make money betting on such an occurrence. The Pakistani team was paid by undercover reporters to foul—bowl no balls—at three specific times in their match against England, which they did. The four faced charges of conspiracy to obtain and accept payments as well as conspiracy to cheat. Two pleaded guilty and the other two ultimately were found guilty of the charges. Amazingly, while all four received prison sentences from between six and 32 months, the three players were not banned from cricket for life, but for five to ten years.

Paul Condon was the head of London's Metropolitan Police Force prior to organizing the International Cricket Council's (ICC) Anti-Corruption and Security Unit (ACSU) in 2000. He headed the ACSU for nearly ten years, stepping down just prior to the arrest of the Pakistani players. Of this scandal, he told BBC Radio Five Live's *Sportsweek* program, "This is a big wake-up call. Cricket is again at a credibility crossroad. I think a number of things have got to happen. I think the ICC have got to renew their efforts and get tougher, I think it has got to be prepared to give the harshest sentences it can—not just to cricketers who are found guilty—but their boards as well….I think if a particular national board does not, or is not doing enough to, prevent corruption then I think they should also suffer consequences as well. The nuclear option is teams would have to be excluded from world cricket if they are not getting their act together."[1] Why would Condon think a "nuclear option" was justified when it came to match fixing in cricket? Because the practice was rampant. Condon told the *London Evening Standard*, "In the late 1990s, Test and World Cup matches were being routinely fixed. There were a number of teams involved in fixing, and certainly more than the Indian subcontinent teams were involved. Every international team, at some stage, had someone doing some funny stuff."[2] Conveniently, none of this appeared to occur on Condon's watch.

However, the one-time head of the ACSU knew of cricket match fixing all over the globe. Some of it was occurring in his home country, England, in its domestic 40-over Sunday league and first-class Championship competitions. Teams out of the running for a title were giving wins away to other teams for future considerations. Condon explained, "If you're Team A and have a higher position in the Sunday league and I'm captain of Team B and my team have no chance in the Sunday league, I might do a deal to ensure you got maximum points in your Sunday league match. You would reciprocate in the County Championship. These friendly fixes quickly became more sinister, probably in the eighties."[3] Though Condon believes match fixing is a no longer a serious concern, he does admit that spot-fixing—the sort of offense that led to the arrest of the three Pakistani players and their agent—is much more troublesome. It is harder to detect and more difficult to prevent than outright game fixing, especially when the legal gambling establishments spread across the globe allow for wagering on the minor in-game events that lead to spot-fixing. Condon's hope? That athletes and coaches step forward to protect their own sport. However, he admitted, "In recent years, there's been very little whistle-blowing from current players."[4]

TENNIS, ANYONE?

In October 2011, the Swedish newspaper *Svenska Bladet* published the names of current tennis players from both the Association of Tennis Professionals (ATP) and Women's Tennis Association (WTA) who were on the London-based Tennis Integrity Unit's (TIU) "blacklist." How did these players earn this distinction? Because research evidence gave very strong indications that these players' matches contained irregular betting patterns, signaling the likelihood of a fix. Along with the blacklist, a second "warning" list of players being monitored for similar irregularities was also published. There were 13 names on the ATP and six names on the WTA blacklist. The warning list contained 16 members of the ATP along with six more from the WTA. That's 41 players in total.

One of the blacklisted names was ranked eighth in the world by the WTA at the time. That was Polish tennis star Agnieszka Radwanska. Mark Harrison of the TIU quickly jumped to her defense, as well as that of the rest of the players named on that list. "I can confirm that the claims made about players' involvement in match fixing are without foundation and should be given no credit whatsoever. The so-called blacklist of players is not from the TIU or any other official tennis body. These are very serious allegations that appear to be based on nothing more than the unsubstantiated claims of an individual. It is highly irresponsible to put players' names into the public domain in this fashion. The TIU would never release information or comment on investigations concerning any player unless it was part of an announcement at the conclusion of a disciplinary hearing."[5]

Though Radwanska and the others on the list may have been wrongly accused, by no means does it mean that tennis is free from match fixing. Far from it. Four months prior to the official formation of the Tennis Integrity Unit in September 2008, the *Environmental Review of Integrity in Professional Tennis* was released. The 66-page report was eye-opening for a number of reasons. Perhaps the most stunning revelation uncovered by the two former London Metropolitan Police officers, Ben Gunn and Jeff Rees (who later became the head of the TIU), commissioned to investigate corruption in tennis was that, "We have examined some 73 matches over the past five years involving suspected betting patterns. We have further examined 45 of those matches and there are specific concerns about each match from a betting perspective which would warrant further review. Patterns of suspected betting activity have been noted on 27 accounts in two different countries and there are emerging concerns about some players which would warrant further attention. Bearing in mind these matches only relate to Betfair [the world's largest legal Internet betting exchange, based in London] account holders, it is reasonable to assume that other suspect betting is taking place using other international legal and illegal betting markets. So there is no room for complacency."[6] The report went on to detail more about the 45 suspect matches, stating, "We judge that cheating at tennis for corrupt betting purposes is the most serious threat and goes to the core of the integrity of the sport. However, although the evidence currently available to prove the precise extent of that threat is limited, as mentioned above, we have examined, more closely, intelligence reports on 45 suspect matches over the past five years. The initial assessment of those matches, supported by other intelligence, indicates that a number of account holders are successfully laying higher-ranked players to lose/backing lesser-ranked players to win. The betting patterns give a strong indication that those account holders are in receipt of 'inside information,' which has facilitated successful betting coups both on 'in-play' as well as 'match' betting. Because of the sensitive

nature of these issues, the Report does not go into detail on those matches but we have shared further confidential information on them with the
Professional Tennis Authorities."[7] All of this information was compiled
by Gunn and Rees in a matter of ten weeks.

The basis for the identifying of these 45 suspect matches was what
Gunn and Rees called "the Sopot Match." This was perhaps the most fa-
mous fixed tennis match in recent history, although both players involved
were cleared of any wrongdoing. On August 2, 2007 in Sopot, Poland,
Russian tennis star and the ATP's fourth-ranked player in the world
Nikolay Davydenko faced off against the 87th-ranked Martin Vassallo
Arguello. Davydenko won the first set 6–2. Suddenly, a disproportion-
ate amount of bets on Arguello to win poured into Betfair. According
to reports, nine people in Russia bet approximately $1.5 million against
Davydenko after he won the first set. Two other American bettors stood
to win $6 million (thanks to the odds) if Davydenko lost. Early in the
third set, Davydenko claimed he had injured his foot and withdrew from
the match, giving Arguello and his betting public the victory.

To its credit, Betfair smelled a rat. Over $7 million had been wagered
on this single match, more than ten times the normal amount. Due to
these suspicions, Betfair declared all bets on the match "null and void"
and reported the incident to the ATP. An investigation was launched
which would consume nearly a year. In the meantime, Davydenko's play
was erratic. Two months after the Arguello match—and while under
investigation—Davydenko was given a code violation by an umpire for
not giving his best effort in a loss to Marin Cilic. He was fined $2,000
by the ATP for the offense (which would eventually be overturned).
Shortly thereafter in a match at the Paris Masters, Davydenko was
warned by a different umpire to again do his best. Davydenko's history
prior to the disputed Arguello match had been checkered as well. In his
three pre-Arguello events, he was knocked out in the first round. And
while he showed signs of an injury in the second set with Arguello, he
had also appeared injured in a match earlier in the same tournament.
Apparently while taking those facts into consideration—but ignoring the
highly unusual betting trends for the match—Davydenko was cleared of
the match-fixing charges against him. Betfair, however, still refused to

pay off any winning bets on Arguello in the match.

Most Americans reading this are probably thinking, "All this fuss over a tennis match? Who cares when you can bet the NFL or NBA?" But that's an extremely narrow view of sports betting. As Gunn and Rees wrote, "Betting on professional tennis is now a global business. In addition to the various onshore betting organisations (the traditional bookmaker) and the state betting agencies in those countries where betting is so controlled, there are currently some 562 on-line betting resources available through the Internet. There is also a thriving illegal market in some parts of the world."[8] They wouldn't even venture to estimate total betting volume on tennis, labeling it a "thankless and probably pointless task." Yet they did reveal that "It is generally acknowledged that, internationally, on the legal markets, tennis is the third most popular sport for betting purposes, following [soccer] and horse racing."[9] Notice the NFL, NBA, and MLB do not crack the top three despite billions being wagered upon them.

Being so popular on an international level, Gunn and Rees quickly realized that for someone with the will, tennis was easy pickings. They wrote, "Tennis is vulnerable to corrupt betting practices. This is borne out by the University of Salford Report 'Risks to The Integrity of Sport from Betting Corruption' (February 2008) in which Professor Forrest comments 'Tennis meets many of the criteria for a sport at risk of betting-related corruption. Contests are one-on-one, so events are easier to fix and the amount available for bribes can be spent on just one individual; pay-offs to fixes can be high because large wagers can be accommodated in a highly liquid market; and betting exchanges provide novel ways of manipulating a match for gain even without necessarily losing it.' Tennis comprises a series of discrete actions ranging from competing for individual points to winning sets and matches and then ultimately achieving tournament success. Betting can and does take place at each level or on a combination of levels, either through the wide variety of legal betting agencies around the world or through the illegal betting market which continues to flourish in some countries."[10] They added, "Individual actions can be manipulated by the corrupt without necessarily affecting the eventual outcome of the set or match. For example, a corrupt participant playing against a weaker opponent can deliberately lose a set or a number of games within a set or even generate a minimum number of double faults without seriously jeopardising the outcome of the match. Any of those eventualities can provide an opportunity for a corrupt player or other individual with 'inside information' to cheat at betting."[11]

Prior to the formation of the TIU, Gunn and Rees attempted to discern which players would be approachable from a fixing standpoint. Their conclusion, which can be echoed in all sports, was that a successful fixer will dig his hooks into a young player and then ride him or her as long as possible. They wrote, "We assess from our enquiries and experience of other sports that the following are vulnerable: young players starting out on their tennis careers who are not earning substantial money and yet have to support the cost of coaching, air fares, hotel bills, etc.; players who have received substantial loans/financial support from sponsors in their early career stages, particularly when there is a doubt about the probity/motives of the sponsors; players nearing the end of their careers who wish to bolster their dwindling earnings; players who become disillusioned because they realise they do not have sufficient skills/commitment to reach the top. These categories do not presume that a top player can never be vulnerable to corruption. Experience in other sports has shown some leading players can be tempted by what they see as easy money; again, once tempted, they are in for life."[12]

Upon the formation of the Tennis Integrity Unit in 2008, these theories seemed to prove true. The players subsequently caught and suspended for illegal gambling were for the most part young and lower-ranked:

Prior to the formation of the TIU but in the wake of the Davydenko scandal, the ATP fined and suspended two players, 31st-ranked Potito Starace and the 258th-ranked Daniele Bracciali, for gambling on tennis matches. Starace reportedly just bet on five matches with a total of $130 wagered, yet he was suspended for six months and fined $30,000 (more on him in a moment).

About six months later, the ATP suspended doubles titlists Frantisek Cermak and Michal Mertinak for gambling. Neither had bet upon their own matches nor attempted to affect the outcome of a match. Yet as a message to others, Cermak was suspended for ten weeks with a $15,000 fine while Mertinak received a two-week suspension and a $3,000 fine.

The 119th-ranked player Mathieu Montcourt was suspended for five weeks and fined $12,000 for gambling on tennis in May 2009. Supposedly he only gambled $3 per match, ringing up a grand total of $192 bet in 36 matches. Were the small bets a tip-off for other gamblers? It's not known, yet less than two months after his suspension, Montcourt was found dead in his Paris apartment building's stairwell. A preliminary autopsy listed cause of death as cardiac arrest. Montcourt was just 24 years old.

In October 2009, the WTA examined the unusual ending of a match featuring U.S. Open finalist Caroline Wozniacki after she unexpectedly retired while leading 7–5, 5–0 (meaning she was a single game away from winning the match). Wozniacki claimed she was injured early in the first set and her father instructed her to quit when she did, fearing further injury. However, betting on the match had swung heavily to her opponent prior to Wozniacki's retirement.

Daniel Koellerer of Austria, at one time the 55th-ranked tennis player in the world, was the first player banned for life for attempted match fixing in June 2011. His banishment was reinforced when he lost his appeal in early 2012.

October 2011 saw the second player banned for life for attempting to fix matches. Serbian player David Savic, ranked 659th, was also fined by the Tennis Integrity Unit $100,000 for three violations. The highest Savic had ever ranked was 363rd.

Of these players, only Potito Starace appeared on the supposed TIU blacklist or warning list as published in the Swedish newspaper *Svenska Bladet*. However, another player appearing on that disputed list, Wayne Odesnik, made news for a suspected fixed match at Wimbledon in 2009. Reporter Nick Harris for the *Independent* in the United Kingdom wrote, "On the morning of Tuesday 23 June 2009, it came to my attention that there was a substantial and suspicious gamble underway on Jurgen Mel-

158

zer of Austria to beat the little-known Wayne Odesnik in straight sets in their first-round Wimbledon match. This was a far from high-profile match. Typically, set betting (forecasting the exact sets score) on that level of low-interest match would attract around £10,000 in bets. Yet £650,000 was matched on Betfair alone *before* that match started (the vast majority on Melzer despite puny odds), and an astonishing £241,000 had been matched on Melzer to win by the specific scoreline 3–0 *before* the match started, with hundreds of thousands of more 'in play.' Melzer duly won 3–0….When Mark Davies, a senior executive at Betfair, told ESPN 'The Integrity Unit is obliged to look at it, but if I were in [TIU head] Jeff Rees' shoes, I wouldn't look at it very long,' he inadvertently sent a strong message that 'there's nothing wrong here, move along.' In fact Jeff Rees and his unit, as well as the Gambling Commission, looked at the case for many months. The Commission nominally stopped its own investigation in 2010, leaving it up to Rees. As the TIU never ever comments on the state of its investigations, it isn't known whether the case remains open as far as the TIU is concerned."[13]

Odesnik's story didn't end there. While the TIU never suspended or fined him for the oddity surrounding his Wimbledon match, about six months later when attempting to enter Australia Odesnik was caught with eight vials of Human Growth Hormone (HGH) in his luggage. This prompted a two-year ban. However, he was able to get that suspension cut to a single year by agreeing to turn whistleblower—on what, no one is really certain, but best guesses relate to both drugs and gambling.

Another of Gunn and Rees' more curious findings was how often players were approached to actually fix a match. They wrote, "A large majority of current and former players we interviewed claimed to 'know of' approaches to players being invited to 'throw matches' presumably for corrupt betting purposes. Only one player admitted being directly approached several years ago. Interestingly, although some players said they would inform the appropriate tennis authorities about any such approach to themselves, there was almost a unanimous view that they would not do so if they knew/suspected another player had been approached."[14] Why not? "The reasons given for adopting that attitude were: concern about their personal safety from would-be corruptors; concern about the confidentiality of any approach made by them to the tennis authorities; a general feeling that informing on other plays was a breach of the trust/ bond that exists between players."[15]

This is of note because some allege that the TIU along with the ATP has not released all they know about the subject of match fixing. Five Italian players who all had been given gambling-related suspensions, including the aforementioned Potito Starace, sued the ATP in 2009 claiming it possessed hidden documents proving higher-ranked players were guilty of gambling and allowed to walk away unscathed. Their argument was based on the notion that the ATP went after what the players' attorney called "the low-hanging fruit" in these lesser-ranked players to (a) look as though the ATP was cracking down on gambling within the sport while (b) preserving the ATP's profitability and reputation by avoiding a scandal featuring a star athlete. The suspended players cited the 45 suspicious matches mentioned in the 2008 *Environmental Review of Integrity in Professional Tennis* along with documents presented to the court which contained depositions of high-ranking ATP officials as well as that of the TIU's Rees which were sealed and considered "for professional eyes only."

On March 1, 2011, a federal judge upheld the ATP's suspension of the five Italian players despite their claims of being scapegoats. Amazingly, coming to their defense (sort of) for questioning what the TIU and ATP truly knows was none other than ESPN. The network requested the federal court unseal those potentially damaging documents. Why? Because ESPN became a major broadcast partner of the ATP and wanted to know what it was getting into. In 2011, ESPN2 committed nearly six hundred hours to professional tennis including Grand Slam, WTA, and ATP events. The network didn't seem confident in what those sealed court records might show as ESPN's senior vice president and director of news Vince Doria was quoted saying, "We have no idea if the allegations are true. We're basically throwing a hook in the water to see if anything's there."[16] Yet in the motion filed to unseal the documents, ESPN argued, "Gambling among professional tennis players has been an ongoing public concern for some time, as this lawsuit demonstrates. Whether professional tennis players—who are public figures—are gambling on their own matches, or the matches of fellow players, is a matter of public concern. Accordingly, ESPN seeks access to the sealed judicial records in this case. It is ESPN's understanding that the documents deal with third parties' gambling accounts or activities."[17]

This action appeared unusual for the so-called Worldwide Leader in Sports as ESPN's news division was in direct competition with its in-house (and larger) entertainment arm. Was there a conflict of interest? As Doria stated, "Virtually everyone we cover is a business partner these days. Most business partners have realized that while some stories are uncomfortable, time moves on. After the story comes out, we're still going to have a relationship with these entities."[18] Even so, ESPN seems to prefer protecting professional sports rather than prosecuting them, as the former is much more profitable than the latter. What ESPN would have ultimately done with the information became a moot point in July 2011. The presiding judge refused to unseal the documents, stressing personal privacy was greater than the public's right to know in this instance.

One scandal did touch two of the world's biggest tennis players, but this blip on the radar did little to either's reputation. The culprit at the center was billionaire Ted Forstmann, chairman and chief executive of IMG Worldwide, a monstrous sports and entertainment agency with clients ranging from Tiger Woods to Gisele Bündchen. Forstmann admitted to betting $40,000 on Roger Federer in the 2007 French Open final against Rafael Nadal. The major problem with this was that both Federer and Nadal were IMG clients at the time. Allegedly, Forstmann received inside information directly from Federer prior to the match (a point Forstmann denies); however, Federer lost to Nadal, costing Forstmann his wager. The ATP did issue a warning to Forstmann regarding "inappropriate behavior," but nothing else. In other words, because Forstmann lost the bet, everything was okay.

Tennis wasn't the only sport Forstmann bet. In a lawsuit filed by his former golfing friend James Agate, it was alleged that Forstmann "bet on college football and the NCAA men's basketball tournament while IMG was representing college coaches…and bet on longtime friend and endorser Vijay Singh against [Tiger] Woods and the rest of the field at the

Masters."[19] Agate claimed he was Forstmann's runner/beard, betting for him in Costa Rica and funneling the winnings through Agate's printing business. "In court documents…Agate lists nearly 600 bets he claims to have placed for Forstmann, including more than $150,000 on the 2007 NCAA basketball tournament alone."[20] Agate also claimed Forstmann bet on the NFL, NBA, NHL, and MLB, all for usually $2,000–3,000 a game. While an original lawsuit brought by Agate against Forstmann was dismissed, documents surfaced indicating that Forstmann paid Agate $575,000 to settle.[21]

Forstmann did admit to gambling on sports, but claims he stopped sometime in 2007. He has since banned gambling on college sports by any of IMG's employees since the firm acquired the Collegiate Licensing Company and moved further into college athletics. In 2011 Forstmann was quoted as saying, "Four years ago I did nothing wrong. OK? And since then I've done nothing at all. So that's a quote. OK? Not only am I saying I did nothing wrong, every governing body, including and most importantly to me, the governing body that governs amateur athletics here—amateur athletics, not pro athletics—said you did nothing wrong."[22] Of course, as IMG has become one of the largest and most powerful entities in college sports by holding exclusive licensing agreements for over 200 college properties, including those of the Heisman Trophy and major colleges like Notre Dame, Duke, and UCLA, why would the NCAA come out and verbally attack their new billionaire business partner?

THE WORLD'S GAME

On September 28, 2011, Michel Platini, head of the Union of European Football Associations (UEFA), gave a speech on match fixing at the Council of Europe. He told the audience, "Ladies and gentlemen, European football is afraid. European football is afraid, and I think I can even say that European sport as a whole is afraid…European sport is afraid because of a match fixing phenomenon that is developing in connection with large-scale online betting activities. The growth of betting-related match fixing is alarming, especially because it is a problem to which no sport and no country is immune. Of course, the sports movement has not been sitting idly by: there have been targeted awareness campaigns, expensive monitoring mechanisms, disciplinary procedures, and so on. However, necessary though they are, these initiatives do not suffice. Especially when match fixing is orchestrated by criminal organizations.

"So what about the criminal codes of European states? Well, experience here shows that, unfortunately, the traditional concepts of money laundering, corruption and fraud are of limited relevance. This is why some countries have established sports fraud as a specific criminal offense, in order to breach the gap. This is the case in Italy, Portugal, Spain, the United Kingdom, Poland and Bulgaria. However, the criminalization of sports fraud is far from universal. And this deficiency is, in part, why match fixing is still going on. Its international nature aggravates the situation further still. This is why I believe the Council of Europe now needs to intervene. It needs to intervene in order to encourage its member states to criminalize sports fraud and it needs to act in order to promote the indispensable cooperation between public authorities and sports governing bodies required in this regard. It is a question of responsibility, a question of ethics, a question of justice."

The UEFA had cause for concern. The attorney the association put in charge of investigating corruption within the sport, Pierre Cornu, flat-out stated in October 2011 that match fixing cannot be stopped. "I don't think we will be able to eradicate this problem. We don't pretend. It's just everywhere."[23] How everywhere is "everywhere"? In February 2012, FIFPro, the worldwide union of professional soccer players, released the results of a survey of thousands of its members from Eastern and Southern Europe. The numbers were shocking. "Almost a quarter of players (23.6%) are aware of match fixing in their league. The stats may cause particular concern for 2018 World Cup hosts Russia, where that figure is as high as 43.5%. The Black Book, a copy of which has been seen by the BBC, shows that 11.9% of footballers have been approached to consider fixing the result of a game, with that figure reaching 30.3% in Greece."[24] The root cause for much of this corruption? "The research found a clear link between non-payment of player salaries and match fixing. As many as 41.1% of players have not had their salary paid on time, of which more than half were approached to consider fixing a match."[25]

There's a reason this survey was conducted. It's the same reason why the UEFA and the International Federation of Association Football (better known as FIFA) are openly discussing match fixing within the game of soccer. The reason comes in the form of one man: Declan Hill. His book *The Fix: Soccer and Organized Crime* alerted the world that soccer was not the clean and pure sport most believed it to be. Games had been fixed. Games were going to be fixed. Something, Hill claimed, needed to be done to combat this before the game of soccer was rife with corruption. At first, he was doubted, ridiculed even. "I was the Old Testament prophet when the book first came out a couple of years ago," Hill told me. "You know, like 'Woe unto you. All will go wrong.'" But since the 2008 release of *The Fix*, as more and more arrests and convictions for match fixing around the world mounted, Hill turned into the expert. A sane voice to turn to and consult in combating this form of corruption. "Now that things are coming out that prove me right," he says, "it's nice to be the guy when they say, 'Ooo, we should've looked at this.' It's good. It's very good."

Not that Hill enjoys seeing a game fixed. It was his love of the sport that sent him on this mission to purify it. The problem for him is in finding those within soccer's hierarchy who possess the same goals as himself. Not all take the notion of reform seriously. "I think inside the halls of power are three types of people," Hill claims. "There are the good guys that are genuinely like 'Okay, let's get the system moving. How do we do this?' The second type are the guys who will mouth some words but are really corrupt themselves or they're going to pretend. And then there's a third group which is the consultants and all these guys trying to make money off the system. They don't care. They just want to make money. They're suddenly anti-corruption experts, saying, 'Oh, match fixing. I've been saying that for years.' And I look around and I'm like, I don't remember seeing *you* six years ago when I stood up and said, 'It's coming, guys.' I don't remember anyone else standing beside me at the podium and I don't remember anyone else from the newspaper articles looking around for confirmation of this crazy Canadian saying this stuff.

But, you know, hey, welcome to the ship."

One of the biggest obstacles to cleaning up the game sits at the very center of soccer. That is FIFA itself. The "association" that oversees the largest sporting event in the world, the World Cup, is itself corrupt. In 2011 alone, FIFA publicly battled against numerous ugly allegations, including officials unethically seeking favors and vote rigging which resulted in two members of FIFA's executive committee being suspended over the awarding of the 2018 World Cup to Russia and the 2022 World Cup to Qatar. When FIFA held its 2011 presidential election, all hell broke loose. Though FIFA's long-standing yet controversial president Sepp Blatter eventually maintained his position, scandal marred the entire process. In the end, Blatter's opponent Mohamed bin Hammam (who is coincidentally from Qatar) was banned for life after FIFA's ethics committee determined bin Hammam arranged $40,000 bribes for 16 Caribbean officials to secure their votes. Bin Hammam denied the allegations and vowed to appeal. Yet FIFA vice president Jack Warner resigned rather than face investigation over his alleged role in the plot. All of this resulted in FIFA president Blatter stating, "Crisis? What is a crisis? Football is not in a crisis. We are not in a crisis, we are only in some difficulties and these difficulties will be solved—and they will be solved inside this family."[26]

"Surely FIFA has no credibility now," Hill pointed out, "and anybody who does more than three minutes of research on the Internet [can see that]." Yet FIFA maintains its want in helping create an international "Integrity Unit" for sport, something designed along the lines of the World Anti-Doping Agency (WADA) which oversees drug testing in a wide variety of international sports. But FIFA is dragging its feet in making the same leap tennis did. Why? "I think they're terrified," Hill explains. "And they're terrified of the issue you see around FIFA, which is if you set up an integrity unit, is it going to investigate their own officials? The sporting officials are terrified that if you set up an integrity unit, the integrity unit is going to do what they are supposed to do which is to investigate anti-corruption of *all* kinds, not just fixing. And that's the huge problem.

"My sense is that there's an internal battle going on inside the international sports organizations. The good guys are saying, 'Look, this is a serious problem. Fixing, particularly linked to the gambling markets, can destroy sports, not all sports, but specific sports can just be destroyed. So we need institutions, we need an international anti-corruption agency.' And then there are other people who are just saying, 'Yeah, yeah,' and basically playing for time, hoping the issue will go away. That's the real danger." At this point, Hill doesn't see FIFA as part of the solution. "I don't think FIFA is doing anything effective against corruption in soccer. I think their guys are just flying around the world holding a series of press conferences and making big statements."

Action, as the saying goes, speaks louder than words. In the case of match fixing in soccer, one can point to numerous countries that have seen such scandals surface. These are not mere rumors or allegations. They are honest-to-goodness plots that have been uncovered, resulting in arrests and convictions for those involved.

Considering the problems faced by the Chinese Professional Baseball League, it should come as no surprise that the Chinese Football Association (CFA) was also rife with game fixing. After a two-year investigation, three referees were arrested by Chinese police on allegations of match fixing in March 2011. One of the three had presided over World Cup games played in the country in 2002. But those arrests were just a warm-up. By the end of the year, nearly 60 Chinese national soccer players, referees, coaches, and officials had been arrested and charged for their involvement in various levels of gambling, corruption, and match fixing. These were not low-level targets. Included were a general manager of the Chinese Super League team Shaanxi, a deputy director of the Chinese Football Administrative Center, the former director of the CFA's referee committee, and not one but two former heads of China's soccer program. The CFA issued a statement regarding the exposure of such widespread corruption within the country which read in part, "Soccer corruption breached the country's law and tarnished the image of the sport as well as the healthy development of soccer in China, leading to a very bad impact on the game....Corruption exposed flaws in the administrative system and imperfections in the supervision mechanism."[27]

One of the reasons match fixing is so prevalent in China is that gambling is an integral part of the Oriental culture, not something merely written off as a vice. Legalized casino gambling now exists in Macau (which surpassed Las Vegas in 2006 as the world's largest gambling center by earning over $7 billion in casino revenue), Singapore, South Korea, the Philippines, Malaysia, Cambodia, Myanmar, Laos, and Vietnam. One country noticeably missing from that list is China. However, in the Chinese territory of Hong Kong, gambling is alive, well, and legal—but only through the Hong Kong Jockey Club. "The jockey club conducts about seven hundred horse races per year at its two racetracks at Sha Tin and Happy Valley. The only other forms of legalized gambling there, including a lottery and betting on soccer matches, is also run from those two tracks. The industry annually rakes in about $12 billion annually [sic]. The organization is the largest taxpayer in Hong Kong and the largest private donor of charity funds. About 750,000 people had telephone betting accounts as of a 2001 account—and in a city that then had a population of six million people, an astonishing one million of them, or 17 percent of the population, placed bets each race day at any of 125 off-track outlets. Here's another measure of Hong Kong's obsessive gambling intensity: the population, which as of 2010 was at seven million, is just 0.1 percent of the world's population of 6.9 billion (as of late 2010). Yet Hong Kong makes up 3.3 percent of the world's total online gambling revenues."[28]

Even though gambling is legal in these countries and those who want to bet have ample outlets to do so, organized crime in the Far East still profits greatly from illegal, underground gambling. And it is here within these criminal organizations that one can witness the genesis of a fixed game. It is where Hill went to infiltrate a notorious group of game-fixers, watching them rig matches right in front of him. As Hill posted on his blog in July 2011, this group "traveled to every single big international soccer tournament—the under-17 World Cup, the under-20 World Cup, the Women's World Cup, the Olympic soccer tournament and the World Cup itself. They have approached dozens of teams and hundreds of players and referees over the last 20 years. I got into the gang. I wore a hidden camera and taped some of their meetings. Then I exposed their activities in the book." That was just one group. There are others.

And they all possess these capabilities. How? Because so much money is pouring into these illegal bookmaking operations from all over the world—including the United States—that the fixers now possess both the capital to finance a fixing scheme as well as the "outs" to bet on the rigged game without fear of being spotted.

INTERPOL secretary general Ronald K. Noble gave a speech at the Global Conference on Asian Organized Crime held in Singapore in January 2008. Its focus was illegal gambling on soccer. Noble was quoted as saying, "I am focusing on illegal soccer gambling because INTERPOL and the Expert Group members identified it as a major organized criminal activity in their jurisdictions, but it is of course not the only one. All of organized crime groups' illegal activities—murder, extortion, money laundering, corruption, trafficking in drugs and people—feed into one another, facilitating and financing the commission of other crimes.

"Gambling on soccer matches might seem as harmless as placing a small bet on your favorite team, but these illegal operations are often controlled by organized criminals who frequently engage in loan sharking and use intimidation and violence to collect debts. If that doesn't work, they force their desperate, indebted victims into drug smuggling and the family members of victims into prostitution. One must remember that organized crime never loses money in gambling operations—one way or another, they make a profit….

"The dangers associated with this type of organized crime have been noted not just in Asia, but in Europe as well. Last year, European soccer's governing body, UEFA, asked police in Europe to investigate the results of at least 26 matches it believed were manipulated by overseas betting syndicates [this included three in the third preliminary round of the 2008 championships, two in the UEFA Cup, and one in the qualifying round of the 2008 Euro]. The matches covered every major European soccer competition and involved countries from almost all corners of the continent. While it is difficult to determine the exact amount of money involved in the match fixing, UEFA claimed an overseas syndicate made five million U.S. dollars on one championship match alone in July 2007."[29]

INTERPOL has in fact done its part to curtail these crimes. Consider this: in his speech, Noble trumpeted the success of INTERPOL's Operation Soga, which was carried out by police officers from INTERPOL's National Central Bureaus as well as Sub-Bureaus in China, Hong Kong China, Macau-China, Malaysia, Singapore, Thailand, and Vietnam. Operation Soga resulted in the arrest of more than 430 individuals and the closing of 272 underground gambling dens which handled an estimated $680 million in illegal bets worldwide. As stunning of a success as that may appear, it was merely a pebble in the path of a runaway freight train. INTERPOL estimates that illegal betting is worth $140 billion a year for organized crime.[30]

In the Far East, China is not the only country to see corruption within its soccer league. Malaysia witnessed the arrest of two team coaches in 2011 as part of a FIFA-led investigation, prompting the Malaysian Football Association to establish its own anti-corruption task force. In March 2008, a writer posted the outcome of a Japanese soccer league game prior to the game taking place. This was not a prediction, but a warning that the game was fixed for a particular outcome—a 2–2 tie which would be won by a certain team during the penalty kick shootout. The game's result was exactly as described. South Korean soccer was devastated by the indictment of 55 professional soccer players on game-fixing charges. Eleven bookmakers were implicated in rigging games as well. Ten players received a lifetime ban from the sport, and one player allegedly committed suicide over the accusations against him. The South Korean K-League later announced it would begin to administer lie detector tests to its players as a deterrent.

Across the world, roundups of players, coaches, and referees involved in fixing soccer games are becoming rampant. For example:

In Greece, nearly 70 players, referees, club officials, and owners were arrested in a match-fixing probe. Among those ensnared were the president of the Greek Super-League and head of the Olympiakos, the country's most popular team. Female prosecutor Popi Papandreou led the charge with backing from both the Greek state police and its national secret service. Papandreou and law enforcement officials spent nearly a year investigating corruption within the country's soccer league. In the end, she produced a 124-page prosecution report to justify the arrests. Those involved were charged with crimes including illegal gambling, fraud, extortion, and money laundering.

Across the Aegean Sea in Turkey, more than 30 players, coaches, and team officials were arrested on charges of fixing at least 19 matches. More were detained and/or interrogated in the probe, including referees, sports journalists, and even sponsors. The corruption touched all four of the country's top teams—Besiktas, Galatasary, Trabzonspor, and league champions Fenerbahce. Two club presidents were detained, as was a former president of Turkey's national soccer federation. The arrests actually postponed the Turkish Super Cup final match. Reigning champion Fenerbahce announced shortly thereafter that it would return the Turkish Cup which it had won the previous season until its deputy chairman and coach were cleared of the charges against them—which included fixing the championship game. Despite all of this, the Turkish Football Federation decided not to punish any of the teams involved citing a variety of Turkish judicial precedents.

Since 2005, Polish police have detained nearly 200 people for suspected soccer game fixing. This included members of the Polish Football Federation, coaches, referees, and players. In early 2009, 17 people associated with the league were found guilty of fixing games and sentenced to prison. The harshest sentence was four years.

In Hungary, three players and four referees were arrested in 2011 by a task force from the National Bureau of Investigation for allegedly manipulating the final scores of games played in Hungary, Germany, Finland, Croatia, and Slovenia. On top of this, three other Hungarian referees as well as three from Bosnia-Herzegovina were suspended for life by FIFA for fixing matches. FIFA found that the six officials manipulated the results of two international "A" friendly matches played in Turkey—Bolivia v. Bulgaria and Latvia v. Estonia.

Then there's the mere "rumors" of fixed games:

- In April 2009, Bulgarian bookies stopped taking bets on several

INTERNATIONAL GAME FIXING

games in the nation's soccer championship for fear of fixed games. A game that had already taken place was suspected of being fixed when a specific result (a 3–1 victory) was bet upon heavily. The game ended in that exact score.

- The Nigerian team's 4–1 victory over Argentina in 2011 was considered suspect. Why? Suspicious betting patterns were noticed in regards to this match, particularly surrounding the game's final goal which came on a penalty kick given to Argentina in the fifth minute of injury time.

- In his 2009 book *Football Dynamo — Modern Russia and the People's Game*, author Marc Bennetts claimed at least one to two games played each season in Russian soccer are "suspicious." One game in particular involving a 3–2 loss by the team Krylya Sovietov was accompanied by irregular betting. The president of the nation's soccer union later stated he was "ashamed" of the team for the game in question.

- Investigations swirled around El Salvador as allegations emerged that teams there were fixing matches in the qualifying stages of its Concacaf Champions League.

- Even in Israel police were investigating game fixing, questioning the head of the country's football federation after having arrested the owners and a former coach of the team Hapoel Petah Tikva. Allegations centered on three potentially fixed games as well as the attempt to influence which referees were assigned to officiate certain games.

- In July 2012, former Southampton defenseman Claus Lundekvam claimed to Norwegian television that spot-fixing was rampant in the English Premier League. While Lundekvam stated no games were thrown, players were rigging which teams received certain in-game events such as the first throw-in or corner-kick, all of which were wagered upon. This, he claimed, went on "nearly every week."

All of this comes on top of the fact that by the beginning of 2012, no fewer than 24 national police investigations were ongoing examining match and/or spot-fixing around the world. And in early 2013, as this book was being finalized, Europol announced to the world that 680 soccer matches worldwide were suspected of being fixed since 2008.

If that were it, that would be bad enough. But there's more. Much more. And it gets worse.

Juventus of Turin was the powerhouse of Italy's top Serie A soccer league. The "New York Yankees of Italian soccer" had won 29 national championships dating back to 1905. However in 2006, after winning their second national championship in as many years, the team fell apart due to accusations of game fixing, dragging much of the Italian soccer league down with it. Italian federal investigators conducted 20 months of wiretapping, attempting to sort out the twisted world of this soccer league. What they discovered was shocking. It was believed that an "elite group" at the very top of Italian soccer formed a criminal organization with the aims of influencing the outcome of games. Investigators pinpointed 33 specific matches between 2004 and 2006 which were in question, investigating 41 people involved in those contests. The revelations included players gambling on games in which they participated, coercion, physical threats, and even a possible kidnapping. One of those suspected players was Juventus' goalie Gianluigi Buffon. While investigators monitored Buffon, he gambled well over $2.5 million on various sporting events. Amazingly, they could not prove he ever gambled on soccer or fixed a game. Even with the revelations of Buffon's habit, he was later selected as the goalie for Italy's World Cup team.

But at the center of it all was Juventus' general manager Luciano Moggi. After winning the 2006 championship, Moggi resigned from his position with the team. When Italian investigators got hold of him soon afterward, Moggi broke down during questioning, claiming he had to defend himself from the "real powers" that ran the game. Who those real powers were remains sketchy, but Moggi's former team was owned by the Agnelli family, who also owns the Fiat Motor Corporation. Despite his cries, investigators accused Moggi of being the mastermind of a system that appointed favored referees to his team's key games. He also held considerable sway over the sale and trade of players throughout the entire league, using those powers to Juventus' notable advantage.

When all was said and done, there was a housecleaning within Serie A. Five teams—Juventus, Fiorentina, Lazio, Reggina, and AC Milan (which was owned by the Italian prime minister)—were punished for their roles in the scandal, with Juventus getting the worst of what lenient sentences were handed down. The club was stripped of their 2005 and 2006 titles while being relegated down from Serie A to Serie B. Meanwhile, the team's entire board of directors was forced to resign. The Italian soccer federation's president and deputy resigned as well. Two top officers in the league's referees' association also quit in disgrace. Moggi was banned for life with 13 others receiving bans ranging from five years to three months. Three were also sentenced to short prison terms. Much of the league's top talent left the country for greener pastures. Even so, corruption still existed. In 2009, three Serie A players were under federal investigation for match rigging. The three were reportedly paid $270,000 by the tried-and-true Italian mafia to throw a particular game which their team lost 2–1 on a late goal.

Despite all of this, the league continues to not just operate, but thrive. The league signed a two-year contract in 2010 for its broadcast rights in Italy for over one billion Euros. American soccer fans can readily watch Italian Serie A games on FOX's cable soccer channels. Do any of these newfound fans realize how corrupt the league was revealed to be just a short time ago…or continues to be? In mid-2012, Serie A was again hit with a game-fixing scandal as large as, if not larger than, the original from 2006. Though details were emerging as this book was written, already Italian officials had arrested 19 people suspected to be involved, including players, coaches, and team officials. Members of Juventus were again under investigation.

In mid-2011 Wilson Raj Perumal, a native of Singapore, was sentenced to two years in prison for fixing a number of soccer games in Finland. Nine players from two Finnish teams, including a pair of brothers from Zambia, were also given suspended sentences for accepting bribes from Perumal though many observers believed more players were involved. But Perumal's reach in the soccer world stretched much farther than Finland. Perumal was brazenly involved in fixing games all over the world. In September 2010, he managed to organize an entirely fake team said to represent the small West African country of Togo, then faced the squad against Bahrain where they (likely intentionally) lost 3–0.

Perumal was also believed to be involved in fixing games with the national team from Zimbabwe. The Zimbabwe Football Association released a report around the time of Perumal's conviction which revealed corruption within the team from 2007 to 2010. When the Zimbabwe team toured the Far East in 2008 and 2009, the team's manager explained how they were met at the airport by four men including one named "Rajah" who they assumed were security personnel. Right away from their first night in the hotel, Rajah began to sink his hooks into members of the team. By the start of Zimbabwe's first game on the tour, Rajah had set up deals with many of the players and team officials to lose by specific scores. When all was said and done, Rajah had paid each player $5,000–$6,000 and each team official $7,000–$8,000.

Perumal was believed to be part of a much larger game-fixing organization, though he was considered only a mid-level member. Authorities were attempting to get him to cooperate and help bring down this ring which had roots in the illegal sports books of the Far East, yet Perumal wasn't revealing much. He had little incentive given his two-year conviction which was called "token at best" by FIFA chief of security Chris Eaton.[31] He added, "If Wilson Perumal's real legacy is a better understanding of how criminals avoid detection while operating globally and freely roaming, and this then enables us to protect football, this is a far better outcome than a short prison term."[32]

At about the same time as Perumal was sentenced, what was labeled as Europe's "biggest ever football betting scandal" made headlines. Not surprisingly, its origins stemmed from an earlier game-fixing incident. In 2005, 28-year-old Ante Sapina was sentenced to three years in prison for his role in fixing games with Bundesliga referee Robert Hoyzer. In a similar fashion as NBA referee Tim Donaghy, Hoyzer, who was once trusted to officiate matches in Germany's top league, turned on the entire German Football Association once the allegations against him became public. He implicated several other Bundesliga members with similar charges of corruption as had been levied against him. German police took his confession seriously and began investigating at least four other referees and 14 players. But also like Donaghy, by the time all was said and done, only one Bundesliga member was sentenced to prison—Hoyzer. It's uncertain if Hoyzer was honest with his allegations against the others or if he was lying to draw attention away from himself. Many believe the former was true and that Germany, which was on the verge of hosting the 2006 World Cup, covered up the situation to save face. Regardless, by the time Hoyzer was sentenced to jail, Sapina was back on the streets. Shortly thereafter, he met his future partner in crime Marijo C. sometime during that 2006 World Cup. Together the pair of German-Croatians, with the aid of a few accomplices, went to work fixing soccer matches all over Europe.

While Sapina was arrested again in 2009, it wasn't until his trial in 2011 that the extent of his reach was revealed. He confessed to bribing multiple players, referees, and UEFA officials to submit to his whims. Exactly how many games that amounted to was in question. Some estimates put the number as high as 200. But for legal purposes the number settled upon was 47 games, including lower-level German league matches, three Champions League games, 12 Europa League games, and even a couple of World Cup qualifiers. "Their creativity had no boundaries. They took over a Belgian second division team, assembled with 'obedient' players, who would perform on the pitch according to the wishes of their bosses without exception. Numerous referees and players, including some from Germany, are believed to have cashed in on bribes. Eventually players themselves became involved in betting, and a dependency developed between players with high debts and the betting fraudsters.

"Marijo C., who owned several betting bureaus in Nuremberg, described one very well-known former Bundesliga player as being so addicted that he had to occasionally lock him into his gaming salon overnight. Convincing professional players to become involved in the manipulation of matches was often all too easy. The most recent confession came from former St. Pauli striker René Schnitzler, who admitted to having been a compulsive gambler since the age of 18 and receiving 100,000 euros from a betting magnate."[33] The money Schnitzler received was to fix five games in 2008.

Just as prosecutors couldn't determine how many games were fixed, they also couldn't total the amount of money Sapina and company profited from those games. Investigators scoured the world for his hidden funds. Accounts were uncovered in the Isle of Man, Croatia, Russia, China, and Malaysia. Sapina himself believed he was making over a million euros a month on sports gambling, but even he didn't seem certain. He was betting on upward of 30 games a day of which at least one was under his control. Not surprisingly, most of those bets were made through contacts in the Asian syndicates, particularly Hong Kong and Malaysia.

Ultimately both Sapina and Marijo C. were sentenced to five years and six months in prison by a German district court. That's 66 months for 47 (known) games, or about 42 days for every fixed match. It's not much of a deterrent to ward off others from attempting to follow in Sapina's footsteps. But something was missing from these sentences. Considering that at least 47 games were fixed, where were the punishments for the players, coaches, and UEFA officials bribed by Sapina's crew? Those men were perhaps more culpable than those called "fixers" because they made the fix a reality. But no arrests followed. Those who were similarly guilty did not face similar sentences. They were free to carry on with their careers.

Meanwhile fans in all of these countries have been burned. An untallied amount of money spent on tickets, concessions, and even wagers was robbed from honest fans conned into watching falsified games. What compensation is coming to them for the loss of their time and money? How many childhood dreams have been crushed by the revelation of these fixed matches? How many have turned their back on what was once thought to be a pure sport?

The biggest question of all is: Does FIFA even care?

THE WORLD CUP

The American sports leagues like the NFL and NBA have a false hatred of gambling. Their public face openly despises wagering on their sport while privately they recognize that the public's ability to bet on their games is extremely beneficial to their overall success. FIFA takes no such stand. Not willing to live the lie the NFL does, FIFA has been seen as ambivalent toward its fans' gambling habits: not necessarily encouraging the practice, but not mandating an outlaw of it either. Instead, it has taken steps to partner with bookmaking firms, not to profit from fans gambling on its games, but in a concerted effort to track betting patterns. In this way it hopes to pinpoint unusual wagering trends and activities to crack down on game fixing. This is what FIFA has labeled as its "early warning system."

The inherent problem in this early warning system rests in finding the telltale "abnormal" wagers among an ocean of legitimate bets. And as with American sports, it also makes the assumption a fixer would bet within the legal market to begin with. Though the illegal betting markets are vast, the current legal form of soccer gambling is itself a monstrous worldwide business. According to the World Lottery Association, an organization of state-authorized lotteries, 90 billion euros are spent each year on legitimate wagers on soccer games. The games of the 2010 World Cup were expected to result in between $1 and $3 billion wagered in the United Kingdom *alone*. "In addition to straight bets on winners and losers, William Hill [the world's largest bookmaker] and other bookies offer a dizzying array of side propositions on—to name just a few—leading scorers, who will be ahead at a certain point in a particular game, the time of the first goal scored and the first player to be seriously injured."[34] Chris Shillington, a spokesman for London-based Extrabet. com, expected his firm would be taking a bet per second—at least—during the 2010 World Cup when England was playing.[35] Even the Las Vegas sports books get in on the World Cup action, though not nearly at the same levels. Jay Rood, director of the MGM Mirage's race and sports book, was quoted as saying that how much gets wagered there "depends on the match. It is really feast or famine. We might book $250,000 for one, and the next might be $5,000."[36] Now within those billions of dollars, try and pinpoint the bets made by the fixers. Maybe they have $100,000 on a fixed World Cup game, perhaps even $1 million. Can that really be noticed within the $1–$3 billion bet?

FIFA doesn't make it easy on itself either. With the 2010 World Cup played in South Africa, FIFA invited bookies to set up shops directly outside of stadiums. The bookmakers were welcomed despite the knowledge that the fixers care not for international borders. But FIFA, like its fans and supporters, took the naïve stance that something as big and well watched as the World Cup was untouchable. Graham Sharpe, spokesman for UK gambling giant William Hill, stated prior to the 2010 World Cup, "There have been proportionately fewer 'rigging scandals' in [soccer], I would suggest, than in some U.S. sports in recent years. Bookmakers are the potential targets of any attempted match fixing, [but] we have no concerns whatsoever about the integrity of the World Cup."[37]

Declan Hill was not so certain. Prior to the 2010 World Cup he issued a statement which was posted on his website and sent to several media outlets. Titled "J'accuse FIFA," it began, "Match-fixers will be at the World Cup in South Africa. They will be there approaching players, referees and team officials and trying to bribe them to fix matches. They will be there because they have been at almost every international football tournament…for the last twenty years. They will be there because there has been no *effective* action on the part of FIFA to clean up this problem." One of the biggest reasons Hill felt confident in making this statement is a fact perhaps few soccer fans realize—players don't necessarily get paid to play in the World Cup. FIFA hands money to the executives of each national team participating in the event. This cash is then to be given to the players. Of course, given the state of corruption within this world, what is supposed to happen compared to what does transpire are two greatly different outcomes. Nationalism be damned; without pay, many players are not going to trot onto the field willing to give it their best effort. Not when they witness the amount of money being shelled out by fans, bettors, and corporations on each and every match as it's televised across the globe. When a wise fixer is aware of such a situation, a little money could go a long way in setting up beneficial results for all involved.

The fact is the World Cup has seen its fair share of controversy over the past 50 years. In some cases, this may be chalked up by some to just conspiracy theory. But in others, the truth may be that games have been fixed on soccer's biggest stage. One would think that the last person to fuel such controversial fires would be a former president of FIFA. Yet in 2008, Brazilian João Havelange, who served as FIFA's president from 1974 until 1998, did just that by stating in an interview with *Folha de São Paulo* that both the 1966 and 1974 World Cups were fixed. Was the 92-year-old Havelange off his rocker? Was he simply bolstering his own national team by making these claims? Or was he revealing a long-held secret? It could be a bit of all three.

The Brazilian team won both the 1962 and 1970 World Cups led by the player who would become an international sensation—Pele. But Havelange alleged that England and Germany conspired to break the country's domination by rigging the other two tournaments in question. There is a case to be made. In the 1966 World Cup held in England, Brazil did not advance beyond the first round. Part of the reason was that two of Brazil's opponents—Bulgaria and Hungary—repeatedly fouled Pele to the point of injuring him with little reprimanding for the offending players. As Havelange pointed out, "In the three matches that the Brazilian national team played in 1966, of the three referees and six linesmen, seven were British and two were Germans....Brazil went out, Pele 'exited' through injury, and England and Germany entered into the final, just as the Englishman Sir Stanley Rous, who was the president of FIFA at the time, had wanted."[38]

England did in fact win the 1966 World Cup on their home field, but not without help. In England's quarter final game against South American powerhouse Argentina, German referee Rudolf Kreitlein red-carded Argentina's captain Antonio Rattin for simply arguing a call. Rattin was so angered by this that British police needed to escort him from the field. Shorthanded, Argentina fell to England 1–0 in what Argentina forever labeled "the robbery of the century." Lending more credence to Havelange's claim is the fact that Germany beat Uruguay in the quarterfinals 4–0 thanks in part to English referee Jim Finney. In this game, the English referee not only sent off a pair of Uruguayan players, but he overlooked a hand stop by a German player which would have been a certain Uruguayan goal.

With the 1974 World Cup, Havelange alleged it was a repeat of 1966 only with England trading places with host country Germany. "In Germany in 1974 the same thing happened. During the Brazil-Holland match, the referee was German, we lost 2–0 and Germany won the title."[39] Interestingly, the final pitted home Germany against the same Holland team that ended Brazil's run. The referee for this match? Englishman Jack Taylor. Germany won 2–1, coming back from a 1–0 deficit with the help of a goal scored on a penalty kick. Were both of these World Cups fixed for the host countries to win, or at least to keep Brazil from continuing its dominance in the sport?

One thing is for certain: in the 1978 World Cup, host country Argentina fixed at least one game for its national team prior to it winning the tournament. And Brazil found itself again on the short end of the stick. This incident was confirmed in 2012 by Peruvian senator Genaro Ledesma. Two years prior to hosting the World Cup, Argentina endured a nasty political coup. The overthrow of the Argentinean government caused some countries to consider not attending. When the games kicked off as scheduled, all was still not well within the country. Jorge Videla's dictatorship was brutal with torture and "disappearances" the norm. As for the soccer, the Argentinean team played well enough to advance to the second round, but to reach the final, one team stood in their way—Brazil. In this era of the World Cup, after the first round, teams did not play a single elimination tournament to determine a final champion. Instead, another round of three games was played with the two teams possessing the best record advancing. In the case of a tie, each team's total goal differential acted as the tiebreaker. As it happened, Brazil won two of its three of its games (tying Argentina 0–0 in the other) by a margin of five goals. Argentina won its first games, but only by a score of 2–0. To advance to the final, it would have to not just defeat Peru, but win by four goals.

This was when the deal was struck. More concerned with the rebelliousness of its own citizenry than soccer, Peru's president Francisco

Bermudez struck a deal with Videla. The Peruvian team would lose by the four-goal margin. In exchange, Videla would allow Bermudez to cast out 13 Peruvian political dissidents to Argentina where they would be held as prisoners. As Senator Ledesma explained, "Videla needed to win the World Cup to cleanse Argentina's bad image around the world. So he only accepted the group if Peru allowed the Argentina national team to triumph."[40] Triumph they did, beating Peru 6–0 to advance to the final match versus the Netherlands. The victory was so easy that the idea the game was fixed was instantly prevalent. Some accusatory fingers pointed squarely at Peru's Argentine-born goalie, and they may have been correct. But this was no fix for betting purposes. Who's to say that had the Peruvian team not obeyed orders that they wouldn't have been left behind in Argentina to suffer a similar unknown fate as those dissidents? An investigation is currently being conducted in Peru to uncover all aspects of this fixed match…35 years too late.

More of these sad shenanigans ensued. In the 1982 World Cup, a critical first-round match between Austria and West Germany was fixed. "Both teams would progress to the second round if West Germany won the game 1–0. The Germans scored in the first eleven minutes, and the rest of the match was an exercise…[in] taking a nap."[41] The team robbed from advancing to the second round by this arranged match, Algeria, protested to FIFA. FIFA allowed the result to stand. Skip ahead to the 2002 World Cup, and once again it appeared as if the host nation was given favorable treatment. Tournament co-hosts South Korea surprisingly advanced to the Round of 16 "knockout" stage. There, their miraculous run continued by beating first Italy then Spain on what many felt were highly favorable calls awarded to the South Korean team by the referees. South Korea would not reach the final match, however, settling for a fourth-place finish. At the ensuing World Cup in 2006, it was alleged that France paid Brazil $25 million to throw its quarterfinals match against their national team. An email was supposedly leaked reading in part, "The Brazilians have taken compensation from the French that exceeds the winners' trophy prize, so they're now very cautious." France won 1–0 with Brazil managing only a single shot on goal in the game. Adding to suspicion was that after the loss, none of the Brazilian star players would speak with the press.

On top of that, Declan Hill chronicled three rigged matches in that same World Cup in *The Fix*. In speaking directly with the mastermind of these fixes, Hill knew ahead of time that Ghana would lose two particular games—a first-round match versus Italy and a second-round game to Brazil—and that the Ukraine would dump one to Italy as well. The fixer named "Chin" lamented to Hill about not making more money from these pre-arranged games. Prior to the 2010 World Cup, the head of the English Football Association, Lord Triesman, resigned his post due to being secretly recorded speaking about how Spanish football authorities were attempting to bribe referees in upcoming tournament. As it turned out (perhaps coincidentally), a Spanish referee controversially red-carded a German player, costing the heavily favored German team a 1–0 loss against Serbia in the first round. Meanwhile, the Spanish team went on to win the entire tournament.

But go back a moment and recall the quote from William Hill's spokesman Graham Sharpe regarding the 2010 World Cup. He said in part, "we have no concerns whatsoever about the integrity of the World Cup." That may have been an entirely honest statement. Or it may have been a statement emanating from a company spokesman doing his job, reassuring a gambling community from which William Hill greatly profits. Because as it turned out, there were serious integrity issues leading up to that World Cup. "South Africa were duped into allowing an Asian match-fixing syndicate to provide them with referees for a series of warm-up games before they hosted the 2010 World Cup, FIFA security chief Chris Eaton said.…The outcome of friendly internationals against Thailand, Colombia, Bulgaria and Guatemala in the weeks leading up to the tournament are all in question after FIFA found the match officials had been provided by a Singapore-based company, fronting for match fixers. Eaton said the South African Football Association had taken up an offer from Wilson Perumal [remember him?], who has since been convicted in Finland on match-fixing charges, to use his company for the procurement of referees for the games."[42] Apparently at least two of these games were fixed for South Africa to win, if not all four. "South Africa were handed two disputed penalties in beating Colombia 2–1 when they played at Soccer City in Johannesburg on May 27. One of the kicks was ordered retaken twice after the initial efforts were both saved. Colombia's goal also came from a penalty. South Africa's 5–0 win over Guate-mala in Polokwane four days later saw them awarded a further two spot kicks. Among the referees was Ibrahim Chaibou from Niger, already suspended by FIFA for involvement in other match-fixing allegations in Bahrain and Nigeria."[43] FIFA security chief Chris Eaton confidently stated that there was no indication that any actual World Cup matches were tampered with, but given Lord Triesman's statement about Spanish soccer officials and the fact that these South African games leading up to the World Cup were rigged, can fans really be so certain?

For many U.S. sports fans, this information should be a roaring warning siren accompanied by flashing red lights. Games—not really "games," but championship-caliber soccer matches on the world's great-est stage—have been fixed and fixed quite recently. How is that possible? How is it that this can happen in soccer's equivalent of the Super Bowl, yet the likes of the NFL and NBA remain untarnished? As Hill wrote, "The amount of money in the Asian gambling market is simply too large not to start flooding into North American sports, even down to a very low level. It is already here in a small way. I have spoken to a number of professionals in the Major League Soccer (MLS). They told me of players working for gamblers—not fixing but just providing them with information, who was injured, who was getting on the bus, who was go-ing to play well. This is where it starts. It is what is known as 'a gateway crime,' and it means that in a few years, unless something is done to stop it, North America will have its own fixing scandals based on this new network of corruption."[44]

With FIFA beginning to wake from its intentional slumber and tak-ing a defensive stance against these Asian-based fixers, is there a danger that instead of abandoning their illegal pursuits these same fixers will simply leave soccer for other gambled-upon sports? Say, for instance, the NFL? Hill's response to this question was immediate: "Of course. The question is why wouldn't they? What's stopping them from doing it now? If you have a smart fixer living in Missouri, and he can make the fix and bet in Antigua, Costa Rica, or Singapore—it's just a couple of clicks of the mouse on the computer. That's the danger. It's not the Asian gangs coming here, it's Americans using the Asian sites to fix. The reason a lot of guys got caught in the past was because they were betting in Vegas. And they were idiots. But now, they just log onto the Internet. They don't bother betting in Las Vegas. They're going offshore and they just can't tell. There's no way to be able to tell what's going on there."

BASEBALL

The history of fixing baseball games dates back prior to the 1876 formation of the National League. As the sport became more organized in those formative years of Major League Baseball, the *New York Times* wrote, "The aim of baseball is to employ professional players to perspire in public for the benefit of gamblers."[1] Though the league made a half-hearted effort to curtail the practice, posting "no gambling" signs within stadiums, gamblers at the ballparks bet on everything: balls, strikes, hits, runs, errors, and wins. It should come as no surprise then that these same gamblers would soon extend their reach onto the playing field to ensure their wagers were made good.

Dubbed the "father of baseball," Harry Chadwick was one of the game's earliest proponents. Among the many refinements he brought to the game, Chadwick is credited with inventing the box score (to the delight of Sabermetrics disciples and fantasy baseball fans everywhere). But by 1876, he was crusading against the corruption recognizable within the game. He wrote, "Baseball has fallen. Yes, the national game has become degraded. At certain match games, large amounts of money changed hands among the spectators. A noted New York club is said to have sold the results of a match. Barked chins and broken fingers may be easily mended, but a disfigured reputation may never be entirely repaired. Once more, abandon the bat, boys, if you cannot keep the game pure."[2] Chadwick's plea fell on deaf ears.

The fevered pitch of gambling and game fixing in baseball reached a mighty crescendo in 1919 when the Chicago White Sox threw the World Series to the Cincinnati Reds. "The Black Sox scandal is not just a riddle wrapped in an enigma inside a mystery. It is a labyrinth of fixers, double-crosses, cover-ups, and a con so big, so audacious, it nearly ruined professional baseball. And manipulating it *all* was Arnold Rothstein."[3] Rothstein pulled off the greatest (known) fix in sports history. Yet, "It was not the perfect crime. Perfect crimes require discretion and intelligence. In 1919, so many players and gamblers flaunted their actions that suspicions surfaced almost immediately. But nearly a year passed before baseball and civil authorities exposed the plot."[4]

Why does this event matter nearly one hundred years after the fact? While there is no doubt the aftermath changed the face of professional baseball, the real intrigue lies in how Rothstein, and to a certain extent the members of the Black Sox who did his dirty work, got away with it.

The fact of the matter is MLB's reaction to the fixing of the 1919 World Series was not much different from the NBA's handling of the Tim Donaghy scandal in 2007. Not only did baseball itself cover up facts, but the media played along attempting to keep the league's good standing intact. This had actually been an unwritten agreement between the two for decades. The men who ran baseball knew there were serious integrity issues within the sport. Gamblers openly talked about which players or umpires they controlled and which games had been rigged. Sportswriters of the era weren't naïve to these issues either, yet they kept these tales under their hat. Even prior to the first pitch of the 1919

World Series—which happened to be a beanball thrown by White Sox ace Eddie Cicotte signifying to gamblers that the fix was in—there were substantial rumors that the players had been bought. "...With the sports pages full of conspiracy theories, with sportswriters and fans wondering if this or that gambler or syndicate was financing the fix, the Brain [Rothstein] began to think that all those loose lips could float his boat. As Rothstein put it, 'If a girl goes to bed with nine guys, who's going to believe her when she says the tenth one's the father?'"[5] By the end of Game 1, many who had such suspicions felt justified. This information trickled up to White Sox owner Charles Comiskey as well as both League presidents, but no one took action to stop the Series once in motion.

Despite baseball's inaction, Chicago sportswriter Hugh Fullerton refused to let the story fade. He attempted to expose the World Series for what it was—outright fixed. His effort wasn't met with great applause. His own paper, the *Chicago Herald and Examiner*, refused to publish his discoveries. He was forced to run the piece in the *New York World*. Even as the evidence mounted, *Sporting News* editor Earl Obenshain ridiculed Fullerton's accurate depiction of the fix, writing in part, "Comiskey has met that by offering $10,000 [it was actually $20,000] for any sort of clue that will bear out such a charge. He might have well offered a million. There will be no takers because there is no such evidence, except in the mucky minds of stinkers who—because they are crooked—think all the rest of the world can't play straight."

Through an odd series of events, including the attempt to fix a 1920 Chicago Cubs-Philadelphia Phillies game, the eight members of the White Sox were finally exposed and brought to court. The problem was no one knew exactly what crime with which to charge them. "No Illinois statute prohibited fixing sporting events, so authorities charged them with conspiracy to defraud bettors [in the case of Chicago resident Charles Nims who lost $250 betting on the Sox] and players [in the form of catcher Ray Schalk who did not participate in the fix], and to injure the business of Comiskey and the American League. If found guilty, they faced up to $2,000 in fines and five years in jail."[6] To the rescue came Rothstein's lawyer, William Fallon. Known as "the Great Mouthpiece," Fallon represented two of the gamblers accused of paying the players to throw the Series, yet his arguments easily applied to everyone charged. He told the court, "The men [the Black Sox and gamblers] undoubtedly are morally reprehensible, but it is my opinion that no crime has been committed. I consider the conspiracy indictment invalid as 'conspiracy to commit an illegal act' means nothing unless you can prove that throwing a ball game is an illegal act. This I am prepared to doubt. If the gamblers who are said to have fixed this series are not profiting by an illegal act, they cannot be prosecuted as such. Profiting as such is not an indictable offense."[7] Strangely, Comiskey himself funded the players' defense for fear of losing a large chunk of his 1921 starting lineup. His lawyer even made the argument that nowhere in the players' contracts did it stipulate they were paid to win. They were merely paid to play. Winning a game was, in a sense, accidental and inconsequential.

Ultimately the players won their court case, celebrating with jurors at a local restaurant after their acquittal. But baseball had a different message for the eight. Having hired federal judge Kenesaw Mountain Landis as baseball's first commissioner in an effort to clean up the sport (publicly at least), Landis banned the eight White Sox from baseball for life with the words "They can't come back. The doors are closed to them for good. The most scandalous chapter in the game's history is closed." Landis went further with his ruling, basically detailing baseball's current anti-gambling rule: "No player who throws a ball game, no player that undertakes or promises to throw a ball game, no player that sits in confidence with a bunch of crooked players and gamblers where the ways and means of throwing a ball game are discussed and does not promptly tell his club about it, will ever play professional baseball."

The biggest "tragedy" to come out of the 1919 Black Sox scandal for many baseball fans is that "Shoeless Joe" Jackson, the team's biggest star, has been banned from the National Baseball Hall of Fame due to his participation in the scheme. Apologists can cry about this all they want. Jackson took $10,000 from the gamblers in bribe money. He signed a confession admitting this, leading to the classic, if false, line "Say it ain't so, Joe." It's true his play during the Series didn't appear overtly suspect. In fact, his professional baseball career was stellar. But Shoeless Joe committed the game's cardinal sin: he associated with gamblers and agreed to fix a ball game. The problem is if Jackson can be banned from the Hall of Fame for these actions, why haven't some others also been kept out?

OTHER WORLD SERIES FIXES

The first World Series was played in 1903. The first attempt to fix a World Series, not so coincidentally, was in 1903. Boston Red Sox catcher Lou Criger, falsely believing he was on his deathbed, confessed to American League president Ban Johnson in 1923 that he was approached by a gambler before the start of the 1903 World Series and offered $12,000 to throw it. Criger claimed he refused the bribe, and though he did commit three errors during the Series, his Boston team beat Pittsburgh five games to three.

There was no World Series played in 1904, but immediately upon its revival in 1905, there was talk of it being fixed as well. At the center of this controversy was Philadelphia Athletics pitcher George "Rube" Waddell who posted a phenomenal 1905 season with a record of 26–11 and a 1.48 Earned Run Average (ERA). The story defending Waddell states that on September 7, Waddell injured his pitching shoulder when he tripped over some luggage at a train station (or more believably, the injury was the result of some friendly team horseplay that turned into a near brawl). A month later when the World Series was set to begin, Waddell's arm still hadn't recovered. He was unable to pitch in the Series and as a result the New York Giants won four games to one. Simple, no? But there are a few holes in this tale, the biggest being that Waddell's arm was good enough to pitch in three separate games after the injury occurred, on September 27, October 6, and October 7 with the start of the Series coming on October 9. Waddell also pitched in a few exhibition games immediately after the Series' conclusion.

The accusations against Waddell stemmed primarily from a 1920 newspaper article written by former owner and president of the Philadelphia Phillies, Horace Fogel. He claimed that "Little Tim" Sullivan (Arnold Rothstein's predecessor) offered Waddell $17,000 to sit out the

Series. This one-time offer amounted to much more than Waddell's seasonal salary under A's owner/manager Connie Mack. And though Waddell wasn't nicknamed "Rube" for nothing (he had a drinking problem, was always borrowing money, and liked to chase fire trucks), Fogel wrote that Waddell was smart enough to take $500 from Sullivan as a down payment. He also added that three of Waddell's teammates later confronted the pitcher about his alleged injury, and that Rube cracked, admitting he took the bribe to sit out. Others in the press doubted Fogel's story, considering it came 15 years after the fact. Some even publicly attacked him for writing the piece. The truth behind the incident remains unresolved, yet it did not stop Waddell from being inducted into the Hall of Fame in 1946.

Skipping ahead seven years, the 1912 World Series between the Boston Red Sox and New York Giants was marred by one highly suspect game. Set to clinch the Series in Fenway Park, the Red Sox felt confident with their ace "Smoky" Joe Wood on the hill as he posted a 34–5 record that season. He lasted an inning. Wood was far from his usual "smoking" self, lobbing in meatballs and allowing six easy runs on seven hits. Wood even pitched out of a full windup with runners on base, allowing the Giants to pull off a double steal. As guilty as Wood appeared that day, he wasn't alone. Star outfielder Tris Speaker was also apparently in on the fix. When Wood threw an errant pickoff throw to second base into center field, the ball somehow squirted past Speaker in center as well. The right fielder had to track it down while Giants runners circled the bases. The Red Sox lost the game 11–4, but won the World Series in extra innings the next day 3–2—with Wood getting the win in relief. Smoky Joe wouldn't earn enshrinement in the Hall of Fame (perhaps rightly so), but Tris Speaker would. A few years after this game, these two players would run a similar con with another Hall of Fame member, Ty Cobb.

Though Arnold Rothstein receives the lion's share of the credit for the 1919 World Series fix, he didn't act entirely alone. One of the other prominent names associated on the gambling end was that of Joseph J. "Sport" Sullivan. Sullivan was a prominent Boston bookmaker, and perhaps had fixed World Series games before. "Sport knew all about baseball. Some even said he had fixed the 1914 Philadelphia Athletics-Boston Braves World Series. Everyone had expected an easy Athletics triumph, but the upstart Braves swept four straight."[8] These were the "Miracle" Braves of 1914, but the true miracle may have been how the members of the Athletics got away with dumping this Series scot-free. While many blame the cheap ways of Charles Comiskey for pushing the eight members of the White Sox into fixing the 1919 World Series, similar actions by A's owner Connie Mack may have triggered his players to do the same. The A's batted a whopping .172 for the Series, and their pitching staff—led by future Hall of Famers Eddie Plank, "Chief" Bender and Herb Pennock—posted a combined ERA that more than doubled that of the Braves' staff. This tale may be truer than baseball purists would like to believe. Evidence lies in the fact that Mack quickly traded away or sold nearly the entire 1914 roster, an act which decimated the franchise for more than a decade, but may have rid him of a team full of cheats.

Sullivan has also been eyed for influencing both the 1917 and 1918 World Series. Oddly, the champions of the 1917 World Series were the Chicago White Sox whose roster was comprised of mostly the same players who would soon be labeled the Black Sox. Taking the loss were the New York Giants, but taking the heat was their third baseman, Heinie Zimmerman. Zimmerman was accused of misplaying a crucial rundown, allowing the winning run to score in what would become the deciding Game 6. Afterward he had to defend himself against allegations of fixing the Series (his .125 batting average didn't help). The disputed play may not have been completely Zimmerman's fault, but it did not help his reputation when Commissioner Landis barred him from baseball a few years later for a career's worth of conduct detrimental to the game.

The case of the 1918 World Series between the Chicago Cubs and Boston Red Sox may have more credence. In 2011, the Chicago History Museum obtained the long-lost 1920 court deposition of Black Sox pitcher Eddie Cicotte. In it, he claimed in a roundabout way that his teammates got the idea to throw the World Series from their crosstown rivals the Cubs, who had done so the year before. Cicotte offered no specifics in his statements, only rumors. Yet he said the White Sox players were clearly in the know about the Cubs tanking. If Sport Sullivan was truly behind the fix, the players' knowledge about it would make sense as he was close friends with Black Sox first baseman "Chick" Gandil.

Bribing members of the Cubs would have been easy given the times. The 1918 baseball season had been shortened due to World War I and attendance had shrunk along with salaries. Players even threatened to strike during the Series due to low gate receipts. In each of the four games the Red Sox won, the margin of victory was a mere one run. Yet one run is fairly easy to give away without looking overly guilty. In this case, three Chicago Cubs players can be questioned: outfielder Max Flack and pitchers "Hippo" Vaughn and "Shufflin'" Phil Douglas. Flack and Douglas each committed errors that led to game-winning runs for the Red Sox (Douglas actually only pitched one inning in the entire Series, yet that inning cost the Cubs Game 4). Douglas was later barred from baseball when in 1922, as a member of the New York Giants, he attempted to sell his services to the St. Louis Cardinals and "disappear," hurting the Giants' chance at winning the pennant while aiding the Cardinals. It's hard to knock Vaughn as he did yeoman's work in the Series for the Cubs, pitching three complete games. Yet in his 27 innings, he walked 17 batters (the Red Sox walked only 18 Cubs in the entire six-game Series) and managed to lose two of those three starts even though his ERA was 1.00. Still, Cicotte's once-lost deposition adds credence to the notion the Cubs dumped the Series to line their pockets.

"HALL OF FAMERS"

In the discussion of potentially fixed World Series games, an important name was omitted. That would be John J. McGraw, Hall of Fame player and manager. McGraw was a rough-and-tumble player turned hard-ass manager who liked his baseball played the same way. He also openly wagered on baseball games. He was arrested for gambling in public in 1904 and a year later placed a winning $400 bet on his New York Giants to beat the Philadelphia Athletics in the 1905 World Series (the same Series "Rube" Waddell sat out). Though he was hardly alone given the culture of the game in that era, the company McGraw kept was extremely suspect. His bookie was none other than Arnold Rothstein. The only consolation in all of this is that McGraw (reportedly) only bet on his team to win. Of course, considering who his bookie was, McGraw *not* betting on a certain game would have been an excellent tip for Rothstein to exploit.

Though the questionable performance of "Smoky" Joe Wood and Tris Speaker in the 1912 World Series has been overlooked, another game-fixing incident involving these two has gained much more attention. The reason may be due to the fact that the legendary Ty Cobb was in on the plot. Very late in the 1919 season, Cobb's Detroit Tigers were playing the Cleveland Indians in a game meaningless to everyone but the Tigers. A win and they would finish third in the American League, earning each player a $500 bonus. With this in mind, Cobb and Tigers pitcher "Dutch" Leonard met with the Indians' Speaker and Wood under the Tigers Stadium stands to cut a deal. They agreed to dump the game to the Tigers with the four betting on the predetermined outcome. Sure enough, the Tigers won 9–5.

After the season ended, the players sent each other money through the mail to settle up on the agreement. But like many others in baseball, Leonard had grown to despise Cobb. By 1926, he decided to further soil Cobb's reputation by selling the letter detailing the pregame arrangement to the press. No newspaper wanted the scoop. Undeterred, Leonard took the letter to American League president Ban Johnson. The last thing Johnson wanted was another gambling scandal on the heels of the Black Sox. He met confidentially with Speaker and Cobb (Wood had since left baseball) and convinced both to retire on the spot. In exchange, the whole affair would be forgotten.

Much to Leonard's delight, the story didn't end there. Commissioner Landis was alerted to the situation. Angered that Johnson arranged this deal outside of his ultimate authority, Landis made the whole affair public. Johnson instantly reneged on his offer, announcing that Cobb and Speaker were henceforth banned from the American League. Landis then held a hearing on the incident. Cobb, Speaker, and Wood admitted to nothing. Behind closed doors, however, Cobb had much more to say. He threatened Landis, warning if he was banned from the game Cobb would publicize all of baseball's dirty secrets, including the entire truth about gambling and game fixing. Landis recognized this was no bluff; if anyone knew these details, it was Cobb. Two months after the hearing, Landis declared the players not guilty. Cobb and Speaker stepped right back onto the playing field for the 1927 and 1928 seasons before retiring on their own terms. They were openly welcomed to the Hall of Fame shortly thereafter.

At about the same time, longtime St. Louis Cardinals and then current New York Giants player-manager Rogers "Rajah" Hornsby was sued by a gambler for not paying nearly $100,000 owed from losing horse-racing wagers. The gambler lost the lawsuit, but the publicity cost Hornsby his job with the Giants, though not within baseball. He spent the next season in Boston, and then bounced around the league going from the Chicago Cubs to the Cardinals (again) and to the St. Louis Browns where he finished his career. Why did the future Hall of Famer, who hit over .400 in three different seasons, play with five different teams in ten years? Rajah couldn't stay away from the track. It wasn't a secret. "Commissioner Landis warned him a number of times that this was unacceptable; baseball couldn't afford any more gambling scandals. Hornsby ignored the warnings and Landis finally went public, telling the *Sporting News* that Hornsby's betting 'has gotten him into one scrape after another, cost him a fortune and several jobs, and he still hasn't got enough sense to stop it.' Hornsby responded by charging that Landis himself had recklessly gambled away baseball's money in the 1929 stock market crash."[9] While no league rule prevented him from betting on races, Landis and other owners worried Hornsby was gambling on more than just horses. A bookie for one sport was a bookie for them all.

Speaking of bookies, long after his playing days Hall of Fame pitcher Jay "Dizzy" Dean was investigated for his association with a nationally known bookmaker (and game-fixer Donald "Dice" Dawson—more on him later). Dean would only be named as an unindicted co-conspirator in the case, but his connection to gambling dated back to his playing days as a member of the St. Louis Cardinals. "In 1934, at the height of

Dean's career, National League president John Heydler hired detectives to shadow the pitcher. When this news leaked out, Heydler implausibly called it a 'routine precaution.'"[10] This was mere spin as suspicion about Dean's gambling habits was rampant. A year after retiring in 1947 the Diz was called before new MLB commissioner A.B. "Happy" Chandler. Dean confessed he had been gambling, but with a caveat that he had never bet on baseball. Chandler countered his denial with an interesting bit of information: Dean had contacted bookmakers for odds on baseball games. Perhaps caught in a lie, Dean claimed he did that for "friends" in Texas who were apparently incapable of picking up a phone themselves. Being finished with baseball, Dean was never reprimanded and entered the Hall of Fame in 1953.

One of the caveats in Commissioner Landis' original banishment of the Black Sox was that players didn't have to participate in fixing a game; they would be kicked out of baseball merely for being in a room where such a plan was discussed if they then didn't inform the league. In other words, pick the wrong friends and a player might be looking for a new career. Remarkably, some of baseball's true legends have had very close mafia ties without a seeming care from the league. Does this mean such a player did a "favor" or two for these questionable friends? Not necessarily. But considering what is known about these associations, a closer look should be taken.

Hank Greenberg was the first Jewish sports superstar. As an outfielder and first baseman for the Detroit Tigers in the 1930s, Greenberg put up Hall of Fame numbers in a nine-year career broken up by distinguished service in World War II as a captain in the U.S. Army Air Force. Though it's hard to take anything away from him, Greenberg was admittedly very close friends with mobsters. The Purple Gang was a collection of Jewish hoodlums in the Detroit area who made a fortune smuggling booze over the Canadian border into the United States. At its head was Abe Bernstein. When Bernstein's brother was serving a life sentence for murder, Greenberg did Bernstein a personal favor. He brought the Army's exhibition baseball team to the prison to play a game versus the prison team. Still active in the military, Greenberg did something unexpected—he suited up and played with the prisoners alongside

Bernstein's murdering brother.[11] Was this a convictable offense in the eyes of MLB? Apparently not. Are Greenberg's mob ties interesting? Quite.

Another mobbed-up superstar was the Marilyn Monroe-marrying, coffee maker-pushing, New York Yankees hero "Joltin'" Joe DiMaggio. While both the Yankees and DiMaggio sold his clean, wholesome image, it was more of a façade than reality. DiMaggio biographer Ben Cramer wrote that murdering mobster Joe Adonis, who built a Broadway-based criminal empire worth millions, supplied DiMaggio with hookers in each city the Yankees visited (DiMaggio wasn't the only player to get such special treatment). Another close buddy of DiMaggio's was Frank Costello, the head of the National Crime Syndicate until nearly assassinated in 1956. Costello set up a mob-financed "trust fund" for Joltin' Joe which supposedly existed only to get DiMaggio to frequent certain mob-controlled nightclubs.

The reason DiMaggio might have been hard up for drinking money stemmed from the lack of sports agents in 1940. At this time, players were usually on their own to negotiate their contracts (though they didn't have much leeway given how baseball's reserve clause locked players to teams). DiMaggio attempted to use his growing star power to leverage more from the Yankees, and brought in a man by the name of Joe Gould to get it. Gould was a well-known boxing manager, but more importantly to Commissioner Landis, Gould was a well-known baseball bettor. Gould never attempted to earn a cent representing DiMaggio, so MLB let the matter slide. Was DiMaggio's connection with a baseball gambler ever investigated? Not likely.

After DiMaggio retired from baseball, the FBI finally called. The Bureau was interested in another DiMaggio friend, Albert "The Mad Hatter" Anastasia, a member of the mafia's Murder, Incorporated whose roster included Frankie Carbo. Despite historically strong mob ties, DiMaggio claimed he had just met Anastasia two weeks before the Mad Hatter was gunned down in a barbershop. DiMaggio then admitted to the FBI he had recently befriended two well-known gamblers, one of which, Joseph Silesi, offered DiMaggio a chance to front a Cuban gambling operation. This operation was linked to Miami-based mob boss Santos Trafficante. Whether DiMaggio knew this or not is irrelevant as he told the FBI he turned down the offer because he didn't want to tarnish his image with the nation's youth.

Another Yankees great, Mickey Mantle, possessed a past that few fans have ever heard about. In his FBI file exists a summary sent "per request of John D. Ehrlichman, Counsel to the President [Nixon]" on July 23, 1969. It does not present The Mick in the best of lights.

"Mickey Mantle, former well-known baseball player of the New York Yankees, has not been the subject of an investigation by the FBI. However, our files reveal that information received in June, 1956, indicated that Mickey Mantle was 'blackmailed' for $15,000 after being found in a compromising situation with a married woman. Mr. Mantle subsequently denied ever having been caught in a compromising situation. Mr. Mantle readily admitted that he had 'shacked up' with many girls in New York City, but stated that he has never been caught.

"A confidential source, who has furnished reliable information in the past, advised in June, 1957, that a very prominent Washington, D.C., area gambler and bookmaker arranged dates for members of the New York Yankees baseball club at a Washington, D.C., house of prostitution. Allegedly, Mr. Mantle was one of the members of the team who was entertained at this house of prostitution.

"In February, 1962, it was alleged that an individual, described as a Dallas, Texas, playboy, night club operator and former boyfriend of a notorious Dallas stripper, was purchasing the University Club, Dallas, Texas, from a former Dallas gambler. It was further noted that the University Club was a private night club, and that Mickey Mantle of the New York Yankees was one of the individuals financially backing this purchase.

"In January, 1963, a confidential source, of unknown reliability, advised that a well-known Dallas, Texas, gambler, who frequently made 'heavy bets' on professional football games and other athletic contests, would make a number of telephone calls to various professional athletes to obtain information concerning certain games. Some of the professional athletes contacted by this individual allegedly included Mickey Mantle of the New York Yankees."

This sordid history, perhaps only known by the FBI and not MLB, was not the cause for Mantle's banishment from baseball in 1983. Well after his playing days, Mantle was hired as a meet-and-greet goodwill ambassador at the Claridge Casino in Atlantic City. Despite the innocence of his position at the casino, as sports gambling was illegal in New Jersey, MLB commissioner Bowie Kuhn wanted to keep baseball's anti-gambling rule strictly enforced. He presented Mantle with an ultimatum: baseball or the casino. Mantle chose the job, and Kuhn followed through on his threat, kicking The Mick out of the game. This ejection, which was rescinded in 1985, never eliminated Mantle from the Hall of Fame which he had entered in 1974.

Mantle and DiMaggio were not the only ones with seedy relationships. In 1963, the FBI learned that the undesirable associations of members of the Kansas City Athletics caused American League president (and former player) Joe Cronin to issue "an edict forbidding Kansas City baseball players and visiting American League baseball players to frequent the following bars and night clubs in the Greater Kansas City area." The list included eight establishments, four of which were within two blocks of each other. As the FBI memo explained, "Kansas City Athletics officials have indicated that the reason for the above mentioned edict is to forestall American League baseball players frequenting these places because of this reputation of either being owned or dominated by Kansas City hoodlum figures." An A's official clarified that "this was done by the ball club because of 'personal escapades' indulged in by the ball players, and not their association with gamblers." However, it was known that gamblers also frequented these places with one, Gigi's Lounge, considered to be "a 'spot' where bookmaking on sporting events took place and 'payoffs' allegedly were handled." Interestingly, A's owner Charles O. Finley "offered to buy this bar [Gigi's Lounge] for a substantial sum of money," going so far as to host the current owner in his personal press box during A's games on numerous occasions. Despite it being labeled a "gathering place for bettors and bookies in Kansas City"

by the FBI, both Finley and A's general manager Pat Friday were known to frequent Gigi's Lounge prior to the offer to purchase. So why was it off limits to players and not management? Apparently much in baseball operated under the philosophy of "do as I say, not as I do."

But Finley was actually quite suspect himself. In 1963, the *Kansas City Star* investigated the A's owner due to his fight with the city to move the team to Oakland (which he eventually did in 1968). Much of the dirt the paper dug up on Finley—which was done as a way to blackmail him to either keep the A's in Kansas City or outright sell the franchise— wound up in the FBI's files. Though "the *Kansas City Star* does not currently possess enough substantial information to support a subpoena of Finley or his General Manager, Pat Friday, before a federal grand jury in Kansas City to question them concerning gambling activities," there was plenty of dirty laundry to report. The FBI spoke to two reporters from the paper who had in turn contacted many people within the baseball world about Finley. The Bureau wrote, "Finley has a reputation among other owners and baseball personages as a gambler. Shortly after his purchase of the Athletics about three years ago, Finley made a statement in the presence of [redacted] that he had a $5,000 bet that the Athletics would finish higher than sixth in the League standings." Other owners, including the legendary Bill Veeck, were apparently suspicious of Finley. "Veeck is alleged to have expressed distrust of Finley and to have posed the possibility that Finley might be a front for other unknown investors in this ball club. Veeck allegedly stated Finley was the only baseball owner he had ever known whose source of funds was an apparent mystery."

One owner who had no issue with Finley was New York Yankees co-owner Del Webb. Recognize that name? It used to be emblazoned above Del Webb's The Mint casino in Las Vegas (now part of the Horseshoe), of which he assumed ownership in 1961 while still controlling the Yankees. Webb was a building contractor mostly known for founding the retirement community Sun City in Arizona, but he also built the Poston War Relocation Center in Arizona which interned several thousand Japanese-Americans during World War II, the Las Vegas Flamingo (now the Flamingo Hilton) for mobster Bugsy Siegel, and the Sahara hotel/

casino in Las Vegas. Webb was also contracted by Finley to build the A's new stadium in Oakland. Missouri senator Stuart Symington contacted Webb and told him if he continued to support the A's relocation efforts, Symington "would support antitrust action against the baseball leagues." Despite the threat, the Yankees still backed the A's move to Oakland.

Finley had other questionable associations as well. The most notorious for the FBI was Carl "Cork" Civella. Civella was labeled simply as a "local hoodlum figure" in this FBI report, but he was much more than that. Civella's brother Nicholas was the head of the Kansas City mob. The brothers must have been baseball fans as both were tailed by the FBI while attending the 1968 World Series played between the St. Louis Cardinals and the Detroit Tigers. In 1977, Nicholas was sentenced to prison on charges of illegal gambling, stemming in part from a $40,000 bet on Super Bowl IV played between the Minnesota Vikings and his hometown Kansas City Chiefs. Around this same time, Carl would assume control of the mob. The fear of Finley's association with Civella wasn't what one would assume, however. Kansas City police chief Clarence Kelly told the FBI "he felt it was a distinct possibility that Finley might desire Civella or criminal associates of the Civellas to cause damage to the facilities at the Kansas City Municipal Stadium which [in] fact would furnish Finley with an excuse to terminate discussions with city officials for leasing the stadium." Police chief Kelly forwarded this information to MLB commissioner Ford Frick who in turn discussed it with Kansas City mayor Ilus Davis. All of this appeared rather interesting, but on March 2, 1964, the FBI was informed that "due to the agreement reached between Charles O. Finley, President of the Kansas City Athletics, and the City of Kansas City in respect to the lease on the Kansas City Municipal Stadium, surveillances on the stadium which had been previously instituted had been discontinued."

Perhaps the king of the "undesirable associations" was Leo "the Lip" Durocher, who has the honor of being the only MLB manager (or player for that matter) suspended for the friends he kept. Durocher reached the majors as a light-hitting infielder, then expanded his repertoire to include craps, poker, and pool hustling. His gambling pals and antics didn't ingratiate him with his Yankees' teammates (including Babe Ruth). Prior

to the 1929 season, "his teammates had, essentially, turned against him in full force. They started to talk about him, not only among themselves but to the writers. They told reporters that he hung out with gamblers, including the infamous Meyer Boston. Leo was accused of every crime in the book. If he met friends at the clubhouse gate, they were gamblers. If he was seen signing autographs—and he loved to—it was part of some slimy underhanded transaction."[12] After two years in New York, the Yankees tired of Durocher and shipped him to the Reds. "In Cincinnati, Leo found himself virtually in the center of the gambling capital of America. He was a short gallop from northern Kentucky, where crap games, bookie joints, casino gambling, and nightclubs flourished. And he loved the action across the river in Covington. There he befriended a legendary Covington gambler named Sleepout Louie, along with Cigar Charley and the Dancer. In later years he regularly visited them even after he had joined the Cardinals and then the Dodgers."[13]

By the time Durocher landed in Brooklyn as a player-manager for the Dodgers, his gambling habits had not subsided. "Leo was out of control. [Winning] the [1941] pennant had overshadowed [Dodgers president and GM Larry] MacPhail's disgust with Leo's gambling and host of unsavory locker room visits. And so Leo's annual dance at the end of a rope was about to begin. Year in, year out, no matter how well the Dodgers had played, there was always some question whether Leo would be back the next year."[14] Winning made Durocher's sins much more tolerable, and as a manager he was successful, though his gambling ways rubbed off on his players. The following year, in 1942, "Leo was involved in high-stakes card games....MacPhail, though, was no respecter of tradition and certainly not of Durocher's feelings. Before the Dodgers went into St. Louis for a four-game series in August, bringing in a 7½-game lead, MacPhail called the players up to the Press Club for an informal get-together, and he started to hit the hard stuff. He was talkative. He told the team he was unhappy with the way they'd been playing lately and he was unhappy with the gambling. He said they had become smug. They weren't hustling. Their 10½-game lead had shrunk thanks to a poor home series against Philadelphia. And now they were headed for St. Louis. 'I'll bet you two hundred bucks right now we'll win this thing by eight games,' blurted out [Dodgers outfielder] Dixie Walker. It was an incredible statement. After all that MacPhail had railed against—the gambling, the smugness—here was Walker betting his own boss. MacPhail roared out of the clubhouse."[15] MacPhail should've taken the bet. The Dodgers blew their lead and finished in second.

Every year Durocher's gambling cropped up, yet he remained entrenched in baseball. In 1943, "Both [Dodgers co-owner Jim] Mulvey and National League president Frick were worried about the Dodgers' behavior under Durocher. It was becoming tiresome, at the very least, to keep fining the guy for beanballs, for cursing out umpires, for agitating the opposition. Worse, the locker room was an open sewer. Gambling of all sorts went on there: craps, card playing, and horse betting. Bookies roamed the clubhouse....One of the bookmakers was Memphis Engelberg, a well-known New York character. He not only touted horses to the players, he booked their bets. [Legendary Dodgers announcer] Red Barber recalled, 'Clubhouse doors could be shut at times to newspapermen but never to Memphis, or George Raft or Danny Kaye or anybody else from Broadway or Hollywood. Leo gambled and therefore was in no position to stop gambling on the ball club.'"[16]

Three years later MLB had reached its breaking point. In 1946, Commissioner Chandler warned Durocher to cut ties with all of the unsavory characters he hung around. Durocher's pals included actor George Raft, his roommate. Raft made a name for himself portraying gangsters, something he knew a great deal about, since, like Durocher, he counted several real-life mobsters as friends. Durocher often was seen in the company of Bugsy Siegel and Joe Adonis (Joe DiMaggio's friend) as well as gambler Memphis Engelberg and Connie Immerman, who had run the Cotton Club in Harlem and was at that time running a casino in Havana, Cuba, likely for Lucky Luciano. Remarkably, Durocher heeded Chandler's warning...until he witnessed MacPhail entertaining a pair of well-known gamblers in his private box during a spring training game (for the record, MacPhail did own race horses). This incensed Durocher and he brought the matter to Chandler. Chandler promptly held a hearing on the state of gambling in baseball. Its conclusion? Suspend Durocher—and only Durocher—for the 1947 season due to "conduct not in the best interest of baseball." Durocher was not suspended for gam-

202

bling despite his history, just for his undesirable associations.

Upon returning in 1948, Durocher mended his ways…at least in the public's eye. But no one forgot his past, especially members of the baseball world. Some 20 years later, Durocher found himself managing the Chicago Cubs. Infamously, in 1969, the Cubs lost 17 of their last 25 games, blowing a seven-game lead over the New York Mets to lose the National League East division. Some wondered if the rise of the "Miracle Mets" wasn't truly miraculous, but the result of something more nefarious. "Newspaper reporters wondered whether Leo was gambling on baseball. They had even heard reports he had gambled against his own team, and that some odd managerial moves were (in retrospect) suspicious. It ended up just talk, and never got beyond that. But some people in the commissioner's office wondered."[17] This sort of speculation haunted Durocher given both his open gambling and mafia relationships. It nearly cost him induction into the Hall of Fame, but the veteran's committee granted him a reprieve, honoring Durocher with induction in 1994.

Durocher wasn't the only Dodgers manager with these sorts of questionable relationships. When MLB commissioner Peter Ueberroth reinstated Mickey Mantle, it didn't come without a warning to all of baseball. Gambling, and related associations, would not be tolerated. "But Ueberroth's strong words failed to prevent [Los Angeles] Dodgers manager Tommy Lasorda from hobnobbing openly with Joseph Peter DeCarlis, a.k.a. Joe DiCarlo, a reputed associate of the late L.A. bookmaker and organized crime figure Mickey Cohen. In a 1982 hearing before the New Jersey Casino Control Commission, a casino security file was introduced that identified DiCarlo, who has worked as an entertainment agent and night club manager, as having allegedly provided organized crime with prostitutes and associated with reputed bookmakers. DiCarlo has been a frequent visitor to Lasorda's Dodger Stadium office and was listed as a bona fide Lasorda pal in the acknowledgments of his 1985 autobiography *The Artful Dodger*.

"Years ago commissioner Happy Chandler suspended Leo Durocher when he couldn't get him to quit hanging around with known gamblers.

When Lasorda was asked by [*Sports Illustrated*] about DiCarlo, he said that he had never heard a peep about the man from baseball's security force or from anybody else. 'I don't know anything about him.' Lasorda insisted. 'Nothing about his past. Not until you told me. I'll not see him again.' Informed of Lasorda's relationship with DiCarlo, baseball's security director, Harry Gibbs, expressed surprise. 'Sure it bothers me, if it's true,' Gibbs said. 'I'll have to look into it.'

"Contacted by [*Sports Illustrated*'s] Greg Kelly, DiCarlo called Lasorda 'a friend of mine.' He indicated that he had also visited at the ball park with Dodger players. Insisting that there was no reason for concern about his relationship with baseball personnel, DiCarlo claimed that he had never been convicted of any crime. When Kelly noted that his record showed a 1948 conviction and prison term for mail theft, DiCarlo said. 'Oh, yes, I remember that.' He also acknowledged having socialized with Mickey Cohen and possibly other bookmakers. But he emphatically denied any involvement in prostitution. And, he said, '[Lasorda] is one of the straightest guys in the world. To say he's tainted for knowing me, that's wrong, 1,000 percent wrong.'

"The question remains why baseball didn't have the same knowledge of the allegations against DiCarlo that the casino industry had. 'It's impossible to know everybody's background,' Gibbs said. 'We do our best.'"[18]

How good was MLB's "best"? Nowhere near good enough. The FBI examined another member of the Dodgers because of his friendship with a high-ranking member of organized crime. In this instance, there was no mention of game fixing, but there were also no details regarding MLB's knowledge of these connections. The Dodger was tied to John Phillip Cerone, a.k.a. "Jackie the Lackey," "underboss of the Chicago family of La Cosa Nostra (LCN) and [who] has served as an upper echelon leader for decades." Cerone's past crimes included arrests for both illegal gambling and bookmaking, and in 1986 he was convicted for his part in skimming $2 million from a Las Vegas casino. The Dodger and Cerone met at Morton's Steak House when the team was in Chicago to play the Cubs in July 1984. This Dodger, "among other sports figures"

according to the FBI, was associated with the Italian-American Sports Hall of Fame (IASHF) in Elmwood Park, IL. In fact, three members of the 1984 Los Angeles Dodgers are enshrined in what's now named the National Italian-American Sports Hall of Fame: manager Tommy Lasorda, third-base coach (and former Chicago Cubs coach) Joey Amalfitano, and catcher Mike Scioscia. As for Cerone, he was on the IASHF's "building foundation committee."

The FBI did admit, "Aside from the fact that numerous Chicago hoodlum figures have been observed at this location, there is no information to indicate the IASHF is involved or used for any criminal activity." So what? If Major League Baseball was serious about the associations of its players and coaches with "undesirables," the fact that an active member of one of its franchises was eating dinner with the underboss of the Chicago mob should have raised numerous red flags. It did for the FBI. Even though the Bureau assumed the Dodger would claim his affiliation with the IASHF as how he knew Cerone, he was still to be questioned. Interviewed on August 17 by the same agent who gave the sports bribery presentation to the team in spring training, the Dodger admitted knowing Cerone, but only through the IASHF as predicted. He stated that he and Cerone were simply discussing entertainment for an upcoming fundraising banquet. The file never reveals whether the Dodger knew what sort of man Cerone truly was, but with this admission, the FBI let the matter drop. As for MLB, it was likely one of hundreds of such associations that were never properly investigated.

FBI INVESTIGATIONS

Baseball clings to its proclamation that no game has been fixed since the 1919 World Series. When Commissioner Landis dropped the hammer on the Black Sox, it forever severed the ties between gamblers and players. No one within the game dared approach that hard-drawn line again. The consequences—banishment—were too much to risk.

Yet there are known and even previously unknown incidents hidden in baseball's past in which players overstepped the boundary MLB

claims has never been crossed. Fans have simply been kept ignorant of these indiscretions. Some are merely the release of inside information, handed out knowingly, however, for gambling purposes. Others are clear approaches made to players for the express purpose of fixing a baseball game.

Occasionally, these lapses in judgment were innocuous. Former head of the Stardust sports book Scott Schettler landed his son a position as batboy for the visitor's clubhouse in Dodger Stadium in the mid-1980s. Schettler himself became good friends with the clubhouse manager who also happened to work in the Stardust's race book in the off-season (apparently MLB didn't mind this conflict of interest). But more to the point, Schettler related, "For those who remember 'the live ball controversy' when the totals began flying over one season, the thinking was the balls were 'live,' purposely being wound tighter than previously. They were jumping off the bats, balls were flying over the fences, and the totals were flying over. Everywhere but Dodger Stadium. The Dodger totals were staying under.

"One day, after that season was over, we're talking and my clubhouse friend tells me he saved the Dodgers a nice piece of change. They told him to dump all the old balls, about 3,500 of them, and begin using these new ones. He didn't do it; in good faith he kept the old balls in play and saved his employers money. On the other side, he cost a few players and bookmakers their money."[19] If a gambler possessed this information during that season, it would've been worth its weight in gold—literally. But apparently this situation was only learned after the fact.

Another member of the Los Angeles Dodgers, however, appeared to be giving away similar information during the regular season with the full knowledge of why it was sought. The FBI possessed an extremely valuable source based in Las Vegas of whom the Bureau wrote: "FOR THE INFORMATION OF ALL OFFICES, LAS VEGAS HAS NO REASON TO DOUBT THE INFORMATION FURNISHED BY THE SOURCE, AND IT IS NOTED THAT THIS SOURCE HAS FURNISHED AND CONTINUES TO FURNISH EXCELLENT

INFORMATION." [emphasis in original] What did this source reveal to the FBI? That a Dodgers pitcher was providing inside information to a Las Vegas-based gambler.

During the 1965 season, the gambler in question rented a hotel room at the Dunes in Las Vegas. The FBI later connected that room to a known New York City bookmaker named David Kossoff who had seven arrests for bookmaking between 1946 and 1963. On at least six occasions, the gambler called a left-handed starting pitcher on the L.A. Dodgers by the name of Claude Osteen. "During their conversations by long-distance phone, [redacted] would discuss [redacted] and the [redacted] and attitude of the Los Angeles Dodgers. Based on these telephone conversations, [redacted], accompanied by the source, would then proceed to the Rendezvous Race Book, Las Vegas, where he would either bet with or against the Dodgers."

The FBI traced these collect toll calls from the Dunes to the Sheraton Palace Hotel in San Francisco where the Dodgers often stayed when in town to play the Giants. The Dodgers were in fact there for a weekend series with the Giants in late August 1965, and "it was on 8/22/65, that the widely publicized incident between San Francisco Giants' [redacted] and Los Angeles Dodgers' [redacted] occurred, culminating with [redacted] for which [redacted] received a suspension for ten days and a fine." This "incident" was the infamous brawl between Giants pitcher Juan Marichal and Dodgers catcher John Roseboro (which demonstrates how controlling the FBI can be with their information). Taking their investigation a step further, the FBI checked with the National League to determine which hotels the Dodgers visited from July through the end of the 1965 season so they could track phone records to see if calls were made to Vegas during those times. This was necessary as the transmission of sports information across state lines for gambling purposes would have been a violation of federal law. It was essential for the case to connect Osteen with the gambler at the Dunes.

The Bureau learned that a popular place for teams to stay while in Pittsburgh was the Carlton House Hotel. There, the FBI made another connection between the Dunes gambler and other major-leaguers. Apparently, two other MLB pitchers—one from the Washington Senators, another from the Cincinnati Reds—may have had a similar relationship with the subject in question (though from the amount of redactions, exactly how these other two pitchers were connected is impossible to clarify). But this growing mound of information was enough for the FBI to bring in Osteen for a chat.

"Following the completion of the baseball schedule of the Los Angeles Dodgers, including any post-game activities, i.e. World Series, that Los Angeles Dodgers Pitcher [redacted] be discreetly interviewed by Special Agents of the FBI away from Dodgers management and premises in an effort to resolve any violation of Federal law. The purpose of waiting until the close of the season is to avert any possible charge that the FBI contributed in any way to a morale decline of the Dodgers' pennant chances or to the mental condition of [redacted] during this current pennant race [this would be the 1965 season in which the Dodgers won the World Series over the Minnesota Twins]. It is noted that information has been received that following the close of the season for the Los Angeles Dodgers, most of the team members will travel on tour in Japan." At that time, Osteen was to be shown a photo and asked if he knew the subject, how they met, etc. They would not bring up the known phone calls unless "he opens himself up to this line of questioning."

This questioning apparently never took place. Though the FBI's respected source witnessed the phone calls and the subsequent bets, phone records "failed to verify" their source's info. The FBI became worried that if Osteen said he didn't know the gambler, then no further questions could be asked. The Bureau wrote, "There appears to be little to be gained and much to lose by attempting these interviews. If both subjects made full admissions, we couldn't bring in any corroborating evidence whatsoever." Though the gambler was later convicted in New York in May 1966 to a year in prison for contempt of court (which at the time was under appeal), the FBI concluded, "Since we have no chance of winning anyway, this case should be closed without interview of either [redacted] and Los Angeles and Las Vegas are being so instructed."

Did MLB know about Osteen's apparent gambling assistance? If so, it did nothing about it publicly. A three-time All-Star, Osteen pitched in the majors from 1957 until 1975, winning 196 games before making the switch to coaching. Of course, the FBI wasn't in the habit of informing MLB (or any other league for that matter) about its activities. It's possible that Osteen —whether guilty or not—didn't even know he was under investigation. The FBI can be that stealthy, and Major League Baseball and its athletes may be that unaware.

A short time after the Osteen investigation, the FBI had another MLB pitcher in its sights. "As you know, allegations have been received by our Detroit office regarding the involvement of [redacted] Detroit Tigers professional baseball player, in gambling activities and [redacted] has acknowledged to Agents of our Detroit office that during 1967 he was a principal in a Flint, Michigan, bookmaking operation. This matter is currently before a Federal Grand Jury in Detroit. Detroit SAC [Special Agent in Charge] Stoddard called this morning to report that he had learned from [redacted — a former SAC], newly appointed [redacted] for Major League Baseball, that [redacted] will be brought before Baseball Commissioner [redacted] about 10:00 a.m. this morning and in all probability [redacted] will be suspended from baseball for at least one year."

This was how the FBI wrote up the case of Detroit Tigers pitcher Denny McLain. Since becoming the last pitcher to win 30 games in a season, McLain's life went into a steady decline. He had a gambling problem, one that the FBI briefly chronicled: "Source advised that [redacted] last month were flown in a private Lear jet from Detroit to Las Vegas, Nev., thereafter to [redacted] appearance in the [1966] All Star Game in St. Louis, Mo., and back to Las Vegas where [redacted] allegedly gambled for three days and nights in the gambling casinos in Las Vegas. Source stated that [redacted] allegedly lost a great deal of money in this unusual gambling visit to Las Vegas."

It was McLain himself who best described how he became a bookmaker while actively pitching for the Tigers. According to his biography *I Told You I Wasn't Perfect*, besides his baseball salary, McLain was earning $15,000-a-year deal from an endorsement deal with Pepsi as

well as having a $30,000 contract to play Hammond organs in the band he fronted. Yet, "I'd begun gambling pretty heavily on basketball and football with a guy named Ed Schober [the Detroit-area merchandising director for Pepsi]. Ed and I started placing our bets through [local bar] the Shorthorn's owner, a guy named Clyde Roberts....One day Roberts came over and said, 'Check it out. You're losing $200 to $300 a week on college and pro basketball. Since I know a lotta other guys who place a ton of action, why don't we start taking the action instead of giving all the money to the bookies?'

"I talked about it with Schober, and we came to the stunning conclusion that it made perfect sense—let us be the bookies. So there you had it—a 22-year-old 20-game winner and the director of merchandising for Pepsi of Michigan bankrolling a bookie operation. We'd make a fortune. We agreed to keep all bets to $100 or less, and Clyde would make certain that any bigger bets were cleared through Schober or me. Clyde also assured me that there would be no need to have mob ties because he had a guy who'd 'protect' the operation."[20]

To get the ball rolling, McLain handed over $4,000 for the group to work with. "Lo and behold, shock of shocks, we bolted out of the gate on a four- or five-week losing streak, and before I left for spring training in February 1967, I had to borrow another $3,000....Like a 20-game winner who felt he had the world by the balls, I was arrogant enough to call in some of my spring training bets from the pressroom in Lakeland. Our general manager, Jim Campbell, was tipped off by a sportswriter and called me into his office to ask if I was doing any betting. Campbell had me by the balls, and the best I could do was distort the truth and tell him I was just betting a little basketball but nothing of any significance. Would Campbell suspend a 20-game winner? Hell no. When you win 20 ball games, you can get away with just about anything. Campbell called me into his office and said, 'If you're going to gamble, Jesus Christ, don't do it in front of the writers.' I never placed a bet in the pressroom or locker room again, although I still studied the spreads, the scoring averages, free-throw percentages, and everything else down to their shoe sizes. God, I just loved everything about gambling, from picking teams to placing bets to watching the action. But the bookmaking dream team wasn't producing results….By midsummer I was down $15,000…."[21]

Come August, McLain wrote that he and Schober quit. At the same time he claimed to have left, a gambler wagered on a long shot in a horse race that won, paying $46,000. It is from this moment that three stories emerge. In his book, McLain wrote that he was forced to help pay off the debt which was settled for 20 cents on the dollar, about $8,000. An alternative version to this story—coming from no less a source than *Sports Illustrated*—claimed that the gambler went to the Detroit mob, and an enforcer crushed two of McLain's toes in order to get the money due. In late September 1967, McLain did in fact miss a start because of such an injury. When he came back to the mound for a must-win, pennant-clinching game, the Tigers lost as McLain barely lasted three innings. According to *Sports Illustrated*, the mob enforcer's brother had bet heavily against the Tigers in that game.

It wasn't until 1970, after both *Sports Illustrated* and *Penthouse* (of all publications) reported on McLain's bookmaking activities, that MLB caught on. Commissioner Kuhn suspended him indefinitely. "Kuhn said I'd been a 'dupe' and all *Sports Illustrated* could say for sure was that I owed some bad guys some money. But you could suspend hundreds of major leaguers for taking action or betting on sports other than baseball. Gambling is part of the baseball culture. We gambled at cards every day on the road. It just didn't add up to suspend me for half a season. When Kuhn had asked us about fixing games, Carpenter shot back at him, 'Bowie, the guy won 108 games in five years—do you really think he threw a game?' Since the fixing rumor was looking like a bogus witch-hunt, Carpenter thought that Kuhn should have allowed me back for the start of the season."[22] Kuhn held firm, but despite baseball's long-standing anti-gambling stance, McLain's suspension amounted to just three months.

The one version of this tale that neither McLain nor *Sports Illustrated* touched upon was the FBI's. "A Detroit informant has reported he is aware that [redacted — McLain] a prominent Detroit Tiger baseball [redacted — pitcher] has in the past **[redacted]** and was approximately **[redacted]** because of these activities. In addition, he stated that [redacted — McLain] lost considerable money immediately prior to and after the All Star baseball game in July and the informant also stated the Detroit baseball club paid off [redacted — McLain's] gambling debts." How much did the Tigers shell out for McLain? According to the FBI, approximately $40,000. Why? Besides protecting their two-time Cy Young Award-winning pitcher, the Tigers wanted "to avoid bad publicity nationally." Which outlet was correct? Ultimately, there's room for all three versions of this story to be true.

About this same time, the FBI became informed about a string of potential game-fixing scandals of which only one ever saw the light of day. The first dated from May 1971. It involved a gambler (or gamblers) in the Washington, D.C. area with ties to members of both the Washington Senators and the Baltimore Orioles. This wasn't the first time someone within the Orioles organization had been examined. Prior to the passage of the Sports Bribery Act when the FBI was simply collecting information on the subject, the Bureau reported in late 1961 that "In connection with an investigation of several gamblers vacationing in Hot Springs [AL], a conversation was reported on 5/16/61. [redacted — 5–6 lines worth] There has been no information uncovered known to the Baltimore Office which would reflect that in fact any of these individuals attempted to, participated in or had knowledge of a 'fixed' or 'thrown' professional baseball game. Subsequently, the Baltimore Office developed information that [redacted] had been dismissed by the Baltimore Orioles although Baltimore newspapers carried stories attributing [redacted] resignation as Oriole clubhouse boy to 'ill health.' Information was developed by Baltimore and subsequently confirmed by Oriole [redacted] that [redacted] name had been found in the address book of a [redacted — another 7–8 lines]."

But in 1971, this talk seemed to point to games in fact being fixed. The FBI wrote, "The latter two individuals indicated [redacted] associated with them in throwing baseball games. [redacted]. They are reportedly paying [redacted]. [redacted] indicated to source that he could get 'in on the action,' that when he opened his [redacted] in the near future, they would send [redacted] and for this service, he, source, would get advanced information regarding 'fixed' baseball games."

The source of this information was connected to a local Washington restaurant. "Source noted that the [redacted] is frequented by sporting figures, both the Washington Senators and Baltimore Orioles. Source said that [redacted] of the Washington Senators and [redacted] of the Baltimore Orioles have been seen by source at this restaurant." Despite knowledge of the gambler, the teams (and players), a location, and the tip that games had been fixed and that the action would apparently continue, the FBI was "unable to develop further information regarding captioned matter to substantiate a sports bribery violation." The case was subsequently closed.

A year later perhaps the last publicly known attempt to fix a MLB game occurred. The effort made by "Louie" on July 22, 1972 was sophomoric to say the least. When the Cincinnati Reds were in Pittsburgh to play the Pirates, Louie called Reds pitcher Wayne Simpson in his hotel room shortly after noon. He offered "two thousand dollars or a new car for [redacted] to lose the night game and [redacted] to get an important hit in the sixth. [redacted] added caller said 'they' are also trying to fix the Houston game so they would also lose and therefore there would be no change in team standings." The non-redacted version of the plot was this: Louie wanted Simpson to lose and serve up a "fat pitch" to the Pirates left fielder Bob Robertson in the sixth inning. To drive home his point, Louie also called Reds catcher Johnny Bench at 1:45 p.m., telling him to "remind [redacted] what he is to do in the sixth." Bench hung up without further discussion. Then he promptly reported the whole incident to team management. Soon afterward, newspapers got wind of the story making it public. Ultimately, Louie's bets didn't come in. The Houston Astros beat the Chicago Cubs 7–2, the Reds won 6–3, and yet oddly enough, Robertson did get a single off of Simpson in the sixth inning.

Less than four weeks later, another similarly weak attempt was made to fix a ball game. Yet this time the caller made a better choice in pitchers—at least quality-wise—asking future Hall of Fame hurler Bert Blyleven to dump a game. The young male caller (assumed to be between 19 and 25) phoned the 21-year-old Blyleven at his parents' home, telling him, "I'll give you five thousand dollars to blow the game tomorrow night." That game was the August 13, 1972 contest between Blyleven's Minnesota Twins and the California Angels. Unbeknownst to the caller, Blyleven's turn in the rotation was scheduled to be skipped. He wasn't going to start the desired game. Blyleven turned down the offer, then informed the Twins who in turn contacted the Commissioner's office. The Twins won 4–3, and nothing was ever heard from the caller again.

These sloppy, disorganized attempts tended to wind up on the FBI's radar. In May 1976, a Milwaukee Brewers player was approached in the wee hours of the morning at the Tittle Tattle Restaurant and Bar in New York City and told that he could "make $75,000 by 'throwing' or ensuring the loss of the Tuesday night [redacted] baseball game." The person making the offer bought the Brewers players there a round of drinks and mentioned at that time he had bet on the second game of the season, which was also a Brewers-Yankees matchup. In discussing it, he told the players that "somebody wants to hurt [redacted — a Brewers player] bad if he walks in here." This may have been Brewers relief pitcher Tom Murphy who gave up four ninth-inning runs, blowing a save attempt in the Brewers' 9–7 loss that day. It was after this conversation that the subject cornered the Brewers player in the back hallway and offered the $75,000. He even sweetened the pot, saying he had a "broad" for the player as well. The player kindly refused. But apparently the approach was legitimate (or frightening) enough for the player to contact Brewers management, the Commissioner's office, and the FBI. The Bureau discovered that the subject making the offer was reported in March 1973 "to be a source of narcotics" in the New York area. Amazingly, the FBI convinced the Brewer to wear a wire and re-establish contact with the subject, which he did. However, no bribe was offered at that time and the case was closed.

All of these attempts were extremely direct. None were made by someone close or even known to the athlete which, one would think, made them easy to refuse. Yet not all approaches were as obvious. A member of the Atlanta Braves in the early 1970s had an unusual relationship with a man both the FBI and MLB questioned. According to the FBI file, "an individual known to [the player] as [redacted] has been closely following his Baseball career since [redacted]. During that period of time [redacted] has spent about $3,000 on [redacted] and recently $500 for a gambling trip to Las Vegas, Nevada. [redacted] maintains close contact with [redacted] and frequently flies from New York to Atlanta to watch [redacted] play. [redacted] has never attempted to bribe [redacted]. In 1973 the Baseball Commissioner's Office conducted a lengthy investigation concerning [redacted]." There was more. The subject spent $1000 "to buy a wardrobe in Philadelphia" for the player, and more importantly, "[redacted] advised that [redacted] has been paying him bonuses when he gets a hit. The bonuses consist of $10 for a single, $25 for a double, $50 for a triple, and $100 for a home run. [redacted] stated, however, that [redacted] has never requested any information concerning either the [redacted] or the Braves and he has never tried to bribe [redacted] in an attempt to alter the outcome of a game."

So if this subject wasn't trying to fix a baseball game, what was he after in spending all this money on the Braves player? Perhaps the player himself. "[redacted] continued that [redacted] has never shown any homosexual tendencies and that he [redacted] has no reason to believe that he is a homosexual. [redacted] continued that he has attempted to discourage [redacted] on numerous occasions, however, [redacted] continues to contact him." Later, the conclusion on the subject's intentions changed. He was described as "an old-time vaudeville entertainer, now is a stand-up comic" and had played in New York City where he supposedly owned a club. He claimed to be friendly with other celebrities including Mickey Mantle and a member of the Cleveland Indians. Neither the FBI nor MLB could substantiate any of this. Yet the player and subject maintained a four-year relationship (to that point) wherein the subject paid the player for good performances. Nothing questionable there, right? The player "added that he has reported all of this to the Baseball Commissioner's Office and to his knowledge no action has been taken." The FBI checked that, discovering, "Investigation by the Security Department, Baseball's Commissioner's Office, New York, New York from May 1971 through June 1973 disclosed no wrongdoing or involvement in illegal activities on the part of [redacted] for the Atlanta Braves Baseball Club."

Baseball, from the FBI's perspective, would be clear from this point onward. Yet the game's biggest gambling scandal had yet to become public.

PETE ROSE

Former FBI Special Agent Tom French made Sports Bribery presentations to several Major League Baseball teams during spring training in the 1980s. One year French met with the Cincinnati Reds and their manager Pete Rose. "I sat down with him and he said, 'What's the big deal about this gambling? I go to the track every day. I don't see a big deal about it.' I said, 'Well, I'm talking about compulsive gambling and the problems of compulsive gambling. I guess if you go to the track once in a while, it's not a bad thing.'" Little did French know that Rose was exactly the sort of gambler about which he and MLB were concerned.

Rose wrote in his book *My Prison Without Bars*, "Outside of baseball and my family, nothing has ever given me the pleasure, relaxation, or excitement that I got from gambling….I started going to the racetrack with my dad when I was six years old and I've been going ever since…. Over the last 30 years, I've hit over a dozen pick-six tickets—all totaled, more than a million bucks in winnings….I'll watch just about any sport on TV—football and basketball are my favorites. And if I had a wager on the game, it made it that much more exciting to watch. But there was a time in my life, after my playing career ended, when my gambling got outta control….The more I gambled, the more I needed to gamble. And the more I lost, the more I tried to double-up to win back what I'd already lost. But ask any real gambler and he'll tell you: 'It ain't about the money—it's about the action!' I kept pushing the limit until I was so mixed up, I didn't know whether to wind my ass or scratch my watch."[23]

Baseball had been concerned with Pete Rose's gambling since he entered the league in 1963. By the early 1970s, MLB had investigated his gambling and associations to no avail. The problem was baseball was soft on Rose, afraid to give the game any sort of black eye. And Rose was smart—he bet through a "beard" which made his gambling invisible to the league. As Rose wrote, "Most real gamblers—guys who will bet a grand or more per game—will always use a 'runner' to call in their bets. The runner provides a buffer between the gambler and the bookmaker in case something turns up the heat. He also handles the pickup and delivery—something I had no time for. I knew that betting with a bookmaker was technically illegal. But my brother-in-law was a cop, who informed me that they had never prosecuted a case against a gambler in the history of the department….

"I preferred not to know the identity of the bookmaker at all or vice versa, but Gio [Tommy Gioiosa] could not get credit for a bet of two grand per game based on his income….So Gio informed his bookmaker, former assistant golf pro Ron Peters, that he was laying action for 'Pete Rose.' I would normally establish a 'settle-up' figure of 30 grand to be paid on Tuesday—right after Monday Night Football….

"Gio and I did pretty well on football and basketball throughout the fall and winter [of 1984]. On any given week, I might have been down 10 or 15 grand with [Peters], but I might have been up with my guy in New York, or Florida, or Dayton. You see, Gio wasn't the only runner I used to place my bets. Over the years, I met many bookmakers at the racetracks. These were honest, working-class guys who had wives and families—not the 'Mafia' guys the press made them out to be."[24]

At this same time, Rose wrote that he went "from cold to ice-cold" and began to show signs of compulsion. He was needing an occasional loan to float his losses until the next win streak. This was a professional athlete—a bona fide superstar—making hundreds of thousands of dollars a year from playing baseball plus endorsements and personal appearance fees, and he could not pay off his gambling debts. It was here in 1987 while managing the Reds that Rose began betting on baseball (if he is to be believed—and even at this late date in his story, that's a big "if"). "Finally, the temptation got too strong and I began betting regularly on the sport I knew best—baseball. This wasn't a no-account playoff bet on a couple of teams I had nothing to do with. I was betting on baseball while I was managing a major league ball club in the regular season. But in all honesty, I no longer recognized the difference between one sport and another. I just looked at the games and thought, 'I'll take a dime on the Lakers...a dime on the Sixers...a dime on the Buckeyes... and a dime on the Reds.' I didn't even consider the consequences."[25]

He should have. Not long after he began betting on baseball, the FBI caught wind of Rose's actions through an unrelated drug and gambling investigation. The Bureau informed MLB, and soon Rose's world came crashing down. Deputy commissioner Fay Vincent handed the reins to attorney John Dowd who worked alongside MLB chief of security Kevin Hallinan and former Cincinnati-area FBI Special Agent Joe Daley. "I had the full powers of the Commissioner," Dowd wrote in an email interview with me. However, MLB gave him very little to start with. "The reports [from MLB's 1970s investigation of Rose] had been inexplicably destroyed." Unlike that earlier investigation, the Commissioner's Office never expressed concerns over what Dowd would ultimately uncover. They wanted the truth. Did MLB attempt to interfere with his investigation? "Never," Dowd emphatically replied. He surprisingly revealed that Rose was not the only player whose gambling habits were examined, yet the "evidence was insufficient" and those results "remain confidential."

Soon after Dowd began his investigation, Rose met with Commissioner Peter Ueberroth, his successor A. Bartlett Giamatti, and Vincent. He denied he bet on baseball. "If the Commissioner had presented evidence or given any indication of his position, I might have handled things differently. But I really didn't believe I had a problem. I knew that I broke the letter of the law. But I didn't think that I broke the 'spirit' of the law, which was designed to prevent corruption. During the times I gambled as a manager, I never took an unfair advantage. I never bet more or less based on injuries or inside information. I never allowed my wagers to influence my baseball decisions. So in my mind, I wasn't corrupt. Granted, it was a thin distinction but it was one that I believed at the time."[26] When he finally admitted to betting on baseball, some 20 years later, Rose wrote, "I got involved because I was rooting for my teams—no, *believing* in my teams. I bet the Reds to win every time. I bet the Phillies [whom he once played for] to win even though they were huge underdogs and on a losing streak. It wasn't the smart way to bet. But it was my gut feeling...and I always bet with my gut. I never—ever—bet against my teams. If I had, I'd be doubting everything I believed in."[27]

John Dowd wasn't so sure. He got the sense that Rose had in fact bet against the Reds. "We had some evidence involving San Diego but not enough to meet our standard. In addition, when certain pitchers pitched, Pete would not bet—a clear signal to the bookmakers that he thought the Reds would lose." Rose's most prominent bookie, Ron Peters, was quick to pick up on this signal of non-action and piggyback on the inside information. Others may have as well.

Dowd's final 225-page report would be the signal flare for Rose's expulsion from baseball. Yet questions surrounded it. Rose's lawyers said it contained "outrageous examples of inappropriate and biased conclusions, inaccuracies, half-truths, slander, and hearsay evidence." In the report, Dowd claimed that Rose was Peters' "only baseball customer in 1987." Though feasible, how could a bookmaker stay in business with just one customer? When Rose's lawyers took the case to court to block MLB from ruling on Rose's future, one of the defense team's witnesses was Sam Dash, former chief counsel to the committee that probed Watergate. Dash claimed, "Dowd's report was not the work of a professional investigator. If I had been given a report like that by one of my deputies, I would have fired him. Pete Rose has been put into an impossible situation. I can't think of another case in this country where a man has been asked to prove his innocence." As a result, Judge Norbert Nadel ruled in Rose's favor, halting MLB's action for 14 days, not believing that newly appointed commissioner Giamatti was going to be an "impartial adjudicator." Nadel added, "To allow the commissioner to continue with his hearing would be futile, illusory, and the outcome a foregone conclusion."[28]

This, of course, all came before Rose admitted the truth. He had committed baseball's ultimate sin. He bet on the game he supposedly loved. The legitimacy of Dowd's report is now much more difficult to question because there was only one real question to ask—did Rose bet on baseball games?—and only one answer that needed to be discovered: yes. The how, who, when, where, and amount were really inconsequential. As for Dowd himself, he could take pride in his work. "I think we re-established the integrity of the game. Many players have thanked us for what we did." As all fans of baseball should.

There is one nagging question that remains from the Pete Rose scandal. How is he the only professional athlete in the past 30+ years to be known as a compulsive gambler? Statistics would mandate that more have to have been sprinkled into the ranks of the major leagues. According to the National Council on Problem Gambling, "Two million (1%) of U.S. adults are estimated to meet criteria for pathological gambling in a given year. Another four–six million (2–3%) would be considered problem gamblers; that is, they do not meet the full diagnostic criteria for pathological gambling, but meet one or more of the criteria and are experiencing problems due to their gambling behavior."[29]

What makes for a compulsive gambler? Gamblers Anonymous lists the following characteristics of such a person: "INABILITY AND UNWILLINGNESS TO ACCEPT REALITY. Hence the escape into the dream world of gambling. EMOTIONAL INSECURITY. A compulsive gambler finds he or she is emotionally comfortable only when 'in action.'…IMMATURITY. A desire to have all the good things in life without any great effort on their part seems to be the common character pattern of problem gamblers. Many Gamblers Anonymous members accept the fact that they were unwilling to grow up. Subconsciously they felt they could avoid mature responsibility by wagering on the spin of a wheel or the turn of a card, and so the struggle to escape responsibility finally became a subconscious obsession. Also, a compulsive gambler seems to have a strong inner urge to be a 'big shot' and needs to have a feeling of being all-powerful. The compulsive gambler is willing to do anything (often of an antisocial nature) to maintain the image he or she wants others to see."[30] These personality traits sound like the mindset of many professional athletes. Yet with the exception of Rose and former NFL quarterback Art Schlichter (who is discussed in the NFL chapter), supposedly no other player has succumbed to either the temptation or compulsion gambling readily offers.

Yet in November 2010, another member of MLB's fraternity seemingly fell down the gambling vortex. New York Mets 27-year veteran clubhouse manager Charlie Samuels admitted to betting on baseball. The source of this was an unnamed MLB investigator, and the admission was to only "one occasion."[31] But Samuels had problems beyond gambling. "Samuels was indicted on charges that he criminally possessed nearly $2.3 million worth of game-used memorabilia—including signed jerseys, bats and baseballs—that belonged to the Mets organization...[and was] also charged with embezzling $24,955 from the Mets by submitting inflated expense claims and failing to report or pay taxes on $203,789 in tips and dues that he received from Mets players and others in 2008 and 2009."[32] The investigation that led to these charges began due to allegations of Samuels gambling with organized crime figures in the New York City area. This led to wiretaps which caught Samuels in the act. Initial reports were that Samuels was gambling primarily on NFL games, but Samuels' nagging admission of betting on baseball remains, as do allegations that he provided inside information on the Mets to area bookies.

Former Mets player Jeff Francoeur had his name tied ever-so-briefly with Samuels when it was revealed he had given Samuels $50,000 in checks. While $15,000 was a "year-end bonus" to be spread around to other Mets' personnel, Francoeur explained away the other $35,000 thusly: "I wrote him a $35,000 check and he gave me cash for it and I bought a car for my mom and dad. And that's what it was all about. That's the whole thing. My parents help pay our bills and stuff while we're away during the season. I didn't want them to see what I paid for the car...I wrote him a $35,000 check and he gave me cash for it and I bought a car for my mom and dad. And that's what it was all about. That's the whole thing."[33] Of course, Francoeur failed to explain why he couldn't stop at a bank for a withdrawal or how Samuels managed to have $35,000 in cash lying around the clubhouse. Was this a cover story? Could he have been using Samuels as a beard? MLB has not publicly admitted to any further investigation of Francoeur or any other Mets in regards to this case to date.

Former Atlanta Braves pitcher Tom Glavine, who was twice honored with the Cy Young Award on his way to winning over 300 games, once said in an interview with T.J. Quinn on ESPN, "Everybody, from the minute they get to the clubhouse, it's 'What goes on in the clubhouse stays in the clubhouse.' And that's team fights or team arguments or team meetings. All that stuff is supposed to remain in-house. That's the culture of the game."[34] Gambling certainly falls within those parameters. The question remains: would a player expose another's gambling habits? Even if it reached the depths of Pete Rose? Even if a game were fixed?

If such a player were going to rat out a fellow player's gambling today, he would likely approach a member of MLB's new Department of Investigation (DoI). Begun in 2008 at the suggestion of the Mitchell Report (which dealt with performance-enhancing drugs) and working alongside its Security Division, the DoI is headed by Dan Mullin who served with the New York City Police Department for over 20 years prior to retiring as a deputy chief. I spoke briefly to Mullin as well as head of Public Relations at MLB, Pat Courtney, regarding the Department of Investigations (a full interview was never granted by either for this book). However, I did learn a few valuable tidbits. For one, the DoI possesses six full-time investigators in the U.S., meaning there is about one investigator for every five teams in the league. The DoI also employs a few investigators in other countries where MLB maintains a significant presence, such as the Dominican Republic. But most importantly, MLB and its DoI have in fact conducted investigations into fixed baseball games as recently as 2012. While I know significant details about one of these investigations (which, for libel reasons, I couldn't discuss here), it's unknown just how many games and/or players have been examined due to game-fixing allegations. Though these numbers remain a MLB secret, there is one number that is known, that being how many of these investigations were publicized in the media: zero.

As baseball's history has proven, gambling is infused within the sport. It cannot be separated from it. But I suppose we should trust MLB's DoI to keep the game free of fixers, even though it has no legal power to subpoena, wiretap, etc., no matter the law enforcement background of the people employed as investigators. This operation also begs another question: what information has the DoI provided to the FBI? Since sports bribery is a federal crime, it is truly the FBI which should be investigating these allegations, not MLB. Yet there is no record that I could find within the FBI's files related to any recent case of game fixing in MLB. Why is that? Is the DoI simply adding a layer of secrecy to MLB's inner workings? Or is it seriously investigating federal offenses? No one will know until MLB makes these cases public.

BASKETBALL

Marvin "Mendy" Rudolph was in trouble. Gambling had gotten hold of him long ago, and its devilish charms decimated his finances. He had cashed in $60,000 from his pension fund and taken a $10,000 settlement from a workman's compensation injury, putting it all toward paying off his debts. Yet this still left him nearly $100,000 short. That's when the NBA referee received a phone call from a Las Vegas gambler offering him enough money to get free and clear in exchange for shaving a few points.[1]

That's right. Tim Donaghy was not the first NBA official to have a gambling problem or to fix a game. Referees in basketball have perhaps more control over a game than any other sports officials. The book *Scorecasting: The Hidden Influences Behind How Sports are Played and Games are Won* recently detailed just how influential NBA referees were when it came to the so-called "home field advantage." The authors wrote, "Home teams shoot more free throws than away teams—between 1 and 1.5 more per game. Why? Because away teams are called for more fouls, particularly shooting fouls. Away teams also are called for more turnovers and more violations….It turns out that offensive and loose ball fouls go the home team's way at twice the rate of other personal fouls. We can also look at fouls that are more valuable, such as those that cause a change of possession. These fouls are almost *four* times more likely to go the home team's way than fouls that don't cause a change of possession….The chance of a visiting player getting called for traveling is 15 percent higher than it is for a home team player."[2] The ultimate conclusion was, "Referee bias could well be the *main reason* for home court advantage in basketball. And if the refs call turnovers and fouls in the home team's favor, we can assume they make other biased calls in favor of the home team that we cannot see or measure." [emphasis in original][3]

Gamblers have never been ignorant of these facts. This is why basketball referees are often approached to shave points. The awarding of a few extra free throws, a change in the possession arrow, a call of "blocking" rather than "charging," and the outcome of a game can be swayed. It should come as no surprise then that such attempts date back to the origins of the professional game. The National Basketball Association (NBA) was founded as the Basketball Association of America (BAA) on June 6, 1946, changing its name to the familiar NBA when the BAA merged with the rival National Basketball League in 1949. Shortly thereafter, an NBA official was caught fixing games. NBA commissioner Maurice Podoloff banished referee Sol Levy after he was accused of fixing three games in the 1949–50 season. This would later be changed to six games, though the true total will never be known.

Levy's modus operandi was the same then as it would be today: he called fouls against star players in order to influence a game's outcome versus the point spread. Yet his scheme ran afoul of sports crusader Frank Hogan, the New York District Attorney. Levy was arrested on November 2, 1951 on charges "to officiate in such a manner that the point spread would be shaved."[4] He was charged with seven criminal counts, and found guilty of six in March 1953. Levy appealed and

226

remarkably won on a technicality in 1954 despite staring down a three-year stretch for his crimes. "The court noted that the section in which Levy was convicted under included commercial fraud, but did not include referees in basketball games."[5] "No one will ever know exactly how widespread the practice was among NBA officials, but at least one player, speaking anonymously to Charley Rosen for his book, contended that there were other officials involved in fixing NBA games. 'Levy wasn't the only ref doing business,' the player told Rosen, 'but all the other guys are safely dead by now. Even after the scandal broke, there were plenty of games dumped in the NBA.'"[6]

At this same time, the NBA was feeling the fallout from the college basketball fixing scandal that forever altered the sport. Just prior to the start of the 1951–52 NBA season, two newly drafted members of the Indianapolis Olympians, Alex Groza and Ralph Beard, were arrested at the annual College All-Star Classic held in Chicago. The pair was accused of fixing games while members of the University of Kentucky in 1948–49. "The NBA acted swiftly. The league couldn't afford the kind of scandal that had so heavily damaged college basketball—not on the eve of a new season, not when the sport was finally gaining a foothold on the pro sports scene. Since Groza and Beard had admitted their guilt, they were out, banned for life from the NBA, and they had 30 days to sell their interests in the Olympians. League officials hoped for the best. With any luck, those stern, decisive actions would mollify fans. They would see that the NBA was capable not only of policing its own players; it was willing, if necessary, to kick out two of its top stars for their actions *before* they even joined the league.

"The fans might have bought it, but players remained skeptical. Many insisted—and would continue to insist for the rest of their lives—that Groza and Beard were far from alone in shaving points while they were playing college ball. Other names were bandied about in private, and at least one other superstar was implicated in New York district attorney Frank Hogan's investigation. There was talk of threats and backroom deals consummated to spare other players of Groza's and Beard's fates. According to Charley Rosen, whose account, *Scandals of '51*, details the scandals at different schools, Maurice Podoloff had been briefed on at least one superstar's involvement in collegiate point-shaving, but Podoloff buckled to pressure. 'The owner of the star threatened to fold his franchise and go home if Podoloff touched his player,' Rosen reported. 'The star remains in orbit.' [That star was likely Boston Celtics legend Bob Cousy who is discussed later.]

"Players, although not sympathetic to Groza's or Beard's actions, strongly felt that the league, while publicly condemning the actions of the point-shavers, had been less than forthright in its investigation of the scandal and the punishment of the guilty. The league, they contended, made scapegoats of the two players, forcing Beard and Groza to pay the ultimate price if, in exchange, it meant saving face and having the problem go away."[7]

On the heels of the banishment of Groza and Beard, yet another NBA player needed to be shown the door, Fort Wayne Pistons' All-Star forward Jack Molinas. Just 29 games into his career, Molinas admitted to having bet on ten games involving the Pistons. Of course, he swore he only bet on his own team to win. In issuing Molinas' ban in 1954, Commissioner Podoloff said, "[Molinas] is a personal psychiatric aberration that will not affect the league."[8] Little did Podoloff know that Molinas had fixed games dating back to his high school days, and that the tradition would continue as he participated in the college basketball point-shaving scandal of 1961 while personally ruining the career of Connie Hawkins.

Many would believe that after this flourish of gambling-related dismissals, the NBA didn't encounter another such case until the story of Tim Donaghy broke; that the league enjoyed 50+ years of corruption-free basketball. This is far from the truth. In fact, after Sol Levy, the next referee to be examined for gambling wasn't Donaghy, it was Hall of Fame inductee Mendy Rudolph.

Rudolph is legendary. Once considered the finest referee in NBA history, he entered the league midway through the 1952–53 season and remained entrenched until ill health forced him to retire in 1975. In between, he officiated 2,112 games, eight All-Star games, and oversaw at least one NBA Finals game for 22 consecutive seasons. In 1966, he

was named referee-in-chief under which he authored the NBA Officials Manual and Case Book. Rudolph was even behind the league changing the officials' uniforms from the zebra-striped black-and-white look to the plain gray jersey worn today. When he left the game, no one had officiated in more important NBA games than Rudolph, whose number 5 has not been worn by another referee.

Unfortunately for the league, Rudolph was a compulsive gambler. "Rudolph would disappear for a weekend at the craps and roulette tables in Las Vegas, or, because he bet large sums at the ticket window, would wear a Groucho Marx disguise at the race track so no one would recognize the widely known official. He had owed a great deal to casinos and to friends and family and business associates he had borrowed from to pay gambling debts and income tax, as well as alimony and child support."[9] Though this sort of gambling was acceptable under league rules at the time, his uncontrolled habit made him an ideal subject to approach for any point-shaving scheme. "There were pleas from the NBA commissioner at the time, Walter Kennedy, for Rudolph to cool his gambling. 'I remember Walter Kennedy calling me with great concern,' said [former NBA referee Earl] Strom. 'He wanted me to speak to Mendy about his gambling. He had been observed at the $50 and $100 ticket windows at the track and buying packs of tickets. I did talk to Mendy. And I think he did try to cool it. But my wife, who handled our finances, used to say to me when I got my paycheck in the mail, 'How much should I put aside for Mendy?' He was always borrowing from us. But he usually paid us back.'"[10]

Around 1973, Rudolph hit bottom. It was then his wife Susan stated he was approached to fix games. She told the *New York Times*, "'And then he told me about a phone call he got. The call was from a gambler in Las Vegas. He offered Mendy a lot of money to shave points in games.' 'It would be the answer to all our problems,' Rudolph said to his wife. 'All I would have to do is look away maybe one time during a game. Maybe twice.'"[11] She couldn't believe he was contemplating it, but he finally told her, "It goes against all my principles. I love the game too much, respect it too much. I couldn't do it to you. I couldn't do it in the memory of my father, and I can't do it to myself. If I have to go into bankruptcy, something I'd hate to do, I'd do it."[12]

Rudolph may have never fixed a game. His integrity might have held. But the FBI seemed to have pretty firm evidence that Rudolph did break the taboo of betting on NBA games while an official. It came in relation into an investigation of the 1967 NBA Finals. The FBI wrote, "As to the game played Sunday, 4/23/67, he noted that Philadelphia only scored 13 points in the fourth quarter which was very unusual [this was Game 5 which the San Francisco Warriors won 117–109 over the Philadelphia 76ers]. Further, in the final game played on Monday night, 4/24/67, he noted that Philadelphia had 64 foul shot opportunities while the Warriors had only 29 foul shot opportunities which in his opinion is very unusual [this was Game 6 which the 76ers won 125–122]. As a result, he had made inquiry as to whether there might have been any irregularities on the part of referees, coaches or players during the playoff. He stated he learned [redacted] that the well-known professional basketball official Mendy Rudolph had been betting during the playoff games. Rudolph supposedly bet on [redacted — about four lines]. Informant stated that he had contacted another source of his, [redacted] indicated he felt the group known as 'The Scholar Group' was handling Rudolph's initial picks and bets." Just how much betting Rudolph did on the NBA remains a mystery, but those known as The Scholar Group will appear again momentarily.

Other officials within the league likely were involved with gamblers as well. Professional sports gambler Lem Banker, who ran with the disgraced Jack Molinas back in his heyday, knew of a gambler who had the Detroit Pistons' timekeeper under control in the early 1980s. This official would run the clock either a little longer or shorter than it should have, depending on a particular game's under/over line. Banker wouldn't reveal whether or not he personally profited off this information, but prior to that he did help protect the NBA's integrity. According to Banker, in the late 1960s or early 1970s, "There was an NBA referee, a young guy, and Bob Martin the bookmaker says, 'Lem, this one guy, he's a small bettor betting $500 a game, but he's been betting much bigger, maybe $5,000, and he's been winning.' So I asked him what's the next game? They were playing on the West Coast and they were playing the Golden State War-

riors. At that time, there were only two officials working each game in the NBA. So I listened to the game and got the names of both referees. Now the next time they played, this guy made another big bet, another game on the West Coast, and sure enough, it's the same referee. After three or four games it became fairly clear that the common denominator was a referee. Now neither of us had any proof, but we made a few calls and, indirectly, brought our suspicions to the league's attention. Pretty soon, that referee wasn't in the NBA anymore, even though nothing formal was filed against him."[13]

The FBI investigated another case of game fixing by NBA officials—that's multiple officials, not just one—in late 1970. A gambler betting through a Los Angeles-area bookmaker informed local police that three upcoming NBA games were going to be fixed and done so by the officiating crew. Initially, the informant didn't know which games because the gamblers controlling the referees were awaiting their game assignments prior to placing their bets. But once those were given and the lines were set for the games, the "bookmaker placed three large bets for informant and told him 'don't worry about money, it's a lock.'" The bets came in winners, but something happened between the informant and the bookie. Communication severed between the pair. The informant lost his inside information, hearing nothing more of fixed games. With that, the FBI's case fell apart.

COCAINE FOR GAMES

Of course, NBA referees weren't the only ones approached to fix a game. Players, too, found themselves in compromising situations in which fixing a game or shaving points may have been an easy way out. As much control as basketball referees have in overseeing a game, the fact that each team only uses five players at a time means that should a gambler get hold of just one starter, possessing 20 percent of a team is enough to influence the final score. Having more players in one's pocket just further ensures the result.

Like in the FBI's files surrounding baseball, several sloppy attempts were made to approach a player out of the blue to get him to agree to fix a game. None appeared to be anywhere near successful, yet in one instance, the FBI used a member of the Atlanta Hawks to lure out a potential fixer. Amazingly, the NBA had no objection to this, or to the player providing inside information to the subject in a show of "good faith." Though the FBI advised the player that the possibility of violence against him was "nil," he ultimately backed out due to spousal concerns and how participating might affect his on-the-court performance.

Unlike baseball, though, gamblers and drug dealers seemed to have better luck infiltrating an NBA player's life in order to get him to do their bidding. The NBA would argue that despite what the FBI discovered and put into its files, none of these schemes ever affected a single game. You can decide for yourself if this is truly the case.

In the mid- to late-1970s, the FBI worked a source in the New York City area who believed that NBA games were being fixed. This source—who was a likely a bookmaker—did not want to be directly involved in any FBI investigation whatsoever, so the Bureau had this initial source shift control of the desired subject to a second informant who was willing to wear a wire and testify should the need arise. What kicked off this intrigue in late 1975? As the original source informed the FBI, the subject in question "expressed a desire to place large bets on National Basketball Association games, especially [redacted] games. [redacted] advised the source that any bets he would place, it would be certain that he would win. [redacted] intimated to source that he [redacted] had control of any game that he would bet through his contacts with the players."

It is here that the investigation complicated itself. The subject with NBA contacts never placed a bet through the FBI's source due to a supposed delay in speaking to certain key players. In the meantime, the FBI agents handling the informant had been granted authorization to use a body recorder, but for only 30 days. When the informant failed to meet with the subject because he wasn't betting as expected, the window on using the recording device closed. This spurred an internal FBI debate whether or not to extend the authorization for using the recorder. One agent saw it as "of the utmost importance," but others did not agree. To make matters worse, the informant set to wear the wire was also involved in another undercover case. A suitable replacement was sought, but none could be found. However, once the NBA season ended in February 1976, all of this became moot. The case was closed. Without basketball being played there were no games on which to bet, meaning if the subject was in cahoots with some players, nothing of interest was to occur until fall.

Come tip-off of the NBA's 1976–77 season, the subject was right back at it according to the original source. "[redacted] has told the source that he can control the outcome of the games he bets by having certain players [redacted] 'shave' points. The source advised that he will keep the Bureau advised of any meets that take place between he and [redacted] for the purpose of placing bets on NBA games. According to the source he will probably be meeting with the players that will be involved in the point shaving. The source went on to advise that he will not testify regarding this matter nor will he introduce a third party to [redacted]. The source stated that he would probably be meeting [redacted] in public places where there would be a possibility of overhearing the conversation." Based off of this information, the source was to be physically tailed as he made it clear that in order to protect himself he would only deal with the contacting agent.

From this point on, the subject became a monumental tease, though one preoccupied with the New York Knicks which boasted a roster featuring future Hall of Famers Earl Monroe and Walt Frazier. For example, "On November 22, 1976, [redacted] telephoned source and advised that the New York Knicks-Philadelphia game, November 26, 1976, was being set up by [redacted] and that he wanted the source to bet for him. [redacted] told source that he would contact the source on November 24, 1976, and make arrangements to get some money to the source to cover the bet." But come that day, "On November 24, 1976, [redacted] telephoned the source and advised him that no bet would be placed on the Philadelphia game. [redacted] told source that [redacted] had played poorly in the New York-Kansas City game, November 23, 1976, and had been criticized in the press for his performance and [redacted] did not want any additional criticism." Shortly thereafter, "On

12/10/76, source advised that [redacted] was interested in placing a bet on the New York Knickerbockers-Phoenix Suns basketball game scheduled 12/11/76. Source advised that [redacted] did not pursue his desire to bet the Knick game due to the fact that no line was established for the game since [redacted]. [redacted] has maintained contact with captioned subject on a regular basis since 12/11/76. [redacted] has advised the source that [redacted] does not want to do anything at the present. [redacted] has told [redacted] that since [redacted] was acquired, the Knicks are expected to at least make the NBA playoffs and that they cannot afford to lose any games. According to the source, [redacted] advised [redacted] that he would look for a game in which the Knicks were heavily favored so that points could be shaved to lose the game by the points, but not by actual score."

The December 9, 1976 trade by the Knicks of their starting F-C John Gianelli to the Buffalo Braves for Bob McAdoo and Tom McMillen apparently created havoc within this supposed fixer's world. Though the subject was to bet $20,000 on the February 18, 1977 Knicks-Bucks game, he again backed out because "[redacted] was trying to control the game through [redacted] and that [redacted] is a doubtful starter for the Bucks game." The bookie and the subject continued to talk, but he never gave money to the source to bet. "It is the opinion of [redacted] that sometime during mid 1977–78 basketball season, [redacted] became apprehensive about dealing with the source. Also with the inclusion of [redacted] on the Knickerbocker roster in December 1976, [redacted] was no longer able to influence the outcome of games as had been the case before his arrival."

Once again, the NBA season ended without the subject betting on a supposedly fixed game with the FBI's informant. Maybe the player(s) connected to the subject was too concerned with the Knicks' playoff chances to participate (though the team finished with a 40–42 record, missing the 1976–77 playoffs). Maybe the subject was suspicious—rightfully so—of his bookie/informant. Maybe the subject was just making up the whole thing. Either way, the FBI believed in the information enough to continue with its investigation.

In the ensuing offseason, the Bureau didn't contact the NBA; the league called the FBI. "On 5/23/77, [redacted] of Security, National Basketball Association (NBA) (retired FBI Agent) appeared at the New Rochelle Office of the FBI. [redacted] met with SAC Besley and advised that on a couple of occasions during the past basketball season [redacted] had alleged to have been betting on basketball games. [redacted] also stated that allegations regarding [redacted] and [redacted] had been received regarding their knowledge and/or participation in such activities. SAC Besley advised [redacted] that agents knowledgeable of sports bribery matters would interview him at a later date." Two days later, other agents did meet with the NBA's security chief, but the league's official wasn't as forthcoming as the Bureau would have appreciated. "On 5/25/77, [redacted] was interviewed at his office in New York City. [redacted] reiterated the information that he had given to SAC Besley previously during this interview. [redacted] stated that he could not reveal the identity of his sources and that he felt that no additional information would be forthcoming regarding the allegations against those he had mentioned."

Even though the FBI's source failed to entrap the subject with apparent connections to a member of the New York Knicks, and despite the fact that the NBA knew more than it was willing to tell the FBI regarding the matter, the Bureau pressed on with its investigation. They made a final stab at getting somewhere and talked to the player all fingers seemed to point to. "On 8/9/77, New York Knickerbocker [redacted] was interviewed at Trenton State College, Trenton, New Jersey. [redacted] was asked if he had ever been approached to 'shave points,' affect the outcome of any ballgame for the purpose of betting or if he knew of anyone in the NBA who had been approached. [redacted] advised that he has never been approached nor has he ever heard of anyone in the NBA being approached or participating in any scheme to shave points or to facilitate sports betting. [redacted] advised that [redacted] with NBA players off the playing floor and felt he would be the last one to ever be approached or to hear of any illegal sports betting or bribery."

Of course, since he wasn't (a) under oath or (b) approached with any incriminating evidence against him besides apparent heresy, the player

had no reason to admit to fixing a game or shaving points or to what this really boiled down to—committing a crime. Right then and there, the FBI's investigation died. But four short years later, the FBI would be back knocking on the Knicks' door, questioning how legitimate some of their games may have been.

In 1982, the FBI seemed to possess very credible information that three members of the New York Knicks were shaving points as a favor to their cocaine supplier. Unfortunately, much of the official record detailing this case has been either sealed or destroyed. What remains publicly available, however, is shocking.

As the FBI detailed, "On March 25, 1982 [redacted] advised that he and a second independent source have determined that [redacted] and a third unidentified player are heavy users of 'cocaine.' Their supplier for 'cocaine' is identified as [redacted] (not to be confused with New York team physician). [redacted] obtains his 'cocaine' from [redacted] subsequently identified as [redacted].

"Source first reported on March 25, 1982 that [redacted], a normal $300 better [sic] per game, began placing large bets on the Knicks games approximately two (2) months ago. As of March 25, 1982, [redacted] had bet seven (7) games and covered six (6) of them. Source at that time stated that he did not think the players were actively participating in 'point shaving' but rather extending a courtesy to their 'cocaine' dealer, regarding inside player information, not known to the general public. On one (1) occasion, [redacted] was told by [redacted] that he [redacted] was simply not going to show up for that night's game and he did not.

"On March 31, 1982, source reported that both of the Knicks' last two (2) games: 1) Chicago Bulls, and 2) Indiana Pacers had been bet heavily by [redacted]. [redacted] has increased his betting to $10,000 per Knick game and wanted to extend it to $12,000 on the Bulls game, but was turned down by bookmakers. [redacted] continues to bet the rest of the games at his regular $300 per game rate. On Sunday, regarding his bet on the Bulls, he told other bookmakers that he was betting $7,000 for himself and $3,000 for [redacted].

236

"Source reports that [redacted] has identified the players by name to the other bookmaker, who is talking to source. After observing the most recent action regarding the Knicks, source now believes that the players are actively engaged in 'shaving points' and possibly even betting against themselves."

The version of the Knicks on display in the 1981–82 NBA season was far from noteworthy. They finished with a 33–49 record, good for last place in the Atlantic Division. Their sole bright spot was former number four overall selection (two picks ahead of Larry Bird) G-F Michael Ray Richardson. In the 1980–81 season, Richardson became the second player in NBA history to simultaneously lead the league in both assists (with a 10.1 per game average) and steals (3.2 per game) in a season, setting franchise records in both categories. But in 1981–82, both of those totals slipped, dropping by three assists a game as well as a steal per game. Why? Michael Ray Richardson had a cocaine addiction. In fact, on February 25, 1986, Richardson, having tested positive for cocaine a third time, would become the first player banned for life by the NBA under its newly developed anti-drug policy. Despite the apparent connection, it cannot be stated for certain that Richardson was part of this FBI investigation.

The dealer working with the players had been previously investigated by the FBI "where he was identified as one of the largest dealers on the East Coast in [redacted]." Yet as the Bureau began to develop the case, the more damning it became toward the players. "In connection with their use of cocaine, all three (3) players use the same dealer. Over a period of the last two (2) months, all three (3) have given their [redacted] tips on when to bet the Knicks to lose. This has occurred seven (7) times and six (6) of the tips were good.

"Source stated that to his knowledge, none of the players receive any money for the tip, but simply do it as a courtesy to their dealer. One such tip was the Knicks-Bullets game in New York about two (2) weeks ago. Another game was the Knicks versus San Antonio last Tuesday, which was good. The type of tips are not regarding point shaving but rather key players not playing. The latest tip was on the Knicks game on March 23,

1982 which was the only one that did not work out." This last game was a 120–97 win by the Knicks over the Cleveland Cavaliers.

As the season progressed, so, too, did the information. The players were throwing their money in with the dealer, making bets by proxy. "Source further stated that at this point, he believes that the players must be betting against the Knicks to lose….Source observed heavy betting by [redacted] toward the latter part of the NY Knicks season, on the Knicks to lose certain games. In each case, the Knicks did lose, or failed to cover the point spread on the game."

The investigation continued into the following season. By early 1983, the FBI had learned that the dealer had indeed bet $10,000 on each of the seven games in question (as opposed to his once-usual $300 a game). They also uncovered from their source "that [redacted] has connections with various professional basketball teams to shave points. Source advised that [redacted] in gambling debts." After reviewing the suspect's phone records, in which he was in contact with another subject in Las Vegas, "it is believed [redacted] these telephones to [redacted] concerning the New York Knicks as well as to coordinate 'point shaving' activity."

The FBI thought so highly of this case, it made a special note regarding its status. This specific file "should be maintained in the Special File Room with access limited to individuals noted above" because of "the sensitivity of the investigation." Yet no front-page headlines followed. The Knicks didn't fall apart in disgrace in a way which would routinely make "top ten" lists of famous sporting scandals. Why?

The lack of physical evidence meant getting anyone to confess proved impossible. Without a confession or the willingness of someone involved to cooperate, the investigation was doomed to fail. After speaking to two specific individuals related to the case, "[redacted] upon interview, denied knowing [redacted] or ever being in contact with any New York Knicks players….[redacted] upon interview admitted knowing [redacted] as a gambler but denied [redacted] was a bookmaker or involved in narcotics….In view of the above and in absence of corroborating witnesses, no further investigation is being conducted and this is being placed in closed status."

Less than a year later, the FBI was on board for another case in which cocaine, gambling and an NBA player were mixed. In this instance a member of the Utah Jazz, while in Atlanta to play the Hawks on March 19, 1983, was contacted by attorneys in the Atlanta area who wanted to meet for dinner. The player agreed as he and at least one of the attorneys had grown up together in the same area of New York. At dinner, an attorney informed the Jazz player that one of his teammates had purchased $250 worth of cocaine, but bounced a check on the dealer. Feeling ripped off, the dealer was going to sue and publicly out the player as a user. This information didn't seem to surprise the player as he claimed his teammate was no longer using, and that he'd kindly cover the check for him. The attorney refused his money. This set off an alarm inside the player's head. He suddenly realized what was happening. "He has concluded that the subjects [the attorneys] wanted a bribe to keep **[redacted]** from being arrested or they wanted information that would help them win bets with bookmakers." This investigation ultimately went nowhere of note; however, it revealed something even more startling than a cocaine-using baller and some crooked lawyers. The Jazz player told the FBI, "He stated he has made some inquiries regarding this matter and has learned that the management of the Atlanta Hawks has repeatedly paid large sums of money to people who make claims that players have committed criminal acts in order to keep them quiet."

At about this same time, the FBI had information concerning another NBA player doing more than just betting on basketball. While this particular file is heavily redacted, certain key phrases paint a clear picture of the information the FBI possessed. "**[redacted]** has furnished information to the effect that subject **[redacted]** has been betting on games involving the **[redacted]** team and alleges in one specific instance point shaving on the part of **[redacted]**....Source gave background information regarding subject and alleged that **[redacted]** fixed four basketball games [redacted — three lines worth]. **[redacted]** is described as a degenerate gambler betting college and pro football and basketball, hockey and often goes to racetracks in **[redacted]** also travels to Las Vegas several times a year....This investigation was predicated upon in-

formation from New York that [redacted] was involved in fixing certain basketball games in the past. One alleged game was when [redacted] played for [redacted] and two games when [redacted]. It is alleged that [redacted] is a degenerate gambler, betting college and professional sports, as well as flats and harness racing." This file paints a picture of an NBA version of Pete Rose, of a player who couldn't control his gambling addiction which led to not just wagering on the sport he knew best, but to shaving points to ensure a winning bet. Why don't we all know this player by name today? Because the game scores and certain game-related facts provided by the informant did not "concur" with the actual results of the alleged fixed games. The Bureau closed the case despite a review of multiple phone numbers that showed the player was calling sports result services multiple times a day and communicating with a bookie known to be associated with the Genovese crime family. To the FBI that was no crime, but for the NBA, perhaps it should have been.

"LEGENDS"

"It's no big deal." That seems to be the NBA's response to a spate of recent gambling-related incidents that have made the rounds on sports websites and blogs. For example, in January 2011, Memphis Grizzlies head coach Lionel Hollins banned gambling on team fights after an "altercation" occurred between teammates Tony Allen and O.J. Mayo when Mayo didn't settle up on his gambling debt (this occurred shortly before Mayo was suspended by the NBA for violating the league's anti-drug policy to boot). It could've been worse. Just a year earlier, a similar incident occurred within the Washington Wizards when gambling between teammates Gilbert Arenas and Javaris Crittenton led to a 50-game suspension for Arenas. But he wasn't suspended for gambling. No, his 50-game ban resulted when Arenas brought four guns into the Wizards' locker room in a "prank" to get Crittenton to pay the money due to him.

The Sacramento Kings claimed in November 2009 that one of its assistant directors of scouting, Jack Mai, was gambling while working for the franchise. Consequently, the NBA banned Mai from the league. The Kings' official statement on Mai's banishment read, "The investigation revealed that Mr. Mai participated in improper wagering activities while a member of this organization." It was not revealed what sort of gambling Mai was involved in nor what amount of money was being wagered, but rumors were that Mai bet on NBA games, including ones involving the Kings. This seems to be a level-headed response except for one minor detail: at the time the Kings were owned by the Maloof family. The same Maloof clan who owns the Palms hotel and casino in Las Vegas featuring a 163-seat race and sports book. So to be clear: betting = wrong, casino ownership = right.

But betting is only wrong to the NBA in certain instances. One would think that meant gambling during a basketball game, but this, too, is mere assumption. Al Horford of the Atlanta Hawks claimed he made a $10,000 wager with the Boston Celtics' Paul Pierce during their teams' 2008 playoff matchup. The bet was that the Celtics would not sweep the Hawks. (Horford was really confident in his team, no?) Horford made the claim during a radio interview, stating "[Pierce] owes me money," since the Celtics did not sweep the Hawks. Horford's statement was backed up by teammate Marvin Williams who was part of the same interview. While this was featured on ESPN.com's TrueHoop blog, the NBA did nothing publicly in response to this story.

Other NBA superstars have had brushes with gambling infamy. Perhaps at the top of that list is Michael Jordan. The man who was once greater than the NBA itself ran afoul of the league when it was revealed that he had been openly gambling on golf matches, including one with a known cocaine dealer. While I make the case that Jordan's initial retirement from the game was in fact an under-the-table suspension for gambling in my book *The Fix Is In: The Showbiz Manipulations of the NFL, MLB, NBA, NHL, and NASCAR*, it is no secret that since leaving the court his gambling acumen has only increased.

Jordan's one-time rival turned chum, Charles Barkley, once admitted he had a gambling problem in an interview with a Phoenix TV station. Then in a different interview with ESPN in 2006, he claimed to have lost $10 million gambling over the years and once lost approximately $2.5 million in a six-hour period. Of course, he didn't feel this was a real problem because he could afford to lose that kind of money. This may have been just a half-truth. In 2008, the Wynn Hotel/Casino filed a civil complaint against Sir Charles for failure to pay off a $400,000 casino marker. Barkley claimed he didn't have money problems; he simply forgot to pay back the casino. Once he did, he publicly vowed not to gamble "for the next year or two."

Former three-time NBA All-Star and member of the 2006 NBA Champion Miami Heat Antoine Walker reportedly ran up over $1 million in gambling debts in the span of a year. His gambling spree began immediately after Walker left the NBA following the 2007–08 season. Approximately $178,000 of that debt was paid back, but another $882,500 remained outstanding. Subsequently, Walker was charged with three felony counts of writing bad checks (ten checks in total) to cover losses at three Las Vegas casinos: Caesars Palace, Planet Hollywood, and the Red Rock. Despite making millions during his NBA career, Walker filed for Chapter 7 bankruptcy liquidation in 2010. In December 2011, Walker was sentenced to five years probation and ordered to pay $770,050 in restitution to the indebted casinos. In an attempt to make some money, Walker stooped to playing basketball with the Idaho Stampede of the NBA Development League.[14]

Immediately following in Walker's footsteps was Allen Iverson. Once known as "The Answer," Iverson appeared to have completely run through the $154 million he had earned while playing in the NBA when he couldn't pay off a nearly $1 million debt to a Georgia jeweler in 2012. But Stephen A. Smith saw this coming two years earlier, for reasons few were willing to mention. Smith wrote, "Allen Iverson is in trouble, folks, deep trouble. The combination of alcohol and gambling—and a once-promising career in tatters because of the first two—won't culminate in anything short of disaster if help does not arrive in short order. If numerous NBA sources are telling the truth—and there's no reason to believe they'd do otherwise in a situation of this magnitude—Iverson will either drink himself into oblivion or gamble his life away."[15] Iverson had been banned from casinos in both Detroit and Atlantic City, but not for incurring debts on the level of Walker or Barkley.

In all of these cases, the yarn the NBA officially spun was that these were "isolated incidents." There was no possibility that players' gambling ever interfered with their on-the-court play, or that with their losses they were tempted to bet on the sport they knew best. Perhaps that is true. But in the FBI's opinion, there are three basketball legends for which gambling on NBA games during their playing days seemed routine.

When the FBI began investigating "Gambling in National Sports" in the late 1950s, one of the first entries—dating from February 1958—dealt with the possible fixing of Boston Celtics games. The file stated:

"A Washington News Service Release of 2/4/58 quoted a letter from Representative Kenneth B. Keating of New York to the Chairman of the House Commerce Committee as requesting an investigation of interstate betting on sporting events including college games. The letter is quoted as saying 'Because so much money is riding on the outcome of games and the point spread, tremendous temptations are being built up.' Keating said an investigation is needed to 'pinpoint' operations of gamblers and to curb illegal betting.

"With regard to Representative Keating's observations, it is noted that a highly confidential informant of the Philadelphia Office has advised that top hoodlum Aldo Magnelli [who was one of 58 mobsters arrested at the famous 1957 "Apalachin Meeting" raid] made several calls on January 30, 1958, to Springfield, Massachusetts, where he discussed the odds on the basketball game to be played on that date between the Philadelphia Warriors and the Boston Celtics of the National Professional Basketball Association. Magnelli was interested in learning whether [redacted] would play for the Celtics that night and whether the game was on the level.

"Magnelli then got in touch with one of his Camden, New Jersey, associates and remarked that the Boston game was supposed to have been fixed, but it 'is all right.' Magnelli was allegedly under the impression that two of the Boston games are supposed to be fixed but that this was not one of them. Magnelli indicated that if [redacted] played he would bet on Boston.

"[redacted] played and scored 16 points, but Boston lost to Philadelphia 116 to 96, indicating that all of Magnelli's precautions were to no avail, and he apparently lost again." The redacted player is likely Bill Russell who was the only Celtics player to score 16 points in that game. Russell's name will appear again shortly.

As the FBI continued its duty, digging into the connection between the sports and gambling worlds, it began to uncover overlooked past transgressions within their own archives. For example, "NY files also reflected that information was received from [redacted], and furnished to the Bureau and interested offices by letter dated 2/3/55, and captioned '[redacted], National Basketball Association; GIIF,' indicating that [redacted], [redacted] is betting on himself and the Boston team and is believed to be attempting to control the point spread and operating in a similar fashion to that which caused the betting scandal in college circles some years ago….By letter dated 2/18/55, the Minneapolis Office advised that an informant of that office had verified the above information and stated that this knowledge was so common that Minneapolis gamblers are not handling bets on game involving the Celtics." The FBI would also hear that some bookies wouldn't take bets on the Detroit Pistons because one of their players was believed to be "doing business" with gamblers.

Though it cannot be ascertained that Bob Cousy was the Celtics player mentioned in the file as betting on himself and the team, it's interesting that the Bureau brought up the connection to the famed 1951 college basketball gambling scandal. Some believe that unlike several other players caught up in that case, Cousy managed to slip the noose. Bill Reynolds wrote about Cousy's connection to the 1951 scandal in his somewhat apologetic biography of the player:

"There were also rumors that the Catholic colleges in New York had been spared due to Cardinal Spellman's influence on [NY district attorney] Frank Hogan. But in the winter of 1953 Cousy was stopped by two detectives while leaving Madison Square Garden after a game against the Knicks. He had heard the rumors that he'd been one of those players involved in dumping games while at Holy Cross. It was almost impossible to be a college star in the late forties and not have your name part of the rumor mill once the scandals broke. Guys on the Celtics were always asking who was next, the rumors everywhere. But that night as Cousy came out of Madison Square Garden, the two detectives said they wanted to talk to Cousy the next time the Celtics came to New York. After that, the rumors only intensified.

"Soon afterward, [Celtics owner] Walter Brown called Cousy into his office, wanting to know if there was any truth to what he'd been hearing. Brown knew that if anything happened to Cousy he might as well put all the basketballs away, burn the uniforms, and put a padlock on the Boston Garden. 'Walter,' Cousy said. 'I have never done a dishonest thing on or off the basketball court.' Brown said that was good enough for him.

"Cousy eventually met with the New York City district attorney in February '53….There were several men present, and almost as soon as he sat down the district attorney said he was sure Cousy had been involved with gamblers when he'd been at Holy Cross, that his name had been on the list of the bookie who had died the previous summer.…A couple more hours went by, Cousy sensing he could proclaim his innocence all he wanted, but no one really believed him. He was allowed to go to dinner, after which he told one of the detectives he wanted a lawyer. The detective told him to wait and went back inside the main office to talk to the district attorney. Cousy waited for four hours. When he went back inside the tone had changed. One of the things they'd asked him about during the afternoon was if he knew two men from St. Albans. He had told them yes, but had never heard their names mentioned in the scandals. As it turned out, while he'd been waiting outside, the district attorney had brought the two men in.

"It seems Cousy had met them before a game in New Haven, Connecticut, against Yale when he was in college, but it was to give them tickets to the game. What he didn't know was that the two men had been telling the dead bookie they had Cousy in their pocket, thus receiving money from the bookie. Paying Cousy for the tickets in New Haven was to show the bookie evidence of this. So the district attorney told him he could go, that the two men corroborated his story."[16] Despite playing innocent here, a few years later Cousy would admit to knowing gamblers, talking to them regularly about inside information, and perhaps even more.

Meanwhile, the FBI continued its fact-finding mission, turning up new evidence under each rock they overturned regarding the Celtics. And the story went from simply betting on games to fixing them. From the Bureau's Boston Office: "On 2/6/59 [redacted] advised in strict confidence that [redacted] Boston Celtics basketball games are being fixed on the 'point spread' because rumors have come to the [redacted] that Worcester gamblers have been bragging about the easy money they have made betting on Celtics games.

"[redacted] stated that, after the National Basketball Association East-West All-Star Game, he heard rumors that the Worcester gambling element had made some 'big money.' [redacted] stated that he regarded it as somewhat significant that [redacted], the [redacted] for the [redacted] who resides in [redacted], Mass., and who had been [redacted] the day of the All-Star game, [redacted] and then, in fact, did participate in the All-Star game." Three Celtics players participated in the 1959 All-Star game: Bill Sharman, Bill Russell, and Bob Cousy.

"[redacted] stated that [redacted], a [redacted] for [redacted], and [redacted] of the Worcester, Mass., PD Vice Squad, conducted a surveillance of [redacted] when the latter returned to Worcester from his playing trips, and they observed [redacted] on two occasions proceed to the home of Francis "Jigger" Santo, a well-known Worcester hoodlum and gambler….[redacted] further stated that [redacted] is [redacted] of an insurance company located in the Bancroft Hotel, Worcester, and [redacted] in the enterprise is Joseph P. Sharry, who is also engaged as the player's representative of the National Basketball Association. According to [redacted], Sharry has the reputation in Worcester of being friendly with the gambling element. In addition, [redacted] stated that [redacted] has in the past manifested an interest in making a 'fast dollar'.

"[redacted] stated he had discussed the above information [redacted], that they regard it as a very important matter but that they are in doubt as to what action to take. **[redacted]** requested that the FBI determine if the fixing of NBA basketball games would constitute a violation within the jurisdiction of the Bureau....**[redacted]** was advised that, on the basis of the information presented, there did not appear to be a violation within the Bureau's jurisdiction."

The latter portion of this file quote may be a bit hard to follow until you learn a few facts. Joseph Sharry's name is not well-known within the NBA. It should be. He helped create the NBA's players' union in the 1950s. But he didn't do it alone. His partner in the endeavor was none other than Bob Cousy who spearheaded the union's formation. Cousy served as the union's first president with Sharry as its secretary. The combination of Cousy and Sharry also shared a partnership in an insurance agency...located in Worcester, MA.[17] Could Cousy be the player whose name is redacted in this gambling-related file? It seems quite possible, considering both the repeated mention of Worcester and the relationship between the redacted name and Sharry.

If the file did pertain to Cousy, then it wasn't the only gambling connection he had. After Cousy had left the NBA following the 1962–63 season (though he came out of retirement to play in seven games for the Cincinnati Royals in 1969–70), Sandy Smith of *Life* magazine interviewed Cousy in 1967. Smith was interested in the persistent rumor that Cousy had been spared from the 1951 collegiate scandal thanks to Cardinal Spellman's influence over New York D.A. Hogan. When Smith unveiled his article, it claimed "the Mob had infiltrated college sports, and that Cousy had been involved with known gamblers....Smith wrote that Cousy's name had been found in the notebook of a gambler. Next to his name was the notation "Skiball," which was the nickname of Francesco Scibelli, an alleged gambler from Springfield, and according to Smith, a friend of Cousy's. Another of his friends, wrote Smith, was Anthony Pradella, also of Springfield, and Scibelli's partner. The article said that, because they always had such excellent information, the Scibelli-Pradella ring was known as the 'Scholar Group.' (Recall that this group allegedly booked NBA referee Mendy Rudolph's bets.) Cousy admitted he knew the two were gamblers and that he often talked to them about pro and college teams and their chances of winning.

"'I'd be having dinner with Pradella and Scibelli would come over,' said Cousy. 'They got together each night to balance the book or something.' Did Cousy realize his friends were using what he told them to fix betting lines and to make smart bets of their own? 'No,' he said. 'I thought they figured the betting line with mathematics. But it doesn't surprise me. I'm pretty cynical. I think most people who approach me want to use me for something.'

"At one point, Pradella invited him to a banquet in Hartford that turned out to be a gangster conclave. 'Police were watching the place,' said Cousy. 'The whole Mob was there.' Cousy defended his actions. 'In this hypocritical world we live in,' he said, 'I don't see why I should stop seeing my friends just because they are gamblers. How can I tell Andy when he calls and asks about a team that I won't talk to him about that?'"[18]

After the article's release, Cousy held a press conference denying most of Smith's article. He stated that the banquet was a simple gathering and that he never claimed the police were watching or that the "whole Mob" was there. However, more important was what Cousy didn't deny: his association with the Scholar Group. Cousy admitted knowing both Scibelli and Pradella for 12 years, but that he only met Scibelli "eight times" in that period. He had golfed several times with Pradella and knew that he gambled "as do most of us." *Life* did not retract anything Smith wrote. In an editorial the publication noted, "the fact that one individual was unwise in his friendship for known gamblers is far less important than the depths of which the Mob is infiltrating spectator sports in America and how much it is using players for its own illegal profit."[19]

Cousy won six NBA Championships as a member of the Boston Celtics, and was later elected to the Basketball Hall of Fame. During his professional career—and perhaps prior to it—he appeared to not just associate with known gamblers, but if the FBI was correct in its information, likely bet upon games in which he played, maybe even shaving points. Could those two opposing ideas—championship-caliber play and game fixing—actually go hand in hand? Of course. That is the beauty of the point spread. A team can thrill fans by winning every game outright, yet at the same time lose those same games in the gamblers' eyes due to the spread. Cousy may have burnt this candle at both ends without a suspicious glance from the NBA.

One of Cousy's teammates was Bill Russell, who would win a total of 11 world titles with the Celtics. Russell is a legend in his own right, a name often spoken with hushed reverence. Yet is it possible that Cousy introduced Russell to this dual lifestyle in the NBA? Of betting on basketball for extra income while still playing at the highest level?

Russell wrote in his autobiography: "Only once during my career did a big-time gambler approach me about fixing a game. He talked casually and indirectly about the proposition he had in mind, but I knew what he was getting at. 'You can't afford it,' I told him.

"This man was a heavy heavy, and the remark offended him. 'What do you mean I can't afford it?' he asked.

"'Look,' I said, 'I'm making over a hundred thousand dollars a year playing ball. During my career I should make over a million dollars. Now, to mess with you I'd have to risk all that, plus my reputation. That's a lot—it's my whole future. So even if I wanted to accommodate you, I couldn't think about it for less than nine or ten million a game—maybe even more. And that's just for me. To make any money, you'd have to be betting enough to have the whole state after you.'

"I reported this incident to the NBA Commissioner, and though nothing came of it, it demonstrates something about game fixing in the modern era: that high salaries are actually a further protection against corruption. A professional athlete would have to be crazy to take bribes today. I've always thought the most likely targets of gamblers would be the referees. They make peanuts, they're highly abused both by the fans and players, and they have more control over a game than anyone else. Moreover, the normal incompetence of NBA referees would be a perfect disguise for a corrupt one."[20]

Russell was right about NBA referees (though I doubt they enjoyed the "incompetent" label). But what about the rest of it? Russell claimed that he turned down the fixing offer because of fear of damaging his reputation, that too much was at stake to take the risk offered by easy money. It's a plausible, though exaggerated claim ($10 million to fix a game?). Yet perhaps Russell whitewashed his own past. Perhaps he didn't realize the FBI had a file implicating him in betting on NBA games, including ones in which he played. Perhaps the risk to his reputation actually wasn't as great as the lure of some extra cash.

The information regarding Russell came to the FBI while it was investigating another NBA legend, Wilt Chamberlain. Much like Jordan some 20 years later, "Wilt the Stilt" had the reputation of a compulsive gambler. This was common knowledge among those who knew him personally. To the FBI, this was news worthy of pursuit.

The FBI would soon discover: "A Boston informant had advised that Wilt Chamberlain, basketball star of Philadelphia 76ers, professional basketball team, is partner with [redacted] New York City bookmaker in restaurant in Harlem, New York. Chamberlain bets heavily on National Basketball Association professional basketball games and is currently betting heavily on basketball championship games between Los Angeles Lakers and Boston Celtics....Discreet inquiries will be made for information which might indicate Federal gambling violation."

This information was expanded upon by the informant on April 20, 1966: "[redacted] advised that he received information from one of his most reliable sources who told him that Wilt Chamberlaine [sic] of the Philadelphia Warriors [sic — 76ers] is a very heavy gambler in basketball games in the NBA. Informant stated that Chamberlain is a partner with [redacted] a well-known NYC bookmaker in the [redacted] of [Big Wilt's] Small's Paradise Restaurant on Seventh Avenue in Harlem, New York. Chamberlain gives all his basketball bets to [redacted] telephonically whenever Chamberlain is not in personal contact with [redacted] in NYC. Informant states that Chamberlain works with [redacted] in fixing a point spread for the various games and then makes his bets. Informant states that Chamberlain is presently betting heavily in the basketball games for the championship of the NBA which is presently underway....Wilt Chamberlain is President and [redacted] Big Wilt-

Small's Paradise Restaurant, NYC, and that [redacted] a.k.a. [redacted] according to [redacted] a source of the informant stated that this is a gambling joint in which [redacted] figures prominently inasmuch as he is a Harlem gambler. It is a general opinion that Chamberlain has shaded points in the professional games that he is a part of and places bets on these shading situations through [redacted]."

The Bureau sensed blood in the waters surrounding Chamberlain. Friendly with known gamblers? Gambling on NBA games? "Shading" points? The hunt was on for more. Shortly thereafter, a "Boston top-echelon informant" provided the following to the FBI:

"On November 2, 1966, [redacted] advised that during the previous week he heard rumors of a possible 'fix' concerning the Philadelphia-Boston Celtics basketball game which occurred October 29, 1966, at Philadelphia, Pennsylvania [the 76ers won this game 138–96]. Informant stated he received this information from a [redacted] named [redacted]. [redacted] indicated to informant that word had been received prior to the game that Philadelphia was to win. The point spread during the week was Philadelphia and five points. On the evening of the game, the game was 'off the boards' in Boston except that bets were being accepted on the Boston Celtics [only Boston bookmakers "in the know" continued to book bets on this game, taking wagers from the squares betting on the Celtics that night]....

"Informant advised on November 3, 1966, that he had received information through [redacted] [a Philadelphia player] had bet $15,000 on Philly on the above-mentioned game in New York. Informant also learned through [redacted] had $11,000 on Philadelphia but either $2,000 or $3,000 of this amount was for [redacted] Boston Celtics player.

"Informant was advised to closely follow this matter and attempt to learn of any additional attempts to either shave points or throw games, particularly the [upcoming] Philadelphia-Boston Celtics game scheduled at the Boston Garden on Saturday, November 5, 1966."

The FBI zeroed in on three players: Wilt Chamberlain, Bill Russell (who was the Celtics player/coach at the time), and a third un-known-due-to-redaction member of the Celtics. The Bureau wanted to interview all three, but were waiting for the best possible information from their informants and sources prior to taking that next step. No open inquiries were being made at that time, nor was the NBA informed. Yet the information continued to come in regarding the looming November 5 match-up between the Celtics and 76ers. "On 11/4/66 [redacted] advised he has learned through [redacted] that [redacted] has bet $15,000 on the game scheduled for 11/5/66 on Philadelphia. Informant also has learned that Bill Russell is betting on Philadelphia for this game, amount not known." Philadelphia-area bookies were consulted regarding this game, but they claimed low volume on NBA games at that time with no games taken off boards there.

The FBI had one huge problem. All of this gambling by the likes of Chamberlain wasn't a crime. "As you know, the fact that players bet on a game or games in which they are involved, does not in itself constitute a violation of the Sports Bribery statute. The Bureau, however, desires to be furnished any information concerning wagering activity on the part of those engaged in professional sports. As you know, it is extremely important that the Bureau be advised in the event information received indicating that an individual or individuals in any way offered a bribe in connection with the outcome of a particular athletic event." This investigation could only go so far. If the FBI discovered that NBA players were betting on NBA games—even fixing them—without a "bribe" instigating this behavior, their hands were tied.

Come the November 5 game between the Celtics and 76ers, the betting line indicated Philadelphia was the favorite, giving anywhere from 6.5 to 5.5 points to the Celtics. What happened in the game? Boston won going away 105–87. If the information the FBI possessed was correct, those betting on the 76ers—including Russell—lost their money. In the initial game between these two franchises, which the 76ers won (and covered the spread) 138–96, Russell posted 12 points for the Celtics with Chamberlain tossing in 13 for the 76ers. In this losing rematch, Chamberlain hammered down 26 with Russell scoring a mere 4. Playing the devil's advocate here, it's interesting to note that both Russell and

Chamberlain were their teams' respective centers. In other words, they matched up against each other. If they were trying to give the 76ers a win in this second game, Russell's low scoring output (4 points when he averaged 13.3 a game in 1966–67) coupled with Chamberlain's high total (26 points, 10 of which came from his 21 free throw attempts) makes their intentions that evening appear suspect.

These two games were not the end of it. "On November 18, 1966, [redacted] advised he had been informed by [redacted] that Wilt Chamberlain of the Philadelphia 76's [sic] has bet $12,000 on Philadelphia for their game of November 18, 1966, with the Chicago Bulls at Boston, Massachusetts. Additionally, [redacted] told the informant that [redacted], [redacted] of the Boston Celtics, has bet $6,000 on Baltimore for the Celtics game with Baltimore on November 18, 1966, at Boston. [redacted] received ten points with Baltimore for this bet and he put up $6,000 to win $5,000. Chamberlain's bet of $12,000 will win him $10,000 if he is correct in forecasting the outcome of the game. Informant did not know the point spread which Chamberlain received regarding the Philadelphia game. Boston will view both games in an effort to determine whether there is any suspicious activity on the part of either [redacted] or Chamberlain." Chamberlain's 76ers won 145–120, likely netting Wilt his $10,000. As for the Celtics player who bet against his team, that bet was a loser as the Celtics won and covered 143–119. This information prompted the FBI to consider closer monitoring of betting lines. "It is suggested the Bureau consider the feasibility of obtaining on a weekly basis the opening lines and closing lines on all national pro sporting events for each week since such information, barring weather and key injuries or other legitimate reasons, might indicate or suggest a fix. It should be noted that when these offices furnish any specific point spread change, they should also offer a reason for the point spread if same is known—such as injury to a key player."

While the FBI monitored the players, a familiar name within the East Coast gambling circles reappeared: the Scholar Group. After Cousy had left the NBA, the Boston-based Scholar Group appeared to maintain its connections with other members of the Celtics. Informants had a difficult time tracking the wagering activities of the group, yet they were never far from the action. "In late February, 1967, informant stated that concerning the Boston Celtics-Philadelphia Pro Basketball game on Sunday February 12, 1967 that [redacted] representing [redacted — two lines]…informant stated that as to the game, Boston was leading by ten points with about three minutes to play when [redacted] fouled out [Russell, KC Jones, and Tom Sanders all fouled out for the Celtics] and apparently Chamberlain during the remainder of this game did not play up to par. [Chamberlain did score 28 points in this game, but was 8 for 24 in free throw attempts.]

"According to the informant, no information had come to his attention as to whether Chamberlain or any of the Celtics' team members had wagered on this game, which Boston won by one point [113–112] thus causing 'The Scholar Group' to lose their bet. Informant also did not know whether [redacted] himself had made any wagers on this game, but he assumes from past history that Boston was undoubtedly a [redacted] selection. Informant stated that the only thing the above incident demonstrated to him that it did not appear that 'The Scholar Group' were controlling the Celtics players, such as [redacted] or Chamberlain. He stated that this was a generalization on his part."

Despite all of this information, the reliable sources, and the apparent betting activities of NBA players, for the FBI, this amounted to nothing criminal. Therefore when the 1966–67 basketball season ended with Chamberlain's 76ers winning the NBA Championship, "no further investigation is being conducted by Boston."

While Russell and the other unnamed member of the Celtics were released from scrutiny, Chamberlain was not off the hook just yet. Come March 15, 1968, "[redacted] has advised that the Philadelphia, Pennsylvania, National Basketball star Wilt Chamberlain has been betting heavily on basketball games involving his team and has bet as high as $10,000 to $15,000 on a particular game. In all instances, he has bet on his own team and the informant had no information that Chamberlain had ever bet against his team or was involved in any point shaving." There was more. "In general conversation with [redacted — a Special Agent] stated that Wilt Chamberlain and [redacted] both of the Philadelphia Warriors [this Agent was a bit "old school," as the Philadelphia Warriors moved to San Francisco in 1962 with the 76ers coming to town the following year from Syracuse], NBA, bet large amounts on NBA basketball games. [redacted] denied knowing who the bets were placed with or the names of any beards that were utilized by the two basketball players to place these bets." A later source would tell the FBI that Chamberlain used a woman to place his bets.

The FBI would later open a file specifically on Chamberlain. Within it, they noted his association with Irving "Ash" Resnick. A friend to boxers Joe Louis and Sonny Liston, Resnick was mobbed up. Though he was one of the original owners of Caesars Palace in Las Vegas, Resnick was thought to be a mafia courier and the Nevada representative for New England's Patriarca crime family. In 1974, eight sticks of dynamite were found under his car. Two years later he was shot at while leaving Caesars Palace, but neither event killed him. Resnick died of cancer in 1989.

"[redacted] and Ash Resnick, who are described as Caesars Palace Casino executives, Las Vegas, along with Joe Louis, ex-heavyweight champion, were in Philadelphia. These individuals were observed in Philadelphia in contact with Wilt Chamberlain, the well-known professional basketball player. This meeting occurred two or three weeks ago. Subsequent to this meeting, a very important game was played involving the Philadelphia team, and there was a considerable amount of gambling money paid on the game. Chamberlain is alleged to have twisted his knee in practice just prior to the game or the day before the game. This resulted in a very poor performance during the game. As a result of Chamberlain's poor performance a heavily one-sided score was made against Philadelphia. As a result of this score, much gambling money is alleged to have changed hands."

The FBI's suspicions were again raised. Chamberlain and another member of the 76ers "spent considerable time with Ash Resnick at Caesars Palace." Both were on Caesars' "comp" list in January 1968, which was no surprise as Resnick is often credited with creating the "high roller" atmosphere in Vegas; bringing whales to town was his specialty. "Inasmuch as 'Ash' Resnick is a friend of such hoodlums and gambling notables as Meyer Lansky, Vincent 'Jimmy Blue Eyes' Alo, and Charlie 'The Blade' Tourine, and has been involved in the past in fixing prize fights, our Philadelphia office is conducting appropriate inquiries to determine if, in fact, a violation of the Sports Bribery Statute exists."

Chamberlain's "injury" that the FBI questioned was publicized on February 10–11, 1968. On Saturday, February 10, Chamberlain's 76ers lost to the New York Knicks 115–97 with Wilt scoring just 16 points. The following night Chamberlain acquired accommodations for Joe Louis and Resnick at the St. Louis Hawks-76ers game which was played in Miami. "Chamberlain did not complain of his knee and in fact played the greatest game of the season and the '76ers' won by more than 20 points in a game in which the '76ers' were the underdog (due to Chamberlain's alleged injury)." The 76ers won 119–93 with Wilt bouncing back to score 21 in the game.

Amazingly, the source of this information for the FBI was Philadelphia-area sports writer George Kiseda. "Kiseda stated on 2/14/68 and again on 4/26/68 that he has absolutely no evidence of wrong-doing on the part of Chamberlain and/or Resnick in regard to point spread or regulating the games, however, the turn of events does look suspicious." Indeed it did. Given the known gambling history of Chamberlain, coupled with his association with Resnick whom the FBI labeled as a fight-fixer, all the ingredients seemed to mix for a potential game-fixing incident. Perhaps the "knee injury" was a true ailment for Wilt. Or perhaps it was the perfect ruse to manipulate the betting lines and make a fast buck over a pair of weekend games. Yet because Resnick was already under investigation for his mafia ties, the FBI closed this case and no further information on sports bribery was made available.

The NBA may have remained ignorant of all this information surrounding Hall of Famers Cousy, Russell, Chamberlain, and Mendy Rudolph. It may not have realized that members of the NY Knicks were involved in betting with their cocaine dealer. There is never a mention within the FBI files that the Bureau shared this information with the league. If so, one could almost—almost—forgive the NBA for these oversights. But the true question to ponder is whether the NBA was in

256

fact aware of the gambling habits of some of their premier athletes and referees, and covered it up. Without a conviction—which the FBI never obtained in any of these cases—it would be easy to do. One would think that if these rumors trickled their way to the FBI, the NBA should have also known something. Chamberlain and Rudolph were both compulsive gamblers. Cousy and Russell may have been betting on NBA games "merely" to make a few extra bucks. And even though the likes of Jordan, Barkley, Walker, and Iverson have had significant public brushes with gambling, we're led to believe nary a single NBA game has been fixed or seen points shaved since Jack Molinas was banned from the league in 1954. Even Tim Donaghy, who nearly every expert would say fixed games, was never found guilty of such a crime. Can this really be the truth?

FOOTBALL

"Game fixing in the NFL is far more subtle, dangerous, and likely than the biased guardians of professional football want the public to believe."
— *former NFL player Bernie Parrish, 1971*

The National Football League (NFL) was founded in September 1920. Between that date and the day you read this, the league proudly proclaims that not one of its games has been influenced by gamblers or organized crime—ever. As former head of the Stardust race and sports book Scott Schettler said upon hearing this boast, "Aw, bullshit. That's just outlandish." Legendary sports gambler Lem Banker echoed those sentiments, saying, "Oh, that's absolute bullshit." Banker then promptly related a story to me about a fixed game played between the Minnesota Vikings and the Tampa Bay Buccaneers. In fact, with the noted exception of former NFL security chief Warren Welsh, every person interviewed for this book, when asked if they believed the honesty of the NFL's claim, responded in a similar negative fashion.

Despite these opinions, the NFL possesses one huge fact in its advantage: history. While the league will admit that twice in its past—prior to the 1946 NFL Championship Game between the Chicago Bears and New York Giants, and before a 1971 Houston Oilers game—gamblers did unsuccessfully attempt to fix a game, never has someone been convicted for this crime. No one has publicly confessed to doing so either. Without this, the NFL is free to maintain its stand.

Yet in his 1989 book *Interference: How Organized Crime Influences Professional Football*, investigative author Dan Moldea uncovered 70 NFL games that had been fixed. These dated between 1951 and 1979 and were backed by statements from some of the men involved. As was discussed in the introduction, Moldea went through hell because of his accusations against the league. But that doesn't mean he was wrong. Instead, the more the NFL went after him, the more Moldea may have been correct, as this has been the league's modus operandi against allegations of game fixing since such stories began to surface.

During the celebration of the Philadelphia Eagles' 1960 NFL Championship Game victory over the Green Bay Packers, a long-distance call came into the Warwick Hotel from Bob Bowie of the *Denver Post*. Tom Brookshier, an Eagles cornerback who was living in Denver at the time, took the call. Bowie told Brookshier he was going to run a story that Packers quarterback Bart Starr was bought off and had fixed the game. He claimed his source was a man named Arley Berry whom Brookshier knew from his college days at Colorado. Upon hearing this, Brookshier, a six-year league veteran, went back into the ballroom and got newly appointed commissioner Pete Rozelle on the phone with the reporter. "The first thing [Rozelle] said to Bowie on the phone was, 'You've got 12 lawsuits as soon as you run that, and the personal lawsuits will follow with all the people that you're going to destroy. The *Denver Post* will never run again.'"[1] The *Denver Post* never published Bowie's story.

This is perhaps what the NFL does better than any of its major-league counterparts. It is able to control both the media and the message, keeping negative stories from becoming stories at all. This art was taught to the league by former commissioner Pete Rozelle, whose background was in public relations. "[Rozelle] was forced to deal with a gambling problem of one kind or another every year since he was elected the NFL's chief executive officer in 1960. The fact that most fans can't recall much about the NFL's gambling scandals is testimony to his ability to enhance the league's public image while he policed the conduct of its personnel. 'We have a basic rule in the NFL,' says a former law enforcement official who advises the NFL on security matters. 'It is to keep it upbeat and keep it positive. But, above all, they want to keep everything quiet.'"[2]

Don Weiss was the NFL's Director of Information during the late 1960s and early 1970s. In his book *The Making of the Super Bowl* he wrote, "Almost overnight, these public relations people gained a status throughout the league they had never enjoyed before…High school students were hired to clip everything that was written about the NFL in the hundred-odd daily papers to which the NFL subscribed. The clips were used to build hundreds of files on players, coaches, and every conceivable football topic. The best—and occasionally the worst—were distributed throughout the league to keep clubs apprised of what various writers were thinking. When the tone of a columnist indicated that some friendly guidance was needed, he'd get a phone call offering it."[3] "Friendly guidance" was not what Bob Bowie received from Rozelle in regards to his 1960 NFL Championship Game fixing article. It was a threat. Whether Rozelle and the NFL would have followed through on it is a different question, but the fear of litigation has kept many from attacking the NFL on any level.

THE PUBLIC CALLS IT SPORT

From an outsider's perspective it appears that NFL owners stand shoulder to shoulder with the commissioner, marching in a lockstep beat in all matters concerning the league. This seems especially true when it comes to gambling and game fixing. Yet at one point in the past an owner broke away from his compatriots and let slip that not all was as it appeared within professional football. Harry Wismer was a one-time broadcaster who did what no one thought possible—he owned two NFL teams at the same time. Wismer first purchased a stake in the Detroit Lions in 1947 with Ralph Wilson (who currently owns the Buffalo Bills), and then in 1950 added shares of the Washington Redskins to his repertoire. Wismer discarded his piece of the Redskins in 1960 (he would hold a stake in the Lions until 1964) to help found the NFL's rival, the American Football League (AFL). There he established the New York Titans. Despite owning a prime franchise in New York City, when Wismer's Titans ran into financial trouble no one would invest to save his team. His three-year tenure in the AFL bankrupted him. None of his AFL partners—including Ralph Wilson—would help him either, preferring to see Wismer sell to entertainment mogul Sonny Werblin who would rename the team the Jets and reinvent not just the AFL, but professional football.

Shortly after leaving the Titans behind and just two years prior to passing away, Wismer published *The Public Calls It Sport*. The book revealed a few well-kept secrets that the NFL certainly would have preferred remained private. For example, Wismer wrote of an incident from 1939 in which one former owner's open gambling habits grated against the NFL's by-laws. "Everyone knew [Detroit Lions owner George "Dick"] Richards gambled, as did many of the other owners. They always bet on their own team….In the letters he had foolishly written to [Lions head coach "Gloomy" Gus] Henderson, Richards revealed that he had bet heavily on a number of the Lions' games and called for everyone's best efforts to win for him.

"Then, as now, it was against the league charter for an owner or player or coach to bet. The rule wasn't enforced but the owners were careful not to put anything in writing. Richards had violated that unwritten covenant and [the recently fired] Henderson saw his chance to embarrass Richards and the league by releasing the letters to [Chicago Bears owner and NFL founding member George] Halas. Halas called me to discuss the matter, and he agreed nothing would be gained by releasing the story to the press, and in Richards' condition, the notoriety might kill him. Halas kept the secret of Richards' betting for years and it only became public knowledge in December of 1964."[4]

Note a few things from this short story. One, not 20 years into the league's existence and multiple NFL owners were gambling on their own sport despite it being against their own rules. Two, it was admitted by a former owner that their own rules weren't readily enforced. Three, despite the Detroit Lions being the Chicago Bears' rivals, Halas refused to damage his opponent and by extension the league by revealing this evidence. And four, this information was willingly withheld from the press for 25 years.

Wismer also wrote an interesting comment about De Benneville "Bert" Bell who served as the NFL's commissioner from 1946 until his death in 1959. Bell's apparent stance on gambling differed greatly from all of the league's subsequent commissioners. "Bert Bell was many things but he was never naïve. He never thought that because pro football was a sport, gambling and gamblers couldn't influence the game. He knew people bet on his games and his slant on betting was grown-up. 'Let them bet. That's their privilege. My job is to keep it from having an influence on our game.'"[5]

Was Bell successful in that endeavor? Wismer for one would say "no." But not in his book. Publicly Wismer would back the league and its officials, writing, "The only way games can be kept free of outside influence is to count on the integrity of the players and officials. When you consider the number of years that the game has been played and the amounts of money that have been bet, the status of pro football today is testimony not alone to its popularity but also its honesty. If I were a gambler and wanted to fix a game, I'd never go to a player or coach. No one player, not even a quarterback, can fix a game...."[6] Privately, when speaking with the FBI, Wismer would tell a completely different story.

The AFL launched in 1960 with Wismer's Titans seen as being the prime franchise in the league. One season later, it's quite possible members of the Titans were fixing games. As this was 1961 and prior to the passage of the Sports Bribery Act, if in fact Titans games were being fixed, it was not a federal crime nor was there reason for the FBI to investigate. However, the FBI did collect information on this incident which has been locked away within its files for the past 50 years. This is

what the FBI wrote:

"On November 24, 1961, Sammy Baugh, head coach of the New York Titans professional football team was interviewed at his request by Agents of our New York Office. Baugh at that time related a series of circumstances which he feels indicates that there are some suspicions that recent games participated in by his team were 'fixed.'

"Baugh advised that on October 22, 1961, the Titans played the Denver Club of the American Football League, with which both clubs are associated. He said that the Titans, the pre-game favorite, lost the game to Denver. Upon returning to his hotel room at the Denver Hilton, Baugh found a written message for him, directing him to [redacted] at the hotel. Baugh said that this [redacted — three lines worth].

"Immediately after receiving this message, Baugh said he called Joe Foss, Commissioner of the American Football League. [redacted — two more lines]. [redacted] went on to state that the following week the ball club played in San Francisco and defeated the Oakland Raiders by a score of 14 to 6, but the team received severe criticism from some sports writers for attempting three passes in the last fifty seconds of the game, when, for all intents and purposes, the Titans had the game won and merely jeopardized the outcome of the game by passing. Baugh defended this action on the part of his quarterback.

"A week later the Titans were defeated by the San Diego Chargers after leading at one point in the first half by a score of 30 to 0. Baugh said that immediately following this game all members of the team and the coaching staff received individual air mail, special delivery letters at their hotel from Harry Wismer, president of the ball club. In his letter [which the interviewing agents saw courtesy of Baugh], Wismer pointed out to the players the serious nature of any possible gambling activities on the part of any members of the staff of the team, and he indicated expulsion from football for life and full prosecution of the law if any were so involved. Wismer indicated that something was amiss during the last three Titans games.

"Baugh went on to state that on November 15, 1961, he received a telephone message which was left with the switch- [redacted — two lines].

"[redacted] in conclusion, pointed out that it is no secret that there is considerable hard feelings between Harry Wismer and himself, and he is of the opinion that Wismer is trying to force him to resign his position as head coach and, thereby, relieve Wismer of paying him for the third and final year of his coaching contract. [redacted — two lines].

"The above facts are all that are known in this regard. It would be appreciated if you would advise if they constitute the basis for a possible violation of a Federal statute and whether you desire any investigation of this matter."

The above memo was sent to the Attorney General, the Deputy Attorney General, and the Assistant Attorney General for review and advice.

A day later, the following was reported: "Foss and Wismer currently engaged in controversy over affairs of American Football League. Wismer and Baugh disputing over terms of Baugh's contract with New York Titans which has one more year to run. Possibility is present that one or all of three men would endeavor to exploit through publicity any open Bureau investigation for their purposes in these controversies. [redacted — two lines]. Recommend Department be consulted as to whether there is possible violation of law. Thus if we conduct investigation it will be on Department authority."

Come late December 1961, the FBI was still intrigued by this brewing scandal, even if it wasn't sure it should be involved. By this time Baugh had been ousted as the Titans' head coach and the Bureau had gathered better statistics—and betting lines—on the games in question. "On October 22, 1961, the Titans were a five-point favorite against the Denver Cowboys. Denver scored 17 points in the fourth period to win 27 to 10. On October 29, 1961, the Titans were a six and one-half point favorite and defeated the Oakland Raiders 14 to 6. On November 5, 1961, the San Diego Chargers were a 17-point favorite over the Titans and although the Titans led 13 to 7 at half time [not by 30 as Baugh had

erroneously reported], San Diego scored 41 points in the second half for a final score of 48 to 13." At the bottom of this memo was a handwritten note, signed simply "H" for Hoover. It read, "If I recall correctly when Baugh was a Red Skin he didn't 'smell too sweetly.'"

The Director's memory was sharp. As the quarterback for the Washington Redskins, Sammy Baugh had allegations of point shaving pinned against him. Vincent X. Flaherty and Dick O'Brien of the *Washington Times-Herald* reported rumors about Baugh and the Redskins gambling on games in December 1943. Like Rozelle with the allegations about the 1960 NFL Championship Game, Redskins owner George Marshall instantly attacked the report and boldly offered a $5,000 reward for proof that any member of the Redskins had gambled on a game. Not even Flaherty or O'Brien could collect. Of course, this meant the story was false, right?

Maybe not. "Baugh did not know that George Marshall had secretly recorded the quarterback's conversations with known bookmakers during the week Flaherty and O'Brien had broken their initial story. The surveillance was arranged through a D.C. police officer, Joe Shimon, who had been hired by Marshall via publisher William K. Hutchinson....The surveillance of the conversations, recorded on old seventy-eight phonograph records...include[d] conversations in which Baugh and other players were heard discussing point spreads, player injuries, inside information, bets, and their bookmaker friends....Although there is no evidence on the recordings that Baugh or any other Redskins player ever threw a game in 1943, the evidence is clear that Baugh and perhaps as many as four other players had personal and/or financial relationships with gamblers and bookmakers."[7]

Setting Baugh aside, the FBI began investigating both the local and long-distance calls made to and from the hotels the Titans stayed at prior to each of the three games in question. But just after the start of 1962, the Justice Department put the kibosh on the whole investigation. "This will confirm an oral request by [redacted] of Assistant Attorney General Miller's office on January 5, 1962, to withhold all investigation involving allegations of questionable practices on the part of members

of the New York Titans professional football team [no reason was given in the memo]. In accordance with this request, all investigation in this matter has been discontinued."

Yet two weeks later, agents contacted Wismer. "Mr. Harry Wismer, President, New York Titans, advised on January 16, 1962, that he has no specific information indicating that members of the Titans were in contact with the gambling element. He advised that he had sent a special delivery letter to each member of the team and the coaching staff following the Oakland game, but this letter was not based on any specific indication he had that any ballplayers had been in contact with the gambling element or might have attempted to alter the outcome of the game. He stated further that letters were sent to warn the team against any such activity as well as to protect his financial interest in the Titans.

"Following the San Diego game, Wismer again verbally warned the players and the coaches that any collusion with gamblers would result in punitive action. At that time he was advised by the players that following the previous Sunday game with Oakland, Coach Sammy Baugh told the players they were free until the following Thursday; consequently, training rules and practice were abandoned until the Thursday before the San Diego game. He stated this fact, together with the high temperature during the game, resulted in the second-half rout in which San Diego scored 42 points against the Titans." Wismer later told FBI in this report that, "in his opinion, basis for gambling contact existed in National Football League since Art Rooney, Pittsburgh Steelers, and the late Tim Mara, New York Giants, were both former bookmakers."

There the matter ended...until Wismer brought it up again. This time he was angered enough to contact the FBI's New York Bureau directly, set to drop a bombshell. "On 10/3/62, Harry Wismer, owner, New York Titans, professional football club of the American Football League, was contacted by [two special agents] as a result of his contact with the [New York Office], alleging that gamblers had influenced the outcome of the Denver-New York game of 9/29/62 [the game was actually played on September 30 in New York and won by Denver 32–10]. Wismer stated that his [redacted — two lines] and, as a result, the Titans lost the game.

Wismer's allegation indicated that the gamblers had some influence in this connection.

"Upon interview, Wismer stated that he had no specific information to report, concerning illegal influence on the outcome of the game in question, but **felt that there is gambling influence present in both the American Football League and the National Football League today.** When questioned in this regard, Wismer could offer no specific information to substantiate this claim, but stated that he is attempting to develop information in this regard, and, when he comes into possession of such information, will immediately furnish same to the interviewing Agents." [emphasis added]

Let's recap. Harry Wismer, one-time owner of three current NFL franchises—the Detroit Lions, Washington Redskins, and New York Jets—set up an interview with the FBI of his own accord, in which he not only stated that his team threw its last game played, but that gambling had influence within both the AFL and NFL as of the 1962 season. Granted, like most, Wismer had no solid evidence of this influence—what could he possess?—but as someone who had been an owner for 15 years and held a position as a league broadcaster for even more, his opinion of the game should be held in the highest regard. If he was willing to walk into the FBI's office and state, "last Sunday's game was fixed, and other games are under gamblers' influences as well," we should all listen, as it flies directly in the face of the NFL's standing policy that no game has ever been fixed.

It is perhaps the "smoking gun" that reveals the NFL has knowingly lied to its fans. What follows is merely the collateral damage.

THE PATRIOTS & THE MAFIA

In 2010, the NFL took great measures to celebrate the 50th anniversary of its one-time rival, the American Football League. Teams that were once part of the hotly debated 1970 merger between the two leagues proudly sported "throwback" jerseys and helmets nostalgically designed

to recall a different time and place. NFL Films produced a five-part documentary titled *Full Color Football: The History of the American Football League* to coincide with this anniversary. Yet nowhere within all of this hoopla did any sportswriter or ESPN talking head bother to mention that during the decade the AFL existed, seven of its ten teams—the New York Titans/Jets, Boston/New England Patriots, Buffalo Bills, Houston Oilers, Miami Dolphins, Denver Broncos, and Dallas Texans/Kansas City Chiefs—had players and/or coaches come under suspicion for either gambling on games or for shaving points.

Shortly after Titans owner Harry Wismer told the FBI that he was certain gamblers were influencing games in both the NFL and AFL, an informant told the Bureau about the gambling habits of at least two members of the Boston Patriots. This information began to trickle into the FBI in October 1962. "Informant reports that two or three members of the Boston Patriots football team are big betters [sic] with [redacted]. An important better [sic] and frequent visitor to [redacted] booking office is [redacted]. On 10/18/62, this informant advised that [redacted] and [redacted] members of the Boston Patriots are indebted to [redacted]. Informant states that bets are placed for these players by [redacted] and believes that these players, along with [redacted], are 'shading points' on Boston Patriots games....Informant stated that a player on the [redacted] named [redacted] is being paid by [redacted] to affect scores of the games. The informant states that he has observed [redacted] giving signals to [redacted] from the stands indicating a bet has been placed for [redacted] by [redacted]."

A little over a month later in December 1962, the FBI had more information to consider. "A confidential informant of the Boston Office who is closely associated with the racketeering element controlled by [Gennaro] Jerry Angiulo, leading hoodlum of the Boston area, has furnished information concerning wagering by members of the Boston Patriots football team of the American Football League with [redacted] in Boston.

"As you are aware, on 11-30-62 [redacted] placed bets against their team in a regularly scheduled league game with the New York Titans

and based on the point spread they won when the Titans were defeated by a score of 24 to 17.

"We have also learned that in connection with the Boston Patriots-Buffalo Bills game on 11-23-62 which ended in a tie, bets were placed by participants in the game [this game was actually played on November 3, not 23, and ended in a 28–28 tie]. These wagers were made contingent upon the point spread between the two clubs which resulted in winnings for the betters [sic].

"[redacted] according to our source, won [redacted] from a six to five bet on the Boston Patriots-Houston Oilers game played on 11-18-62. The point spread being five points in favor of Houston and Houston being victorious 21 to 17...."

What was the FBI to do with this solid information? Nothing. If players on the Patriots were shaving points in 1962, no federal crime was being committed; therefore, the FBI had no jurisdiction. They were not the AFL's police force. In fact, they hadn't even informed AFL commissioner Joe Foss of this information, though the Bureau did note, "A review of Bureau indices relative to Joseph Foss, Commissioner of the American Football League at Dallas, Texas, fails to indicate any derogatory information and it was noted that on 12-18-43 the Director [Hoover] designated Foss as his number one choice candidate to receive the National Distinguished Service Award of the United States Junior Chamber of Commerce in its selection of the ten outstanding young men of America of 1943."

On December 14, 1962, a memo from the Director gave the go-ahead to the Dallas Bureau to contact AFL commissioner Foss about the Boston Patriots betting. What Foss and the AFL did with this information is unknown. Whatever was done—if anything—wasn't overly effective, because once the Sports Bribery Act passed, the FBI investigated members of the Patriots in earnest for gambling on football games.

In September 1967, the FBI heard a very interesting story from an informant regarding members of the Patriots. "[redacted] advised on 9/11/67 that he had been approached the evening of 9/8/67 by [redact-

ed] Boston Patriot football players to place a bet on the San Diego Chargers to win an AFL football contest between the two teams the evening of 9/9/67....**[redacted]** introduced the betting proposition to informant by stating the **[redacted]** at the Stardust Hotel [in San Diego, not Las Vegas] had advised him the informant could possibly be of help to him. **[redacted]** is unknown to the informant. Initially, **[redacted]** gave him a hundred dollar bill and then another four one-hundred dollar bills were given to the informant. The informant decided that he did not want to hold $500 and returned $300 to **[redacted]**. The players indicated that up to $2,000 would be forthcoming to bet on the game and the informant would get half the proceeds for placing the bets. Informant attempted to place a bet with a bookmaker friend who made a telephone call and then advised the informant that he could only accept the Chargers with a six-point spread. Informant did not place a bet for the Patriots players and returned their money to them because while in negotiation to place the bets, he read a newspaper account that indicated that **[redacted]** had been connected with Life Magazine to gamblers and he did not want to get involved. He telephonically advised **[redacted]** of his inability to place a bet well before game time. When he advised **[redacted]** that he could not make the bet, **[redacted]** made a comment to the effect that it did not matter as they were probably going to win anyway."

Who was that player connected to gamblers in *Life* magazine? It was the former All-American quarterback from the University of Kentucky, Vito "Babe" Parilli. The story was in a two-part series on the mafia that *Life* published September 8, 1967. Titled "$7 Billion on Illegal Bets and a Blight on Sports," the article detailed the connection between Patriots players and a notorious Massachusetts mob haunt, Arthur's Farm. The article stated: "Another potentially explosive situation involves the strange affinity that several members of the Boston Patriots pro football team have for a ramshackle roadside store in suburban Revere, Mass. named Arthur's Farm. Behind its shabbily humdrum front, Arthur's Farm turns out to be a beehive of Mob activities. It does a fast business in sports betting and the exchange of stolen property, and doubles as an informal conference hall where gangsters can get together with people who are of use to them.

"The proprietor is Arthur Ventola, a convicted fence [who would be murdered by Whitey Bulger's Winter Hill Gang in 1976]. Among the regular habitués are Arthur's kinsmen—Nicholas (Junior) Ventola and Richard Castucci, both active bookies. [Castucci was allegedly a FBI informant. When famed Boston mobster Whitey Bulger learned of this, he began betting football with Castucci, keeping him alive as long as he was winning his bets. When Whitey's luck ended, so did Castucci's, who was found in the trunk of his car with a bullet in his head.] Another is Henry Tameleo, a lieutenant of New England Cosa Nostra boss Raymond Patriarca who, with Tameleo, is now awaiting trial for an interstate gambling-and-murder conspiracy.

"Another regular at the farm, it turns out, is Babe Parilli, quarterback of the Boston Patriots. 'Half the team goes there,' Parilli told *Life*. 'One of the coaches, too. But we're not doing anything wrong.' Parilli admitted knowing Arthur and 'Junior' and to having met Tameleo. He insisted he did not know they were mobsters, or that they used information garnered from Parilli and the other Patriots to make a killing on 'informed' bets.

"Why, then, do Parilli and his teammates visit Arthur's Farm so often? 'We stop on the way home from practice,' says Parilli, 'to buy toys, razor blades and things we get at wholesale prices.'"[8]

While this might have seemed like a scoop, the FBI knew much of this information at least a year prior to the *Life* article's publication. In many ways, the *Life* piece mirrors the FBI's file from November 20, 1966. It reads, "[redacted] advised that for the last several weeks the following members of the Boston Patriots pro-football team have been in contact several times a week with [redacted] notorious thief and fence, at Arthur's Farm in Revere, Massachusetts....[redacted] has introduced this other group, and possibly other members of the Patriots team, to [redacted] who ingratiates himself by furnishing them toys and other articles which he has purchased from thieves and which were stolen in the Boston area. The friendship with [redacted] is very close at the present time and, in fact, [redacted] invited [redacted] to be his guest for a weekend in Miami, Florida when the Boston Patriots play the Miami

Dolphins.

"Informant has never observed [redacted] bet but does know that both [redacted] and the above-described coach have bet because he personally has placed the bets for them with 'Junior' [redacted] a relative of [redacted]. The bets were: $200 for [redacted] and $300 for the coach on the game two week ago, which would have been the Denver game. [redacted] lost his bet and the coach won his bet….Relative to the Denver game, the informant said he was accompanied by Henry Tameleo, LCN [La Cosa Nostra] member from Providence, Rhode Island. Tameleo asked [redacted] how the game looked; [redacted] told him to bet on Boston; Tameleo bet on Boston and lost."

The good thing here was it appeared as though Mafioso "lieutenant" Tameleo lost his bet, meaning it's doubtful this particular game in question was fixed. The bad thing was…well, everything else. Clearly, members of the Patriots were more than just chummy with the New England mobsters hanging around Arthur's Farm. How many of the Patriots? According to a 1967 *Sports Illustrated* source, "At least 20 of the Patriots, including 12 who are still with the club, have shopped at Arthur's Farm."[9] Couple that with the known fact that sports gamblers worked from there and, for the AFL, it should have been a recipe for disaster. However, team president Billy Sullivan was quick to defend his embattled quarterback, stating, "I've been in professional sports for 32 years and I have never met a nicer man, a man with a better character than Babe. He'll sit for hours talking to little kids. I've never even heard him swear. In some ways he reminds me more of a violinist than of an athlete."[10] Even so, Parilli's confession of sorts to *Life* raised a few eyebrows within the league. Shortly after the article's publication, "Parilli was polygraphed by the NFL, but the results were not made public."[11] However, Parilli's seven-year stint as the Patriots' starting quarterback came to an immediate halt after the 1967 season. He never started another game. In 1968, he suited up as Joe Namath's backup for the Jets and won a Super Bowl ring with the team in 1969.

There was still the matter of the 1967 Patriots-Chargers game on which the FBI believed members of the team attempted to bet. Patriots' defensive captain, linebacker Tom Addison, wrote a statement on a Stardust Motor Hotel place mat regarding Parilli and the *Life* article. It read in part, "We stand behind Babe 100 percent on and off the field because he is the type of person that is beyond reproach as a quarterback or as an individual. It is outrageous to think that Babe should be picked from so many of us—including myself—that have entered the doors of this so-called Arthur's Farm. If I had an Italian name, and was a quarterback, it could have been me. Why did they not use the name of an Irish or English player? Babe Parilli has done nothing wrong, nor have any of the other players who have shopped there. We want to drop the matter now and forget about it. It has not hurt our morale for this game with San Diego because we are a team and we will play like a team."[12]

The Patriots did play like a team against the Chargers—a team on the take. As *Sports Illustrated* reported, "Parilli deserved a better fate than he received Saturday night. His receivers dropped half a dozen passes. The Chargers scored a third touchdown after Boston, attempting to kick, lost the ball on a high pass from center. Trying to pull the game out, Parilli was hit while passing, and the ball went to San Diego's Kenny Graham, who ran it back for a touchdown and a 28–14 win. Parilli's substitute, John Huarte, late of Notre Dame and the Jets, finished the last couple of minutes of the game while Parilli and [Patriots head coach Mike] Holovak, old friends, exchanged some words that made them look like old enemies. Later nobody was talking. The Boston locker room was as gala as a polio ward."[13]

The FBI's informant who supposedly did not make the players' wager told the Bureau that the only line he could get on the game was six points. Yet according to the FBI, "Local newspapers carried the Patriots as a one to two point favorite in the contest." A big difference, but perhaps because in a game against Denver the week before—played immediately after the *Life* article ran—Parilli threw six interceptions in a 26–21 loss, bookmakers were having trouble setting a line. Even with the scrutiny on the team, the players wanted to bet, warning their potential beard, "The Patriots players in contact with the informant apprised him of the perilous position they were in by betting against their own team and cautioned him to make sure that any bets he placed were on his own account."

All in all, the FBI came to one determination. "No bribery violation [exists] as the players initiated the betting and the bet was not consummated." In other words, had the players bet against themselves and lost to the Chargers 28–14, they wouldn't have violated the Sports Bribery Act. No "bribery." Also, since the intended bettor chickened out and didn't bet—even though the Patriots' players wanted him to and they still went out and lost—again, no law was broken. Of course, the FBI had no idea if the players went out and found someone else to bet on their behalf once the informant backed down. This may not be entirely out of the realm of possibility. When the Patriots returned to San Diego three weeks later to again play the Chargers, the informant met with several of the players and was given tickets to the game, but no Patriot brought up the subject of wagering. Considering that he failed them the first time, why would the players use him again?

OFF THE BOARD

Rumors surrounding the AFL weren't confined to the Patriots. By the mid-'60s, the entire league seemed to be under suspicion. The same *Life* article discussing Parilli revealed another interesting tidbit, an investigation "of the relationship between a star American Football League quarterback and two bookies, Carmello Coco and Philip Cali. The inquiries were stepped up after the player's teammates were overheard in the locker room angrily accusing him of 'throwing' the game they had just lost. But no public accusation has yet been made."[14] Writing in the *Boston Globe* in 1966, Will McDonough published an article discussing the AFL investigating "certain of its players" for betting on games. He quoted AFL commissioner Milt Woodard as saying that his office "is looking into aspects of several recent AFL games." Woodard added that, "I have been aware of the reports for two weeks, and we have been, and still are, investigating the games in question." Woodard would later backtrack on these public statements, claiming he had been misunderstood and that no players were being investigated. How could the AFL investigate the games without investigating its players? No explanation of that contradiction followed.

The FBI wasn't about to leave these matters for the league to determine. As Hoover himself wrote on an FBI memo in regards to the AFL, "I want to bear down on these fixes in football games." The question was where to start? AFL games were being taken off the board by illegal bookmakers across the nation week after week. Did this mean bookies believed AFL games were suspect? Or was it that the overall play in the AFL was too inconsistent compared to the NFL, compromising bookies' abilities to set solid lines? Could it have even meant both? Hoover and the FBI wanted to know. This was laid out in a letter from the Director, FBI, to the Special Agent in Charge in New York dated November 3, 1966: "As in previous years, numerous allegations have been received during the current football season with respect to irregularities in American Football League (AFL) contests. On three recent successive weekends, bookmakers have taken one or more AFL games 'off the board.' While this action on the part of the bookmakers may be attributed to a lack of confidence in the AFL teams, the frequency of such action by bookmakers is somewhat suspect. In view of our responsibilities in the Sports Bribery field, you are instructed to determine through the established liaison with officials of the AFL whether they are in possession of any current information bearing on this matter. At the time of your contact, once again remind these officials of our responsibilities under the Sports Bribery statute."

As the Bureau pounded the pavement seeking leads and information, they may have gleaned the truth from one particular informant. The FBI contacted a Des Moines, IA bookmaker who was the subject of several previous FBI cases, including a May 1965 conviction in U.S. District Court on a federal gambling charge which he later "gloated" to the FBI about getting reversed. He told the interviewing agent: "The big bookmakers in the United States, particularly [redacted] are responsible for the 'wave of allegations' regarding AFL football games being 'taken off the board.' [redacted] told [informant] that [redacted] and his cohorts prepare a 'football line' each Sunday evening prior to the following weekend games involving both collegiate and professional teams. Because the AFL football teams are erratic in their weekly play, [redact-

ed] and associates have been preparing 'false and erroneous lines' which they disseminate and sell to other bookmakers throughout the Unites States. This 'false and erroneous line' will be off as much as three to six points whether it involves the so-called favorite or loser. Immediately after this line has been disseminated, the big bookmakers take certain games 'off the boards' because this 'erroneous line' will involve only those games and the big bookmakers cannot afford to accept wagers on these particular games. These big bookmakers then dispatch 'whiskers' (close associates who are gamblers and are known by other bookies throughout the United States) to all areas of the United States where these particular people then place wagers with local bookmakers on the AFL games for which **[redacted]** and associates have put out an 'erroneous line.' **[redacted]** further told [informant] that when the smaller bookmakers complain to the larger bookmakers about games 'being taken off the boards'—the answer is that a substantial sum of money has been placed upon either a favorite or loser and the bookies are 'afraid of this game.' **[redacted]** alleged to [informant] that the big bookmakers have 'really cleaned up' through this method in betting on certain AFL games." A Denver-area gambler echoed these sentiments, informing the FBI that AFL lines weren't coming out until Thursday as bookmakers were having issues setting a good number, and because of discrepancies between bookies, some gamblers were making a killing middling games.

That may have been an excellent explanation for why so many games during that time frame were suspect, but it did not exonerate players and coaches from betting on games in which they participated. One of those suspected by the FBI was former Boston Patriots and Buffalo Bills head coach, then-current Denver Broncos head coach and general manager Lou Saban. Colorado law enforcement had observed Saban associating with known Denver hoodlums. Why? The Broncos rented the top floor of a building to use as team offices apparently without recognizing that the restaurant and bar located on the first floor was operated by a former runner who was known to book bets. Of course, the team had received a "very attractive financial deal" to rent out that floor. None of this was going to be an issue, Saban told the FBI, since players wouldn't have any real reason to visit these facilities, and "if any gambling or illegal activities take place in the restaurant he will immediately rule this restaurant off limits to Broncos personnel."

"Coach Saban, at the beginning of this interview, told of his respect for the FBI and advised he wanted to make it clear that he was in complete charge of the Bronco operation and desired that he be the Bronco individual contacted in the event any problems came to the FBI concerning Bronco personnel being involved in any illegal activities including gambling activities. For information Boston and Buffalo, no mention was made to Saban at this time concerning the allegations previously made by top-echelon informant in Boston that Saban and some of his former Boston Patriot football players had in the past placed a bet or bets with a Boston bookmaker." One of those bets was the previously mentioned Bills-Patriots game played November 3, 1962. At that time, Saban was in his first year as the Bills' head coach, having just come to the team after coaching the Patriots the previous two seasons. An informant told the FBI "that [redacted] of the Buffalo Bills football team of the American Football League bet $2,400 on Buffalo, three point underdog in the game between the Buffalo Bills and the Boston Patriots on November 3, 1962. The odds were 12 to 10 and [redacted] won $2,000 as the game's final score was a 28 to 28 tie. [redacted] bet this game directly with [redacted] according to the informant."

Another AFL team under suspicion was Lamar Hunt's Dallas Texans who would soon move to Kansas City to become the Chiefs. The FBI learned in late 1962 that, "In 1960 unverified information was received that some Dallas Texan football players, namely [redacted] and Max Boydston as well as Ray Collins were involved in point fixing of AFL games....Although it was never actually verified, the Dallas Texans subsequently got rid of all three ball players." A month later, more information fleshed out the tale. "The information was furnished from [redacted — a lieutenant of the Dallas PD] to [redacted] who in turn gave it to owner, Lamar Hunt and Head Coach Hank Stram. [redacted] stated he even reviewed movies of all games in which these three men participated. He advised that the only thing that he could definitely state was that their performance was erratic and on several occasions, caused the Texans to either win by less than the point spread or even lose. He advised there was no concrete evidence of any point fixing by the three

men other than the above. As a result **[redacted]** subsequently retired
from professional football after the 1961 season and prior to the beginning of the 1962 season, **[redacted]** was traded to the Oakland Raiders,
Boydston was 'dropped' and thereafter signed a contract and played
with the Oakland Raiders during the past season." The fate of the three
players noted in the file is correct. Texans defensive tackle Ray Collins'
last season was 1961. Boydston was the Texans' tight end in 1960 and
1961 and played the following season, his last, for the Oakland Raiders. It's likely the third, redacted player was Texans quarterback Francis
"Cotton" Davidson. He was the Texans' starter in both 1960 and 1961,
but was then traded to Oakland in 1962 after sitting on Dallas' bench for
the first game of the season.

In the meantime, the FBI was visiting teams from coast to coast due
to rumors of players betting, points being shaved, and games taken off
the boards. A game between the Miami Dolphins and Houston Oilers
played on October 23, 1966 raised suspicions due to a tremendous line
movement which changed from Houston -18 down to the Oilers being
favored by -13½. Houston lost outright 20–13. Though the FBI chalked
this up to the fact that the Dolphins acquired "two top-notch players"
prior to the game, it still took the time to talk with team owner Joe
Robbie.

Robbie informed the FBI he was aware of the variations in the
Dolphins' point spreads and knew "that there was only one game that he
had heard was 'off the board' and that was with the Houston Oilers. He
indicated that through his contacts with other League personnel, he felt
the main concern of the investigation re these irregularities in American
League football games was focused on the Houston football team." This
was true, as will be revealed in a moment. Also, "Mr. Robbie was made
aware of certain 'hot' spots where Miami Dolphins football players have
been observed. It is noted that one of the spots brought to his attention
is operated by **[redacted]** the subject of an IGA investigation by the
Miami Division. Mr. Robbie informed those at the conference that he
would take immediate steps to make this restaurant and lounge off limits
to the players and personnel of the Miami Dolphins."

The FBI then contacted Oakland Raiders general manager Scotty Sterling. He had no information of note. FBI Special Agents also met with New York Jets owner David "Sonny" Werblin and Buffalo Bills owner Ralph Wilson—both of whom reportedly knew nothing of these gambling allegations surrounding their league. How true that was could be debated. When the FBI contacted Denver Broncos owner Gerald Phipps, he told the Bureau that at an AFL owners meeting, gambling and sports bribery were matters of importance, yet they had no "specific information" on fixed games. NFL commissioner Pete Rozelle also met with the AFL owners and said the same thing, that all of this lacked concrete evidence.

It is interesting that the NFL in 1966 was already involved in AFL matters. At this point, the notion of the two leagues merging was simply in the negotiating stage, but the rumors of rampant player gambling by AFL members were troublesome for both leagues. A major gambling scandal would have dealt a severe blow to the credibility and profitability of the merger. Even if it was deemed "just an AFL problem," NFL fans would have looked suspiciously at it, given the 1963 gambling-related suspensions of Green Bay Packers star Paul Hornung and Alex Karras of the Detroit Lions (which is discussed later). A fixed football game would have been seen just as that by fans, regardless of the league affiliation of the players involved. Therefore, the NFL decided to flex its Security Division's muscle and assist in the matter at hand. "With [William G.] Hundley [the NFL's director of security in 1966], [William] Cahn [Nassau County, NY, prosecutor] wanted to discuss 'reports that certain points in at least nineteen [professional football] games…were rigged.' Pete Rozelle had stated in November 1966 that Hundley 'was conducting a general investigation of continuing rumors in the American Football League.' Cahn said that he had discovered that [Gil] Beckley [bookmaker and head of the mafia's national layoff system] had 'picked nineteen out of twenty winners' and had actually picked the point spreads of each winner."[15]

The AFL did have its own Security Division, but it was not as well established as the NFL's simply given that the league had only been in operation for six years. Even so, it did things slightly differently than its

NFL counterpart. Both possessed a security agent for each of its teams, but the AFL's investigator reported to his assigned team whereas in the NFL the agent reported directly to the league. When FBI agents did get to sit down and discuss this with AFL commissioner Milton Woodard and the AFL security chief in December 1966, both said they "were unable to ascertain any possible violation of the sports bribery statute." Though they shouldn't have been the ones to determine this, their combined statement did not mean that players weren't betting—that didn't violate the Sports Bribery Act; they just couldn't tell if games were being fixed. A significant difference, and one that they may have assumed would keep the FBI out of the league's business.

Despite pleading informed ignorance regarding players gambling, Woodard, even in this meeting, repeated to agents one allegation that the FBI had heard time and again. A supposed "rumor" that had spread across the sports gambling nation. One that involved a quarterback, strange line fluctuations, erratic play, and constant rumors of point shaving.

THE OILERS

Miami Dolphins owner Joe Robbie mentioned it to the FBI. Denver Broncos owner Gerald Phipps did, too. Even AFL commissioner Woodard and the league's security chief brought it to the FBI's attention. Something was rotten with Houston Oilers games. Phipps went so far as to tell the interviewing agents that he knew the individual who operated the Ohio Sports Service which put out the "Canton line" on football games. This man, according to Phipps, "has for the past two years never put out a line on a Houston Oiler football game and has told him the reason for this was that he did not trust [redacted]."

Phipps wasn't the only one with this information. The FBI had multiple sources telling them a similar tale. One Denver gambler, who "at one time enjoyed a reputation as being the biggest" in the area, "recently advised SA [redacted] that the books continue to suspect [redacted] is involved with gamblers and that it was difficult to get a line on the

Houston Oiler games from them and that he had stayed completely away from any Oiler games when betting with books. When it was pointed out to **[redacted]** had not been the starting quarterback for the Oilers in recent games and had done little playing other than kicking extra points, **[redacted]** stated that the books were still afraid of Oiler games inasmuch as they did not know ahead of time whether **[redacted]** would be the starting **[redacted]**."

Another informant "said according to information he has received, there are allegedly a number of members on Houston football team who have been placing large wagers each week during the 1966 season with sports bookies in Houston and also in other cities, but specific team members not known. [Informant] said Houston **[redacted]** bet on Houston to win New York game, 10/16/66, and they bet on Houston to lose Miami game 10/23/66. New York was favored and lost [the Oilers beat the Jets 24–0] while Houston was heavy favorite against Miami [sources stated the spread was Houston from -15 to -19] and lost [final score was 20–13 in favor of the Dolphins]. According to [informant], point spread on these two games fluctuated widely, ten points with some bookies, during the week prior to the games, which is a sure indication that a fix or an attempt to fix the games was being made. [Informant] said in contrast point spread of National Football League games will fluctuate at most two points from the time spread comes out Monday until game time. [Informant] advised he doubts bookies will accept bets on Houston games remainder of 1966 season."

Subsequently, the FBI learned that the Houston-Kansas City game scheduled for October 30, 1966 was taken off the boards across the country. Why? "Knowledgeable gamblers in the country, such as **[redacted]** of Houston, and others are of opinion Houston quarterback George Blanda is shaving points in games played during 1966 football season; that possibly the gambling group known as **[redacted]** and **[redacted]** of Las Vegas are controlling Blanda; that **[redacted]** and **[redacted]** the Las Vegas gamblers, have apparently been suspicious of Blanda for some time, as they would not accept any wagers on the Houston-Miami game played 10/23/66." Houston lost the game versus Kansas City 48–23. Two weeks later, the story was the same. "**[Redact-**

ed] advised 11/9/66, sports bookies are not accepting bets for the Houston-Boston [which Houston would lose 27–21] or Kansas City-Miami games scheduled 11/13/66. [Informant] said bookies suspect any game in which Houston quarterback George Blanda is playing. Blanda and unknown other members of Houston team are supposed to be placing large wagers on games each week."

George Blanda is enshrined in the Pro Football Hall of Fame. He ranks sixth in career scoring with 2,002 points, having played 340 games in 26 seasons in both the NFL and AFL. Nicknamed "The Grand Old Man," Blanda holds the record for being the oldest person ever to play in an NFL game, which he did at the age of 48 in 1975. He also may have been gambling on football games for a large portion of his career.

Blanda began his life in professional football as a member of the Chicago Bears in 1949. He was mainly the team's kicker, though in three seasons he was also the Bears' starting quarterback. After the 1958 season, Blanda was out of football at the age of 31. Yet in 1960, he joined the AFL as the Houston Oilers' starting quarterback and kicker. Why the gap in time? Why did he switch leagues? It may have had something to do with gambling on NFL games. While the bulk of the FBI's investigation into Blanda derived from his 1966 season, in fact, the Bureau had information concerning his betting habits dating back to 1962. "Informant stated that when the Houston Oilers of the American Football League are in Boston, [redacted — Blanda] of that team is a big bettor with **[redacted]**, Boston **[redacted]**. **[redacted]** told the informant on December 14, 1962 that [redacted — Blanda] often bets $500 or more on a game. The informant stated that [redacted — Blanda] is extremely cautious and circumspect because, allegedly, he had been in trouble with the management of the Chicago Bears Football Team for prior bets while a member of that team." It's quite possible that Chicago Bears owner and head coach George Halas, whom Harry Wismer revealed had hidden gambling information regarding another owner in the past, did the same with Blanda. Only, in this case, Blanda may have been secretly banished from the Bears and blacklisted from the NFL. When the AFL formed, he may have discovered a backdoor into pro football and then fell right back into his previous gambling habits.

When the FBI began examining Blanda in 1966, it discovered that it had previously interviewed him in early 1963. Not for betting while a member of the Bears, but rather "this interview concerned allegations that there had been betting activities in the American Football League on the part of Blanda of the Houston Oilers and Lou Saban, coach of the Buffalo Bills." The notes of the FBI's 1963 interview with Blanda were rather, well, bland, with one exception. "[Blanda] stated he played professional football for about ten years with the Chicago Bears, then became inactive and about three years ago resumed football during which time he has played quarterback for the Houston Oilers. He stated he is of the opinion that the year 1964 will be his last year as an active player [recall Blanda played through the 1975 season]....He advised that he is friendly with several members of the Boston Patriots Team, especially with an end named [redacted — most likely Gino Cappelletti] who formerly played football with the University of Minnesota. He advised that in view of the fact that his athletic status keeps him in the public eye, he has made an effort to refrain from cultivating the friendship of any person of questionable character. In this regard he said that in view of the numerous persons he comes into contact with as a professional player, it is possible he may have in the past experienced chance meetings with a hoodlum or bookmaker; however, he never encouraged the friendship of the person past the initial meeting....He stated that as a result of professional football and his employment with Spector Freight Lines, his yearly income averages between $35,000 and $45,000. He stated this amount fulfills all of his financial requirements and eliminates any temptation to consort with or place bets with gamblers...."

"In regard to place betting activities, Blanda advised that betting activities on his part had never been discussed with him by any member of the Chicago Bears Management nor had he ever been reprimanded for such type activities during his tenure with that team. Blanda advised that he has read newspaper publicity concerning [redacted — running back Rick Casares] for the Chicago Bears. He advised that he was very friendly with [redacted — Casares] when both were teammates with the Bears. He continued that he recently attended a birthday party given for [redacted — Casares] by his girl friend, **[redacted]** on July **[redacted]**, 1962 [Casares' birthday is July 4] in the Rush Street area of Chicago.

During that party Blanda said he recalled being introduced to a man named [redacted] who was described as a close friend of [redacted]. He advised that he never saw [redacted] again, but assumed after reading newspaper reports that this person is identical with a bookmaker named [redacted]. Blanda stated with the exception of information appearing in newspapers he had no personal knowledge of betting or gambling on the part of [redacted]." Casares, as will be revealed, was gambling on football with his friend Paul Hornung of the Green Bay Packers. While Casares may have been connected to the mob, it's likely in his case that Bears owner Halas once again covered up a growing scandal for the good of his team, the NFL, and football in general.

Blanda ended his interview with the FBI by swearing he was a good boy and that he would be right there for the Bureau if needed. "Blanda said that professional football players' contracts include a statement reflecting that betting or gambling on the part of a player is prohibited. He stated that with this in mind, any professional player including himself would be foolish to jeopardize his career by violating this phase of his contract. Blanda concluded by telling the agents that he could be counted upon to recontact in the future if he should obtain any information relative to gambling activities within the realm of professional football. He said that he did not condone betting action on the part of players because subsequent publicity was injurious of the game of football in general."

Even before the AFL's 1966 season kicked off, Blanda's alleged gambling habits were tipped off to the feds. "[Special Agent in Charge], Houston, on 1/17/66, received information from W.P. Hobby, Jr., President and Executive Editor of the *Houston Post* to the effect that there was a possible planned abduction of the daughter of [redacted] of the multi-millionaire [redacted] family of Houston. The lead on possible [redacted] proved to be false, but in checking the source of the story, information was received that former professional baseball player [redacted — Johnny Temple, former second baseman for the Cincinnati Reds, Cleveland Indians and Houston Colt 45s] now employed by station KHOU-TV in Houston, claimed to have received a call from a woman who identified herself as the wife of [redacted] Washington,

D.C., gambler. The woman allegedly asked [redacted — Temple] if he had heard a rumor that George Blanda, **[redacted]**, and Charlie Tolar of the Houston Oilers professional football team had received a $100,000 bribe to control points in Oiler football games. [redacted — Temple] passed the information on to the general manager of the TV station. The manager of the TV station gave the information to K.S. "Bud" Adams, owner of the Houston Oilers. Adams and a private investigator named **[redacted]** and an unnamed police sergeant interviewed Temple. The police sergeant indicated privately to Temple that he had an informant who had some information about this alleged bribe, but he would not furnish it to **[redacted]** because **[redacted]** was untrustworthy."

Here the story gets a little weird. The woman who made the call was married to a well-known Washington, D.C.-area bookmaker/gambler who was once used as an FBI informant. However, he was convicted on gambling charges, served prison time, and upon his release became "unproductive." "Prior to his incarceration, he was considered one of the leading gambling figures in the Washington area." This gambler claimed to the FBI his wife never made such a call or claim. However, "he readily admitted knowing [redacted — Temple]. He stated he knew [redacted — Temple] when [redacted — Temple] played professional baseball for the Cleveland Indians and that he met him on one occasion in Washington. He said [redacted — Temple] is aware of **[redacted]** former gambling activities and was aware of the fact **[redacted]** was a bookmaker when he met him." The gambler's wife was interviewed and denied making the call as well. So despite the odd fact that KHOU's sports reporter Johnny Temple knew the D.C.-area bookmaker whose wife allegedly called in the tip, the bookmaker and his wife weren't saying a thing to the FBI.

Meanwhile in Houston, the FBI was discussing the matter with the concerned Oilers owner, Bud Adams. Yet Adams' first priority didn't seem to be catching the crooked players. "Mr. Adams stated he was primarily concerned over this allegation in that if it were made public he was certain that the reputation and public image of the Oiler organization would suffer. He emphatically stated at the same time that if there should be any substance to the allegation he would be the first person to want the matter investigated to the fullest and if a law violation was indicated he would want vigorous prosecution to follow. Adams said although he felt the allegation was totally without merit he engaged the services of [redacted] a private investigator in Houston, to attempt to determine if either of the three named players were known to be in contact with local gamblers or were living beyond their means. He said in this connection [redacted] interviewed [redacted] who also had apparently told a police sergeant about this allegation. Adams stated [redacted] submitted a report to him indicating he had contacted a number of gamblers and bookmakers in Houston and as far as Austin, Texas, and that he had developed absolutely no information to indicate Blanda, [redacted] or Tolar had in any way been consorting with undesirable characters or gamblers. Adams stated he had not confronted the Oiler players with this allegation due to the fact that nothing had been shown to him to indicate the allegation had merit."

Notice here that Adams didn't use AFL security in this matter. He hired his own private investigator who conducted a wide-ranging search from Houston all the way to Austin in search of bookmakers or gamblers working with these players. This proved fruitless. When the FBI interviewed this P.I., he told the FBI, "[redacted] said he had interviewed [redacted — Temple] on several occasions concerning this telephone call and that he is convinced in his own mind that [redacted — Temple] is not telling the truth about this alleged phone call. He said each time [redacted — Temple] recounted the facts to him about this alleged call they were at variance in some respects and that he had contacted numerous gamblers and prominent Texas bookmaker [redacted] in Austin, Texas, and had developed no information to indicate a member of the Oiler team either bets on football or was believed to in any way attempt to control the outcome of Oiler games....[redacted] stated he had learned of many nonspecific and groundless rumors mostly from bettors who had lost money on the Oiler football team suggesting that possibly there was an attempted fix on some of the Oiler games but that none of the allegations he heard were of any substance or subject to any type of verification." Adams' P.I. apparently could tell Temple was lying about the phone call—for what purpose, he doesn't say—and could also tell that all of the fixing rumors he heard, of which there were apparently several, were clearly make-believe and unverifiable. Some investigator.

His answers to the FBI mirrored exactly what his employer Adams would want them to hear.

Because the origin of these allegations came from the D.C. book-maker's wife who suddenly refused to cooperate, the FBI put the matter on hold…until the rampant rumors of Blanda and the Oilers gambling cropped up during the 1966 season. Then the investigation continued, wisely using sources outside of the Oilers' front office. In doing so, they may have revealed why Adams' P.I. couldn't discover where Blanda was betting. He was placing his bets outside of Texas. "On 11/29/66, [re-dacted] advised that a rumor is circulating that George Blanda, quarter-back of the Houston Oilers Football Club, is placing bets regularly with a Lake Charles, LA, bookie. The identity of the bookie is not known to source at this time." This information came from the New Orleans Bureau which asked the Houston office if it should attempt to determine who that bookie was. The Houston Bureau, for its own reasons, apparently did not request a follow-up on this information.

Despite the official denials, Adams must have taken both the phone call to KHOU's Johnny Temple in January 1966 and the rumors of Blanda's point shaving during the season to heart. After the two alleged-ly tainted Oilers games played on October 16 and 23, and prior to the October 30 game against the Kansas City Chiefs which was taken off the boards, Adams "specifically requested" an attorney from the U.S. Department of Justice visit the team to discuss gambling. "On 10/27/66, AUSA [redacted] Houston, personally appeared before entire squad of Houston Oiler team and coaching staff, outlined Federal statutes in sports bribery field, and in a straight-forward unequivocal manner warned that prosecutive action would surely result for any participation on their part in point shaving, bribery, attempted bribery, etc. and that any dealings they might have, legitimate or otherwise, with gamblers, bookmakers and the like would render them suspect. No questions were asked by squad members, and nothing occurred during the meeting which suggested possible involvement in this activity by any team mem-bers."

But rumors of Blanda's gambling abounded. Another informant told a more amazing tale which, given the mindset of Texas in the 1960s, may not have been as crazy as it appears. "[redacted] advised 12/1/66, sports bookies in [Washington, D.C.] understand certain unnamed players of the Houston and Kansas City football teams are close personal friends with some 'Texas Millionaires' who like to bet thousands of dollars each week on football games, and who are not necessarily professional gamblers. These individuals like to win bets for prestige purposes and winning money is probably a secondary consideration in most cases. Also, for prestige purposes, these individuals like to be associated with professional football players. [redacted] said certain members of the Houston and Kansas City football teams in order for their rich acquaintance to be a winner have been known to influence the outcome of a game and in return these players have reportedly received substantial rewards from the grateful gamblers. The informant said the players betting themselves through a bookie could not possibly win enough to warrant them placing their jobs in jeopardy."

Despite all of this information, the rumors against Blanda and the other members of the Oilers remained too elusive to prove for a court of law. That did not mean they were false. In fact, one of the AFL's own seemed to confirm that at the very least, members of the Oilers were certainly gambling on games. Before the 1966 season was even over, the FBI reported "On 12/1/66, [redacted — most likely Bill Hundley] in charge of [redacted — security] for the NFL and AFL, advised that the allegations with respect to the Houston Oilers Football team, had already been furnished by him to [redacted] Chief of Special Investigative Unit at the Bureau. [redacted] stated briefly that the allegations with respect to the Houston team came as a result of contact by a [redacted] with the vice detail of the Houston PD, who advised an individual named Wolf, a TV cameraman who worked with the [redacted] that an informant advised him of a meeting and a payoff at a motel in Houston in which funds were paid to [redacted] of the Houston team for their part in fixing a football game. The money reportedly was supposed to come from the city of New Orleans. This [redacted] is no longer with the vice detail of the Houston PD and has been reduced to a uniform status. He was unable to produce the informant and according to Mr. [redacted] the story was based upon an informant who was never located and the story of an 'amoral' private detective of the Houston Oilers Football team, namely one [redacted]. [redacted] stated that the entire incident was a 'bizarre' one and as far as they could determine, certain players named [redacted] and possibly [redacted] were betting on Houston Oilers games, but they were betting on themselves to win. He had no indication of any irregularities either in the NFL or the AFL which would fall under the jurisdiction of the Bureau and in particular the Sports Bribery Statute."

That was the story told to the FBI. The one for public consumption was different. John Wilson of the *Houston Chronicle* wrote an article on February 16, 1967 quoting Bill Hundley, the new director of security for the AFL/NFL, as saying his investigation into the Oilers in the fall of 1966 "failed to turn up any evidence of tampering with the outcome of games." Apparently Hundley failed to mention to Wilson what he readily admitted to the FBI: that members of the Oilers were betting on games against league rules. No player was disciplined by the league—publicly at least. Houston's record in 1966 was 3–11. Blanda finished the season with 17 touchdown passes against 21 interceptions. He started only eight of the team's 14 games as quarterback, getting benched late in the season in favor of Don Trull. Blanda was outright released by Houston in March 1967 only to be picked up by the Oakland Raiders where he would spend the remainder of his career as the team's kicker. Coincidentally (or not), Charley Tolar's seven-year career—all of which was spent as a member of the Houston Oilers—came to an immediate halt after the 1966 season as well. The third named player and his fate remain unknown.

EARLY NFL

If the NFL was so inclined, it could argue that all of the above information relates to the defunct American Football League, not the still-in-existence National Football League; therefore, if one were to believe AFL games were fixed, that does not mean NFL games have been fixed. Mere semantics? Perhaps. But let's grant the NFL that luxury because such a stance does not affect anything that follows from this

point onward.

Bernie Parrish played in the NFL as a defensive back from 1959 through 1966, serving at one point as vice president of the National Football League Players Association (NFL PA). In his scathing book *They Call It A Game* published in 1971, Parrish wrote, "There are four basic ways to fix a football game: (1) Through a referee; (2) through an important player, or, more subtly (3) through the coaching staff and team management, or (4) by drugging a key player or a number of them. I have played in NFL and AFL games that left me with an uneasy feeling that something was wrong; a penalty called at a bad time, a score on a field goal that looked no good, interceptions in the flat, a quarterback eating the ball and getting sacked when he could have thrown it, a poor game plan, bad strategy, or a win that was just too easy. With $139 million at stake for the owners, $84 million for the television networks, and up to $66 billion for organized crime's bookmaking syndicates, and with what I learned as a player, no one will ever convince me that numerous NFL games aren't fixed."[16]

One of the two "attempts" the NFL admits is the 1946 NFL Championship Game played between the Chicago Bears and the New York Giants. Two members of the Giants, fullback Merle Hapes and quarterback Frank Filchock, were accused of taking a bribe to throw the game for the Bears. Each player was to receive $2,500 plus a $2,000 bet in their honor (and perhaps a cushy off-season job) for not covering the ten-point spread. A wiretap on gambler Alvin Paris' phone tipped off authorities who sprang into action, bringing the matter straight to the NFL's attention less than 24 hours before the game was set to kick off.

Hapes and Filchock were brought to Gracie Mansion in New York City where mayor William O'Dwyer, NFL commissioner Bert Bell, and Giants owner Tim Mara's sons Wellington and Jack were waiting. They separated the players, interviewing them individually. Hapes confessed to being offered the bribe—though not to accepting it—as he was the only player mentioned by name on the wiretap (however, the wiretap indicated other NFL games may have been fixed in the past). Filchock claimed innocence. Hapes was suspended for the game; Filchock was allowed to play. Out on the field, Filchock appeared to be representing the gambling interests of which he claimed ignorance. He threw two touchdowns but six interceptions, and the Giants lost by exactly the point spread, 24–14.

It was soon revealed that Paris was merely a front for three other gamblers who had bet at least $20,000 on the Bears. Paris and his three compatriots were all eventually convicted for their role in attempting to fix the game. But at Paris' trial another revelation came to light: Filchock admitted under oath to being offered a bribe to throw the game.

"NO! NO! A thousand times NO! Tell me this is not true!" So wrote J. Edgar Hoover in a FBI memo related to this incident. Hoover, however, was not truly upset at these revelations; the Director was being sarcastic. Hoover highlighted several passages in a *New York Daily Mirror* article dated January 9, 1947, including one which read, "Professional football has blundered through this crisis by the skin of its teeth....Reports persist, however, that two other National League forward passers are dominated by the mobs....It is no secret that, in the private boxes of some team owners, bookmakers are weekly guests." Following this, Hoover wrote, "This can't be true! The 'dear boys' would never let their 'dear public' down like this!!!"

Filchock's lie which allowed him to play in the 1946 Championship did not sit well with the NFL. "At the January 1947 meetings, owners gave the commissioner the latitude to suspend for life any player or team official involved in a game-fixing attempt. Hapes and Filchock were suspended indefinitely; Hapes, reinstated in 1954, never played in the NFL again, while Filchock, reinstated in 1950, threw three passes for the Baltimore Colts that season and retired [he would later become the head coach for the AFL's Denver Broncos in 1960–1961]....Bell was convinced that the league needed to do more. In announcing the Hapes and Filchock suspensions in April 1947, he stated, 'Professional football cannot continue to exist unless it is based upon absolute honesty. The players must be not only absolutely honest; they must be above suspicion. In short, the game and its players must be kept free from corruption, from all bribes and offers of bribes and from any possible 'fixing' of games.'"[17]

Harry Wismer, who coincidentally was the radio broadcaster for the 1946 NFL Championship Game, would later write, "Bell's action [suspending Hapes prior to the 1946 championship] established in the public's mind the idea that gamblers were ever under his watchful eye and could never hope to influence pro football while he was commissioner."[18] As harsh as Hapes' and Filchock's suspensions seemed and as convincing as Bell's announcements were, in fact it did little to curb the association between footballers and gamblers.

The NFL's popularity swelled in post-World War II America for two main reasons: television and gambling. The growth in popularity of the recently developed point spread coupled with the advancements of televised sports pushed the NFL slowly but surely to the forefront of gambling Americans' minds. This is why there seems to be no record of an attempt to fix an NFL game prior to the 1946 Championship—the NFL simply wasn't popular enough for gamblers to bother. Baseball was the predominant game, both for casual and betting fans. But as the NFL ratcheted up through the 1950s and 1960s, more and more rumors of fixes developed. This is no coincidence. The more people bet on football, the more money flooded the betting market, and the easier it became to hide the "unnatural money" needed to make a fixed game worthwhile.

In 1951, Los Angeles mobster Jimmy Fratianno was $35,000 in debt at the beginning of the NFL season and was looking for a way out. According to Fratianno, "a friend of mine" called and told him "they had this referee for the [Los Angeles] Rams, and to start betting on the Rams." Fratianno took the advice. For his part, the referee had a $2,500 bet placed in his honor for "just call[ing] penalties, you know." As was detailed in the book *Interference*, the first fixed game he bet on was the September 28, 1951 Rams-New York Yanks game that the Rams won 54–14. They followed that up with an attempt on the October 28 Rams-San Francisco 49ers game, but the 49ers won 44–17 as the Rams played so badly, having the referee in their pocket did nothing to save the game. The final fixed game was the December 16 Rams victory over the Green Bay Packers, 42–14. Soon afterward, an investigation began, causing the referee to quit working with the mobsters. According to Moldea, "All the games named by Fratianno were officiated by the same game officials, a

crew headed by Rawson Bowen."[19]

At this same time in the early 1950s, "The Blonde Bomber" Bobby Layne was winning back-to-back championships as the quarterback of the Detroit Lions. He was also fixing games. Notorious gambler/ bookmaker Donald "Dice" Dawson confirmed this. "Dawson admitted to [author Moldea] that he did business with Lions quarterback Bobby Layne. 'It was Bobby Layne who was the bettor, who I bet for,' Dawson says. 'I knew him better than [I knew] my own brothers. And he did plenty. He'd be playing in his own game, and he'd be betting all over the board. He'd bet five, six, seven games on a Sunday.'"[20] Moldea elaborated on Dawson's confession regarding Layne's habits. "Layne was thought to have shaved points or participated in the fixing of several NFL games, according to several bookmakers and law enforcement officials. One was the final game of the 1956 season in which the 9–2 Lions played the 8-2-1 Chicago Bears on December 16. Layne left the game in the second quarter supposedly with a concussion. The Bears won the game, 38–21, and the Western Division title."[21] Dice Dawson didn't believe Layne fixed this game—though he wasn't personally involved in it—because he believed Layne would have wanted to play in order to keep control of it. However, Layne may not have been above faking an injury. Bernie Parrish wrote, "Howard (Hopalong) Cassady came to the Browns in a trade with the Detroit Lions in 1963. Hoppy was a receiver and kick-return specialist. The stories he told me about hoodlum associations and player betting and the game he thought Bobby Layne, the Detroit quarterback, had thrown, were extremely disturbing. Two games he suspected were the 1958 All-Star game and a Chicago Bears game when Layne had gotten knocked out and had to be carried off the field. Hoppy thought Layne had faked his injury."[22]

In fact, many single out the antics of Layne for the creation of the NFL's injury report which continues to be issued each week. This labels each injured player as either "probable," "questionable," "doubtful," or "out" for each game. Though the NFL claims the injury report has no correlation with fans' gambling interests, many would doubt that, as a player's health status is the sort of inside information that has always mattered to the gambling public. Despite the fact that when Layne

retired after the 1962 season as the NFL's all-time leader in both passing yards and passing touchdowns, as well as having led the Lions to championships in 1952 and 1953 (while losing the 1954 championship game to the Cleveland Browns), the Lions traded him to the Pittsburgh Steelers two games into the 1958 season. Why? The official reason was that Layne had lost a step following a serious knee injury which shortened his 1957 season. But perhaps the reality was that the Lions shipped Layne to Pittsburgh because they tired of his gambling ways. It didn't seem to alter Layne's habit in the least. As Dawson told Moldea, "Layne had fixed games or shaved points in no fewer than seven games over a period of four years—while Layne played with Detroit Lions and later the Pittsburgh Steelers."[23] Prior to a 1960 Steelers-Redskins game, Layne was photographed holding his "injured" passing arm. Instantly the line on the game dropped. Having begun the week as a seven-point favorite, the line dropped to the Steelers -1, and by kickoff—thanks to Layne's "injury"—the bookmakers took the game off the boards. Perhaps unremarkably, Layne played in the game which ended as a 27–27 tie. Shortly thereafter, teams were required to officially announce any and all potential player injuries.

The name of Dice Dawson will appear again later, but before leaving him, "On the subject of whether there were other players who fixed games and shaved points, Dawson told [Moldea], 'There were a lot of players who did business. That's all I can say. I wouldn't want to say anything else because they are still alive and have families. Bobby [Layne] was one of several players I knew. Naturally, I wanted to do business with the quarterback because he handles the ball on every play. And a lot of quarterbacks were shaving points. Sure, it happened. The players didn't make any money [from playing football], and so they bet. In those days, they were barely getting by. They were getting their brains beaten out for almost nothing.

"'I was involved with players in at least 32 NFL games that were dumped or where points were shaved. I knew a lot of players and then through them I got acquainted with other players and then did business with them.'"[24]

Though Dawson preferred to work with the quarterback, getting to the man playing that position wasn't an absolute necessity. As Parrish wrote, "Quarterbacks are not the only players with opportunities to affect point spreads. Offensive tackles miss blocks and get their quarterbacks smeared on crucial third-down passing situations. Detective Captain Gene Phaff of the Cleveland Police Department used to go to Browns games looking for a certain offensive tackle to miss his block on crucial passing downs, hoping not to see it; then, futilely having to watch it happen. Captain Phaff could not prove his suspicions, but he was convinced the tackle was doing it deliberately."[25] Running backs can miss open holes, foolishly cut back against the blocking, or fumble away the ball. Defensive backs can miss tackles, drop easy interceptions, or allow wide receivers to get behind them in coverage. Kickers can miss field goals or shank punts. In fact, it's difficult to think of a position where a player can have a "bad game" which would not affect the final score, or more importantly, the final score against the point spread. All a corrupting influence needed was an in, and it seemed as if more gamblers were doing just that.

What wouldn't help this situation would be if an owner was gambling for—or against— his own team. But in the case of Carroll Rosenbloom, who owned the Baltimore Colts then later traded the franchise for ownership of the Los Angeles Rams, this appears to be what happened. As a result of a lawsuit brought against Rosenbloom over the purchasing of the Hotel/Casino Nacional in Cuba in 1958, a damaging set of depositions taken in 1960 were made part of the public record a year later thanks to the *Miami Herald*. Conveniently for Rosenbloom, he had sponsored Pete Rozelle for his commissionership in 1960, and Rozelle would come to Rosenbloom's defense in this affair, stating, "No proof whatsoever was uncovered in an extensive investigation that Rosenbloom ever bet on any National Football League game since he bought the Colts ten years ago." Remember, the lawsuit from which these statements sprung had absolutely nothing to do with Rosenbloom gambling on NFL games.

Robert McGarvey (member of Philadelphia Detective Bureau): "After Mr. Rosenbloom purchased the Baltimore Colts, which was in 1953,

one of the several services I performed for him during the period of 1953–1954 was placing his bets, or assisting in the placing of his bets, on professional football games. During this period Mr. Rosenbloom bet frequently and in large amounts on professional football games.,.,,Mr Rosenbloom wagered to win and when he felt his own team would not win, bet against the Colts on such occasions."

Larry Murphy: "After first meeting Mr. Rosenbloom in 1953, I had occasion to learn that he was a big bettor and frequently bet on golf matches, horse racing, baseball and football. I particularly remember that in 1953 when his team, the Colts, was playing against the Forty-Niners out on the coast, he bet a large amount of money against his own team, and because of the point spread, won the bet. I know that he frequently bet on professional football games and many times bet against his own team."

Richard Melvin: "In the course of my social and golfing relationship with Mr. Rosenbloom during this period of time, I had occasion to learn from conversations of his on the golf course and other places that he frequently bet on professional football games. I distinctly remember that during one professional football season he made nine straight winning bets on professional football games."

Michael McLaney: "One of the other transactions was my betting knowledge and background, and a business relationship was formed for the purpose of betting large sums of money on football games. It was Mr. Rosenbloom and myself usually in partnership. These bets were made on professional and college games and were for large sums of money. On some occasions we would not be equal partners because Mr. Rosenbloom had much more money than I had and was able to bet higher. On one occasion, for instance, he bet as high as $55,000 against his own team, the Baltimore Colts, against the Pittsburgh Steelers." [This was incorrect—it was against the 49ers—and McLaney corrected himself later] When asked where the game was played, he responded, "It was played in Pittsburgh [San Francisco], and the reason for the large bet was that Mr. Rosenbloom had decided to leave several of his fine players at home because it was the end of the season and the game wasn't very important."[26]

Rosenbloom even had the audacity to bet $1 million on his own team in what's been called "The Greatest Game Ever Played," the 1958 NFL Championship Game between his Baltimore Colts and the New York Giants. This was the first and only NFL title game which went into sudden death overtime. The Colts eventually won 23–17 on an Alan Ameche one-yard touchdown run instead of attempting a very short field goal. The reason being, many felt, was that had the Colts kicked the field goal, Rosenbloom would have lost his bet due to the point spread. If the Colts scored a touchdown, they would cover. During a chance meeting with legendary broadcaster Pat Summerall, who played in the game as the Giants kicker, I asked if he had ever heard of this rumor. Summerall denied it, seemingly surprised by the question. But another player in that game, Colts Hall of Fame defensive tackle Art Donovan, had not just heard the rumor, but seemed to believe it. He wrote in his autobiography, "More to the point, there are a lot of people who feel that [Colts head coach] Weeb [Ewbank] went for the sudden-death touchdown, instead of playing it safe with a field goal, because the Colts' owner, Carroll Rosenbloom, had a big bet on the game. The scenario does make sense. The Colts were laying anywhere from three and a half to five points that day, and old Rosey definitely struck me as the kind of man who didn't mind playing it fast and loose."[27] Dan Moldea did Donovan one better. He verified the wager with the bookie who took the action. "Once and for all, Rosenbloom did indeed bet on the game, and it was for a million dollars, which he split with a friend. Oddsmaker Bobby Martin confirmed the wager to me....Also, an official with the NFL told [Moldea] that [commissioner] Bert Bell knew about the bet and had scolded Rosenbloom for his gambling activities."[28]

As the FBI began to ramp up its duties in regards to the looming Sports Bribery Act, it began to hear more and more rumors of NFL players gambling on games. In late 1960, the Chicago Bureau wrote, "In this regard, it is noted that [redacted] is the [redacted] of sports events in the world. It is his business to determine the point spread or 'line' on all professional baseball, college and professional football, and college and professional basketball games in the country. He then furnishes this service at the cost of $30 per week to bookmakers and gamblers throughout the United States, Canada, and Mexico. In view of his business, it would be anticipated that he is in an advantageous position to know of any 'fixes' in national sports. This informant was contacted by SA William F. Roemer in this regard on 11/15/60. He advised that he has heard rumors in the past that [redacted], Sammy Baugh, and [redacted] all of whom have been outstanding quarterbacks in the National Football League (NFL), are known to be heavy betters on professional football games. He stated that in view of their proclivities in this regard, he was always somewhat dubious when handicapping games in which they were involved. It is noted that the former two [redacted] are no longer active, whereas [redacted] remains one of the outstanding stars of the NFL. It is also noted that information has been developed by the Chicago Office that while [redacted] was [redacted] the Chicago Bears he was rooming with [redacted]. [redacted] is a former Chicago bookmaker who is a close associate of Murray Humphreys and Gus Alex, Chicago top hoodlums, as well as [redacted] who are also notorious Chicago hoodlums."

Speaking of Chicago, it appears a 1961 game between the Bears and the Los Angeles Rams may have been fixed, but not by the Bears. A criminal informant for the San Francisco Bureau came forth in 1963 to reveal this information. He had waited two years to do so because of his previous criminal history and the fact that he feared that law enforcement would have assumed he took part in the plot even though he swore he did not bet on the game in question. In May 1963, the informant signed a statement which read in part, "We had some conversation about the Los Angeles Rams, Chicago Bears exhibition football game the following weekend [this was the September 23, 1961 game played in Los Angeles]. The Rams were 24-point favorites and [redacted] told me to take any bets I could at 12 points even money. [redacted] and [redacted] stated that [redacted] possibly [redacted] would be the Rams [redacted] and when the Rams got close to the Bears goal, [redacted] would pass to [redacted] who would drop the ball." The Bears won 21–17. Though the informant's statement focused on the Rams throwing the game, it's interesting that he also mentioned Chicago Bears owner/coach George Halas as well, claiming, "Halas…allegedly was met by well-known gambler when he arrived in Los Angeles for game in question." The FBI wanted to question Halas to see if this was true, but for unknown reasons they apparently did not.

HORNUNG & THE PACKERS

The FBI wouldn't have to do much come 1963 as the gambling antics of NFL players would finally catch up with the league and explode on the front pages of newspapers everywhere. Publicly, the tipping point came when Detroit Lions defensive lineman Alex Karras was interviewed on *The Huntley-Brinkley Report* in January 1963. Karras was asked, "Have you ever bet on a game in which you were playing?" He responded, "Yes, I have."[29] Karras' honest answer would ignite a PR disaster the likes of which the NFL has not since seen. When all was said and done, Karras would be suspended indefinitely and five other members of the Lions— guard John Gordy, defensive back Gary Lowe, middle linebacker Joe Schmidt, linebacker Wayne Walker, and defensive end Sam Williams—who had each bet $50 on the 1962 championship game between the Green Bay Packers and New York Giants were fined $2,000 apiece. The Detroit Lions organization was hit with a $4,000 penalty for minimizing information concerning the "undesirable associations" of their players as well as for allowing unauthorized personnel on the sidelines during games.

NFL commissioner Pete Rozelle and Jim Kensil, a former sportswriter who became Rozelle's right-hand man, wrote an eight-page press release which was made public hours after the players were informed of their punishments on April 17, 1963. It began: "There is no evidence that any NFL player has given less than his best in playing any game. There is no evidence that any player has ever bet against his own team. There is no evidence that any NFL player has sold information to gamblers. There is clear evidence that some NFL players knowingly carried on undesirable associations which in some instances led to their betting on their own team to win and/or other National Football League games."

This last statement was certainly true in the case of Karras. The FBI had been investigating him and other members of the Lions for some questionable business associations prior to this announcement. But Karras' sins were minimal compared to those of the second player suspended indefinitely—Paul Hornung. The Green Bay Packers' "Golden Boy" was awash in a sea of hard partying, women, gambling, and mafia connections.

The FBI knew of these relationships prior to the NFL getting wind of them. "On August 2, 1962, information was received from a reliable source who is [redacted] the Sahara Inn Motel on Manheim Road in Schiller Park, Illinois, a suburb of Chicago....The Sahara Inn is a large Las Vegas-type motel which contains four lounges and is where the biggest names in the entertainment field are featured. The Sahara Inn has taken the place of the now defunct Chez Paree, as the Chicago night club offering entertainment stars such as [redacted] etc. It is owned ostensibly by Manny Skar, and also operated by him. Skar is a former small-time thief and burglar who is known to have been in close association with several of the Chicago top hoodlums including Marshall Caifano, Sam Giancana, and Murray Humphreys. Undoubtedly, he is also in contact with many others. Several allegations have been received, although none verified, indicating that Skar is merely a front for the Chicago hoodlums, and that therefore the Sahara Inn is owned by the hoodlum element in Chicago."

The following day, August 3, surveillance was conducted based off a tip. "Many of the individuals whom we had references to had been invited by Skar to spend the afternoon on the boat of Skar located on Lake Michigan at Burnham Harbor, near the Loop area of Chicago. This boat is named the Sahara....[redacted] advised that he had come into town for the All Star Football Game, which was held in Soldier Field in Chicago, on the evening of August 3, 1962. [This game was the Chicago College All-Star exhibition played yearly between the previous season's NFL champions—in this case, the Green Bay Packers—and a group of college all-stars. Green Bay would win 42–20.] He stated that [redacted — two lines] with Manny Skar. He stated that Skar seems to "go all out" in cultivating the coaches and athletes involved on both sides in the All Star Game....[redacted] advised that on the evening of August 2, 1962,

Skar extended an invitation to [redacted] and several other coaches and players to spend the afternoon of the All Star Game day on the boat of his, the Sahara. Skar advised that he would stock the boat with 'plenty of food and women,' and that since Soldier Field is located in the immediate vicinity of Burnham Harbor, they could all walk over to the ballgame following the afternoon on the boat."

According to this FBI report known gamblers were on board this party boat. And in fact, they did attend the game with "some 30 tickets…located in the mid-field." One of the people present was "being investigated by the Nevada Gaming Commission, due to the fact that he is investing several million dollars in the Tropicana Hotel and Gambling Casino."

Then the report turned its attention to Paul Hornung, albeit in a redacted form. "[redacted], who is a [redacted] of [redacted] and who has accompanied [redacted] on several of his nocturnal escapades, advised that he is extremely fearful that [redacted — Hornung's] reputation is in danger of being tarnished not only due to his association with Skar and [redacted] but with other individuals whom [redacted — Hornung] has associated with during his travels in night clubs throughout the United States. [redacted] advised that no information has come to his attention indicating that [redacted —Hornung] has thrown football games or 'shaved points,' and that he would be very surprised if such was the case. However, he advised he would not be so surprised if he learned that [redacted — Hornung] feels obligated to individuals like Skar and [redacted] for the [redacted — about three lines worth] which would directly influence the outcome of football [redacted] which [redacted] is engaged in. [redacted] also noted that [redacted] in view of his propensity for night life, has on many occasions [redacted] sometimes in the company of Skar and makes himself a tool of the people like [redacted] and Skar who undoubtedly are able to control his [redacted]. [redacted] noted that inasmuch as [redacted] being the [redacted] the possibilities presented to people like Skar and [redacted] in maintaining a close relationship with [redacted — Hornung] are extremely interesting, even without any suspicion that [redacted — Hornung] would consciously throw ballgames or shave points. [redacted] stated that due to the moral background and character of [redacted] he is sure that [redacted] but that the problem involved is that [redacted] in some instances is not in the best possible condition in order to perform in his top efficiency, and that in most cases where this is true, it is within the knowledge of gambling individuals like [redacted] who are then able to take large bets either for or against [redacted] as the case may be."

In his autobiography *Golden Boy*, Hornung wrote that he first met Manny Skar (which he misspelled as "Scar") in 1955, adding he "was rumored to be somewhat connected to the mob."[30] There is no doubt Manny Skar was mobbed up. After the party boat incident in 1962, Skar's life went into freefall. Within a year his hopeful "little Las Vegas," the Sahara Inn, went bankrupt. Then in 1965 the 42-year-old Skar dropped his wife off at the front of their Lake Shore Drive apartment building, drove into the nearby parking garage, and was promptly shot dead as he exited the car. Why? Skar was about to turn state's evidence and testify against the mafia. The hit man was Joseph "The Clown" Lombardo, who had followed Skar for two days prior to picking out the murder location. The hit on Skar was Lombardo's initiation into the mafia.

Ten days after the College All-Star game, the FBI decided it wanted a few answers. "In view of information contained in the referenced communications, it is felt that contact with [redacted — Vince Lombardi] coach, and general manager, Green Bay Packer Football Team, in the National Professional Football League, and [redacted — Hornung] will be desirable. It is felt that contact with [redacted — Hornung] may result in information pertaining to hoodlums that he reportedly has been in contact with. It is felt that contact with [redacted — Lombardi] may result in useful information and would generally have beneficial results for the Bureau. The Milwaukee Office contemplates discreetly discussing [redacted — Hornung's] activities with Lombardi and contact with [redacted] unless some information is present in Bureau files that would indicate such contacts are undesirable. In view of the status of Lombardi and [redacted — Hornung] as national sports figures, the approach to Lombardi and to [redacted — Hornung] through Lombardi will be made in the vein of seeking their cooperation in matters of possible interest to the Bureau. It is noted, however, that through this contact

Lombardi will be apprised discreetly of the facts of possible significance relating to [redacted — Hornung's] activities. It is noted, however, that no information has come to the attention of Milwaukee that [redacted — Hornung], in his reported contacts with hoodlums, has engaged in illegal activities or gambling or thrown or shaved points in football games."

Two days after the Packers demolished the Chicago Bears 49–0, Vince Lombardi sat down with a pair of FBI agents to discuss his MVP running back. "Vincent Thomas Lombardi, coach of the Green Bay Packers football team, a member of the National Professional Football League at Green Bay, Wis., was interviewed by [redacted — two agents] on 10/1/62. Lombardi appeared extremely cooperative and willing to discuss activities of the various players in the National Football League and, in particular, activities of **[redacted]** presently a **[redacted]**.

"Lombardi at the outset of the interview advised he desired to assure the FBI of his 100% cooperation in furnishing any information that came to his attention regarding hoodlums, contacts of football players or any information to help the FBI. In this connection, he pointed out that he is presently managing and operating a two-million-dollar yearly business in regards to the Packers Football Team and well realizes the dangers involved should a sports scandal in any way even touch players in the league and, particularly, Green Bay Packers players.

"Lombardi pointed out that actually the league rules and practices are such that the minute any suspicious contact is made with a football player or anyone connected with the professional football league, this contact is immediately to be reported to the head coach and eventually to the Football Commissioner that same day [this did not seem to happen in the case of Skar's party boat stocked with mobsters, gamblers, women and Packers...unless none of this was considered "suspicious"].... Other than this, personal investigations are constantly being made by investigators hired by the league who on the other hand make their reports directly to Pete Rozelle's office and not to the various coaches.... Lombardi pointed out that as far as participation in gambling of any sort pertaining to football games by players, strict league rules call for immediate banishment from the league of the violator. He advised he has no information or suspicion on this point in regard to his team...."

While it's impossible to discover what Lombardi really knew in regards to his players' gambling habits, it seems as though he was either extremely naïve or outright lying to the interviewing agents. The general assumption regarding St. Vincent here would be that Lombardi was too busy watching game film and developing the legendary Packers' sweep to recognize what his players were sneaking off to do. Could there have been motivation for an all-knowing Lombardi to lie? As head coach and GM of the Packers, he was sitting pretty with a championship team led by the league MVP in Hornung. An admission of guilt to either the NFL or FBI would have likely resulted in a gambling scandal—something he admitted to—which would spell an instant end to the Packers' 1960s dynasty, perhaps even Lombardi's job. For according to Hornung, he wasn't the only Packers player betting on games. In a 1986 *Sports Illustrated* article, "Hornung told [*Sports Illustrated*] that there were 10 or 12 other Green Bay Packer players who regularly wagered on NFL games in the team's glory days. He said that betting on games by players was rampant throughout the league."[31]

Returning to the FBI's interview with Lombardi: "Following the All-Star Game in Chicago and following the Green Bay Packer-Chicago Bear exhibition game in Milwaukee at the beginning of the present football season, Pete Rozelle, Commissioner of the NFL, called [redacted — Hornung] in for interview in Milwaukee and discussed with him his reported association with **[redacted]** and apparently Manny Skar. In this connection, Lombardi advised specifically he knew neither of these individuals and knew nothing about them except that, as a result of the above interview of [redacted — Hornung] by Rozelle, the presence of some football players at various times at the Sahara Inn in Chicago and contact with Manny Skar and **[redacted]** was made known, as well as the fact that **[redacted]** reportedly made a huge bet on the All-Star Game. [redacted — Hornung] was forbidden by the Commissioner to have any further association or contact with these individuals, and it appeared [redacted — Hornung] claimed a longtime personal friendship with **[redacted]** and intended at one time to have gone into business with him in the future. This was reportedly some legitimate type of

business activity, having no connection with football. Nonetheless, [redacted — Hornung] was forbidden to have further contact with these individuals....

"Lombardi pointed out [redacted — Hornung], of course, is a national sports figure, is much sought after by all levels of the 'sporting fraternity' and, in his own estimation, he is immature and has a 'lot of growing up to do.'

"Lombardi pointed out he has never had any reason to believe that [redacted — Hornung] is anything but honest and reliable, but he is well aware of his penchant for night clubbing and women and, for this reason, is constantly on the alert and 'somewhat worried' concerning [redacted — Hornung]. He was very careful in making this statement to point out that he has no reason to believe that [redacted — Hornung] has ever thrown a game, shaved points or given aid or information to anyone in the hoodlum or gambling elements, but as an illustration of things that constantly are being examined by himself, his staff and the league, he pointed out during the Chicago Bear game just finished, [redacted — Hornung] after only a few plays took himself out of the game claiming a pulled muscle [Hornung in fact rushed only twice in the game for 14 yards]. Lombardi pointed out he has no reason to believe [redacted — Hornung] was other than honest in pulling himself out of a game, but it is the kind of thing that is not provable in any way, and he as coach cannot help but wonder in his own mind if the injury were true...." Lombardi then complained to the interviewing agents that George Halas would not list certain players on the injury report as per NFL rules, adding "this is the kind of information that is a bonanza for gamblers if such are interested in the game and gives them opportunities for inside information."

Lombardi concluded with a promise...of sorts. "He stated, however, he would appreciate receiving any information regarding participation by [redacted — Hornung] in any unsavory contacts and vehemently stated that, regardless of [redacted — Hornung's] position on the team, if he makes any further contacts or gets out of line he will be summarily fired." This guarantee was made prior to Hornung's suspension in

1963, which one would think would be just the sort of incident damning enough for Lombardi to "fire" him. But as Hornung wrote in his book, when talk of his suspension being lifted prior to the 1964 season was publicized, Lombardi told reporters, "Any trade talk is ridiculous. I positively have no thought of trading him If Hornung plays, he'll play for us."[32]

Two days after Lombardi's interview, it was Hornung's turn in the hot seat. "[redacted — Hornung] pointed out he has knowledge of the fact that [redacted] is known as a bettor, a man who bets on anything, but stated he has no idea what events [redacted] bets on or how much money he bets with the exception that [redacted — Hornung] had been advised by Commissioner Pete Rozelle, of the NFL, at the beginning of this season that [redacted] had bet $20,000 on the All-Star Game, and that [redacted — Hornung] was to have no further contact with this man. [Hornung later told the FBI that he spoke with this gambler who denied betting $20,000, saying it was "impossible" to make such a high bet on a football game—especially the All-Star game—and that he had only wagered $2,000 on the game.]

"[redacted — Hornung] stated he told Rozelle of the close relationship between [redacted]; that he felt [redacted] was not a hoodlum but was a wealthy businessman, and that he would find it extremely difficult to sever his association with him or not to contact him at all. [redacted — Hornung] stated he had agreed not to seek [redacted] company, but he did not know what he would do in the event [redacted] called him up in view of the past favors and in view of his hope to go into business with [redacted] company in the future.

"In this connection, [redacted — Hornung] pointed out that [redacted] is an extremely close friend of George Halas and the entire Chicago Bear Football Team. He said he told the Commissioner that, in fact, [redacted] of the Chicago Bears at the present time holds a job in [redacted] organization."

Hornung appeared to be rather forthright with the interviewing agents. He admitted he knew Skar dating back to his Notre Dame days, some five to six years at that point. Hornung added that Skar never asked him for information, nor did his associates which Hornung did not know or realize may have been mob-connected. Hornung said he had not seen Skar "this football season, had not seen him either before or after the All-Star game," but merely talked with him by phone. However, the FBI knew this wasn't completely true. Then Hornung admitted being acquainted with Gil Beckley. "[redacted — Hornung] did advise he has an acquaintanceship with [redacted — Beckley] whom he volunteered is presently under indictment by the FBI as a bookie and knew this individual at Newport, KY. He stated [redacted — Beckley] invited him [redacted — Hornung] to sit with him at the [redacted — Floyd Patterson-Ingemar Johansson heavyweight title] fight but then pointed out to [redacted — Hornung] that he probably would not want to be seen with him, and they both agreed that it would be unwise for [redacted — Hornung] to ever be seen in [redacted — Beckley's] presence." Hornung wrote about this escapade in *Golden Boy,* including a tidbit not shared with the FBI: Beckley placed a winning $1,000 wager on the fight for Hornung.

Hornung's relationship with Beckley was perhaps more dangerous than with Skar. Beckley was the mafia's top layoff bookmaker in the 1960s who, according to Moldea, participated in fixing 19 football games in 1966 (many of which were likely the AFL games described earlier). He wasn't alone in possessing such an opinion of Beckley. "When asked whether Gil Beckley had ever influenced the outcomes of professional football games, FBI supervisor Ralph Hill replied, 'The records would show that, yes. They would have been manipulated in many ways. One is getting to the ballplayers, to get the coaching staff to manipulate the points down and then ensure that they are within the spread.'"[33] Beckley would later vanish, assumed to be murdered by the mob.

Hornung wasn't as honest when facing Commissioner Rozelle and the NFL. Like his compatriot Rick Casares of the Chicago Bears, whose betting ways actually started the NFL's 1962 investigation into player gambling, Hornung took a lie detector test on January 10, 1963. Unlike Casares, who passed two polygraph examinations (despite betting on NFL games, if Hornung's book is to be believed), Hornung failed. Casares skated through the NFL's investigation without a scratch thanks mostly to his coach George Halas protecting him. But Hornung had to devise his own safety net. Hornung outright threatened Commissioner Rozelle that should the NFL come down too hard on him, he'd appear before Congress—which was investigating gambling at the time—and expose everything he knew within the NFL. Rozelle took him seriously. As a result, when Rozelle announced Hornung's suspension he "spoke highly of Hornung's honesty, never mentioning that the player had lied during the initial polygraph examination ('When I told Hornung of the charges, he admitted them,' said Rozelle)."[34]

Hornung claimed that after his suspension he never bet on a football game while still a player. Not that he wasn't tempted. But he stayed on the straight and narrow for the remainder of his career, entering the football Hall of Fame in 1986. Whether or not he ever bet against himself or the Packers prior to his suspension cannot be determined as the FBI dropped its investigation of Hornung when the NFL suspended him; however, it is quite possible other members of the Packers—perhaps some of the ten or 12 Hornung outed to *Sports Illustrated*—did throw a game. Oddly, it was one in which Hornung did not play: the Packers' Thanksgiving Day game against the Detroit Lions on November 22, 1962.

The first Packers-Lions game in 1962 was considered suspect by many gamblers as the heavily favored Packers failed to cover the spread in a tight 9–7 victory. "Large bets and unnatural money had appeared on this game, which had been placed by beards who had received money from supposedly untraceable sources."[35] Come their Thanksgiving Day match-up, the Packers' record was 10–0 with the Lions close behind at 8–2. But by the fourth quarter the Lions were demolishing the Packers 26–0 before the Pack scored two late, meaningless touchdowns to make the final score 26–14. Though the Lions turned the ball over five times in the game, their defense sacked Bart Starr ten times (compared to just once in the first game), forcing three fumbles and two interceptions. After this beating, the Packers wouldn't lose another game all season, including the championship versus the New York Giants.

Shortly thereafter, the FBI began to hear rumors about the fix

being in that day. On December 14, 1962, the FBI learned from an informant that "the only restriction on betting on professional football teams during the current football season, to his knowledge, was that the Green Bay Packers were 'off the board' (bets not accepted on this team) for three of their past four games, the reason being, according to the informant, was that the Packers were prohibited favorites. The exception was their game with the Detroit Lions on Thanksgiving Day." Four days later, the Los Angeles Bureau, which had just obtained information from a raid on bookmakers conducted by the LAPD, wrote, "The [redacted] on the Green Bay Packers football team, according to several sources on the LAPD, are actually [redacted] on the events in which they participate and are suspected of [redacted]. Certain bookies have lost considerable money on Green Bay Packers bets and as a result few wagers are accepted prior to day of Packers games. Material taken in a gambling arrest by the LAPD, according to that department, substantiates to a degree the allegations against the Packers." Even with this information, the L.A. Bureau was told, "Conduct no investigations at this time which might infer we are investigating activities of the Green Bay Packers or, in fact, any other professional football team. Any information, however, that is furnished concerning questionable activities on the part of Packers or players on other teams should be noted."

Yet that may not have been the end of gambling on the part of Packers players. Even after Hornung received his indefinite suspension, the FBI had information that at least two Packers players were betting on Packers games through a Milwaukee bookie—and not on the Packers to win. This information came from a "top-echelon criminal informant," but most of the information obtained remains redacted. What is able to be determined was that these players bet against the Packers in their September 22, 1963 game against the Detroit Lions. This wasn't the wisest investment as the Packers won 31–10. The FBI's information had it that these same players were going to bet on the November 3 game versus the Pittsburgh Steelers as well (it wasn't known which side their money would be bet). Assuming the bookie was going to meet with the players, the FBI tailed him but only did so the day before the game. No observed meeting took place, and the Packers beat the Steelers 33–14. The file ends with contact wanting to be made with the informant prior to the Packers-49ers game played November 24, which was also won by the Packers 28–10.

RAMPANT RUMORS

Two weeks prior to the announcement of the suspensions of Hornung and Karras, NFL commissioner Pete Rozelle came to the FBI seeking an olive branch. "Rozelle wants to make as complete a statement as possible at the time he announces the action taken, in an effort to show the public his inquiry was thorough and the action taken is justified. In this way he hopes to prevent any extensive follow-up publicity and to gain the reassurance of the public in the integrity of his league." Notice here that Rozelle wasn't saying that the NFL did in fact conduct a 100 percent thorough investigation. What he wanted was for his statement, the suspensions and associated fines to act as a stopgap for the media, to prevent them from digging any deeper while assuring NFL fans that all was good within football. In this effort, the PR master Rozelle was successful.

Continuing from the FBI file: "Rozelle's purpose in contacting the Bureau was twofold. First, he wanted to discuss the new Federal gambling statute covering the interstate transmission of wagering information. He asked for advice as to the extent of the application of this statute. It was pointed out to the Commissioner that an answer to his question encompassed a legal opinion relating to the statute; that the Bureau was strictly a fact-finding organization; and that a decision as to prosecution and other legal interpretations were properly within the province of the Department of Justice proper.

"The second item covered was a desire that, should the FBI at any time in the future receive any information of irregularities on the part of his football players, we feel free to communicate directly with the Commissioner, where it was proper for us to do so. Rozelle stated he recognized the FBI's responsibility to investigate reported violations of Federal statutes and that these investigations had to be handled on a confidential basis. It was his hope, however, that in other situations where information of interest to the National Football League was received and no Federal violation was indicated, we would be able to at least alert him to the potentially troublesome spot."

FBI director J. Edgar Hoover read this memorandum and added a personal, handwritten note. It began, "I don't put too much faith in Rozelle. I don't question his integrity but I doubt his determination to get to the bottom of this filthy mess." Hoover may have been correct, for after Rozelle made his April 1963 announcement regarding the gambling investigation, little appeared to change in terms of NFL players gambling. In fact, it may have gotten worse as the FBI opened more investigations into possibly rigged games.

It was just three weeks into the 1965 NFL season when the FBI looked into the October 3, 1965 contest between the Washington Redskins and the Detroit Lions. As the FBI wrote, "On 10/12/65 [redacted] advised that he had heard 'rumbles' that captioned game had been fixed. The 'line' furnished by Multiple Sports News Service opened at 7, changed to 6½, and finally closed at 5½ favoring Detroit [this downward line movement signaled more money was coming in on the underdog Redskins than the home favorite Lions]. It is noted that the Washington Redskins, scoreless until the fourth quarter, scored their ten points in the last part of the fourth quarter. Even the TV sportscaster made mention of the fact that [redacted] Detroit Lions [redacted] some strange plays in protecting the Detroit 14-point lead. It is noted that the Washington Redskins scored their touchdown through an interception of a pass [redacted]." The Lions won 14–10, but the Redskins covered the spread in an apparently sloppy game. The two Redskins quarterbacks, Sonny Jurgensen and Dick Shiner, threw a combined six interceptions to go along with two team fumbles. Yet Lions quarterback Milt Plum—the one seemingly singled out for strange play in the file—countered by throwing four interceptions himself.

Of all the people the FBI could have gone to for more information on this game, the Bureau couldn't have made a worse (or better, depending on your viewpoint) selection. They approached Multiple Sports News Service "consultant" Frank "Lefty" Rosenthal—the man nationally known for fixing games. "Rosenthal volunteered that this was not an unusual point change in a professional football game. He further stated that [redacted] is known in the trade as a mediocre [redacted]. [redacted] play selection in the fourth quarter of captioned game was indeed unusual in protecting a 14-point lead." Who knows, Lefty could've fixed this game himself. Because according to another informant, "[redacted] telephonically advised SA [redacted] from Pittsburgh, PA, that he had heard nothing questionable about professional football games played this season, except for captioned game. Informant stated that the word was out to bet on Washington."

One month later, the FBI had a report that two members of the San Francisco 49ers had bets against themselves in a November 7 game versus the Dallas Cowboys. "In view of information set out in reairtel concerning Unknown Subjects betting heavily against their team in captioned game….On 11/16/65, [redacted] who is well acquainted with bookmaking activities in Dallas, advised he had not heard anything about any San Francisco players betting on the game, however the point spread, in Dallas, opened with Dallas as a four-point favorite, and later dropped to two points, because of the heavy betting in Dallas, on Dallas." As Dallas won the game 39–31, meaning the losing players would have been winners if they did indeed bet against themselves, the FBI brought them both in for an interview. "Both [redacted] advised that betting on professional football games by any member of the team was strictly forbidden and both offered their full cooperation and assistance." They had "no knowledge" of any team member betting on NFL games, but they acknowledged gambling was done, though simply on horse races and in poker games.

While that case was closed, a year later a similar investigation began, focusing on a team just down the California coastline. "Information had been received from [redacted] regarding rumor circulating among the gambling element in Bridgeport, Connecticut, that [redacted] the Los Angeles [redacted] had bet [redacted] in the game vs. Minnesota on 10/16/66. Informant advised the newspaper account of the game indicated that [redacted] played worst game of his career. The Rams, which were a two-point favorite, were defeated by Minnesota 35 to 7. Infor-

313

mant advised that Bridgeport gamblers, including **[redacted]**, allegedly bet heavily on Minnesota and won." The player who "played [the] worst game of his career" that day was most likely Rams quarterback Roman Gabriel. Against the Vikings that October afternoon, Gabriel went 9 for 22 passing for 125 yards. He threw three interceptions and was replaced by Bill Munson. The Rams didn't score until the fourth quarter when they were already down by 35 points.

Soon, as the cliché goes, the plot thickened. "**[redacted]** Berkshire County House of Correction, Pittsfield, Mass. And who is awaiting sentencing in **[redacted]** and **[redacted]** has provided information to Bureau Agents concerning a variety of topics including the possible fixing of National Football League contests during the years 1968, 1969, and 1970. **[redacted]** stated that during these years, **[redacted]** who plays for the Los Angeles Rams, as an **[redacted]** and **[redacted]** for the Los Angeles Rams, were both involved in the fixing of Los Angeles Rams football contests and that these fixes were coordinated by **[redacted]** of Springfield, Mass.....**[redacted]** as a result of a Bank Fraud and Embezzlement investigation, alleges that **[redacted]** well-known Massachusetts gambling figure, coordinated the fixing of National Football League (NFL) contests during 1968–1970. **[redacted]** claims that **[redacted]** Los Angeles Rams **[redacted]** and **[redacted]** for the Rams, were involved. The alleged fixing was by way of 'point shaving.' There have been previous allegations regarding **[redacted]** and **[redacted]** which were not substantiated by investigation. The United States Attorney, Boston, requests investigation to determine the accuracy of **[redacted]** statement. Discreet investigation being conducted in this matter."

Already in custody, this criminal informant had more to share, making his confession seem all the more legitimate. This source had been known to FBI for five years, but his information ranged from very reliable—including being used in Grand Jury testimony which was corroborated entirely—to questionable. However, the FBI felt in this instance their source was being forthright. "**[redacted]** has indicated that the sports fixes were accomplished in the sense that the point spread for contests was held to within the line set by **[redacted]** and not in the sense that Los Angeles lost games on account of activity by [redacted]. He stated that on numerous occasions, he, [redacted] was sent by [redacted] to Las Vegas, Nevada, where he placed bets of considerable amounts based on the information provided to [redacted]. [redacted] has stated their subsequent to the contests, [redacted] demonstrated to him while watching game films, particular plays where [redacted] conducted themselves in such a manner as to accomplish the fix….It is noted that during the years 1968–1970, rumors consistently persisted that the [redacted] Brothers of Springfield, Mass. were using [redacted], the [redacted] to obtain information pertinent to the Los Angeles Rams football team so that this information could be used in setting football lines and placing wagers."

While gathering background information and further debriefing their informant, the FBI sent a memo to its Los Angeles Bureau. This had one standing order: "In no way should the football team be made aware of the nature of the investigation." Despite Rozelle's earlier pleas with the Bureau, the FBI apparently did not trust the NFL or its security division enough to share this information. They played this close to the vest. Almost too close. Just as it appeared to ramp up, the FBI decided the source should undergo polygraph examination. The informant agreed… as long as his attorney could see a list of questions first. The FBI decided that without the polygraph test, it would go no further with the case. Sadly, it appears that test never occurred as the file suddenly ends.

Three years later, however, another FBI investigative file opened again centering on the Los Angeles Rams. This investigation focused on the December 14, 1969 Rams-Lions game. "[redacted] interviewed by [Bureau] Agent 1/21/70 and stated that one [redacted] had told him on the day of the football game that [redacted] had advised an unknown person, who had bet $800 on the Los Angeles Rams, to switch his bet to the Detroit Lions because 'the fix was on the game.' [redacted] stated that [redacted] told him the Los Angeles Rams' [redacted] was in on the fix because [redacted]."

The next day, another possible source regarding this allegation was interviewed. This person, however, was not as open. "[redacted] was inter-

viewed by [Bureau] Agent 1/22/70 and refused to furnish any information, stating 'talk to my attorney'....**[redacted]** said that he did not like
FBI agents." Whoever this uncooperative source was, he was no saint.
He was the subject of two other FBI investigations—one in Louisville,
the other in Detroit—and had an arrest record which included serving
a sentence for grand larceny. However, this person of interest "willingly
assisted Bureau Agents in fugitive matters and bank robbery matters,
however, he was uncooperative concerning investigations into gambling
activities."

Unfortunately, the FBI could find no further leads in Los Angeles
or Detroit concerning this possible fix. Instead, the Bureau did what it
refused to do the last time they investigated the Rams—they went to the
NFL. The FBI reported that the NFL "did not conduct any investigation of the captioned game. He stated that the Rams had sewed up their
conference title and had notified the office of Commissioner Pete Rozelle
that they were not going to play their first string and would probably play
[redacted] a great deal." This was a bit of a falsehood. The 1969 Rams
indeed began the season 11–0, easily locking up the title in the Coastal
Division. Then they lost to the Minnesota Vikings 20–13 a week prior to
taking on the Lions in the game in question. In that contest, the Lions
crushed the Rams 28–0. But the Rams didn't take the field with their
second string offense. Leading the charge that day was a familiar name:
quarterback Roman Gabriel. That afternoon, Gabriel completed seven
passes for 41 yards on 13 attempts. He also tossed a pair of interceptions
before backup Karl Sweetan finished off the game.

Twice the FBI had information concerning a fixed Rams game,
and twice their starting quarterback Roman Gabriel played a very
poor game. Coincidence? In the first instance, the desired lie detector
test apparently was never given and the case faded. In the second, the
informant wasn't fond of FBI agents and refused to discuss any matter
related to gambling. Without those leads, neither investigation was going
anywhere. It is interesting to note that if the first source was right and
that perhaps two members of the Rams were shaving points in the 1968,
1969, and 1970 seasons, it was during great seasons record-wise for the
team. In 1968, the Rams finished second in their division with a 10-3-1

record. Then as stated above, they won their division in 1969. And in the first year of the merged NFL and AFL, the Rams again finished second, posting a 9-4-1 record. Of course, a team need not lose a game when shaving points. It can win, just not against the spread. If players on a winning team such as the Rams were doing both—winning games but making sure not to cover the spread when necessary—it must have been a difficult tightrope to walk. But it would have been incredibly effective. The on-the-field wins would have kept the Rams as a constant betting favorite, allowing the fixers to remain in control of everything. But their failure to cover the spread would have been maddening to bettors across the country.

Other games and teams appeared on the FBI's radar in this era as well, though beyond the initial information, investigations couldn't uncover more. The Bureau examined a Chicago Bears vs. St. Louis Cardinals game played on Halloween night in 1966. "Information set out that official in National Football League Game between the Chicago Bears and St. Louis Cardinals which was won by St. Louis 24 to 17 had been corrupted. Major gamblers [redacted] reported as having bet on St. Louis." The report continued, "On November two last [redacted] advised [redacted] nationwide bookmaking figure, advised [redacted] another interstate bookmaking figure to bet five thousand dollars through [redacted] bookmaking office on St. Louis. [redacted] told [redacted] that if St. Louis did not win, his money would be returned. According to informant, one of game officials was involved."

In 1968, just one year after joining the NFL, the FBI was swarming over the New Orleans Saints. While investigating rumors of game fixing by members of the LSU football team—which turned out to be accurate—the Bureau received information regarding the Saints as well. Several players appeared to be associated with the "hoodlum" element in New Orleans leading the FBI to dig further into the team. Regarding one member of the Saints organization: "in the past he has been known to associate with such nationally known gamblers as [redacted] who operates out of Miami and New York City." But more importantly, "[redacted] advised he received information from a source he did not desire to reveal that [redacted] who is connected with the operation of the

New Orleans Saints Football Team of the National Football League, was in Dallas, Texas, sometime during the football season of 1968 attempting to place a large bet on a Saints football game as a player or players on the Saints team was or were in the 'tank.' Informant said he did not know which game or amount of money involved although he might be able to determine this through a person with whom he is acquainted. Informant stated he understood the person on the New Orleans team involved in this matter was [redacted]. Informant said he understands [redacted] was an active player; however, [redacted]. Informant said [redacted] has a poor reputation and [redacted] has repeatedly been warned that he should get rid of [redacted] before he damages his team and professional football in general by his activities." This informant was tight with New Orleans mob boss Carlos Marcello and asked him if he knew of fixed games. Marcello said no; however, one player "reportedly is living beyond his means, which possibly indicates he has an outside source of income."

Then there were the oddities surrounding a game played between the New York Giants and Philadelphia Eagles on November 17, 1968. The day prior to this game a former FBI special agent was at a cocktail party in Wilmington, DE. He learned that "[redacted] related to a group at the party that he had heard the 'fix was on' in captioned game. Complainant understood that the 'fix' was a point-shaving fix and not one designed to throw the entire game." This information originated in a conversation in the Concord Country Club locker room in Concordville, PA. "During lunch [redacted] made the comment that the boys in the locker room said that if the Eagles ever won one—tomorrow is the day… [redacted] then commented that the word was out that the gamblers were going to unload on this game and there would be as much as five million dollars bet on the game." There was a question of which team was going to do what. Though it would seem the Giants were going to tank the game, the source revealed that "by inference, [redacted] did take conversation to mean Eagles had been lying down all year to 'set up for this game.'" Yet the 6–3 Giants opened as 14-point favorites against the winless Eagles and had beaten them earlier in the season 34–25. By game time, heavy betting on the Eagles caused the line to drop five points to the Giants -9. Lo and behold, despite the Giants outgaining the Eagles in yards 274 to 107, the Giants won by a score of only 7–6. This triggered the former special agent to send a Western Union telegram to commissioner Pete Rozelle, detailing the information he had learned before game time. What Rozelle did with this is unknown. As for the FBI, since neither the former special agent nor the FBI knew the name of the person with the loose lips in the locker room, the investigation quickly faded.

And let us not forget the legend of Joe Willie Namath. In his biography *Namath*, author Mark Kriegel quotes from Namath's FBI dossier, "The same source also advised that there have been rumors among members of the New York sports world that Namath had 'thrown' several games while quarterbacking the New York Jets during the 1966 season. It is also understood that Namath's association with 'hoods' and cheap gamblers will soon be revealed publicly in New York City." It's no stretch to say that Namath was in fact friends with known members of the mafia, some of whom wanted Joe to stay away from them for his own sake. His name and number were discovered in Dice Dawson's address book (along with other quarterbacks') when the notorious gambler/game-fixer was arrested in the late 1960s. But Namath lived his life his own way. While it was his co-ownership of the nightclub Bachelors III which led to Commissioner Rozelle's ultimatum where Namath was forced to choose between football and the bar (he chose the bar and briefly quit football), the question remains: did he gamble on games?

Kriegel's biography would seem to indicate yes. "'Joe used to put all the bets through me with the bookies,' says Art Heyman, an avid bettor then knocking around the lower rungs of professional basketball. 'He used to bet all the football games….College. He did all the college games.' How much Namath bet—Heyman recalls his usual wager as $200 a game—and whom he bet on remain unclear. There is no question, however, that he enjoyed gambling. If it wasn't football, it was pool, or horses."[36] Was it just college games Namath bet? Again, Kriegel's book makes one wonder. "For years, there have been whispers that Namath and [Lou] Michaels made a bet [on the Jets in Super Bowl III] that night at Fazio's. And while owners like Rosenbloom could brag with impunity about a quarter-million-dollar wager [which Rosenbloom allegedly made on his Colts against Namath's Jets in Super Bowl III], woe to the player who made any kind of bet."[37] Kriegel couldn't pin down the rumor. Lou Michaels said they never bet, but his brother Walt said they did—just not on that game. Namath's teammate, Jets defensive back Jim Hudson, said there was a bet. But Namath's lawyer, Mike Bite, denied these allegations. Yet Hudson countered by claiming Bite collected the winning wager on Namath's behalf.

Prior to Namath winning Super Bowl III and perhaps taking home a few extra bucks to boot, several questioned if he was fixing games during the 1968 season. Two games stood out: a Week 3 loss to the Buffalo Bills and a Week 5 loss to the Denver Broncos. In losing to the Bills 37–35, Namath threw five interceptions—three of which were returned for touchdowns by the Bills. He duplicated that feat in the 21–13 loss to the Broncos, tossing five interceptions albeit without the Broncos scoring on any of the plays. Namath confronted these rumors in his own book *I Can't Wait Until Tomorrow…'Cause I Get Better Looking Every Day* writing, "Hell, you'd have to be an idiot to make it that obvious. If you want to throw a game, you don't have to allow a single pass to be intercepted. You just screw up one or two handoffs, and the running back can't handle them, and he fumbles the ball, and he takes the blame. Then maybe you throw a critical third-down pass a little low, and you let the punter come in and give the ball to the other team. You don't give it away yourself."[38] It's easy to agree with Namath; however, it is interesting how the Hall of Fame quarterback seems to know ways to shave points in a game without looking guilty.

THE FINK ON THE CHIEFS

When I interviewed legendary sports gambler Lem Banker, one of the questions I asked was if he knew of NFL games fixed during the 1960s and 1970s. "Yeah," he said. "Kansas City Chiefs. Big moves with Len Dawson. Big money."

Dan Moldea also investigated members of the Kansas City Chiefs for shaving points in *Interference*. He wrote, "According to FBI records, nearly twenty games played by the Kansas City Chiefs over a period of two and a half seasons, 1966–68, were the targets of unnatural money. In a vast majority of these games, the side where the unnatural money turned up was the winner."[39] Who was behind this unnatural money appearing on Chiefs games? "Federal agents investigating the Kansas City Chiefs were interested in Gene Nolan because his brother Joseph Lee had been convicted in 1968 for participating in a conspiracy to bribe football players at Louisiana State University to fix four LSU games. The case became the first successful use of the Federal Sports Bribery Act of 1964. 'Jo-Jo' Nolan was to have paid the LSU players off in upfront cash—through a middleman—and lay down bets for them. An FBI source in New Orleans told special agents that Gene Nolan had been doing business with the Kansas City Chiefs, particularly Johnny Robinson, a 1960 LSU graduate and a teammate of the legendary All-American halfback Billy Cannon, who had been playing for the Houston Oilers and later the Oakland Raiders before he joined the Chiefs."[40]

Throughout the 1968 season, both gamblers and bookmakers could not get a good read on the Chiefs. One week the Chiefs' game would be on the board, the next week it'd be off. One week they'd crush the Broncos 34–2, easily covering the spread; the next week they'd face a hapless Bills team lacking their star quarterback and barely win, much less cover the spread. This would go back and forth all season. "The NFL concluded that the Chiefs' games had been taken off the boards because the team was 'too unpredictable' in 1968. NFL executives failed to note that during the 1968 season, the Chiefs had compiled a 12–2 record, which was best in the AFL that year."[41]

The real trouble for the team started the following season during their march to Super Bowl IV. The IRS began a massive investigation of gambling and bookmakers which ultimately led to the arrest of Dice Dawson and 13 others. During that time, wiretaps revealed that Dawson had called MLB players, three NFL quarterbacks—the Chiefs' Len Dawson, Lions' QB Bill Munson, and Rams' QB Karl Sweetan (Roman Gabriel's backup)—plus four other "big-name players" in the NFL[42] (recall that Joe Namath's name and number were also found in Dawson's address book). Years later, Dice Dawson would tell Moldea that he "knew [Len Dawson] was doing a lot of gambling over there. In Kansas City the Civellas [the crime family with whom Kansas A's owner Charles Finley was friendly] were betting really big money. Some of these people got ahold of Lenny, and they made a shithouse full of money."[43] In other words, Len Dawson the quarterback wasn't working with Dice Dawson the gambler, but others were.

This all came to a head just before Super Bowl IV, which showcased the Chiefs and the Minnesota Vikings. NBC News broke the story on January 5, 1970, detailing how from this IRS investigation a grand jury was to be convened which would subpoena NFL players and personnel, including Len Dawson. Author Michael MacCambridge would write of this incident in his book *America's Game*, "And once again, all the attention leading up to the [Super Bowl] game centered on the AFL quarterback at the eye of a media hurricane. This time, though, Len Dawson did nothing to bring it on himself....Rozelle was on a boat in Bimini when the news hit, and could do little but release a statement from the league office that evening, noting that the league had 'no evidence to even consider disciplinary action against any of those publicly named.'"[44]

Len Dawson suddenly found himself in the middle of a media frenzy, one even more intense than usual leading up to a Super Bowl. To combat this, NFL security chief Jack Danahy wrote up a signed statement for Dawson to read to the press. In it he confessed, if only to the slightest of charges, by saying, "I have known Mr. [Dice] Dawson for about ten years and have talked to him on several occasions. My only conversations with him in recent years concerned my knee injuries and the death of my father. On these occasions, he contacted me to offer his sympathy." A reporter on the scene immediately asked Dawson if he had ever met Dice Dawson personally, to which Len replied, "Are we going to get into all this?"[45] Chiefs head coach Hank Stram then stepped in and saved his star quarterback, directing questions away from Dawson to the game about to be played. In Super Bowl IV, Dawson led the Chiefs to a crushing victory over the Vikings 23–7. And as MacCambridge wrote, "Ultimately, that's all there was to the story."[46]

Not exactly.

By prematurely running its story, NBC News actually wrecked the federal government's investigation. The feds hadn't yet secured further wiretap authorizations nor had it obtained the cooperation of the gamblers involved, meaning confessions weren't forthcoming. As a result, the grand jury probe never took place. Instead, about a month after the Super Bowl, charges against most of those arrested were dropped, though a few, including Dice Dawson, would serve short prison sentences. Len Dawson was later audited by the IRS to little effect; meanwhile, he continued to play in the NFL until 1975, later entering the Hall of Fame in 1987.

The NFL was able to quickly erase this ordeal from its history. Yet 13 years later, PBS—the only network not funding the NFL by broadcasting its games—would investigate the connections between the league and organized crime in a January 17, 1983 episode of *Frontline*. Featured in a segment was a bookmaker named John Charles "Butch" Piazza (a.k.a. John Petracelli). He revealed on the program "that between 1968 and 1970 he had been involved in payoffs to a particular team's head coach, quarterback, and defensive captain. 'With the quarterback,' Piazza said, 'if he knew the perimeters of the score that we wanted to hold…he'd throw a bad pass or throw it out of bounds and only kick a field goal. We also bagged the defensive captain, a defensive back, so he could slip and fall down and let the other team score.' The head coach was needed to guarantee that neither the quarterback nor the defensive back were pulled out of the game. Piazza added that he had known of the fixing of four games in each of those years. He said that the players had received and split an average of $300,000 per game, plus 10 percent of what the fixers made gambling. Their biggest payoff, he claimed, was $795,000 for a single fixed game, which he had personally delivered."[47]

Many doubted Piazza's confession. They believed with the amounts of the payoffs he claimed, millions would have had to have been wagered on the games in question and that would not have been possible given the era. Also, PBS did not broadcast any evidence of which games those were, so nothing could be fact-checked, and Piazza did not reveal the names of the players nor the team involved. Even so, Piazza did pass a PBS-sponsored polygraph test and the network ran with his story. If

true, it's most likely Piazza was referring to the Chiefs with Len Dawson being the quarterback, Johnny Robinson as the defensive back, and Hank Stram as the head coach. Dawson was connected to both Dice Dawson and allegedly the Civella crime family while Robinson was connected to the New Orleans gambling brothers the Nolans. And as coincidence would have it, MacCambridge revealed in *America's Game* that Dawson and Robinson were roommates while on the Chiefs. Further information contained within the FBI's files seems to bear out this theory.

Random information concerning the Chiefs first appeared in FBI files in 1966. On November 1, 1966, the FBI heard from the "operator of Harold's Club" in Kansas City who knew a well-known area bookmaker. He informed the Bureau that this bookie took the October 23, 1966 Kansas City vs. Denver game off the boards which the Chiefs won handily 56–10. This bookie then did the same with the Kansas City vs. Houston game played the following week, but then put the game back up later in the week, limiting bets to just $50 as the Chiefs were favored by 14 points. The Chiefs won this game and covered as well, 48–23. When asked why KC games were off the boards, the source told the FBI, "[redacted] replied he had received information from Chicago that members of the Chiefs had been betting on their recent games." Later in November, a different informant told the Bureau, "players involved in irregularities on Kansas City team not known, but he understands more than one player is involved."

In 1967, the Kansas City Bureau decided to look into the actions of the hometown Chiefs. The trigger appeared to be the fact that Chiefs games were routinely taken off the boards due to oddities in wagering. "[redacted] during a contact on the night of 10/11/67, advised the reason none of the [redacted] gave a line on the Kansas City Chiefs-San Diego game being played this Sunday, 10/15/67, was that the [redacted] source for [redacted] Omaha gambler [redacted] has informed the [redacted] that he suspects Kansas City [redacted] is 'doing business with the gamblers.'" Another source in the Denver gambling community had a similar claim as he "had indicated [redacted] that the line on the Kansas City-Oakland game played on 10/1/67 at Oakland suddenly

changed the last hour before this game and Kansas City went from a 6.0 favorite to a 2.0 favorite. [redacted] to both of these informants and other gamblers contacted by the Denver Office that he suspected that something was happening in this game and suspected Kansas City had 'laid down' in this game." In the Oakland game played on October 1, 1967, Kansas City never led, losing 23–21. Dawson was 12 of 25 for 160 yards, throwing one touchdown and one interception. Two weeks later in the suspect game against San Diego, the Chiefs were upset 45–31, again without ever holding a lead. Dawson was a very respectable 24 of 37 for 364 yards, but three interceptions, including one returned 100 yards for a touchdown by the aptly named Speedy Duncan, did not help the Chiefs' cause.

The problem with Chiefs games wasn't a localized issue, as sources and information came from all corners of the country. "[redacted] told [criminal informant] that the local bookies in Omaha were not taking bets on the Kansas City Chiefs football games because there were stories circulating in Omaha that someone on the Chiefs football team was doing business with the gamblers. [redacted] told [criminal informant] that the recent Oakland-Kansas City game 'smelled' and there was a lot of talk about the San Diego-Kansas City game which was to be played during the PM of 10/15/67. [redacted] told [criminal informant] that he had no concrete information as to why the Kansas City Chiefs football games were 'being taken off the board' by the bookies. [redacted] told [criminal informant] that he guessed that if anybody on the Kansas City Chiefs team was doing business with the gamblers, it would logically be [redacted] because he is in the position to 'throw the game.' [redacted] further advised this [criminal informant] that the Las Vegas, Nevada, gamblers for the past couple of Chiefs games have bet heavily on the Chiefs' opponents and have won a great deal of money."

The FBI attempted to turn this Omaha bookie into an informant. In his interview with the Bureau, he told the FBI the Chiefs "stink." He didn't know if the Chiefs were fixing games, but had "circled" a few and would only take small bets or parlay plays on the Chiefs. He had also heard "there is considerable dissension between Chiefs' [redacted] and the Chiefs' two Negro ends, especially [redacted]. [redacted] suggested

the Chiefs might trade these two ends at the close of the current season because of this problem." This source also "admitted he had abandoned his conservative line on the Chiefs and accepted heavy betting on the Chiefs for their Thanksgiving game with Oakland, 11/23/67. [redacted] stated the local line was Kansas City plus 7 points. [redacted] noted Chiefs were still contenders and this was a 'must' game for them."

In the weeks leading up to that Thanksgiving Day matchup against the Raiders, the Chiefs were rolling. They demolished the Broncos 52–9, whipped the Jets 42–18, and stomped the Patriots 33–10. In the last two games, the FBI had information that the Chiefs were at least ten-point favorites and covered easily. But then the team had a misstep against the Chargers, losing 17–16. This set the stage for the 6–4 Chiefs to take on the 9–1 Raiders in this "must"-win game played in Kansas City on November 23, 1967. The Chiefs lost 44–22. Dawson barely connected on 30 percent of his throws, going 11 for 32 for 130 yards with four interceptions, two of which were returned for touchdowns. Dawson would even be benched for backup Jacky Lee in the fourth quarter. The Omaha bookie told the FBI, "[redacted] acknowledged he had 'made a bundle' when Oakland soundly beat the Chiefs. [redacted] denied any inside knowledge that the Chiefs were going to 'lay down' or that any players had sold out the team."

Despite the apprehension of the gambling community, by December 1967 the FBI shut down their investigation because they could "not produce any information which would substantiate the allegation that [redacted] Kansas City Chiefs [redacted] was involved with gamblers." The reason the Chiefs' lines would not be set, according to the FBI? "This reluctance was based in part on the erratic play of the Kansas City Chiefs, lack of physical conditioning, and squad dissension."

Yet almost immediately after one investigation ended, another one opened. This, however, did not begin as a gambling investigation; it was a narcotics matter. And the "reliable source and contact of the Kansas City office" was a player on the Chiefs. "[redacted] allegedly is a [redacted] for narcotics. [redacted] reportedly is supplying narcotics to [redacted] Minnesota Twins baseball player, and to [redacted — two] members of the Minnesota Vikings NFL football team." The informant/ player had more to add. "[redacted] further said he had contacted one of his scouts, [redacted] indicated that source of funds for [redacted] new Cadillac, flashy clothes, and large amount of spending money was 'bad.' [redacted] requested Coach [redacted] not to have him 'squeal' on [redacted]. [redacted] advised he intended to confront [redacted] with allegations PM Sept 15, 1967, in order to make decision whether to retain or dismiss [redacted] from football squad."

As this second investigation continued into 1968, narcotics no longer seemed to be an issue. The primary concern became game fixing, and the FBI wasn't going to necessarily share their information with the NFL or AFL. "If Kansas City feels that the coach of the Kansas City Chiefs is reputable enough to be contacted on a confidential basis, he should be so contacted and advised that information has come to the attention of the Bureau that there may have been a possible fix of captioned game [Chiefs vs. Jets played on September 15, 1968] and that possibly the [redacted] may be involved. He should be asked to review the game film of 9/15/68 for an opinion as to whether [redacted] or any other player or individual officiating at the game acted in such a way as to create a point-shaving situation [the Chiefs were a seven-point favorite and lost 20–19. Len Dawson was 12 of 20 for just 98 yards] ….The coach should not be informed at this time of the possible involvement of [redacted] or [redacted]. He should also not be informed of details of the various betting activity by various individuals at this time. It is felt that the coach may be obligated to notify the American Football League and it is not felt too advisable to provide further details at this time as it may compromise the informant or otherwise interfere with the Bureau's sports bribery investigation if the American Football League conducts an investigation of their own based on information developed by the Bureau."

Chiefs head coach Hank Stram was later informed of the investigation into this game. He received word from Chiefs owner Lamar Hunt, who had in turn been contacted by NFL commissioner Pete Rozelle. Rozelle also contacted Stram personally. For his part, "Stram said he possessed no info RE Chiefs-Jets game being suspect." Though there is no information within the FBI files directly related to Stram outside of the report of this contact, recall that the bookmaker Piazza featured on *Frontline* stated he worked with a head coach as well as two players. If this was in fact the Chiefs and Stram he was referring to, it would have certainly behooved Stram to play dumb.

This September 15, 1968 game between Kansas City and New York was allegedly fixed by members of the Chiefs working in cooperation with a New Orleans gambler. Remarkably, one of the Chiefs—which does not appear to be the same player the FBI was using as a source— contacted NFL commissioner Pete Rozelle directly with this information. The FBI in turn wanted to speak to Rozelle about what this disgruntled Chief had told him. In the meantime, information regarding this plot was flowing in freely.

"Our New Orleans Office has independently learned from informants that prominent Baton Rouge, Louisiana, gambler [redacted] who was recently convicted in connection with a Sports Bribery case involving Louisiana State University football players, is allegedly receiving excellent information regarding the Kansas City Chiefs football team. [redacted] is said to receive telephone calls from Kansas City in this connection and furthermore, on Sunday morning prior to the Kansas City-New York game, he reportedly placed substantial bets amounting to between 30 and 50 thousand dollars on the New York Jets even though the Kansas City team was favored." This "prominent Baton Rouge gambler" was one of the Nolan brothers. Of that, there is no doubt. Yet which brother was it? Author Moldea believed it was Gene Nolan, yet the FBI's information here seemed to finger his brother "Jo-Jo" as it was Jo-Jo who was directly connected to sports bribery within the LSU football program.

Whichever brother it was, an old connection from LSU was apparently talking with him while a member of the Chiefs. As the New Orleans Bureau reported, "[redacted] who owns and operates New Orleans Novelty, Co., New Orleans, La., and who is known to the New Orleans Office as a big bettor and amateur handicapper on college and professional baseball, had told the informant during a conversation on 9/24/68, that [redacted] contact on the Kansas City Chiefs Professional Football team is [redacted] the former football star in Louisiana State University (LSU)...." This was Chiefs safety Johnny Robinson. Graduating from LSU in 1959, Robinson became the Chiefs' defensive captain as well as a seven-time Pro Bowler and a six-time All-Pro during his 12-year career. According to the FBI's source, Robinson was "allegedly heavily in debt."

The FBI knew the two subjects—one in Kansas City, the other in New Orleans—were communicating by pay phone. This made them difficult to track; however, both were under surveillance (although the FBI wondered if they worked through an unknown intermediary). When the bets were made, they were placed in a way "so as not to influence betting market." But the FBI weren't the only ones working this case—NFL security was, too. The FBI soon discovered that the Southwestern Bell Telephone Company agreed to give the NFL toll-call information on the telephones owned by both Len Dawson and Robinson. But despite being headed by a former FBI man, NFL security stuck out like a sore thumb in the field. While the FBI had Nolan under surveillance in Baton Rouge, the agents working the case noticed "that two automobiles appeared to be very closely following [redacted — Nolan]." They identified the cars, noting that one was licensed to "a New Orleans detective agency operated by former agent [redacted]. [redacted] has been on retainer to the National Football League regarding their investigations in the New Orleans area." But that was just the tip of the iceberg. This "investigator" trailed Nolan "in an old-type car and that this individual virtually rode on his bumper during various parts of the day and went as far as even following him in a bathroom."

Rozelle had a "promise of cooperation" with the FBI in this case. Saying and doing, though, were two completely different things. The FBI went to the NFL's headquarters only to discover that Rozelle, the league's chief of security, another investigator and another ranking member of the league were all unavailable. Rozelle's assistant promised to put Rozelle in contact with the FBI as soon as he was available. Soon afterward, the FBI wrote in its report, "It would appear [NFL investigator] Waechter, possibly on instructions of NFL-AFL League office, will not disseminate any info RE this case to FBI because of possible embarrassment and scandal to professional football. Fact that none of league

officials were available in New York on Sept. 20 last reflects that the league office is attempting to circumvent the FBI's jurisdiction in this case. Both New Orleans and Kansas City FBI offices have encountered separate surveillances of subjects in this case, which indicates the league office possesses positive relevant information RE this case which should be made available to FBI. **From actions of league officials, it appears they have no intention of advising FBI as to information they have developed but intend to handle this matter in their own way, which could consist of 'whitewash' or expose with resulting embarrassment to FBI.** [redacted] and [redacted] were formerly associated with Department of Justice, and extent of any possible cooperation on their part is undoubtedly known to Bureau." [emphasis added]

Spurred by the NFL's refusal to cooperate, the FBI agents felt it was time to talk to the player who instigated the NFL's side of this investigation. That was Chiefs defensive end Jerry Mays, a seven-time Pro Bowler and two-time All-Pro who apparently squealed on his teammates Dawson and Robinson. "Kansas City suggests **[redacted – Mays]** of Kansas City Chiefs be interviewed by Bureau Agents for all information he possesses regarding initial allegation in this matter. Upon completion of this interview, logical interviews should thereafter be conducted with other members of Chiefs. In event Mays declines to discuss matter, Bureau permission is requested to discuss this case with [United States attorney], Kansas City, Mo., for purpose of having **[redacted]** and other appropriate players or officials of Chiefs subpoenaed before a federal grand jury."

As the FBI in Kansas City was ready to take this case all the way, the rug was ripped out from beneath them. "On nine twenty five last [five days after the Kansas City Bureau requested permission to interview Mays], Pete Rozelle, Commissioner, National Football League, telephonically advised SA **[redacted]** that he had spoken to chief investigator William Hundley at three thirty AM and had been informed investigation RE **[redacted]** and **[redacted]** was decidedly negative." Hundley said the players had no contact with gamblers or bookmakers, but that Robinson had merely called "friends who had attended LSU." The NFL also informed the FBI that Dawson and Robinson had been "interviewed and voluntarily answered all questions in presence of their attorneys." The Bureau was to get the results of these delivered to its New York City Bureau.

This was the end of the FBI's investigation into Dawson, Robinson, and the Chiefs. Even though J. Edgar Hoover's handwritten note regarding the NFL's conclusion read, "I don't like this reliance by us on self serving [?] by NFL," the FBI never appeared to interview anyone on the Chiefs. Not Dawson, not Robinson, not even Mays who went directly to the NFL to inform the league that he believed the first two fixed his team's game against the Jets. The NFL effectively told the FBI, "we have this, it's our domain, and there's no problems," and the FBI bought it. Why, exactly, this is difficult to determine. As soon as the FBI's file mentions Rozelle informing the FBI that their investigation found nothing, the FBI shut the doors on theirs. All this information was set aside and forgotten.

Even so, this would not be the FBI's last foray into a fixed NFL game.

THE 1970S

The 1970s started with a bang for the NFL as it witnessed its second and final admitted attempt to fix a game. Two friends and former teammates—one retired, one still playing—met on December 3, 1971 for a night out on the town. After having several drinks while partying with women until the wee hours of the morning, they began to have "a discussion concerning the hypothetical possibility of someone throwing a football game and how easy it would be for the [redacted] during a punt or extra point or field goal or to [redacted] when they were down at the goal line, causing a fumble." This conversation lasted about 15 minutes.

The following day, December 4, retired Denver Broncos running back Donnie Stone phoned his former teammate and then-current center for the Houston Oilers, Jerry Sturm, with an offer. "He then asked him to shave points on the next three Houston games stating 'Let Pittsburgh, Sunday, beat you by more than seven points and it's worth ten thousand dollars a game.' He stated to [redacted – Stone] that he thought he was kidding and that [redacted – Sturm] was not interested in that kind of money. [redacted – Stone] said, 'Would you turn down that kind of tax-free money?' to which [redacted – Sturm] said, 'I would.'"

Sturm's salary in 1971 was $30,000. The offer his former teammate was allegedly making was equal to that, offering $10,000 per game for the final three games of the season. At the time, the Oilers were awful. Their record was a paltry 1-9-1. Who would have noticed if the Oilers didn't cover in their final three games? Even so, Sturm didn't accept and instead went to the FBI. He reported the bribe attempt Sunday morning prior to the December 5 game versus the Steelers (which the Oilers won 29–3; in fact, they won their final three games of the season—the three in which Stone allegedly wanted Sturm to shave points). The meeting was held in a "small supply room" and afterward, this information was relayed to the NFL's security representative in Houston. "[redacted – Sturm] advised he and [redacted – Stone] were very close friends....[redacted – Sturm] advised that [redacted – Stone] in his opinion was a good guy and never talked like a gambler before and never indicated any gambling connections." Sturm told the FBI that he felt he was placed "in a very untenable situation" due to his friendship, but stated he would testify against Stone if need be. That never came to pass. Because Sturm was the only witness in this case, it was dropped without any attempt to prosecute. After the season, the Oilers dropped the 11-year veteran Sturm as well.

Most would find it odd to approach a center to fix a game or shave points. But the fact is such a player could be as useful as a quarterback, if not more so. He could miss a crucial block, be slow pulling on a play, cause a false start, be flagged for holding, or as Stone allegedly mentioned, mishandle a snap. All of these plays would affect an offense, stall a drive and perhaps force a kick or a turnover to the other team—none of which would appear overtly suspect. But what if a fixer had a quarterback under control? Thus far, most of the cases discussed revolved around that position—Sammy Baugh, Bobby Layne, Babe Parilli, George Blanda, Frank Filchock and Len Dawson—and any football fan can understand why the quarterback would be the most beneficial player to control.

So it should come as no surprise that in 1973, some conniving gambler attempted to purchase control of the Atlanta Falcons quarterback for the entire season.

"[redacted] advised on 8/16/73 that [redacted] operating in north Georgia, possibly Atlanta, has 'bought' the [redacted – quarterback] of the Atlanta Falcons Professional Football Team for $100,000 and that point spreads on Atlanta football games this season can thus safely be predicted. Informant could not provide identity of the [redacted] but stated he would attempt to learn his identity." This informant had "only recently been opened as a top-echelon target and thus informant's reliability has not been determined. However, informant appears to have unlimited potential and thus any investigation conducted by Atlanta in this matter should be conducted in such a manner so as to protect the fact that information came from someone close to [redacted] and also protect the fact that the information came from the [redacted] area."

The subject who supposedly bought the Falcons' quarterback was well-known and had an arrest record in both Georgia and Tennessee dating to the 1950s. He once operated a "plush gambling house" in Marion County, Tenn., and at the time was running a "night club in the underground section of Atlanta." The informant was apparently closely associated with him. "On 08/24/73, [redacted] advised that he recently observed [redacted] in the company of [redacted] is one of the oldest and largest bookmakers in the Atlanta area. Informant continued that [redacted] is short of money presently, and as a result informant speculates that the purpose of [redacted] being in contact with [redacted] was for [redacted] to furnish financial assistance to him in his book operation." A few days later, the informant shined further light on the plot. "On 8/29/73 [redacted] advised that on 8/23/73 he conversed with [redacted] and captioned matter came up. [redacted] indicated that it was 'safe' to bet on Atlanta Falcons football games and again mentioned that the Atlanta quarterback has been [redacted]. [redacted] advised he was unable to get the actual identity of the quarterback from [redacted]." It was at this point the FBI decided, "On the basis of the information obtained to date any consideration to disseminate to the National Football League or the Atlanta Falcons should be held in abeyance."

But there was good reason why the informant could not get the identity of the Falcons quarterback. The team had a quarterback controversy, and no one knew who was going to win the coveted starting role. "From information available to the Atlanta Division, it appears extremely doubtful that the information provided to [redacted] is accurate inasmuch as at the time the informant received this information, the identity of the starting quarterback for the Atlanta Falcons was unknown even to the Falcons coaching staff. There were at that time three potential starting [redacted — quarterbacks] namely [redacted] was designated as the starting quarterback for the first regular season game which was with the New Orleans Saints, 9/18/73. It should be noted however, that during August, when the informant obtained this information, [redacted] was not the leading candidate for the starting quarterback job and both [redacted] and [redacted] were rated ahead of [redacted]. [redacted] replaced [redacted] as the [redacted — quarterback] in the second half of the Atlanta-San Francisco game played 10/7/73, and has continued as the regular starting quarterback since that time. [redacted] has since been traded to the New England Patriots. The Atlanta Falcons have won their last three games since [redacted] has been starting [redacted] and they have won by scores far exceeding the point spreads established by the betting line."

After the 1972 season, the Falcons traded starting quarterback Bob Berry to the Vikings in exchange for Bob Lee. Lee's competition for the starting role was Berry's backup Pat Sullivan and journeyman Dick Shiner. Who would have been the prime candidate to bribe? Who knows? Lee would have been seen by many as the apparent starter given that the Falcons traded for him while Sullivan was a second-year player, and Shiner had never distinguished himself on any of the four teams he played for prior to joining the Falcons. However, it was Shiner who was tapped to start the season as the Falcons' quarterback. He posted a weak 1–3 record, was replaced by Lee and promptly traded to the Patriots. Lee remained the starter for the remainder of the 1973 season. Was a bribe ever really made, or was it just boasting talk from an old-time gambler? It's not known as the FBI canceled the investigation due to the surrounding circumstances.

Strangely, Bob Berry was traded from the Falcons to the Minnesota Vikings to be the backup for future Hall of Fame quarterback Fran Tarkenton, who would be the subject of the FBI's next sports bribery investigation involving an NFL game. Stranger still, this investigation came at the end of the same season in which Berry was traded, 1973, and centered around the NFC Championship Game between the Vikings and the Dallas Cowboys played on December 30. As the FBI noted in this case, "It should be recognized this is a serious allegation and if not promptly put to rest could have serious ramifications in the sports world."

The initial allegation appeared dangerous for the NFL. "A group of Dallas gamblers, including one [redacted] are attempting to fix the outcome of Sunday's football game between the Dallas Cowboys and the Minnesota Vikings with a $350,000 payoff to [redacted] both of the Minnesota Vikings. [redacted] is to receive $85,000 of this money and [redacted] is to receive the remainder for their parts in this fix. [redacted] advised that the source of this money is the National Bank of Commerce, Dallas, Texas, and that [redacted] and [redacted] (last name unknown) delivered this money to one [redacted] in Dallas. Further, [redacted] advised that [redacted] was to leave Dallas on Braniff International Airlines Flight [redacted] on [redacted] in route to Minneapolis, apparently to deliver money to [redacted]." The players singled out in this were Tarkenton and Vikings running back Chuck Foreman. According to the FBI's information, the players were to receive their share of the money in Tulsa, OK, where the Vikings were training prior to the game.

This story circulated well before kickoff. According to the FBI, both the *New York Times* and the *Atlanta Constitution* newspapers received tips about the bribe offer to the Vikings players. Both newspapers in turn called the FBI with the information, including unusual stories behind how they received the tips. Soon afterward the FBI received a similar tip as a source called the Bureau on three separate occasions on December 26 detailing the plot. In the last of these three calls, the source changed the bribe amount from $200,000 to $350,000, and added that it had been handed off from whoever picked it up at the National Bank of Commerce to the mule tasked with taking it to the players. The Bureau

checked, and indeed the name of the mule was registered on a Braniff flight that day. The FBI also looked into the names mentioned by this mysterious source, and these, too, checked out as well-known Dallas-area bookmakers and gamblers. But the source refused to meet with anyone, explaining that he only gave up this information because both the director of the Dallas FBI and the Dallas chief of police had done the source a "great favor" in the past.

Given that the source spoke to the FBI five days prior to the game, the Bureau went to the NFL with the information. "In connection with the alleged attempt to fix the outcome of Sunday's professional football game between the Dallas Cowboys and the Minnesota Vikings by a payoff to [redacted — Tarkenton] and [redacted — Foreman] both of the Vikings, the following individuals have been appraised of the alleged attempt:

"Dallas Cowboys: [redacted], President and General Manager, who advised coach [redacted] immediately after the secret practice session yesterday.

"Minnesota Vikings: Jim Finks, General Manager, contacted at Tulsa, Oklahoma, where the Vikings are working out....Finks advised of basic allegations set forth in referenced teletype, however, 'Bud' Grant, Head Coach of Vikings, unavailable. Finks stated he would notify appropriate Viking management regarding this matter. Finks further advised he is taking under advisement matter of notification of alleged involved players.

"National Football League: Former Special Agent [redacted], Chief of Security, who stated he would advise Pete Roselle [sic], National Football League Commissioner. Roselle is unavailable as he is honeymooning."

Not everyone was buying this tale. "[redacted] of the Dallas Cowboys advised the SAC, Dallas, that he felt this was a scheme of some gambler who already had his bets down on the basis of the point spread, three points in favor of Dallas, with the hope that the resulting publicity of the payoff would change the odds to give him additional insurance

for his bet." This unknown member of the Cowboys was likely correct, albeit misguided as once a bettor's wager is placed, a line movement is inconsequential. The FBI determined that the National Bank of Commerce in Dallas showed no large withdrawal of cash on December 26 as the source claimed. The line on the game never wavered from favoring the Cowboys by three. And perhaps most importantly, the Vikings beat the Cowboys soundly, winning 27–10. As a result, the FBI chalked this entire affair up as a hoax. It never interviewed the source or either member of the Vikings in question. One thing the FBI failed to consider was if this "hoax" was meant to get the FBI looking at the Vikings while the Dallas-area gamblers did business with the Cowboys. For if anyone looked guilty of throwing a game that day, it was Cowboys quarterback Roger Staubach. He threw for a meager 89 yards on 10 for 21 passing with four interceptions. Granted, that was against the Vikings' vaunted Purple People Eaters defense, so Staubach's ineptitude appears justified.

The city of Dallas played a role in another potential bribe offer when a member of the newly formed Seattle Seahawks was approached to fix games in 1977. "[The player] stated that in late January, while visiting the [Pyramid Club in Dallas] with friends, he [redacted] was called aside by [redacted]. He stated [redacted] asked him if he was interested in making some extra money. According to [redacted] explained that he [redacted] could get paid anywhere from $50,000 to $100,000 depending on the game that was to be fixed and the number of players involved in fixing the contest." According to a friend of the player, the person who approached him had "the reputation of being a 'hit man.'"

Despite this player being offered $100,000 per game by a hit man should he be able to recruit other players to join in on the fix, the player did nothing until training camp in August 1977 because "he feared repercussions." At that point, he went to the league with the story which in turn came to the FBI. When the FBI discussed the matter with the player, he did not want to fully cooperate, refusing to sign a statement or testify if need be. He may have had good reason to fear this potential fixer. The FBI was well aware of the suspect who had "been engaged in a variety of criminal activities which would fall under Federal jurisdiction." The problem for the FBI was that "a clear-cut sports bribery violation has not been established which could be used in the prosecution of **[redacted]**" as the suspect was "not openly engaged in gambling, prostitution, or bribery violations at the present time." The likely reason for his inactivity was due to the fact that two of his closest associates were already under investigation for murder. The FBI believed the suspect knew the feds were investigating him, which was indeed the case as the FBI had an IRS agent working undercover, wearing a wire, and engaging in knowingly receiving bribes from Ft. Worth-area gamblers at that same time. Because of all this, the case revolving around the Seahawks player was moved to "inactive status."

Also in 1977, the NFL investigated ten members of the Miami Dolphins for their association with a suspected bookmaker named J. Lance Cooper who had been arrested in 1976 along with four other bookmakers. The problem for the NFL was that Cooper had the names of Dolphins starting quarterback Bob Griese, his backup Earl Morrall, defensive end Bill Stanfill, and Dolphins head coach Don Shula in his address book. Cooper had his home and office wiretapped during the probe which showed that he had been granted access to the Dolphins' locker room and practice field for seven years leading up to the time of his arrest. "[Cooper] later admitted during a polygraph examination that he had passed on information about the Dolphins to organized-crime figures."[48] What did the NFL do about this evidence and Cooper's admission? Nothing...publicly at least.

A year later, a similar incident came to light when two NFL players, Jake Scott of the Washington Redskins and recently retired Detroit Lions tackle Craig Hertwig, were caught in the home of a convicted bookmaker, Bennie Fuqua, during a raid of his home in December 1978. Scott admitted he and Fuqua had been lifelong friends. While looking quite incriminating, the NFL didn't bother to question either of the players. Instead, "this matter was hushed up for nearly four years, even after a state law enforcement agency notified the NFL, in writing, of the problem."[49]

REFEREES

So far only players have been discussed as the focus of NFL game-fixing probes. But there are other men out on the playing field who can influence the outcome of a football game: the officials. One-time NFL and AFL owner Harry Wismer wrote of fixing a game, "The person I would go to [for a fix] would be an official, probably the umpire. The umpire is the man whose primary duty is to observe the blocking and the use of hands by both the offense and defense. Players and coaches say it is almost impossible for a play to be run without an infraction of some kind. Holding is the usual call and the officials could probably call it every time a play is run. If my partner in crime were the umpire, he could control the scoring by dropping his flag whenever the wrong team scored. There is another logical reason why the officials would be the ones to try to fix. They are underpaid and overcriticized. They are a perfect target for a player or a coach who is anxious to alibi on a poor performance."[50] He's not alone in these thoughts.

Gambling expert and author Larry Grossman told me something similar. "Look, who's to say in an NFL game or college game you throw a flag in the end zone or you throw a flag on a defensive guy or holding—there's holding on every play—I mean refs can affect a lot of the action without making it obvious. A couple calls here, a couple calls there, you know, throw a flag on a runback play or not throw a flag… it's those little edges, those little things that can make the difference in a game." Complementing that notion was legendary Philadelphia sports radio host Howard Eskin who said to me in an on-air interview on WIP in 2010, "Years ago I think officials, I'm talking maybe 15, 20 years ago, weren't making enough money, did have other jobs, and it's easy [to fix a game]. In the NFL, you can call a hold anytime you want and change if a team's on a drive, you can only have so many 15-yard penalties and be able to recover from that. I believe that could happen because the money is different for officials than it is for players."

Despite this, the FBI rarely possessed information causing the Bureau to investigate NFL officials. In 1976, a source gave "some information RE officials in the NFL who are allegedly being paid by the hoodlum figures to assist in the outcome of a game. The identity or location of these hoodlum figures is not known." This same source alleged that these hoodlums also worked with NBA officials as well. As a result, "`[redacted]` of the NFL and `[redacted]` of the NBA `[redacted]` have been contacted in NYC and expressed an interest in helping the FBI by plotting the calls of the various officials to determine if there is any pattern and validity to the information being received." This particular investigation went nowhere of significance; however, there was no further mention of either league providing the FBI with any officials' phone records.

But in 1979 another more invasive investigation began, centering around two NFL referees. As Dan Moldea wrote, "Oddsmaker Bobby Martin told me that during the late 1970s, he suspected one particular referee of being involved in gambling and influencing the outcomes of NFL games. 'There was too much unnatural money showing up on the games he was officiating,' Martin says. 'So I put the word out on [the referee] to see what I could find out.' One of those whom Martin called was Las Vegas gambler Lem Banker, who told [Moldea], 'Yeah, we had suspicions about certain games with some of the officials during the late 1970s. I remember Bob called me and wanted me to check out one particular referee. We watched some of the games, and a lot of unnatural money did show up. But we could never prove anything.' A third gambler told [Moldea's] associate, William Scott Malone, that two particular referees had been involved in game fixing since 1977. But the source refused to provide any details—because he was personally involved in the scheme. However, the same referee was named by Martin, Banker, and the confidential source, who also named the second referee."[51]

The investigation was a three-pronged affair. On one side was the FBI. On another, the IRS. And on the third was NBC reporter Chuck Collins. All seemed to begin with similar information, but in the end each reached somewhat different conclusions. The basic story was the FBI received information from an informant claiming that New York mobsters were paying two or three NFL referees $100,000 apiece for each game fixed. The referees' job was to ensure that the mobsters won their bet by covering the spread and/or shaving points. These games were mostly Monday Night affairs, and according to the information were:

Seattle Seahawks vs. Atlanta Falcons, fixed for Seattle; played Monday, 10/29/79 — Seattle won 31–28 and covered in most places

Cleveland Browns vs. Kansas City Chiefs, fixed for Cleveland; played 9/9/79 — Cleveland won 27–24 and covered

Pittsburgh Steelers at Houston Oilers, fixed for Houston; played Monday, 12/10/79 — Houston won 20–17 as the underdog with the Steelers favored by 3 or 4

New York Jets at Minnesota Vikings, fixed for the Jets; played Monday, 10/15/79 — Jets won 14–7 and covered

New York Giants at Washington Redskins, fixed for the Redskins; played Monday, 9/17/79 — Washington won 27–0 and covered

Dallas Cowboys at Cleveland Browns, fixed for Cleveland; played Monday, 9/24/79 — Cleveland won 26–7 as underdog with Dallas favored by 3

San Diego Chargers at Oakland Raiders, fixed for Oakland; played Thursday, 10/25/79 — Oakland won 45–22 and covered

Miami Dolphins at Oakland Raiders, fixed for Oakland; played Monday, 10/8/79 — Oakland won 13–3. Game was pick'em, but Oakland was favored in some areas, Miami in others. It was thought the mobsters did not win their bets on this game.

The source first overheard the information regarding the September 17 Redskins-Giants fix while playing in a Houston-area high-stakes poker game. The FBI trusted him enough to attempt to record conversations between himself and the person of interest. But then the problems began. The informant was caught attempting to sell this same information to IRS agents. Then the source's information was considered "nebulous and third- and fourth-hand." Then, despite passing a polygraph examination, the FBI dropped its investigation because it received information that the source was a pathological liar.

Another significant problem with this information was that these two referees did not work every game mentioned. As the FBI report stated, "The enclosed 1979 season officiating assignments for the National Football League were provided by [redacted] Security, National Football League (NFL). [redacted] advised that officials for all NFL games are assigned as a team. This officiating team, as reflected on enclosed assignment sheets, consists of seven individuals. The team headed by [redacted] and [redacted] were the only officiating teams who were assigned to two games each of the eight suspected games reflected in Houston teletype to the Bureau." So the two referees in question officiated only four of the suspected eight games.

Of note, however, was that the NFL revealed to the FBI how it rated its officials and that other internal NFL investigations had been conducted regarding referees in the past. "[redacted] advised that the officials for each NFL game are scored by a panel of three NFL officials after each game. The purpose for this scoring is to judge which officials will be assigned to the league playoff, championship, and Super Bowl games. [redacted] stated that officials are penalized points for missing calls, being in the wrong position to make a call, or making an erroneous call. [redacted] further advised that each official in the NFL is investigated by his office and watched closely during the first three years which he is assigned as an official. [redacted] further advised that his office regularly investigates all claims of game fixing involving officials in the NFL. [redacted] stated that the usual complaint is that erroneous calls were made by the officials to beat the point spread. [redacted] stated that to date, all complaints investigated by his office were unfounded." Who made these complaints, why they were made, regarding which referees and which games remains unknown.

Though the FBI gave up, the IRS did not. Why? Because the same informant whom the FBI blew off managed to give the IRS the outcomes of the eight allegedly fixed games prior to them being played. That wasn't all. The IRS trailed the beard betting for the mobsters in Las Vegas and watched him place bets large enough on the games in question to alter the betting line. Despite this credible information and the urging of the agent in charge of the case, the IRS squashed the investigation

and refused to continue.

The NFL, of course, looked into these allegations and found nothing to substantiate the source's claims. "[redacted — from the NFL] advised that on the basis of a full and complete investigation conducted by his office, a review of the closing line spread sheets, and the fact that no one official was involved in all or most of the games on the dates listed above, he is of the opinion that the allegations regarding game fixing are unfounded."

But NBC Chicago reporter Collins didn't quit so easily. Collins "advised that he had received additional information tending to support alleged bribery of NFL officials to fix football games. NBC investigation apparently indicates that car dealers are acting as agents for organized crime money and betting on fixed football games." These were high-end car dealers, owning Rolls-Royce and Fiat dealerships in Las Vegas, Los Angeles, and Honolulu. As Collins continued his probe, few were willing to lend a hand—least of all the NFL. "[redacted — Collins] has been in touch with the NFL and they have refused to furnish information. He indicated that NFL had his name apparently given them by the FBI. Inasmuch as [redacted] is furnishing information to the ASAC, Houston, concerning the developments in this matter, the fact that [redacted] is talking with the FBI should not be disclosed." Though the FBI's report stated that Collins "alleged that he has determined that two of the games involved alleged payoffs" and expected a transcript of the recording that backed these claims, it appears as though he never publicized his findings.

This appears to be the last major game-fixing investigation conducted by the FBI in regards to the NFL. Could no one have successfully fixed or even attempted to fix an NFL game since 1980? It's possible, though quite unlikely. In 1983, the NFL suspended Baltimore Colts quarterback Art Schlichter for the entire season because he was gambling on NFL games, though reportedly not on his team's games. Yet on Sundays, he readily admitted that he'd pay more attention to the scoreboard detailing other ongoing games—on which he had bet—rather than the play right in front of him. Schlichter was a compulsive gambler, but he wasn't caught betting by the NFL even though his habit had emptied his bank account. His downfall came when the bookmakers to whom he was indebted threatened to break his passing arm. Seeking help, Schlichter didn't turn to the NFL; he went to the FBI. His career and life never fully recovered. Amazingly, no other player in the NFL has since had a similar condition which has ever been made public. Yet in 1986, the NFL revealed to *Sports Illustrated* that "it issues 10 to 12 warnings a year to specific players about associating with gamblers and, like the other professional sports leagues, it likes to give the impression that it has an efficient security staff that pounces on cases involving improper associations."[52]

While the NFL has not publicly released any information regarding the current standing of how many players it must admonish for their associations with gamblers, the problem has not completely vanished. When Michael Vick was arrested on charges of running a multistate dogfighting operation, no one seemed to mention that the reason dogs are fought is to wager on the outcome. Who was Vick betting with, how many other gamblers were involved, and was football ever discussed at these events were highly relevant questions that never seemed to be asked or answered. In 2011, a reported 25 NFL players, including Terrell Owens, Santonio Holmes, Santana Moss, Gerard Warren, and Adalius Thomas, invested $20 million or more into a failed Alabama casino named Country Crossing. NFL rules forbid its employees from any involvement in a gambling operation. Fines and suspensions should have followed. Instead, this story, like many others of such impropriety, vanished.

Former FBI Special Agent Tom French doesn't seem to believe the NFL is as free from outside influence as it contends. He told me, "I think when they [the NFL] say that [none of its games has ever been fixed] it means that no one's ever been convicted of doing that. Let's put it that way, because with the amount of money that's bet on sports today and…well, look at the characters that play professional sports for the most part, football, basketball…baseball, well, I don't know. Baseball got more heat from Pete Rose, probably more than the other two sports, you know? But the other two sports are the ones that most easily can be

fixed....Look at it this way: you've got a third and goal to go, and say the line is—well, it doesn't matter what the line is, but it's third and goal and you run the ball in, okay? Holding. The flag goes down. You push them back ten yards and now you take the field goal instead of the seven. I mean, in a sport where betting is so big and half a point is huge, what do you think four points is? So I mean you have people who have women problems, drug problems and everything else, and everyone would say, 'Why would a multimillionaire guy fix a sport?' Well, it could be any one of a million reasons. It could be financially, even though he's making all that money, believe it or not. Or it could be that someone's shaking him down, that he knows something and is extorting him. Maybe he's got a girlfriend or something and he's portrayed as a family guy, and he doesn't want this to get out. So you don't have to lose, you just have to knock a couple of points off. Instead of getting 15 tonight, you get 12."

Everyone I talked with, including some who would not go on the record, had suspicions regarding certain NFL games, certain players, and at least one official. Every gambler has a "bad beat" story that often turns into how a game was fixed. And many fans, too, have a game in their memory in which things just did not seem right. Are all these people crazy? Or have they correctly sensed when something was amiss within the NFL? Strange things often happen in NFL games in conjunction with the betting line. A famous case in point is the November 16, 2008 San Diego Chargers-Pittsburgh Steelers game. The Steelers were 4½-point favorites and most of the money was bet on them to cover. The Chargers had the ball on their own 21-yard line, down 11–10 with five seconds remaining in the game. They attempted a hook-and-ladder play wherein the receiver catching the ball repeatedly laterals it to a teammate in an attempt to confuse the Steelers' defense, hoping against hope that a hole opens for a miracle score. Instead, on the second attempted lateral, Steelers safety Troy Polamalu knocked the ball out of a Chargers player's hand. Polamalu scooped up the live ball and ran it in for a touchdown. Steelers win 17–10 and cover the spread, right? Wrong. For some reason, the play was reviewed by the officials even though, no matter what, the Steelers were going to be winners...but not against the spread. After a lengthy review, the referee ruled that the Chargers had committed an illegal forward pass during one of the two laterals and therefore the play was dead. No touchdown. This official's call was 100 percent incorrect, but oh well. Game over, 11–10.

In Las Vegas, this caused an instant uproar. Bettors who had cashed their winning Steelers tickets—that's how long the delay was on the field—were literally chased down by casino security in at least one sports book to get back the house's money. At the same time, Chargers bettors were scrambling on the floor to find the pieces of once losing tickets that had been ripped up and thrown away. There's no way to say this outcome was fixed, but it is an excellent example of what one ruling by an official—an incorrect ruling to boot—can do in regards to the wagering public.

Former chief of NFL security Warren Welsh believes that with all the reviews and discussions, both by the league and by the media, if the same official was intentionally making bad calls this referee would be publicly discovered. Though he did admit, "You can't do this in the case of one game," only if it were an ongoing action. When I reminded Welsh of the case of Tim Donaghy in the NBA and asked if a similar situation could occur within the NFL, where a dirty official could fall through the cracks of league security, he told me, "I think potentially all these things can happen. I just think that there's so much oversight by not only the officials that are working the game, but the integrity of the players, instant replay, these analysts that are talking and talking, I think it would be fairly hard to escape something. But again, there are things that can happen. Just passing on information. Like your best friend. You don't gamble, but your best friend does. And you're chatting about girls and this, that, and the other thing, and the conversation turns to, 'What do you think is going happen this week?' Innocent things can turn into real things, too. I think if you look historically at some of this stuff, it started in a real naïve way and then it just got out of control."

CONCLUSION

"Gambling is inevitable. No matter what is said or done by advocates or opponents of gambling in all its various forms, it is an activity that is practiced, or tacitly endorsed, by a substantial majority of Americans."
— Commission on the Review of National Policy toward Gambling, 1976, p.1.

Sports and gambling are inseparable. Not only that, they are mutually beneficial. No league official will admit it, but the rise in prominence of professional sports and its hold upon its fan base is directly tied to people gambling upon their games. "The NFL wouldn't exist without gambling, and it wouldn't thrive especially without gambling," Larry Grossman said. "I know for a fact the NBA would never have made it without gambling. I've talked to people like [legendary sports gambler] Sonny Reizner, who was a very good friend, who used to be at the Boston

Garden, and gambling is pretty much what brought people in to watch the games back in the '50s. There was a section for gamblers. At Fenway Park, they'd bet on every pitch. There were all sorts of action going on during the game. The leagues knew about it, and told them not to be so obvious, to keep it under control."

I believe if the leagues could overtly profit from sports gambling, each and every one of them would happily support its legalization. NFL, NHL, and MLB teams have allowed their team logos to be incorporated with state lottery scratch-off tickets. Among others, the Green Bay Packers, New Orleans Saints, Washington Redskins, Baltimore Ravens, and Cleveland Browns in the NFL; the Boston Bruins, Pittsburgh Penguins, and Philadelphia Flyers in the NHL; and the Chicago Cubs, Chicago White Sox, and St. Louis Cardinals in MLB have all been featured on lottery tickets without sanction from their respective league offices. For a taste of those billions of dollars being wagered on the games, I'm certain each league's anti-gambling attitude would be markedly different. Since that is not the case as yet, officially every league is against any advancement in the legalization of sports gambling.

Jay Moyer, Special Counsel for the NFL, made a statement before the Congressional Committee to Study Sports Gaming in Delaware in 2002. He said, in part, "The NFL's policy on this issue has been consistent for decades. Simply put, gambling and sports do not mix. Sports gambling threatens the integrity of our games and all the values our games represent—especially to young people. For this reason, the NFL has established strict policies relating to gambling in general and sports betting in particular. The League prohibits NFL club owners, coaches, players, and anyone else connected with the NFL from gambling on NFL games or associating in any way with persons involved in gambling. Anyone who does so faces severe disciplinary action by the Commissioner including lifetime suspension. We have posted our anti-gambling rules in every stadium locker room and have shared those rules with every player and every other individual associated with the NFL. The League has also sought to limit references to sports betting or gambling that in any way are connected to our games. For example, we have informed the major television networks that we regard sports gambling

CONCLUSION

commercials and the dissemination of wagering information as inappropriate and unacceptable during football game telecasts. NFL teams may not accept advertising from gambling establishments, and our broadcast partners may not do so on NFL programming."[1]

In late 2012, as the legal battle between the sports leagues (which in a sense had been deputized by the federal government) and New Jersey heated up over the state's attempt to legalize sports gambling, each major league commissioner wrote a "declaration" regarding their stance in this fight. Mirroring in many ways what Moyer stated on the NFL's behalf ten years prior, MLB commissioner "Bud" Selig wrote, "Another likely result of sports gambling is that fan loyalty would diminish, as many fans would focus less on their allegiance to certain teams, players, or cities and instead focus more on the outcomes of individual bets. The inevitable shifting 'loyalties' that would result from sports gambling could forever alter the relationship between teams and their fans. Players would not be viewed by fans as exceptionally skilled and talented competitors, but as mere assets to be exploited for 'fast money.'"

The problem for the leagues with this potential shift in the mindset of fandom is that, as NBA commissioner Stern wrote, "The NBA cannot be compensated in damages for the harm that sports gambling poses to the fundamental bonds of loyalty and devotion between fans and teams. Once that special relationship has been compromised, the NBA will have been irreparably injured in a manner that cannot adequately be calculated in dollars."

Can the leagues prove this certain harm? No. And in reality, they already actively support an institution which does exactly what they "fear" legalized gambling would do: fantasy sports. In these leagues, "owners" root for "their" players often over and above their supposed real-life team affiliations. Yet the professional leagues all actively encourage fans to join these fantasy leagues where money often exchanges hands between participants.

"Sure, they're against it," former bookmaker Scott Schettler opined, "but they'd be the first ones to squawk if people quit putting odds on the games. That's the last thing they want is for people to quit putting odds on the games. They love it. They love the betting, but they want to be holier-than-thou. They're not stupid, either. They know half the people watch games because they've got a bet on it. They don't watch because the Steelers are 40 points ahead of the Raiders and they want to keep cheering, you know? They can't be that stupid, that they think everybody's a fan. But it is what it is."

Grossman agreed without mincing any words. "The NFL is just totally full of shit. I remember when they asked Rozelle, if he could pull a handle and all sports betting, all football betting would be stopped immediately and never happen again, would he pull the handle? And he never answered the question." Grossman was right. Rozelle was asked on NBC's NFL '85 pregame show on November 17, 1985, if a "magic button" existed that could stop gambling on NFL games, would be push it? He "danced"[2] around the question without giving a definitive answer. "Many, many, many people watch football just because of gambling," Grossman continued. "They wouldn't watch it to the extent they watch it now, by any means. It's not even close. I mean, when a team's leading 17–7 and there's three minutes left and there's a touchdown point spread and you're holding your audience for the advertisers on television, why are they holding the audience? They're holding the audience because everybody's involved in the point spread. The outcome is done. It's just ludicrous to think that football would be anywhere *near* as successful without gambling. Anybody that believes that is an idiot. I have no respect for them whatsoever. And they can lie through their teeth and they can say whatever they want. It's not the truth. And that's all there is to it. They want to hold their audience. They want to keep their fourth-quarter advertisers happy. Why is the point spread in every newspaper in the country? It's only legal in Nevada. Why does everybody talk about it? Why are there television shows about the point spread? It's absurd. As soon as the Super Bowl game's announced, they ask what the number is. Everybody wants to know."

Whether it's $80 billion or $380 billion (depending on the source of the estimate) that's illegally wagered on sporting events each year within the United States, the fact of the matter is no one is going to stop. Bookies have little fear of the legal ramifications in breaking the law. Bettors

350

don't care that their money is funding organized crime. People are going to bet on the games because they've always bet on the games. They enjoy it. It's the frosting on the cake. The natural solution would be to lift the national prohibition on sports gambling, and let the states decide if they want to legalize it and reap the tax revenues from those billions of dollars wagered.

"I think it is crazy that sports betting is not legal everywhere," the Philly Godfather stated. "Legalize and tax would be the best route for everyone. South America took in $124 billion in online gambling in 2011 while the Hollywood movie business took in $24 billion. Imagine what the U.S. would do...."

"You would have to do it like they do in Las Vegas," Schettler theorized. "You couldn't let the government run it. I could imagine the headline, 'New York City gets middled for $200 million.' You'd have to keep them out of it as they'd screw it up anyways. Let private money do the booking and the government just tax, that's all. The government can regulate it and tax it, but tell them to just stay the heck out of it. But it would work. It sure would."

Larry Grossman agreed that it should be legalized as well. In doing so, he offered another often overlooked reason why. "The thing with legalized sports betting is that it really protects the public at large because there's no credit. That's how people really get hurt. All of a sudden they have a telephone and they're watching the [college football] games on Saturday and they have six games bet, $100 a game, and they lose all six. So now they're down $600 going into Sunday. They're doing it pretty much for entertainment, but they're down $600 knowing they've got to settle on Tuesday. So now on Sunday they play the early [NFL] games. They bet $300 a game and they lose three more games. Now they're down $1,500. So now they're betting $500 or $1,000 a game to get back. And now all of a sudden they were betting $100 for laughs, but they owe the bookmaker $3,500. They don't even have $3,500. But what does it take to say 'gimme $300 on a game' or 'gimme $50 on a game'? It's the same amount of breath. So it's the bookmakers and the credit that really hurts just the average sports bettor. I'm not talking about the sophisticated professional. I'm talking about Joe America that gets involved and gets killed because he just loses control and he has credit. So I think it's much more dangerous the way it is now than if the state controlled everything. And then they would get their taxes and they would make sure they're getting paid off. Nobody gets their knees broken, and nobody gets their families threatened. It's much cleaner."

While most everyone I interviewed for this book agreed that sports gambling should be legalized, there were a few dissenters. One of those was former FBI agent and NFL security chief Warren Welsh. "I just think if you introduce gambling—legalized gambling—you're going to get a lot more people that haven't been gambling that now are going to gamble," he said. "And a lot of those people can't afford the money that they are now putting down on legalized betting. I don't see the other side of it. The revenue issue is not a big issue. There's just not that much money involved for the states. I don't see any upside." However, when we discussed how much money may in fact be involved in the illegal sports wagering market, and then the ties to organized crime, Welsh slightly relented. "It's very true," he admitted. "It's very pragmatic that there is probably not too much investigating of bookmakers. There's too much going on in the world, and enforcement agencies don't have the manpower. It's a tough thing. The things that do bring the attention are when the gambling turns into shylocking [loan sharking] and drugs and those sorts of things, prostitution to some extent. When the innocent person puts down $5 to their local bookie and thinks that's the end of it, well, the money is probably traveling up some chain somewhere that's going to get into the wrong hands sooner or later, and to me, that's the bigger picture."

While this debate could fill an entire book of its own, perhaps the only angle overlooked is one which the leagues want us to ignore: legalizing sports gambling would actually bring *more* integrity to the games.

The leagues, of course, disagree. "The spread of sports betting, including the introduction of sports betting in New Jersey," MLB commissioner Selig wrote, "would threaten to damage irreparably the integrity of, and public confidence in, MLB. The more pervasive the sports gambling culture, and the more that culture is actively promoted by governments, the more likely it is that games will be perceived by the public with increased cynicism. Specific plays, coaching decisions, and umpiring calls would be questioned by fans who suspect that the 'fix is in.' If fans suspect that plays, decisions, and umpiring are in any way influenced by sports gambling, they will more likely disengage from what they perceive to be a tainted sport rather than continue to invest their energy in it. Beyond fostering increased suspicion of underhanded dealing, increased sports gambling also makes it more likely that people will actually attempt to 'fix' games or obtain inside information from people directly involved in the sport."

Selig's writing, which was parroted by his fellow commissioners, is incredibly offensive. In Selig's own sport, no game has admittedly been fixed since 1919. Is Selig's stance truly that legalized sports gambling will upend nearly one hundred years of history? What about each league's vaunted Security Division? Can't those law enforcement professionals prevent game fixing? There are other league-mandated precautions already in place as well, including contractual language demanded by the players' collective bargaining agreement. In the case of the NFL, paragraph 15 of every player's contract states, "Player recognizes the detriment to the League and professional football that would result from impairment of public confidence in the honest and orderly conduct of NFL games or the integrity and good character of NFL players. Player therefore acknowledges his awareness that if he accepts a bribe or agrees to throw or fix an NFL game; fails to promptly report a bribe offer or an attempt to throw or fix an NFL game; bets on an NFL game; [or] knowingly associates with gamblers or gambling activity…[he is subject to fine, suspension, or termination of his contract]." Yet despite all of these precautions and more—including the federal crime of sports bribery—legalizing sports gambling is actually going to make game fixing *increase?*

In fact, the opposite is true. Keeping sports gambling underground is leading to more corruption and fixes than anyone is even aware of. Legalization would aid in integrity, not degrade it. How? For starters, by monitoring all betting action within the United States as opposed to

the mere one percent which now occurs in Nevada. As previously shown, soccer, tennis, and cricket have all seen recent match-fixing scandals erupt in several different countries. And the public knows about these incidents. Why? With sports gambling being legal in much of Europe and Asia, the corporate bookmakers there constantly monitor their clients' betting and react when something out-of-the-ordinary takes place. These reactions led to investigative actions which have resulted in the arrests of literally hundreds of gamblers, mafiosi, players, coaches, and referees around the world.

But here in the United States? Nothing. Outside of a handful of game-fixing scandals within college football and basketball—which have all come about through other non-sports bribery-related investigations—a crime that's rampant across the globe has supposedly never infected our borders or our beloved professional leagues. Are we really so naïve to believe this is true?

As this book has shown, the leagues believe their own historical propaganda and are not looking for fixed games (and it's highly unlikely they would tell fans if they discovered one). The sports gamblers neither care about nor watch for fixed games. The legal sports books don't even consider the possibility of a fixed game. The sports media isn't investigating for fixed games. The FBI has given up, no longer even possessing a designation within its file system for sports bribery, and only pursues such cases if they fall into their lap. All have reasons why they should continue to be vigilant, but each has built-in excuses to let someone else be a watchdog for trusting fans. Yet with all of the finger-pointing between these entities, no one has pulled their head out of the sand to actually take the burden onto their shoulders and do the work.

Legalization would force everyone back into the game, so to speak. Taken out of the hands of the illegal bookies and organized crime, a system similar to the one employed in Europe would undoubtedly reveal irregularities in need of further investigation. These would be a matter of public record. Everyone would know, and there'd be nothing to hide behind.

The NFL acknowledged this in a "policy paper" it issued in 1972 (a copy of which ended up in an FBI file). In the paper, 12 questions were "asked" regarding legalizing sports gambling. In question seven, the NFL asked itself, "What is the difference between betting on a game and betting on a horse race?" Within its own answer, the NFL revealed one of its greatest fears. It wrote, "In racing, a State Commission sets dates and sites of meetings, licenses trainers, owners, jockeys and drivers. It hands down suspensions, assesses fines and takes a generous slice of the betting action. This tight supervision has become necessary to guard against drugging, fixing of races and false identification of horses. Any similar governmental obligation to control team sports would involve far-reaching changes in their present structure of operations and place a costly and staggering burden to not only oversee sporting events in its own state but also presumably everywhere a sporting event is held, if legalized bets are accepted on that event."

If some type of government regulation over the professional sports leagues came with the legalization of sport gambling, wouldn't that also add to the integrity of the games? Granted, the argument can be made whether a state or federal government should involve itself in the affairs of a private entity like the NFL, but when billions of tax dollars are funding the stadiums in which these games are being played, perhaps that money should come with a bit of oversight attached. Imagine the differences in the drug-testing programs, the fines/suspensions issued, and the regulations of health concerns like concussions if a state-controlled sanctioning body was allowed to police professional sports leagues? Take the control of the NFL, NBA, and MLB out of the hands of a privately appointed commissioner and turn it over to maybe a publicly elected official, and every league's makeup would turn on a dime. Of course corruption would still exist (when hasn't it in politics?), but what was once kept behind closed doors could be a much more public affair.

Perhaps this is exactly what the professional leagues fear. If all of this information were out in the open, it would show that the players, coaches, and referees are not immune to outside influences. That they can be—and have been—corrupted. That not every game is truly pure. Perhaps then "integrity" would not just be a word bandied about, but a true state of being in the world of professional sports.

ACKNOWLEDGEMENTS

First and foremost, I must thank my wife Sarah for her love, support, understanding and patience. Without her, this book would not exist. I also must thank my family and friends whose support, advice and promotion run deeper than I can probably imagine.

Thanks, too, to Adam Parfrey, Jessica Parfrey, and all at Feral House for taking the risk to bring me on board and for delivering this book to the masses.

Much of the information in this book would not be available without the willing and generous help of the following: Michael Ravnitzky, Lauren McGuinn, Dan Moldea, Scott Schettler, Ryan Rodenberg, Tom French, Vegas Runner, Larry Grossman, Warren Welsh, Declan Hill, Lem Banker, Greg Stejskal, the Philly Godfather, Brian Mack, Howard

Schwartz and all at the Gambler's Book Club, Katarina Pijetlovic, Tim Donaghy, Beth Harper, Patrick Hruby, Graham Sharpe, John Dowd, Dave Cokin, Howard Schlossberg, Patrick Hruby, Matt Youmans, Michael Falkner, Matt Agosta, The Society of Former Special Agents of the FBI, the FOIA Agents of the FBI, and all of the authors willing to write insightful books and articles which were quoted here. Also a wink and a nod to those who provided vital information yet preferred to remain unnamed. I thank you all.

A thank you is also in order for all of those in the media world willing to help me promote this message, including: Ian Punnett, Chris Boros, Lisa Lyon & all at Coast to Coast AM, Steve Czaban & Steve Solomon, Chris Myers, Charlie Bernstein, Dino Costa, Erskine, Howard Eskin, Richard Syrett, Joe Boesch, Anthony Urciuoli, Sam Bourquin, Joe Anderson, Rob Long, Sandy Clough, Rob Kerr, all at The Raw Feed, Jason Gregor, all at The Flow of Wisdom, Tim Unglesbee, Claire B. Lang, Mitch Nelles, Colin Cosell, Doug Warren, Mo Egger, Kate Delaney, Tom & Lisa, The Final Word with Jay Reelz & JD, The Outlaw Michael Tomsik, all at The Fan vs. Fan Show, Freedomizer Radio, Derrick Oliver, Jim Harold, Dave Luhrssen, Mark Yost, and Victor Thorn.

There are several I'd like not to thank, but they shall remain anonymous except for those at the M Resort sports book who kicked me out for asking too many questions.

A tip of the cap to all of my fans and followers—I wish I had space to name you all.

WORKS CITED

INTRODUCTION

1 – Howard Cosell with Peter Bonventre, *I Never Played the Game* (New York: William Morrow and Company, Inc., 1985), 110.

THE SAGA OF TIM DONAGHY

1 – Sean Patrick Griffin, *Gaming the Game: The Story Behind the NBA Betting Scandal and the Gambler Who Made It Happen* (Fort Lee, NJ: Barricade Books, 2011), 286–288.

2 – Ibid., 146.

3 – Ibid., 286–288.

4 – Ibid., 147–148.

5 – Ibid., 150.

6 – Ibid., 153.

7 – Ibid., 288.

8 – Ibid., 159.

9 – Ibid., 171.

10 – Ibid., 296.

11 – Ibid., 282–283.

12 – Jack Mccallum, "Game-Fixing and Dogfighting Rock Pro Sports," SportsIllustrated.com, July 24, 2007. sportsillustrated.cnn.com/vault/article/web/COM1061870/1/index.htm

13 – Griffin, *Gaming the Game*, 213.

14 – Tim Donaghy, *Personal Foul* (Sarasota, FL: Four Daughters, LLC, 2009), 206.

15 – Ibid., 207.

16 – Griffin, *Gaming the Game*, 270.

SO YOU WANT TO BE A PROFESSIONAL SPORTS GAMBLER

1 – Joseph B. Verrengia, "Ancient Olympics were a mix of sacred, profane," Associated Press, July 25, 2004. corinth.sas.upenn.edu/dgr/sitecache/clips/sacredprofane.htm

2 – Larry Grossman, *You Can Bet On It: Volume 2 — Sports Betting* (New York: Cardoza Publishing, 1994/2004), 27–28.

3 – Scott Schettler, *We Were Wiseguys and Didn't Know It* (self-published, 2009), 28.

4 – Ibid., 17.

5 – Ibid., 22–23.

6 – Ibid., 79.

7 – Ibid., 92.

8 – Grossman, *You Can Bet On It: Vol. 2 — Sports Betting*, 46.

9 – Ibid., 39–40.

10 – Ibid., 47.

11 – Schettler, *We Were Wiseguys and Didn't Know It*, 96–97.

12 – John L. Smith, "IRS giving messenger bettors close look during March Madness," *Las Vegas Journal Review*, March 20, 2011. www.lvrj.com/news/irs-giving-messenger-bettors-close-look-during-march-madness-118320759.html

13 – Schettler, *We Were Wiseguys and Didn't Know It*, 112.

14 – Sam Skolnik, *High Stakes: The Rising Cost of America's Gambling Addiction* (Boston: Beacon Press, 2011), 119–120.

15 – Anthony Cabot, "The Absence of a Comprehensive Federal Policy Toward Internet and Sports Wagering and a Proposal for Change," *The Villanova Sports and Entertainment Law Journal*, Volume 17, 273–274.

16 – Dan Moldea, *Interference: How Organized Crime Influences Professional Football* (New York: William Morrow & Co., 1989), 31.

17 – Grossman, *You Can Bet On It: Vol. 2 — Sports Betting*, 24.

18 – Griffin, *Gaming the Game*, 39.

19 – Ibid., 67–69.

20 – Moldea, *Interference*, 240.

21 – Michael Franzese, *Blood Covenant* (New Kensington, PA: Whitaker House, 2003), 19.

22 – Declan Hill, *The Fix: Soccer and Organized Crime* (Pittsburgh, NY: McClelland & Stewart Ltd., 2010), 138–139.

A GOOD DEFENSE...

1 – Harry Wismer, *The Public Calls It Sport* (Englewood Cliffs, NJ: Prentice-Hall, Inc., 1965), 53–55.

2 – Chad Brown and Alan Eisenstock, *Inside the Meat Grinder: An NFL Official's Life in the Trenches* (New York: St. Martin's Press, 1999), 76–77.

3 – Tony Softli, "NFL Security is No Joke," 101espn.com, March 6, 2012. www.101espn.com/category/tsoftli-blogs/20120306/NFL-Security-is-No-Joke/

4 – Ibid.

5 – Mark Kriegel, *Namath: A Biography* (New York: Viking/The Penguin Group, 2004), 293–294.

6 – Moldea, *Interference*, 23.

7 – Ibid., 340.

8 – John Underwood, Robert H. Boyle, Douglas S. Looney, Armen Keteyian, Greg Kelly, Austin Murphy, Martin Dardis, and Jack Tobin, "The Biggest Game in Town," *Sports Illustrated*, March 10, 1986.

9 – Aaron Skirboll, *The Pittsburgh Cocaine Seven: How a Ragtag Group of Fans Took the Fall for Major League Baseball* (Chicago, IL: Chicago Review Press, 2010), 125.

10 – Ibid., 145.

11 – Ibid., 158–159.

12 – Ibid., 216.

13 – Moldea, *Interference*, 349.

14 – Don Reese and John Underwood, "I'm Not Worth a Damn," *Sports Illustrated*, June 14, 1982.

15 – Moldea, *Interference*, 28.

16 – Franzese, *Blood Covenant*, 358.

BOXING

1 – Jack Cavanaugh, *Tunney: Boxing's Brainiest Champ and his Upset of the Great Jack Dempsey* (New York: Random House, 2006), 81.

2 – Ibid., 81.

3 – Ibid., 81.

4 – David Pietrusza, *Rothstein: The Life, Times, and Murder of the Criminal Genius Who Fixed the 1919 World Series* (New York: Carroll & Graf Publishers, 2003), 232.

5 – Cavanaugh, *Tunney*, 306.

6 – Ibid., 287.

7 – Ibid., 306–307.

8 – Pietrusza, *Rothstein*, 240–243.

9 – Cavanaugh, *Tunney*, 341–343.

10 – Ibid., 64–67.

11 – Ibid., 64–67.

12 – Nick Tosches, *The Devil and Sonny Liston* (New York: Little, Brown, and Company, 2000), 74–75.

13 – Ibid., 116.

14 – Barney Nagler, *James Norris and the Decline of Boxing*, 1964.

15 – Tosches, *The Devil and Sonny Liston*, 80.

16 – Ibid., 202–203.

17 – Ibid., 204–205.

18 – Ibid., 207–208.

19 – Ibid., 211.

20 – Ibid., 212.

21 – Ibid., 213–214.

22 – Vic Ziegel, "Ali, Spinks, and the Battle of New Orleans," *New York* Magazine, October 2, 1978. Accessed online at: nymag.com/news/sports/48897/

23 – Ibid.

24 – Ibid.

25 – Jack Newfield, *Only in America: The Life and Crimes of Don King* (New York: William Morrow and Company, Inc., 1995), 47.

26 – Ibid., 46.

27 – Ibid., 102.

28 – Cosell, *I Never Played the Game*, 183.

29 – Newfield, *Only in America*, 102.

30 – Ibid., 104.

31 – Ibid., 125.

32 – Cosell, *I Never Played the Game*, 184.

33 – Newfield, *Only in America*, 134.

INTERNATIONAL GAME FIXING

1 – "Condon calls for tougher stance," *London Evening Standard* online, November 6, 2011. www.thisislondon.co.uk/sportheadlines/condon-calls-for-tougher-stance-6365143.html

2 – "Former ICC anti-corruption unit head Paul Condon reveals all cricket nations rigged games," The *Telegraph* online, November 16, 2011. www.dailytelegraph.com.au/sport/cricket/former-icc-anti-corruption-unit-head-paul-condon-reveals-all-cricket-nations-rigged-games/story-e6frey50-1226196285943

3 – Ibid.

4 – Ibid.

5 – "Tennis anti-corruption unit slams Radwanska 'cheating blacklist' slur," *News from Poland* online, October 24, 2011. www.thenews.pl/1/5/Artykul/57328,Tennis-anticorruption-unit-slams-Radwanska-cheating-blacklist-slur

6 – Ben Gunn and Jeff Rees, *Environmental Review of Integrity in*

Professional Tennis, September 2008, 1. Accessed via: www.howtofix-asoccergame.com/Report%20on%20possible%20fixing%20in%20Tennis%20for%20the%20ATP.pdf

7 – Ibid., 1–2.

8 – Ibid., 37.

9 – Ibid., 37.

10 – Ibid., 10.

11 – Ibid., 10.

12 – Ibid., 12.

13 – Nick Harris, "The curious case of Wayne Odesnik, a tennis betting mystery, a drugs ban and a whistleblower's deal," *SportingIntelligence*, January 3, 2011. www.sportingintelligence.com/2011/01/03/the-curious-case-of-wayne-odesnik-a-tennis-betting-mystery-a-drugs-ban-and-a-whistleblower%E2%80%99s-deal-03010/

14 – Gunn and Rees, *Environmental Review of Integrity in Professional Tennis*, 11.

15 – Ibid., 11–12.

16 – Daniel Kaplan and John Ourand, "ESPN seeks to unseal ATP gambling info," *Sports Business Journal*, December 6, 2010. www.sportsbusinessjournal.com/images/articles/SBJ201012060301-2.jpg

17 – Ibid.

18 – Ibid.

19 – Michael McCarthy, "IMG's Ted Forstmann talks gambling, global sports growth," *USA Today*, January 12, 2011. www.usatoday.com/sports/2011-01-11-ted-forstmann-img-gambling-woods_N.htm

20 – Greg Couch, "IMG Boss Teddy Forstmann Alleged to Have Used Hush Money to Quiet Accuser," *AOL News*, October 28, 2010. www.aolnews.com/2010/10/28/img-boss-teddy-forstmann-alleged-to-have-used-hush-money-to-quie/

21 – Ibid.

22 – McCarthy, "IMG's Ted Forstmann talks gambling, global sports growth".

23 – Matthew Holehouse, "Match-fixing in football cannot be wiped

out, says Uefa lawyer Pierre Cornu," The *Telegraph*, October 20, 2011. www.telegraph.co.uk/sport/football/8839671/Match-fixing-in-football-cannot-be-wiped-out-says-Uefa-lawyer-Pierre-Cornu.html

24 – Dan Roan, "Report shows match-fixing rife in Southern and Eastern Europe," BBC, February 7, 2012. www.bbc.co.uk/sport/0/football/16923742

25 – Ibid.

26 – "Sepp Blatter: 'We are not in a crisis'," Associated Press, May 30, 2011. espn.go.com/sports/soccer/news/_/id/6607533/fifa-difficulties-not-crisis

27 – Sabrina Mao and Ken Willis, "Soccer-China starts corruption hearings against officials," Reuters, December 19, 2011. blogs.reuters.com/sport

28 – Skolnik, *High Stakes*, 71–72.

29 - Opening remarks by INTERPOL Secretary General Ronald K. Noble, Global Conference on Asian Organized Crime. Singapore, January 23–24, 2008. www.interpol.int/public/ICPO/speeches/sgAOC20080123.asp#

30 – "IOC pushing governments to act on illegal betting," Associated Press, February 1, 2012. sports.espn.go.com/espn/wire?section=oly&id=7526953

31 – Paul Kelso, "Global match-fixing investigation claims major scalp as Wilson Raj Perumal is jailed for two years," The *Telegraph*, July 19, 2011. www.telegraph.co.uk/sport/football/8648454/Global-match-fixing-investigation-claims-major-scalp-as-Wilson-Raj-Perumal-is-jailed-for-two-years.html

32 – Ibid.

33 – Srecko Matic, "The rise and fall of Berlin gambling king Ante Sapina," *Deutsche Welle*, May 19, 2011. www.dw-world.de/dw/article/0,,15087442,00.html

34 – William Spain, "Billions expected to be wagered on World Cup 2010," MarketWatch, June 1, 2010. www.marketwatch.com/story/billions-set-to-be-wagered-on-2010-world-cup-2010-05-28?pagenumber=1

35 – Ibid.

36 – Ibid.

37 – Ibid.

38 – "1966 & 1974 World Cups Were Fixed — Former FIFA President," Goal.com, June 26, 2008. www.goal.com/en/news/9/england/2008/06/26/753029/1966-1974-world-cups-were-fixed-former-fifa-president

39 – Ibid.

40 – Martin Rogers, "Argentina's 1978 World Cup win against Peru was fixed in a brutal political deal, former senator says," Yahoo Sports, February 11, 2012. sports.yahoo.com/soccer/news?slug=rogers_argentina_peru_fixing_scandal_world_cup_021012

41 - Hill, *The Fix*.

42 – Mark Gleeson, "South Africa duped by fixers before World Cup: FIFA," Yahoo Sports, March 5, 2012. sports.yahoo.com/soccer/news;_ylt=AriacWheTxFNCFqvIpbK6mYmw7YF?slug=reu-soccerafricasafricafixers

43 – Ibid.

44 – Hill, *The Fix*, xv–xvi.

BASEBALL

1 – Ken Burns, *Baseball (First Inning)* film.

2 – Ibid.

3 – Pietrusza, *Rothstein*, 149.

4 – Ibid., 148.

5 – Kevin Cook, *Titanic Thompson: The Man Who Bet Everything* (New York: W.W. Norton and Company, 2011), 98–99.

6 – Pietrusza, *Rothstein*, 184.

7 – Ibid., 176.

8 – Ibid., 151.

9 – Zev Chafets, *Cooperstown Confidential: Heroes, Rogues, and the Inside Story of the Baseball Hall of Fame* (New York: Bloomsbury, 2009), 57.

10 – Ibid., 62.

11 – Ibid., 63–65.

12 – Gerald Eskenazi, *The Lip: A Biography of Leo Durocher* (New York: William Morrow and Co., 1993), 49.

13 – Ibid., 57–58.

14 – Ibid., 143.

15 – Ibid., 148.

16 – Ibid., 151–152.

17 – Ibid., 22.

18 – Underwood, et al., *The Biggest Game in Town.*

19 – Schettler, *We Were Wiseguys and Didn't Know It*, 127–128.

20 – Denny McLain with Eli Zaret, *I Told You I Wasn't Perfect* (Chicago, IL: Triumph Books, 2007), 65–66.

21 – Ibid., 65–66.

22 – Ibid., 153–154.

23 – Pete Rose with Rick Hill, *My Prison Without Bars* (Rodale, 2004), x–xi.

24 – Ibid., 115–118.

25 – Ibid., 134.

26 – Ibid., 147–148.

27 – Ibid., 135.

28 – Ibid., 163–167.

29 – National Council on Problem Gambling website. www.ncpgambling.org/i4a/pages/Index.cfm?pageID=3315

30 – Gamblers Anonymous website. www.gamblersanonymous.org/ga/content/questions-answers-about-gamblers-anonymous

31 – "Report: Mets' Samuels admits bet," ESPNNewYork.com, November 5, 2010. sports.espn.go.com/new-york/mlb/news/story?id=5768114

32 – Ian Begley, "Charlie Samuels indicted in Queens," ESPNNewYork.com, May 12, 2011. sports.espn.go.com/new-york/mlb/news/story?id=6526209

33 – Craig Calcaterra, "Jeff Francoeur explains why he gave Charlie

Samuels $50,000," Hardball.NBCSports.com, May 11, 2011. hardball-talk.nbcsports.com/2011/05/11/jeff-francoeur-explains-why-he-gave-charlie-samuels-50000/

34 – Skirboll, *The Pittsburgh Cocaine Seven*, 140.

BASKETBALL

1 – Ira Berkow, "The Temptations of a Man of Integrity," *New York Times*, May 31, 1992. www.nytimes.com/1992/05/31/sports/the-temptations-of-a-man-of-integrity.html?pagewanted=all&src=pm

2 – Tobias J. Moskowitz and L. Jon Wertheim, *Scorecasting: The Hidden Influences Behind How Sports Are Played and Games Are Won* (New York: Crown Archetype, 2011), 152–154.

3 – Ibid., 155.

4 – Henry Abbott and Peter D. Newmann, "When an NBA Referee Was Convicted of Shaving Points," ESPN.com True Hoop blog, July 24, 2007.

5 – Ibid.

6 – Michael Schumacher, *Mr. Basketball: George Mikan, the Minneapolis Lakers, and the Birth of the NBA* (New York: Bloomsbury, 2007), 195.

7 – Ibid., 194–195.

8 – Alan Goldstein, "Foul Play: History of Point Shaving Calls Into Question Integrity of Today's Games," Pressbox Online, Issue 2.42, October 18, 2007. www.pressboxonline.com/story.cfm?id=2697

9 – Berkow, *The Temptations of a Man of Integrity*.

10 – Ibid.

11 – Ibid.

12 – Ibid.

13 – Lem Banker and Frederick C. Klein, *Lem Banker's Book of Sports Betting* (reprint, originally published 1986), 35.

14 – "Antoine Walker sentenced in casino case," Associated Press, December 6, 2011. msn.foxsports.com/nba/story/Antoine-Walker-sentenced-after-pleading-guilty-to-failing-to-pay-Las-Vegas-casino-gambling-debts-120611

15 – Stephen A. Smith, "Iverson needs more than a prayer," *Philadelphia Inquirer*, March 7, 2010. articles.philly.com/2010-03-07/sports/24956781_1_train-wreck-allen-iverson-pat-croce

16 – Bill Reynolds, *Cousy: His Life, Career, and the Birth of Big-Time Basketball* (New York: Simon & Schuster, 2005), 109–110.

17 – Bill Doyle, "Sharry aided NBA players," *Worcester Telegram & Gazette*, September 14, 2007. www.telegram.com/article/20070914/NEWS/709140465/1009/SPORTS

18 – Reynolds, *Cousy*, 250–253.

19 – Ibid., 253.

20 – Bill Russell and Taylor Branch, *Second Wind: The Memoirs of an Opinionated Man* (New York: Random House, 1979), 106–108.

FOOTBALL

1 – Jeff Davis, *Rozelle: Czar of the NFL* (New York: McGraw-Hill, NY 2008), 121–122.

2 – Moldea, *Interference*, 33.

3 – Don Weiss with Chuck Day, *The Making of the Super Bowl: The Inside Story of the World's Greatest Sporting Event* (Chicago: Contemporary Books, 2003), 312.

4 – Wismer, *The Public Calls It Sport*, 25–26.

5 – Ibid., 53.

6 – Ibid., 53–55.

7 – Moldea, *Interference*, 54–56.

8 – "$7 Billion on Illegal Bets and a Blight on Sports," *Life*, September 8, 1967.

9 – Edwin Shrake, "For Babe, a week to forget," *Sports Illustrated*, September 18, 1967. sportsillustrated.cnn.com/vault/article/magazine/MAG1080314/1/index.htm

10 – Ibid.

11 – Moldea, *Interference*, 166.

12 – Shrake, "For Babe, a week to forget."

13 – Ibid.

14 – "$7 Billion on Illegal Bets and a Blight on Sports."

15 – Moldea, *Interference*, 162.

16 – Bernie Parrish, *They Call It a Game* (New York: The Dial Press, 1971), 182.

17 – Michael MacCambridge, *America's Game* by Michael MacCambridge (New York: Random House, 2004), 49.

18 – Wismer, *The Public Calls It Sport*, 53.

19 – Moldea, *Interference*, 73–74.

20 – Ibid., 84.

21 – Ibid., 84.

22 – Parrish, *They Call It a Game*, 186.

23 – Moldea, *Interference*, 85.

24 – Ibid., 85.

25 – Parrish, *They Call It a Game*, 186.

26 – Ibid., 199–202.

27 – Arthur J. Donovan, Jr. and Bob Drury, *Fatso: Football When Men Were Really Men* (New York: William Morrow and Company, Inc., 1987), 47–48.

28 – Moldea, *Interference*, 91.

29 - Alex Karras with Herb Gluck, *Even Big Guys Cry* (New York: Holt, Rinehart, and Winston, 1977), 162.

30 – Paul Hornung, *Golden Boy: Girls, Games, and Gambling at Green Bay (and Notre Dame, Too)* (New York: Simon & Schuster, 2004), 45.

31 – Underwood, et al. *The Biggest Game In Town.*

32 – Hornung, *Golden Boy*, 160.

33 – Moldea, *Interference*, 180.

34 – MacCambridge, *America's Game*, 178.

35 – Moldea, *Interference*, 114–115.

36 – Kriegel, *Namath*, 205.

37 – Ibid., 79.

WORKS CITED

38 – Joe Namath with Dick Schaap, *I Can't Wait Until Tomorrow...'Cause I Get Better Looking Every Day* (New York: Random House, 1969), 31–32.

39 – Moldea, *Interference*, 183.

40 – Ibid., 185.

41 – Ibid., 187–188.

42 – Ibid., 209.

43 – Ibid., 210–211.

44 – MacCambridge, *America's Game*, 268–269.

45 – Moldea, *Interference*, 214.

46 – MacCambridge, *America's Game*, 269.

47 – Moldea, *Interference*, 358.

48 – Ibid., 297–298.

49 – Ibid., 300–301.

50 – Wismer, *The Public Calls It Sport*, 54–55.

51 – Moldea, *Interference*, 307–308.

52 – Underwood, et al., *The Biggest Game In Town*.

CONCLUSION

1 – Statement of Jay Moyer, Special Counsel National Football League, before the Committee to Study Sports Gaming in Delaware Established by House Resolution No. 63, December 18, 2002.

2 – Underwood, et al., *The Biggest Game in Town*.

INDEX

Entries in *italics* denote titles of books.

ABOUT THE AUTHOR

Brian Tuohy is considered to be America's leading expert on game fixing in sports. While *Larceny Games* discusses game fixing from a sports gambling aspect, his previous book *The Fix Is In: The Showbiz Manipulations of the NFL, MLB, NBA, NHL, and NASCAR* examined how the professional leagues influence the outcome of their own games for TV ratings and profit. He has appeared as a guest on over one hundred radio programs throughout the United States and Canada, and has spoken at Florida State University, Columbia College in Chicago, and at the 2012 AEJMC National Conference. Another book of Brian's based largely on government files, *Disaster Government: National Emergencies, Continuity of Government and You*, was published in 2013.

For more, visit: TheFixIsIn.net, DisasterGovernment.com, or LarcenyGames.com